THE PSALMS OF SOLOMON

EARLY JUDAISM AND ITS LITERATURE

Rodney A. Werline, General Editor

Editorial Board:
Randall D. Chesnutt
Kelley N. Coblentz Bautch
Maxine L. Grossman
Carol Newsom

Number 54

THE PSALMS OF SOLOMON

Texts, Contexts, and Intertexts

Edited by
Patrick Pouchelle, G. Anthony Keddie, and Kenneth Atkinson

Atlanta

Copyright © 2021 by SBL Press

All rights reserved. No part of this work may be reproduced or transmitted in any form or by any means, electronic or mechanical, including photocopying and recording, or by means of any information storage or retrieval system, except as may be expressly permitted by the 1976 Copyright Act or in writing from the publisher. Requests for permission should be addressed in writing to the Rights and Permissions Office, SBL Press, 825 Houston Mill Road, Atlanta, GA 30329 USA.

Library of Congress Control Number: 2021940328

Contents

Abbreviations vii

Introduction
   Patrick Pouchelle and G. Anthony Keddie 1

Psalms of Solomon 16.10 and Its Biblical and
   Hellenistic Backgrounds
   Eberhard Bons 23

Changing Contexts: Psalms of Solomon 11 and
   Its Parallel in Baruch 4:5–5:9
   Johanna Erzberger 35

Understanding the History, Theology, and Community of the
   Psalms of Solomon in Light of the Dead Sea Scrolls
   Kenneth Atkinson 57

Poverty and Exploitation in the Psalms of Solomon:
   At the Intersection of Sapiential and Apocalyptic Discourses
   G. Anthony Keddie 81

The Same Scholarly Fate? A Short Comparison between
   the Psalms of Solomon and the Assumption of Moses
   Patrick Pouchelle 111

Violators of the Law and the Curse of the Law:
   The Perception of the Torah in the Psalms of Solomon
   and in Paul's Letter to the Galatians
   Stefan Schreiber 139

Coping with Dissonance: Theodicy, Genre,
    and Epistemology in the Psalms of Solomon
    Shani Tzoref 165

The Imaginative Experiencing of Psalms of Solomon 8
    Angela Kim Harkins 203

Social Memory Features in the Psalms of Solomon
    Rodney A. Werline 221

A "Song with a Happy Heart": A Response
    Rodney A. Werline 243

Bibliography 257
Contributors 293
Ancient Sources Index 297
Modern Authors Index 315

Abbreviations

2 Clem	2 Clement
AB	Anchor Bible
AcBib	Academia Biblica
A.J.	Josephus, *Antiquitates judaicae*
AJEC	Ancient Judaism and Early Christianity
ALGHJ	Arbeiten zur Literatur und Geschichte des hellenistischen Judentums
AOAT	Alter Orient und Altes Testament
APOT	Charles, Robert H., eds. *The Apocrypha and Pseudepigrapha of the Old Testament.* 2 vols. Oxford: Clarendon, 1913.
As. Mos.	Assumption of Moses
b.	Babylonian Talmud
BA	La Bible d'Alexandrie
BBB	Bonner biblische Beiträge
BBR	*Bulletin for Biblical Research*
Bell. civ.	Appian, *Bella civilia*
Ber.	Berakhot
BETL	Bibliotheca Ephemeridum Theologicarum Lovaniensium
BGBH	Beiträge zur Geschichte der biblischen Hermeneutik
BHQ	Schenker, Adrian, et al. *Biblia Hebraica Quinta.* Stuttgart: Deutsche Bibelgesellschaft, 2004–.
B.J.	Josephus, *Bellum judaicum*
BJS	Brown Judaic Studies
BN	*Biblische Notizen*
BNP A	*Brill's New Pauly* Antiquity
BZAW	Beihefte zur Zeitschrift für die alttestamentliche Wissenschaft
CBQ	*Catholic Biblical Quarterly*
CD	Damascus Document
CEJL	Commentaries on Early Jewish Literature

Cher.	Philo, *De cherubim*
Civ.	Augustine, *De civitate Dei*
col.	column
ConBNT	Coniectanea Neotestamentica or Coniectanea Biblica: New Testament Series
CurBR	*Currents in Biblical Research*
DCH	Clines, David J. A., ed. *Dictionary of Classical Hebrew*. 9 vols. Sheffield: Sheffield Phoenix, 1993–2016.
DCLS	Deuterocanonical and Cognate Literature Studies
Det.	Philo, *Quod deterius potiori insidari soleat*
Deus	Philo, *Quod Deus sit immutabilis*
DJD	Discoveries in the Judaean Desert
DSD	*Dead Sea Discoveries*
DSSSE	García Martínez, Florentino, and Eibert J. C. Tigchelaar, eds. *Dead Sea Scrolls Study Edition*. 2 vols. Leiden: Brill: 1995.
EJL	Early Judaism and Its Literature
EKKNT	Evangelisch-Katholischer Kommentar zum Neuen Testament
Ennarat. Ps.	Augustine, *Enarrationes in Psalmos*
ep.	epistle
EncRel	Eliade, Mircea, ed. *The Encyclopedia of Religion*. New York: Macmillan, 1987.
Eth.	Ethiopic
FAT	Forschungen zum Alten Testament
Flac.	Cicero, *Pro Flacco*
FRLANT	Forschungen zur Religion und Literatur des Alten und Neuen Testaments
Fug.	Philo, *De fuga et inventione*
H	Codex Harris
HAL	Koehler, Ludwig, Walter Baumgartner, and Johann J. Stamm. *Hebräisches und aramäisches Lexicon zum Alten Testament*. 3rd ed. Leiden: Brill, 1995, 2004.
HBCE	The Hebrew Bible: A Critical Edition
Heb.	Hebrew
Hen	*Henoch*
Hist.	Herodotus, *Historiae*; Polybius, *Historiae*; Thucydides, *Historiae*
Hist. rom.	Dio Cassius, *Historiae romanae*

Hypoth.	Philo, *Hypothetica*
IEJ	*Israel Exploration Journal*
Int.	*Interpretation*
Ios.	Philo, *De Iosepho*
JBL	*Journal of Biblical Literature*
JAJ	*Journal of Ancient Judaism*
JJS	*Journal of Jewish Studies*
JQR	*Jewish Quarterly Review*
JR	*Journal of Religion*
JRS	*Journal of Roman Studies*
JSJ	*Journal for the Study of Judaism in the Persian, Hellenistic, and Roman Periods*
JSHRZ	*Jüdische Schriften aus hellenistisch-römischer Zeit*
JSJSup	Journal for the Study of Judaism in the Persian, Hellenistic, and Roman Periods Supplement Series
JSNT	*Journal for the Study of the New Testament*
JSOT	*Journal for the Study of the Old Testament*
JSOTSup	Journal for the Study of the Old Testament Supplement Series
JSP	*Journal for the Study of the Pseudepigrapha*
JTS	*Journal of Theological Studies*
KlT	Kleine Texte für theologische Vorlesungen und Übungen
LD	Lectio Divina
Leg.	Philo, *Legum allegoriae*
LHBOTS	The Library of Hebrew Bible/Old Testament Studies
LNTS	Library of New Testament Studies
LXX	Septuagint
m.	Mishnah
MT	Masoretic Text
Mut.	Philo, *De mutatione nominum*
N	Codex Nitriensis
NEA	*Near Eastern Archaeology*
NETS	Pietersma, Albert, and Benjamin G. Wright, eds. *A New English Translation of the Septuagint*. New York: Oxford University Press, 2007.
NovT	*Novum Testamentum*
NovTSup	Novum Testamentum Supplement Series
NTL	New Testament Library
NTOA	Novum Testamentum et Orbis Ant

NTS	*New Testament Studies*
NRSV	New Revised Standard Version
OBO	Orbis Biblicus et Orientalis
OG	Old Greek
OTP	Charlesworth, James H., ed. *The Old Testament Pseudepigrapha*. 2 vols. Garden City, NY: Doubleday, 1983–1985.
PAAJR	*Proceedings of the American Academy of Jewish Research*
Pis.	Cicero, *In Pisonem*
Post.	Philo, *De posteritate Caini*
Praep. ev.	Eusebius, *Praeparatio Evangelica*
Prot.	Plato, *Protagoras*
Prov. cons.	Cicero, *De provinciis consularibus*
Pss. Sol.	Psalms of Solomon
PTSDSSP	Princeton Theological Seminary Dead Sea Scrolls Project
QC	Qumran Chronicle
RB	*Revue biblique*
RBL	*Review of Biblical Literature*
REJ	*Revue des études juives*
RevQ	*Revue de Qumrân*
Sacr.	Philo, *De sacrificiis Abelis et Caini*
SBLSP	Society of Biblical Literature Seminar Papers
SCS	Septuagint and Cognate Studies
SemeiaSt	Semeia Studies
Sent.	Menander, *Sententia Antiquae*; Pseudo-Phocylides, *Sententia Antiquae*
Sest.	Cicero, *Pro Sestio*
SJLA	Studies in Judaism in Late Antiquity
Somn.	Philo, *De somniis*
SNTSMS	Society for New Testament Studies Monograph Series
SNTW	Studies of the New Testament and Its World
Spec.	Philo, *De specialibus legibus*
SR	*Studies in Religion*
STDJ	Studies on the Texts of the Desert of Judah
StPatr	Studia Patristica
SUNT	Studien zur Umwelt des Neuen Testaments
SVTG	Septuaginta: Vetus Testamentum Graecum
SVTP	Studia in Veteris Testamenti Pseudepigraphica
SymS	Symposium
Syr.	Syriac

t.	Tosefta
T. Benj.	Testament of Benjamin
T. Levi	Testament of Levi
TRev	*Theologische Revue*
TZ	*Theologische Zeitschrift*
TSAJ	Texte und Studien zum antiken Judentum
TUGAL	Texte und Untersuchungen zur Geschichte der altchristlichen Literatur
Unit. eccl.	Cyprian, *De catholicae ecclesiae unitate*
VL	Vetus Latina
VTSup	Vetus Testamentum Supplement Series
WGRW	Writings of the Greco-Roman World
WUNT	Wissenschaftliche Untersuchungen zum Neuen Testament
ZAW	*Zeitschrift für die alttestamentliche Wissenschaft*
ZNW	*Zeitschrift für die neutestamentliche Wissenschaft und die Kunde der älteren Kirche*
ZWT	*Zeitschrift für wissenschaftliche Theologie*

Introduction

Patrick Pouchelle and G. Anthony Keddie

Sometimes proceedings seem cursed. We would have been very happy to see this book published at an earlier date. Unfortunately, a cluster of events—personal, professional, and even global in the case of the COVID-19 pandemic—delayed the publication of this book. We wish to ask the reader to forgive us this delay and to enjoy reading this volume's excellent contributions in spite of these events.

It is a great pleasure to introduce these essays, most of which were originally delivered and discussed at the Second International Meeting on the Psalms of Solomon in Paris from 7 to 9 July 2015. The first part of this introduction is dedicated to the Jesuits, who hosted the meeting, and to their contribution to the early research on the Psalms of Solomon. The second part of this introduction will present the research done on the Psalms of Solomon between 2013 and 2015. Finally, the third part will introduce the different contributions to this colloquium.

1. The Contribution of the Jesuits to Early Research on the Psalms of Solomon

The Second International Meeting on the Psalms of Solomon was organized by Patrick Pouchelle and held at the Centre Sèvres, the Jesuit Faculty of Paris. This Jesuit institution served as an especially appropriate setting for this meeting since the Jesuits played a major role in the modern rediscovery of the Psalms of Solomon almost exactly four hundred years ago. The Jesuits were involved in the first studies on this text: the person who saw its first manuscript (André Schott), its first editor (Juan Luis de la Cerda), and its first commentator (Juan Eusebio Nieremberg) were all Jesuits. When we observe the interactions of these intellectuals more attentively, it is clear that Jesuits were not the only intellectuals interested in the

Psalms of Solomon in the early seventeenth century; they were engaged in the scholarly world of their time.

However, since the involvement of Jesuits in the earliest studies on the Psalms of Solomon is not well known by scholars, we begin this introduction with a brief history of the earliest modern scholarship on this text. This examination of the rediscovery of the Psalms of Solomon reveals the intellectual milieux that set the tone for research on this text. It also situates Jesuits among the diverse humanist intellectuals who delighted in the study of ancient literature at the beginning of the seventeenth century, just before rivalries between Catholics and Protestants culminated in the Thirty Years' War in Central Europe.[1]

André Schott was born in 1552 in Antwerp and was educated at the university of Leuven.[2] He was a personality dedicated to humanism—dedicated to the idea that *litterarum iuvandarum studio nemini secundus* ("Follower of nobody regarding the zeal of supporting the letters" [personal trans.]), according to the Dutch philologist David Ruhnken.[3] He probably fled from Antwerp to Paris around the time that the city was sacked by the Spanish in November 1576 with the formation of the Dutch Republic as its consequence. There, being qualified as *bonitas ipsas* ("the goodness itself"), he managed to maintain contacts between adversaries, notably Protestants and Catholics. He was the first modern author ever to allude to the Psalms of Solomon in a written document. In 1614, he wrote a letter to Johannes Meursius (or van Meurs), a famous Greek philologist and professor at Leiden:

> Hœschel engaged himself to publish in Greek the books of Cyril of Alexander "against Julian *the transgressor.*" He also found a very old copy of Solomon, brought from Constantinople in which there are eighteen psalms of Salomon, until now *unpublished* and unseen.[4]

---

1. This part of the introduction is a modest contribution to the attempt of recent scholars (e.g., Mordechai Feingold, preface to *Jesuit Science and the Republic of Letters*, ed. Mordechai Feingold [Cambridge, MA: MIT Press, 2003], vii–xi) to challenge the traditional view that it is meaningless to study the contribution of Jesuits to science in the seventeenth and eighteenth centuries because Jesuits were only "committed to shunning innovation and to defending Aristotle in philosophy and Saint Thomas in theology" (viii).

2. See especially Luciano Canfora, *Convertire Casaubon* (Milan: Adelphi, 2002).

3. See Léon Maes, "Lettres inédites d'André Schott," *Muséon* 9 (1908): 410.

4. Hœschelius græce pollicetur editurum se Cyrilli Alexandrini adversus Julia-

After the Act of Abjuration in 1581, Antwerp still belonged to the Spanish Netherlands whereas Leiden was Dutch. Although Protestant, van Meurs tried to remain far from the religious polemics of his time, notably the rise of Arminianism. In the letter, the person mentioned by Schott is the Protestant Hœschel. He was the head of the Public Library of Augsburg and director of a new publishing house, *Ad insigne pinus*, whose aim was to edit newly discovered Greek texts. This publishing house was the reason that Schott and Hœschel came to know each other. Around 1595, Schott brought a manuscript to Hœschel containing the *Library* of Photius, and Hœschel edited it. Unfortunately, Hœschel retired in 1614 and passed away in 1617, without being able to produce an edition of the Psalms of Solomon.

Until Oscar von Gebhardt, it was believed that the manuscript Schott had mentioned belonged to the Public Library of Augsburg. However, the manuscript could no longer be found in Augsburg and was never mentioned in its catalogue.[5] Juan Luis de la Cerda,[6] who produced the *editio princeps* of the Psalms of Solomon, could be understood as saying that Schott sent him the actual manuscript:

> Hitherto, the most respectable Father André Schott of our community sent these Psalms of Solomon, recently discovered in the very old parchments of the library of Augsburg.[7]

---

num παραβάτην libros. Nactum se quoque Solomonis exemplar vetustiss. Cp. adlatum, in quo Psalm. XVIII Salomonis hactenus ἀνέκδοτοι et invisi (personal trans., italics: presented in Greek in the original text). Johannes Meursius, *Opera* (Florence, 1763), 11: ep. 343, col. 249C. The epistle is dated 23 October 1614, as noted by Oscar von Gebhardt, *Die Psalmen Salomo's zum ersten Male mit Benutzung der Athoshandschriften und des Codex Casanatensis*, TUGAL 13.2 (Leipzig: Hinrichs, 1895), 1; J. Viteau, *Les Psaumes de Salomon: Introduction, texte grec et traduction, avec les principales variantes de la version syriaque par François Martin*, Documents pour l'étude de la Bible (Paris: Letouzé et Ané, 1911), 192. The date is curiously misgiven by Herbert E. Ryle and Montague R. James in *Psalms of the Pharisees Commonly Called the Psalms of Solomon* (Cambridge: Cambridge University Press, 1891), xxvii, and Robert B. Wright in *The Psalms of Solomon: A Critical Edition of the Greek Text*, Jewish and Christian Text in Contexts and Related Studies 1 (London: T&T Clark, 2007), 34. The former authors mentioned 1615 while Wright gave 24 September 1616 as the date.

5. The manuscript was also not present in Munich, where some manuscripts from the old library of Augsburg were purchased (von Gebhardt, *Die Psalmen Salomo's*, 2).

6. Juan Luis de la Cerda, *Adversaria Sacra* (Lyon: Louis Prost, 1626).

7. Misit adhuc Reuerentissimus Pater Andreas Schottus Societatis nostrae hos Psal-

Moreover, de la Cerda seems to attest at several points in his edition that he had consulted the manuscript: he wrote *obscure in meo Graeco codice* (obscure in my Greek codex) for Pss. Sol. 2.4 and 4.19 and *in Codice quem vidi* (in the codex that I saw) for Pss. Sol. 4.21 and 5.16.[8] These allusions by de la Cerda are not completely decisive, however, for they do not explicate whether the manuscript that he received was the original or a copy. Indeed, Von Gebhardt demonstrated that Schott's manuscript is to be identified with one of the witnesses in Vienna.[9] Moreover, as the psalms have always been found within a biblical manuscript, Schott would not have sent the whole codex and also would not have cut pages out of the codex. It is more probable that Schott only sent de la Cerda a copy.[10]

In his recent critical edition, Felix Albrecht explains that this manuscript was delivered by Ogier Ghiselin de Busbecq (1522–1592).[11] This mention deserves a short commentary. This Flemish intellectual and diplomat was known as a good negotiator, a well-educated person who mastered several languages, and more surprisingly an herbalist. He was sent in 1555 by the emperor Ferdinand I to Suleiman the Magnificent to conclude a treaty. During the negotiation that lasted seven years, Busbecq made a trip to Ankara and discovered an inscription presenting an ancient copy of the Res Gestae Divi Augusti (The Deeds of the Divine Augustus), the funerary inscription of the first Roman emperor. He later communicated a copy of it to Schott, who published its first edition in 1579.[12] During his

---

mos Salomonis recens in membranis antiquissimis Bibliothecae Augustanae repertos. "Our community" obviously refers to the Jesuit company. The idea that the text was "discovered in … the library of Augsburg" is the source of the error made until von Gebhardt. The Psalms of Solomon were discovered in Augsburg but from a manuscript belonging to the imperial library of Vienna.

8. See Ryle and James, *Psalms of the Pharisees*, xiii–xiv for other examples.

9. See von Gebhardt, *Die Psalmen Salomo's*, 1–8.

10. See von Gebhardt, *Die Psalmen Salomo's*, 1–8, Viteau, *Les Psaumes de Salomon*, 193.

11. Felix Albrecht, *Psalmi Salomonis*, SVTG 12.3 (Göttingen: Vandenhoeck & Ruprecht, 2018), 23–24.

12. See Pierre Cosme, "Les *Res gestae divi Augusti*: Une autobiographie d'Auguste?," in *Autobiographies souveraines*, ed. Pierre Monnet and Jean-Claude Schmitt, Histoires anciennes et médiévales 112 (Paris: Sorbonne, 2012), 34–35; William Stenhouse, "Greek Antiquities and Greek Histories in the Late Renaissance," in *Et Amicorum: Essays on Renaissance Humanism and Philosophy in Honour of Jill Kraye*, ed. Anthony Ossa-Richardson and Margaret Meserve, Brill's Studies in Intellectual History 273 (Leiden: Brill, 2018), 187–88.

stay in Turkey he gathered around 250 manuscripts, which he gave in 1576 to the Imperial Library of Vienna. Among them was found the manuscript known today under the number 147, the source of the first edition of the Psalms Solomon.

Von Gebhardt rightly observed that, in that period, Sebastian Tengnagel was the head of this library. Tengnagel was born in 1563 and was renowned for mastering not less than fifteen languages. He had worked as an assistant to Hugo Blotius, the head librarian of the Imperial Library prior to taking over the post in 1608. He was one of the foremost scholars of oriental languages in Europe and was actively engaged in collecting and preserving ancient manuscripts.[13] That Tengnagel and Hœschel exchanged some manuscripts is demonstrated by the correspondence between the two as well as the presence of Hœschel's annotations in the Vienna manuscript, which contained the Psalms of Solomon as well as the version of Sirach he used for his edition of that text in 1604.[14] He even mentioned our eighteen psalms in a letter to Tengnagel in 1616:

> There are who want that I give the priority to the proverbs of Solomon with three manuscripts, I have collected. These should be printed according to a shape which is before Sirach and to which I will add eighteen psalms *unpublished*, found in a handwritten codex, bought in Constantinople, similarly ascribed to Solomon.[15]

A last indication may be the addition of τέλος σὺν θεῷ ("the end, thank God!") to the text. This phrase occurs at the end of the psalms as edited by de la Cerda but is not present in any known manuscript of the text. It is possible that Hœschel reproduced this medieval monk's assessment at the end of his copies.[16]

Therefore, the manuscript's journey from Vienna could be reconstructed as follows. At an unknown date, Tengnagel sent Hœschel a Greek

---

13. See G. J. Toomer, *Eastern Wisedome and Learning: The Study of Arabic in Seventeenth-Century England* (Oxford: Clarendon, 1996), 39.

14. Von Gebhardt, *Die Psalmen's Salomo's*, 7.

15. Sunt qui velint primum locum Proverbiis Salomonis cum tribus m.s. quae contuli, ut dem, ea imprimendis forma qua ante Siracidem, iisque subjungam Psalmos XV[III] ἀνέκδοτους qui in codice membranaceo, Constantinopoli empto, leguntur eidemque Salomoni adscribuntur. Quoted by von Gebhardt, *Die Psalmen's Salomo's*, 7.

16. von Gebhardt, *Die Psalmen's Salomo's*, 8.

manuscript. Hœschel used it for his edition of Sirach. Either Hœschel or Schott noticed the importance of this previously unknown collection of eighteen psalms. Thereafter, Hœschel or Schott[17] copied the Psalms of Solomon, perhaps shortly before the death of Hoeschel. Sometime after that, presumably, Schott sent this copy (including the addition τέλος σὺν θεῷ) to de la Cerda.

The cooperation and the relationship between the Catholics Schott (a Jesuit) and Tengnagel (a layperson) and the Protestants Hœschel and Meursius[18] sheds light on a scholarly vitality that was above the religious and political divisions of that time. What was important for them was studying and transmitting ancient literature in order to make progress in the production of knowledge and to build the Republic of Letters.[19]

With de la Cerda, the history of early scholarship on the Psalms of Solomon changes its focus from central Europe to Catholic Spain. This Spanish Jesuit from Toledo was born around 1558. De la Cerda and Schott possibly met each other when the latter was in Toledo from 1579 until 1584. In fact, in 1580, Schott was in Salamanca copying manuscripts when he was called to hold the position of Professor of Greek in Toledo. Schott was still a layperson at that point, for he was only ordained to the priesthood in 1584 and then entered the Jesuit community in 1586 or in 1587. When Schott was a teacher in Toledo, de la Cerda was about twenty-four or twenty-five years old. We do not know whether he was a student of Schott.[20] In 1583, Schott went to Tarragona for seven years. At this time, de la Cerda became Professor of Grammar at Murcia before teaching from

---

17. It also remains possible that Schott was the one who copied the Psalms of Solomon and added the τέλος σὺν θεῷ.

18. Meursius tried to remain neutral as long as possible before more explicitly confessing being a Protestant.

19. In his popular book, *The Swerve: How the World Became Modern* (New York: Norton, 2011), Stephen Greenblatt has similarly shown how a Catholic and former papal secretary named Poggio Bracciolini became a leading humanist dedicated to making ancient texts such as Lucretius's *De rerum natura* available to other humanists, who were also devoted to progress in the study of Latin, poetry, and philosophy.

20. For some biographical accounts, see Andrew Laird, "Juan Luis de la Cerda and the Predicament of Commentary," in *The Classical Commentary: Histories, Practices, Theory*, ed. Roy K. Gibson and Christina Shuttleworth Kraus, Mnemosyne: Bibliotheca Classica Batava (Leiden: Brill, 2002), 174.

1597 onward in Madrid at the renowned Jesuit institution known as the Colegio Imperial de Madrid.[21]

When Schott sent the Psalms of Solomon to de la Cerda, the latter had already become famous for his commentary on the work of Virgil published between 1598 and 1617. He is one of the first to produce a systematic and exhaustive commentary of a classical author that not only paraphrased and explicated the ancient texts, but also elucidated difficult words and referred to many other Latin authors.[22]

After having received the text of the Psalms of Solomon from Schott, de la Cerda decided to put it in his *Adversaria Sacra*. This type of collection requires some explanation. *Adversaria Sacra* refers to a kind of "gathering of ideas related to sacred things." These *adversaria* constituted a literary genre on their own—a genre that is famously exemplified by the *adversaria* of Adrianus Turnebus, which were published in 1604. Humanists had something like a notebook in which they recorded any ideas they found interesting, especially while reading a book. This way of collecting ideas in an efficient manner while reading was integral to Jesuit pedagogy.[23] It was around 1614 that an Italian Jesuit named Francesco Sacchini published his influential *De ratione libros cum profectu legendi libellus*.[24] In this book, Sacchini suggested that students should use two notebooks, the first

---

21. For a survey of the history of this institution, see Bernabé Bartolomé Martínez, "Educación y humanidades clásicas en el Colegio Imperial de Madrid durante el siglo XVII," *Bulletin hispanique* 97 (1995): 109–55.

22. For recent studies of this commentary in its historical context, see Giuseppe Mazzochi, "Los comentarios virgilianos del Padre Juan Luis de La Cerda," *AISO: Actas II* (1990): 663–75; Sergio Casali, "Agudezas virgilane nel commento all'Eneide di Juan Luis de la Cerda," in *Esegesi dimenticate di autori classici*, ed. Carlo Santini and Fabio Stok, Testi e studi di cultura classica 41 (Pisa: Edizioni ETS, 2008), 233–61; Craig Kallendorf, "Epic and Tragedy—Virgil, La Cerda, Milton," in *Syntagmatia: Essays on Neo-Latin Literature in Honour of Monique Mund-Dopchie and Gilbert Tournoy*, ed. Dirk Sacré and Jan Papy (Leuven: Leuven University Press, 2009), 579–95; Laird, "Juan Luis de la Cerda."

23. See Jean-Marc Chatelain, "Les receuils d'adversaria aux XVIe et XVIIe siècles: Des pratiques de la lecture savante au style de l'érudition," in *Le livre et l'historien: Études offertes en l'honneur du professeur Henri-Jean Martin*, ed. Frédéric Barbier et al., Histoire et civilisation du livre 24 (Paris: Droz, 1997), 169–86.

24. Francesco Sacchini, *De ratione libros cum profectu legendi libellus* (Ingolstadt: Elisabeth Angermaria, 1614), recently republished as a facsimile by Iveta Nakládalová, Bibliotheca Sphaerica 5 (Barcelona: Seminario de Poética Europea del Renacimiento, Instituto Séneca, 2009).

one for noting unorganized ideas emerging from reading and the other for classifying these ideas according to different fields of thought. The literary genre of the *adversaria* is akin to the publication of the first type of notebook: an accumulation of ideas and quotations without specific organization.[25] As for philologists like de la Cerda, an *adversaria* was firstly a collection of emendations or explanations of rare words.[26] Hence, his *adversaria sacra* contains 187 chapters trying to elucidate rare or obscure words in the Vulgate[27] and Latin fathers. To this he added an edition of the Psalms of Solomon and an edition of Tertullian's *De Pallio*. This latter edition was further developed in his commentary on Tertullian, which was published between 1624 and 1630. In light of the conventions of the *adversaria* genre, the presence of the Psalms of Solomon in the appendix of his *adversaria sacra* is surprising. We do not know why this text did not merit its own edition. De la Cerda introduced the psalms with these words *ad lectorem*:

> If only they allow, in honor of God, to be useful to you (the reader) and to make me possible to succeed that these psalms see light by me, a light from which so many generations were deprived.[28]

Hence, our psalms were first presented as part of the vast erudition of de la Cerda, which was somewhat denigrated (time has changed!) by Diderot in his *Encyclopedia*:

> Jean-Louis de la Cerda: ... the books of this Jesuit did not make a fortune; they are also long and boring because he explains the clearest things to extol his erudition, and because, otherwise, he is always off topic.[29]

---

25. Chatelain, "Les receuils d'adversaria," 172–74. But Laird, "Juan Luis de la Cerda," 175 qualifies it as "a treatise on sacred eloquence."

26. Chatelain, "Les receuils d'adversaria," 177–78.

27. Including the so-called Velezian variant allegedly confirming some readings of the Vulgate, but which have now been demonstrated as a retroversion from the Latin probably made by the Marquis of Velez.

28. Utinam cedant in honorem deo, tibi in utilitatem, mihi enim tantum volo profecisse, ut hi psalmi lucem per me videant, qua tot seculis caruere.

29. Jean-Louis de la Cerda: ... Les ouvrages de ce jésuite n'ont pas fait fortune; ils sont également longs et ennuyeux, parce qu'il explique les choses les plus claires pour étaler son érudition, et parce que d'ailleurs il s'écarte sans-cesse de son sujet (s.v. "Tolède").

A last word regarding the choice of Lyon for publishing the *Adversaria Sacra* should be added now. The publisher was Louis Prost, heir of Guillaume Rouillé. In France, Lyon was the unique city able to compete with Paris regarding the publication of books in the seventeenth century.[30] Owing to its situation in the south of France, Lyon was a cosmopolitan city, relatively tolerant and open to the market of the Italian peninsula as well as Spain.[31] Hence, the Jesuits, well established in Lyon,[32] were well situated to publish Spanish authors in this city so as to grant them a wider audience in Europe.

In 1614, Juan Eusebio Nieremberg entered into the Jesuit company.[33] His father was from Tyrol and his mother from Bayern. They came to Spain with Maria of Austria, the daughter of Charles V, when she returned to Madrid in 1582. This Jesuit was very prolific. His bibliography gathers books on various subjects, such as natural histories on animals living in the Americas, as well as the holy scriptures, spirituality, theology, philosophy, and astronomy. Regarding astronomy, Nieremberg was a proponent of the geocentric theory of Tycho Brahe, and he even quoted Galileo's new discoveries. Nieremberg was a professor of humanities, natural history, and sacred scriptures in Madrid. His vast erudition was at the service of preaching: knowledge, for him, was a way to the Lord, and he believed that science should only be scrutinized so as to discern God at work.[34]

In his work devoted to the study of the Old Testament, *De origine sacrae scripturae* (1641), Nieremberg treated the Psalms of Solomon after analyzing the canonical psalms with particular attention to their authorship.

---

30. Henri-Jean Martin, *Livre, Pouvoir et Sociétés à Paris au XVIIe siècle (1598–1701)*, 2 vols. (Genève: Droz, 1969), 1:324.

31. See Lyse Schwarzfuchs, *L'hébreu dans le livre lyonnais au XVIe siècle: Inventaire chronologique* (Lyon: ENS éditions, 2008), 46.

32. See Etienne Fouilloux and Bernard Hours, eds., *Les jésuites à Lyon: XVIe–XXe siècle* (Lyon: ENS éditions, 2005).

33. For further detail, see Hugues Dider, "La vie et la pensée de Juan Eusebio Nieremberg" (PhD diss., Université de Lille, 1974); Víctor Navarro, "Tradition and Scientific Change in Early Modern Spain: The Role of the Jesuits," in *Jesuit Science and the Republic of Letters*, ed. Mordechai Feingold (Cambridge, MA: MIT Press, 2003), 331–87; Scott Hendrickson, *Jesuit Polymath of Madrid: The Literary Enterprise of Juan Eusebio Nieremberg (1595–1658)* (Leiden: Brill, 2015).

34. This is the main thesis of Hendrickson (*Jesuit Polymath of Madrid*) who argues that Nieremberg's scrutinizing of science involved applying the exercises of Ignatius of Loyola.

His concern was to determine whether some psalms could be ascribed to the actual Solomon.[35] He then gave the Greek text and a Latin translation of Pss. Sol. 1 and 18, considered whether Solomon could have been the author of them, and disregarded this hypothesis.[36] Thus, about seventy years before the Protestant scholar Johann Albert Fabricius published the first collection of Old Testament pseudepigrapha (*Codex pseudepigraphus Veteris Testamenti*) in 1713, some Jesuit intellectuals were already casting doubt on the attribution of these eighteen psalms to Solomon.[37] This suggests that some Catholics, like some Protestants, were already raising concerns over the authenticity of extracanonical religious texts in the period of the Reformation and Counter-Reformation.

Nieremberg's seems to have been the last contribution to the study of the Psalms of Solomon by a Jesuit during this early modern period.[38] After Nieremberg, the Psalms of Solomon were used by Louis Ferrand (Ludovicus Ferrandus), a French Catholic layperson, in his commentary on the canonical Psalms (1683). The first book ever dedicated to the Psalms of Solomon, however, was written by Georg Janenski under the supervision of Johann Georg Neumann, a Lutheran theologian in Wittenberg (1687).[39]

---

35. *An Salomon psalmographus fuerit?* ("Was Solomon a psalm writer?") (9.36, pp. 336–37).

36. *Exscribuntur duo Salomonis psalmi ex repertis in Bibliotheca Augustana* ("Two psalms of Solomon were copied from their discovery in the library of Augsburg") (9.37, pp. 337–39); *Considerantur quæ possint derogare authoritat Salomonici psaterii* ("They are considered as able to contradict the Solomonic authorship of the Psalter") (9.38, pp. 339–40). He disregarded the Solomonic authorship of Pss. Sol. 1 because he understood it as describing persecution in a Jerusalem without a king. He disregarded the Solomonic authorship of Pss. Sol. 18 because he considered its mention of Christos Kyrios in Pss. Sol. 17.32 as probably Christian, and because Pss. Sol. 2.1 mentions a battering-ram, a machine that he presumed to have been invented by the Carthagians. After dealing with the issue of authorship, Nieremberg observed for the first time in print that the Psalms of Solomon are quoted by none of the fathers of the church.

37. On Fabricius and the origins of the Old Testament pseudepigrapha, see Annette Yoshiko Reed, "The Modern Invention of 'Old Testament Pseudepigrapha,'" *JTS* 60 (2009): 403–36.

38. For a later contribution by a Jesuit, see Ferdinand Cavallera, "Un chef-d'oeuvre de la littérature apocryphe: Les Psaumes de Salomon; Bulletin de Patrologie," *Études* 118 (1909): 789–805.

39. Georg Janenskius, *Dissertationem historico criticam de Psalterio Salomonis* (Wittenberg: Christian Fincelius, 1687).

Three Jesuits were at the foundation of the modern study of the Psalms of Solomon—Schott, de la Cerda, and Nieremberg. Their work on the Psalms of Solomon was not carried out in religious isolation, however, but through collaboration with Catholic laypersons like Tengnagel and Protestants like Hœschel and Meursis. These proceedings of the Second International Meeting of the Psalms of Solomon at the Centre Sèvres should be considered as not only a commemoration of the significant contributions of Jesuit intellectuals to the modern study of the Psalms of Solomon during the Renaissance, but also as a tribute to Schott's willingness to collaborate with others to advance humanistic inquiry through the preservation and discussion of little-known ancient texts during times of interreligious strife.

2. What Has Happened since the First Meeting?

The Second International Meeting on the Psalms of Solomon pursued the same general objectives as the First International Meeting, which was convened in Strasbourg, France, in June, 2013: "to take a fresh look at established views and to develop perspectives for future research."[40] The proceedings of the First International Meeting were edited by Eberhard Bons and Pouchelle and published in early 2015 as *The Psalms of Solomon: Language, History, and Theology* (SBL Press). Since these essays were published prior to the Second International Meeting, they helped to orient some of the research questions addressed in Paris in July, 2015. Moreover, several of the same scholars participated in both conferences. It is important to note, however, that a number of studies have been published since the First Meeting (and even since the Second Meeting), which shed new light on the Psalms of Solomon and will also help to shape future research on the text. Much of this research contributes, in particular, to the three areas that Kenneth Atkinson identified in his formal response to the papers from the First Meeting as ripe for further inquiry: the text's language of composition, literary structure, and historical setting (especially, its sectarian background and messianism).[41]

---

40. Eberhard Bons and Patrick Pouchelle, introduction to *The Psalms of Solomon: Language, History, Theology*, ed. Eberhard Bons and Patrick Pouchelle, EJL 40 (Atlanta: SBL Press, 2015), 1.

41. Kenneth Atkinson, "Response," in Bons and Pouchelle, *Psalms of Solomon*, 188–91.

Prior to the First Meeting, there was a consensus among scholars that the Psalms of Solomon was originally composed in a Semitic language, with most preferring Hebrew to Aramaic. During and since the first meeting, this question has been reinvigorated. Some scholars now think that at least parts of the text were originally composed in Greek. Two main arguments have been put forward: first, that the Psalms of Solomon employs Greek vocabulary that relies on idiosyncratic Septuagint translations; and, second, that in some cases, the psalms convey Greek philosophical concepts that could not have been represented by Hebrew vocabulary.[42] Atkinson signaled in his response that this challenge cannot be ignored, even if, in his mind, Greek should ultimately be rejected as the original language of the text. He has suggested, on the one hand, that some Septuagintalisms in the text could have been introduced by the Greek translator of an original Semitic text and, on the other hand, that parts of the text (e.g., 9.4) may have been written in Greek.[43] This debate has demonstrated the need for improved methods for determining the original languages of the pseudepigrapha in particular. As James Davila and Daniele Pevarello have remarked (independent of this renewed debate), the Psalms of Solomon is an "ideal candidate" for this quest.[44]

This issue of the text's language of composition overlaps to some degree with both of the other foci of current research—the literary structure of the text and its historical setting. Whereas it has been common to view the psalms as independent compositions, betraying different forms and even dates, some recent scholarship has detected more literary coherence across the collection (if *collection* is the right term) than is often assumed. By arguing that the psalms are transected by a common Deuteronomic ideology of history typical of biblical prophecy, for instance,

---

42. Eberhard Bons, "Philosophical Vocabulary in the Psalms of Solomon: The Case of Ps. Sol. 9:4," in Bons and Pouchelle, *Psalms of Solomon*, 49–59; see also the discussion in Albrecht, *Psalmi Salomonis*, 181–82.

43. Atkinson, "Response," 179, 181. See also Atkinson's more recent analysis of the Greek and Syriac texts and their history of transmission: "Psalms of Solomon: Greek" and "Psalms of Solomon: Syriac," in *Deutero-Canonical Scriptures*, vol. 2 of *The Textual History of the Bible*, ed. Matthias Henze and Frank Feder (Leiden: Brill, 2019), 332–50.

44. James R. Davila, "(How) Can We Tell If a Greek Apocryphon or Pseudepigraphon Has Been Translated from Hebrew or Aramaic?," *JSP* 15 (2005): 3–61; Daniele Pevarello, "Psalms of Solomon," in *The T&T Clark Companion to the Septuagint*, ed. James K. Aitken (London: T&T Clark, 2015), 432.

Brad Embry has challenged the genre categorization of the text as a series of individual psalms.[45] Moreover, Embry has suggested that the text's similarity to biblical prophecy raises questions about its invocation of Solomon, who was sometimes associated with prophecy in Second Temple literature.[46] Solomon was not exclusively, or even primarily, tied to the genre of prophecy in Second Temple literature, however. What Thomas Elßner has called *Salomonisierung* was much more widespread and particularly common with proverbs, psalms, and wisdom texts.[47]

Independent of Embry, Matthew Gordley has called for a reconsideration of the text's association with Solomon, which is usually viewed as ornamental at best and a later imposition at worst. Drawing on Hindy Najman's work on "Mosaic discourse,"[48] Gordley has argued that the Psalms of Solomon should be viewed as "Solomonic discourse." This proposal has numerous implications—that the position of Solomon in the titles of some of the psalms reflects an early stage of transmission; that the text's psalmic form, didactic function, Deuteronomic view of history, and emphasis on the Davidic messiah all invoke Solomon; and that the text's Solomonic discourse sought to subvert Herod's appropriation of Solomonic propaganda.[49] As Gordley concludes,

> It is not that these multiple themes are uniquely Solomonic. Rather, it is the combination of these themes and their deployment in psalms and prayers that is uniquely Solomonic: Solomon is the one figure around whom these varied but inter-related themes cohere. Thus the *Pss. Sol.* represents one particular instance of the development of the tradition of

---

45. Brad Embry, "Some Thoughts on and Implications from Genre Categorization in the Psalms of Solomon," in Bons and Pouchelle, *Psalms of Solomon*, esp. 68.

46. Embry, "Some Thoughts on and Implications from Genre Categorization," 77. Cf. Embry, "The Name 'Solomon' as a Prophetic Hallmark in Jewish and Christian Texts," *Hen* 28 (2006): 47–62.

47. Thomas R. Elßner, "Das Wagnis der Hoffnung: Ein Bund auch für uns geschlossen (PsSal 9,10)," in *Weisheit als Lebensgrundlage, Texte imprimé: Festschrift für Friedrich V. Reiterer zum 65. Geburtstag*, ed. Renate Egger-Wenzel, Karin Schöpflin, and Johannes Friedrich Diehl, DCLS 15 (Berlin: de Gruyter, 2013), 125.

48. Hindy Najman, *Seconding Sinai: The Development of Mosaic Discourse in Second Temple Judaism*, JSJSup 77 (Leiden: Brill, 2003).

49. Matthew E. Gordley, "Creating Meaning in the Present by Reviewing the Past: Communal Memory in the Psalms of Solomon," *JAJ* 5 (2014): 368–92; Gordley, "Psalms of Solomon as Solomonic Discourse: The Nature and Function of Attribution to Solomon," *JSP* 25 (2015): 52–88.

Solomonic discourse, rooted in the biblical idea of Solomon and going beyond it.[50]

Gordley's emphasis on Solomon's influence throughout the text might receive additional support from the recent proposal by Nathan Johnson that it is "David's son," not Israel, who is characterized as the Lord's "servant" in 17.21.[51] To what degree the Davidic messiah of the psalms may be viewed as *Salomo redivivus* is an issue that merits further attention.[52]

This proposal that Solomon is a more important figure in the ideological framework of the psalms than has been assumed might also find support in recent scholarship that stresses the sapiential character of the text. Both Stefan Schreiber and Pouchelle have detected hitherto downplayed affinities with wisdom literature and Proverbs in particular.[53] These arguments pose a challenge to Embry's categorization of the psalms with biblical prophecy and have significant implications not only with regard to genre, but also with respect to historical setting. Whereas scholarship that asserts or assumes a prophetic impulse in the text tends to view the text as a reaction to the alienation caused by the Roman conquest, associations with wisdom literature might imply different functions. Pouchelle, for instance, has noted that several of the psalms are didactic and idealize discipline and self-sufficiency like sapiential texts; they are not necessarily historical reflections of a situation of suffering and poverty. Several of the essays in the present volume contribute additional perspectives to this debate over the genre of this text and its historical implications.

Another aspect of the discussion of literary structure that has received special attention in recent scholarship is the use or perfor-

---

50. Gordley, "Solomonic Discourse," 88.

51. Nathan C. Johnson, "Rendering David a Servant in *Psalm of Solomon* 17.21," *JSP* 26 (2017): 235–50.

52. Pablo A. Torijano, *Solomon the Esoteric King: From King to Magus, Development of a Tradition*, JSJSup 72 (Leiden: Brill, 2002), 109; Gordley, "Creating Meaning in the Present," 389.

53. Stefan Schreiber, "Can Wisdom Be Prayer? Form and Function of the Psalms of Solomon," in *Literature or Liturgy? Early Christian Hymns and Prayers in Their Literary and Liturgical Context in Antiquity*, ed. Clemens Leonhard and Hermut Löhr, WUNT 363 (Tübingen: Mohr Siebeck, 2014), 89–106; Patrick Pouchelle, "The Simple Bare Necessities: Is *Pss. Sol.* 5 a Wisdom Prayer?," in *Tracing Sapiential Traditions in Ancient Judaism*, ed. Hindy Najman, Jean-Sébastien Rey, and Eibert J. C. Tigchelaar, JSJSup 174 (Leiden: Brill, 2016), 138–54.

mance of the psalms in communal contexts. What has become clear is that very little is known with certainty about the uses of the Psalms of Solomon. The way that the psalms were used in different communities in antiquity could shed light on their literary structure. For instance, the circulation of the text in Christian communities alongside the Odes of Solomon might support the idea that the psalms had liturgical functions as prayers or hymns,[54] but this does not entail that this was how they were intended or first used. Daniel Falk found little evidence of liturgical use in the structure of these psalms, but Atkinson has rejected this argument, proposing that they were used in synagogue settings in their earliest communities.[55] Rodney Werline has drawn on theoretical insights from religious studies and the social sciences in order to illuminate the potential functions of the psalms in their earliest settings: "Most likely these psalms were performed, whether by an individual in communal gatherings or the entire community seems unclear."[56] He has suggested, for instance, that the psalms provided a form for the emotive performance of God's righteousness and the concomitant formation of pious subjects through discipline (παιδεία).[57] One future avenue of

---

54. See further Michael Lattke, "Die Psalmen Salomos: Orte und Intentionen," in *Die Septuaginta—Orte und Intentionen: 5. Internationale Fachtagung veranstaltet von Septuaginta Deutsch (LXX.D), Wuppertal 24.-27. Juli 2014*, ed. Siegfried Kreuzer, Martin Meiser, and Marcus Sigismund, WUNT 361 (Tübingen: Mohr Siebeck, 2016); Lee Martin McDonald, "The Odes of Solomon in Ancient Christianity: Reflections on Scripture and Canon," in *Sacra Scriptura: How "Non-canonical" Texts Functioned in Early Judaism and Early Christianity*, ed. James H. Charlesworth and Lee Martin McDonald, with Blake A. Jurgens, Jewish and Christian Texts in Contexts and Related Studies 20 (London: T&T Clark, 2014), 108-36.

55. Daniel K. Falk, "Psalms and Prayers," in *The Complexities of Second Temple Judaism*, vol. 1 of *Justification and Variegated Nomism*, ed. Donald A. Carson, Peter T. O'Brien, and Mark A. Seifrid, WUNT 140 (Tübingen: Mohr Siebeck, 2001), 36; Kenneth Atkinson, *I Cried to the Lord: A Study of the Psalms of Solomon's Historical Background and Social Setting*, JSJSup 84 (Leiden: Brill, 2004), 211–22.

56. Rodney A. Werline, "The Formation of the Pious Person in the Psalms of Solomon," in Bons and Pouchelle, *Psalms of Solomon*, 152.

57. Werline, "Formation of the Pious Person in the Psalms of Solomon," 152. Werline, "The Experience of God's *Paideia* in the *Psalms of Solomon*," in *Linking Text and Experience*, vol. 2 of *Experientia*, ed. Colleen Shantz and Rodney A. Werline, EJL 35 (Atlanta: Society of Biblical Literature, 2012), 17–44. See also, Patrick Pouchelle, "Prayers for Being Disciplined: Notes on παιδεύω and παιδεία in the Psalms of Solomon," in Bons and Pouchelle, *Psalms of Solomon*, 115–32; Pouchelle, *Dieu éducateur:*

research would engage both this question of use and the matter of the text's language of composition. Partial or full composition in Greek by scribes might suggest more restricted social settings but does not necessitate that the psalms were not performed.

Investigations of the text's language of composition and literary structure, genre, and use are thus inseparable from questions of its historical settings. While the psalms have been attributed to the full spectrum of Jewish sects, the dominant view in the twentieth century was that they were produced by the Pharisees. In his *I Cried to the Lord*, Atkinson challenged this paradigm, concluding that there is not enough evidence to associate the text definitively with any known sect. Recent scholarship has, for the most part, followed Atkinson on this point.

Two recent books have, however, disputed Atkinson's cautious assessment. Heerak Christian Kim has described the Psalms of Solomon as "Zadokite propaganda" like the Dead Sea Scrolls.[58] Although Kim makes some intriguing points about the text's scriptural intertexts, his thesis is unlikely to be accepted.[59] That the psalms share a critique of the Hasmoneans with some of the scrolls is clear, but far too little is known about the so-called Zadokites in the Second Temple period to support the idea that they were a dominant self-identifying group and that this group was responsible for the Psalms of Solomon.[60]

The second book that advocates a specific sectarian attribution is František Ábel's *The Psalms of Solomon and the Messianic Ethics of Paul* (2016).[61] This is the most extensive study of the Psalms of Solomon since Atkinson's *I Cried to the Lord* (2004). As a comparison of the theologies of the Psalms of Solomon and Paul, this book builds upon the founda-

---

Une nouvelle approche d'un concept de la théologie biblique entre Bible Hébraïque, Septante et littérature grecque classique, FAT 77 (Tübingen: Mohr Siebeck, 2015).

58. Heerak Christian Kim, *Zadokite Propaganda in the Late Second Temple Period: A Turning Point in Jewish History* (Lanham, MD: University Press of America, 2014).

59. Many of the methodological issues that Joshua Schwartz noted in his review of an earlier book of Kim's are also found in this study. See Joshua Schwartz, review of *Jewish Law and Identity: Academic Essays*, by Heerak Christian Kim, *RBL* 10 (2006).

60. See further Deborah W. Rooke, *Zadok's Heirs: The Role and Development of the High Priesthood in Ancient Israel*, Oxford Theological Monographs (Oxford: Oxford University Press, 2000); Alice Hunt, *Missing Priests: The Zadokites in Tradition and History*, LHBOTS 452 (London: T&T Clark, 2006).

61. František Ábel, *The Psalms of Solomon and the Messianic Ethics of Paul*, WUNT 2/416 (Tübingen: Mohr Siebeck, 2016).

tion set by Mikael Winninge's *Sinners and the Righteous: A Comparative Study of the Psalms of Solomon and Paul's Letters* (1995). Like Winninge, Ábel has detected very similar theologies in the psalms and Paul's letters and has therefore concluded that the strand that connects them is Pharisaism. Without taking a clear position as to the form in which, or mode through which, Paul came to know the Psalms of Solomon, Ábel has made a strong case for the psalms and Paul sharing a distinctive form of Davidic messianism:

> Paul's message and the theology of the Psalms of Solomon are related by way of expressing the same crucial theological themes, particularly the idea of the coming of the messianic age including the concept of a Davidic Messiah and a Last Judgment according to deeds, where God's righteousness, grace, and mercy are manifested in their entirety and where the universal nature of God's purpose in salvation history—the salvation of "righteous" Jews and Gentiles—is realized.[62]

Whereas Winninge viewed one of the main innovations of Paul vis-à-vis the psalms as an emphasis on suffering as an individual's means of maintaining a status of righteousness,[63] Ábel seems to view both theologies as stressing that God's discipline prepares the righteous and pious for the messianic age. For Ábel, the main difference between the psalms and Paul is that the latter believed that the messianic era had already begun.[64] Although particular points of his argument may be questioned, Ábel's study constitutes the strongest case yet made for theological continuity between the psalms and the Pharisaic messianism of Paul.

An underlying theme in Ábel's study that has recently been developed by other scholars is that this variety of Davidic messianism is a reaction to the "deep disappointment and conflicts related to the dominance of the Roman Empire."[65] Whereas scholars have typically construed the psalms as both anti-Hasmonean and anti-Roman, Nadav Sharon has argued that the text is only anti-Roman.[66] In his view, 17.4–6 is the only

---

62. Ábel, *Psalms of Solomon and the Messianic Ethics of Paul*, 286.
63. Mikael Winninge, *Sinners and the Righteous: A Comparative Study of the Psalms of Solomon and Paul's Letters* (Stockholm: Almqvist & Wiksell, 1995), 213–332.
64. Ábel, *Psalms of Solomon*, 286.
65. Ábel, *Psalms of Solomon*, 290 (cf. 257).
66. Nadav Sharon, "Between Opposition to the Hasmoneans and Resistance to Rome: The Psalms of Solomon and the Dead Sea Scrolls," in *Reactions to Empire:*

clear condemnation of the Hasmoneans and should be considered an instance of hindsight introduced into the text during Herod's reign.[67] The other psalms, Sharon asserts, focus their attention on the Romans as God's instrument for disciplining the people for their sins. This supports Sharon's more comprehensive claim in his *Judea under Roman Domination* (2017) that most Jews supported the Hasmoneans and resented the Romans between 67 and 37 BCE.[68] While future studies will have to measure Sharon's arguments about the Hasmoneans against Atkinson's analysis of allusions to the Hasmoneans and temple priests throughout the psalms,[69] there can be little doubt that his historical reconstruction of the events of this neglected period will stimulate further discussion of the specific historical settings of the psalms.

Sharon's argument that the psalms set out to undermine Roman imperial ideology finds support in James Scott's recent study of the role of the Judean conquest in Pompeian propaganda, *BACCHIUS IUDAEUS: A Denarius Commemorating Pompey's Victory over Judea* (2015).[70] On the one hand, Scott has argued that the allusion to the Romans trampling God's altar in their sandals (2.2) implies that they sacked the temple on Yom Kippur (cf. m. Yoma 8:1).[71] On the other, Scott has suggested that the depiction of Pompey as a dragon in 2.25 parodies Pompey's propagandistic presentation of himself as the New Dionysus.[72] Scott's book has thus generated fresh questions about the psalms as a reaction to imperial ideology. Methodologically, his study demonstrates the importance of taking material evidence and Greco-Roman literature into account when analyzing the psalms and contemporaneous Jewish texts. With this more holistic

---

Sacred Texts in Their Socio-political Contexts, ed. John A. Dunne and Dan Batovici, WUNT 372 (Tübingen: Mohr Siebeck, 2014), 41–54.

67. Sharon, "Between Opposition to the Hasmoneans and Resistance to Rome," 46, following Benedikt Echkardt's theory of Pss. Sol. 17 as a composite text: "PsSal 17, die Hasmonäer und der Herodompeius," *JSJ* 40 (2009): 465–92.

68. Nadav Sharon, *Judea under Roman Domination: The First Generation of Statelessness and Its Legacy*, EJL 46 (Atlanta: SBL Press, 2017).

69. Among others: Atkinson, *I Cried to the Lord*; Kenneth Atkinson, "Perceptions of the Temple Priests in the Psalms of Solomon," in Bons and Pouchelle, *Psalms of Solomon*, 79–96.

70. James M. Scott, *BACCHIUS IUDAEUS: A Denarius Commemorating Pompey's Victory over Judea*, SUNT 104 (Göttingen: Vandenhoeck & Ruprecht, 2015).

71. Scott, *BACCHIUS IUDAEUS*, 110–11.

72. Scott, *BACCHIUS IUDAEUS*, 117.

approach to the historical setting of the psalms, Scott has demonstrated that the psalms may have subverted imperial ideology in much subtler ways than scholars have typically noted.

The three main areas of inquiry that have occupied scholars working on the Psalms of Solomon in recent years, then, are the text's original language of composition, its literary structure, and its historical settings. Debates that seemed settled prior to the First Meeting have surfaced again, generating fresh perspectives and instigating the refinement of methodologies. The studies presented at the Second Meeting and included in revised form in this volume are contributions to these current scholarly debates.[73]

3. The Contents of This Volume

The areas of research addressed in the past colloquium and in recent scholarship are also the focus of many of the contributions in this volume. At the same time, a number of the essays pay special attention to the literary contexts and intertexts of the Psalms of Solomon. The choice of appropriate literary *comparanda* for this text is an essential step in establishing its historical contexts, literary structure, and even original language.

The volume begins with a section on questions of original language, sources, and the history of the textual tradition. Eberhard Bons continues his work on Greek concepts in the Psalms of Solomon in his contribution. By focusing on Pss. Sol. 16.10, Bons sets out to determine how we might best contextualize this text's emphasis on eschewing unreasoning anger. He shows that the LXX regularly employs the same language of anger as Pss. Sol. 16.10, namely, θυμός and ὀργή, but the MT and LXX show very little concern for the control of anger. Bons calls particular attention to the term ἄλογός ("unreasoning"), noting that it appears only twice in the translated LXX texts and seems to be drawn from non-Jewish Greek literature. The idea of unreasoning anger in Pss. Sol. 16.10 is not biblical, according to Bons, but instead derives from a Greek moral philosophical tradition with roots in Aristotle.

Johanna Erzberger takes the question of the text's original language in new directions through an extensive analysis of the common tradition in

---

73. Albrecht's important new critical edition, *Psalmi Salomonis*, was published in 2018, after the manuscript of this volume had already been completed. Nevertheless, some authors took the opportunity to engage with Albrecht's book in late-stage additions to their essays.

Bar 4:5–5:9 and Pss. Sol. 11.2–7a. Unlike previous research on this parallel, Erzberger argues that the interdependency is between the Greek versions of these texts. She maintains that both passages are based on a common Greek source, which each author has reworked in different ways to fit their broader literary aims and structures. Although the author of the psalms has modified the common source less than the author of Baruch, Erzberger avers that the traces of its reworking betray the author's efforts to situate this material in the broader text at the time of composition. Psalms of Solomon 11 did not, therefore, exist in its final form independent of the rest of the text, as is sometimes argued.

The essays in the second section focus on literary and historical contexts more than language and structure per se. Kenneth Atkinson discusses potential intertexts among the Dead Sea Scrolls, demonstrating greater reflexivity about the choice of *comparanda* than is typical in scholarship on the Psalms of Solomon. Following recent trends in research on the Dead Sea Scrolls, Atkinson emphasizes that many of the scrolls were not originally sectarian and would have been influential among the wider Jewish population. Atkinson suggests that a considerable number of Hebrew prayer and poetic texts and collections (e.g., Words of the Luminaries, Daily Prayers, Festival Prayers, the Hodayot, the Cave 11 Psalms Scroll, and the Psalms Pesher) share much in common with the Psalms of Solomon—some combine Deuteronomic and deterministic perspectives in the form of petitionary prayers, some reflect on historical events, and some demonstrate that texts continued to be developed over time and thus remained living. Most importantly, Atkinson contends that the Dead Sea Scrolls intertexts show that the Psalms of Solomon would have developed into a collection over time and would have had a liturgical usage, but this use of prayers in communal worship did not entail the rejection of the temple cult.

G. Anthony Keddie similarly uses intertexts as a window into the historical context and purpose of the text but comes to different conclusions. He argues that the common understanding of the Psalms of Solomon as "literature of the oppressed," like apocalyptic texts, is flawed. Drawing on insights from religious studies and the social sciences, he proposes that religious texts often generate class subjectivities that shape individuals' perspectives on their economic position and agency but do not necessarily align with their actual socioeconomic conditions. Keddie proposes that the Psalms of Solomon combines sapiential and apocalyptic discourses on socioeconomic inequality while alluding to some of the structural sources of economic inequality in the early Roman period. Like apocalyptic texts, the psalms downplay human agency in social change. Like sapiential texts, they connect excessive wealth and sin. In the text's paradoxical alignment of apocalyptic and sapiential perspectives in order to advance a class subjectivity for the pious as the poor and exploited, Keddie finds proof that its producers were not economically destitute.

Patrick Pouchelle continues the search for appropriate intertexts by engaging in the first thorough comparison of the Psalms of Solomon and the Assumption of Moses (a.k.a. Testament of Moses). In a systematic fashion, he addresses similarities of language, dating, and provenance. He begins by noting that recent scholarship on both texts has reconsidered the possibility that they were originally composed in Greek rather than a Semitic language. He then demonstrates that the Psalms of Solomon and Assumption of Moses evince similar strategies for understanding the sieges of Jerusalem by outsiders (Pompey and probably Varus, respectively) and the success of Herod. Moreover, they both depict the altar as trampled or defiled (As. Mos. 5.4; Pss. Sol. 8.12). Pouchelle hesitates to attribute both texts to the same community without further evidence but nevertheless concludes that these texts have much in common and that these similarities deserve further attention as a window into poorly understood communities in early Roman Judaea.

Stefan Schreiber enters the discussion of Paul and the Psalms of Solomon with an essay that was written prior to the publication of Ábel's book on the topic (see above). Schreiber takes as his point of departure the perception of the Torah in Galatians and the psalms and especially its implications for gentiles. Much like Ábel, he views the timeframe of the messianic age as the main difference between Paul and the psalms, arguing that the latter can only conceive of gentile inclusion in the covenant in eschatological terms. For Paul, according to Schreiber, the demarcation between Jews and gentiles has already been abolished by Christ and the works of the law rendered obsolete.

The third and final section appeals to fresh analytical methods to illuminate the literary structure, use, and experience of this text. Shani Tzoref draws on recent work on theodicy in order to demonstrate the genre hybridity of the psalms. She finds elements of three main types of theodicy in the psalms—retribution theodicy, educative theodicy, and eschatological theodicy. Moreover, the text may constitute a reaction to a different type of theodicy, the mystery of theodicy, according to which divine justice cannot be known: even the concept of hiddenness in the psalms affirms that divine retribution is tangible. These different theodicies correspond to different genres in the Hebrew Bible and thus illustrate the genre hybridity of the Psalms of Solomon. Tzoref concludes that the text exhibits aspects of the genres of psalms, prophecy, and wisdom through its form, content, and worldview, respectively. It rejects the epistemological anxiety of apocalypticism by asserting that divine justice may be known through personal and national experience.

Angela Kim Harkins has brought the theoretical approach that she has developed elsewhere in her work on emotions, subjectivity, and cognition in the Dead Sea Scrolls to the Psalms of Solomon. Her particular interest is in the ways that the liturgical use of this text could have shaped the emotional experience of its readers and hearers. Harkins maintains that the text rhetorically constructs embodied experiences that would arouse its readers' and hearers' emotions, vividly provoking them to be afraid of divine punishment. This is especially clear in Pss. Sol. 8, where cues referencing the embodied experience of a theophany (e.g., the sound of war, the feeling of tremors) help to cultivate a religious subjectivity inclined towards scrupulous adherence to the law. Moreover, the particular descriptions of experiences enable readers and hearers to identify with foundational moments in the history of Israel, such as the Sinai theophany, which seems to be invoked in Pss. Sol. 8.

Rodney A. Werline explores some similar questions of memory and experience in the Psalms of Solomon, building on his prior work on these topics. Werline applies social memory theory, largely from a cultural anthropological perspective, in order to illuminate some of the ways that the text's authors constructed the past to make sense of their present. He demonstrates that even those psalms which are ostensibly focused on the individual rely on memories that were developed in communal settings. The memories that the Psalms of Solomon express are not simply a matter of mental reflection but are connected to embodied actions such as rituals that perform remembrance. Werline suggests that the time lapse and crisis of the beginnings of Herod's reign induced the updating of Pss. Sol. 17. As the product of marginalized scribes, the memories conveyed by the Psalms of Solomon may be viewed as an attempt to falsify hegemonic memories, to contest the memories communicated by imperial powers.

The volume concludes with a response essay by Werline in which he summarizes the main contributions of the Second Meeting and outlines some directions that future research might take.

Psalms of Solomon 16.10 and Its Biblical and Hellenistic Backgrounds

Eberhard Bons

1. Introduction

In a previous study on the Psalms of Solomon, I asked the question of what we can say about the theological and intellectual context of this collection of eighteen texts.[1] I argued that it is striking, on the one hand, that the Psalms of Solomon take over numerous typical words and phrases of the LXX Psalter, for example, ἐν τῷ θλίβεσθαί με, "when I am afflicted" (Pss. Sol. 1.1; 15.1; Ps 17:7 LXX) and μὴ παρασιωπήσῃς ἀπ' ἐμοῦ, "do not pass me by in silence" (Pss. Sol. 5.2; Ps 27:1; see also Pss 34:22; 38:13; 108:1 LXX). On the other hand, it is evident that the Psalms of Solomon employ a vocabulary that is not at all typical of the LXX, for example, words like ἀκρασία, "lack of self-control" (Pss. Sol. 4.3); αὐτάρκεια, "sufficiency, self-sufficiency" (Pss. Sol. 5.16); ἀμαθία, "ignorance" (Pss. Sol. 18.4). Therefore, the following question arises: to what degree do the Psalms of Solomon diverge from the LXX and other contemporary Jewish literature? On the assumption that they diverge from other literature of Jewish origin—the so-called pseudepigrapha of the Old Testament—can we observe parallels or similitudes with texts of non-Jewish origin, both on the level of terminology and that of ideas? In my previous study, I came to the conclusion that Pss. Sol. 9.4 shows the specific influence of Stoic vocabulary and ideas of Stoic philosophy, in particular the first line of the verse: τὰ ἔργα ἡμῶν

I would like to express my gratitude to my colleagues Christoph Kugelmeier (Saarbrücken) and Ralph Brucker (Hamburg) for their precious hints and suggestions.

1. Eberhard Bons, "Philosophical Vocabulary in the Psalms of Solomon—The Case of Ps. Sol. 9:4," in *The Psalms of Solomon: Language, History, Theology*, ed. Eberhard Bons and Patrick Pouchelle, EJL 40 (Atlanta: SBL Press, 2015), 49–58.

ἐν ἐκλογῇ καὶ ἐξουσίᾳ τῆς ψυχῆς ἡμῶν, "our works are in the election and power of our soul."

In this essay I will focus on another quotation, Pss. Sol. 16.10, in particular its last line: ὀργὴν καὶ θυμὸν ἄλογον μακρὰν ποίησον ἀπ' ἐμοῦ, "anger and unreasoning wrath put far from me" (NETS). It is not my intention to give an interpretation of Pss. Sol. 16 as a whole.[2] Rather, my aim is more limited: how can we explain the last line of Pss. Sol. 16.10 against its biblical and nonbiblical background?

The following considerations are not based on the assumption that the Psalms of Solomon are a translation from a lost Hebrew text, an assumption held by many contemporary scholars.[3] Although the presence of numerous Hebraisms or Semitisms in the Psalms of Solomon can hardly be denied, the presence of a typically Greek vocabulary and of specific Greek syntactic features, especially word order,[4] are a strong case for the opposite hypothesis. In fact, my contention is that the Psalms of Solomon imitate the Hebraizing style of the LXX, combining it with a terminology borrowed at least partially from contemporary nonbiblical Greek.[5] Hence, it can be concluded that these features—syntactic phenomena as well as

---

2. For a brief interpretation of Pss. Sol. 16, see, e.g., Kenneth Atkinson, *I Cried to the Lord: A Study of the Psalms of Solomon's Historical Background and Social Setting*, JSJSup 84 (Leiden: Brill, 2004), 187–88; František Ábel, *The Psalms of Solomon and the Messianic Ethics of Paul*, WUNT 2/416 (Tübingen: Mohr Siebeck, 2016), 171–74.

3. See, e.g., the following authors: Sven Holm-Nielsen, "Die Psalmen Salomos," JSHRZ 4 (1977), 53: "Daß der griechische Text eine Übersetzung aus dem Hebräischen ist, unterliegt kaum noch einem Zweifel"; Otto Kaiser, *Die poetischen und weisheitlichen Werke*, vol. 3 of *Grundriß der Einleitung in die kanonischen und deuterokanonischen Schriften des Alten Testaments* (Gütersloh: Gütersloher Verlagshaus, 1994), 41: "Die eigenartige, sich nur mittels einer sklavischen Wiedergabe eines semitischen Originals erklärende Verbalsyntax und weitere, offensichtlich auf Lesefehlern beruhende Ungereimtheiten des griechischen Textes sprechen für die Annahme, daß das Buch ursprünglich hebräisch abgefaßt war"; Albert-Marie Denis, *Introduction à la littérature religieuse judéo-hellénistique*, 2 vols. (Turnhout: Brepols, 2000), 1:521: "La langue de composition a été probablement l'hébreu"; 243; Antonio Piñero Sáenz, "Salmos de Salomón," in *Libros poéticos y sapienciales*, vol. 3 of *La Biblia griega Septuaginta*, ed. Natalio Fernández Marcos and María Victoria Spottorno Díaz-Caro (Salamanca: Ediciones Sígueme, 2013), 239–69, esp. 243: "Sin embargo, el análisis del texto griego conduce irremisiblemente a postular un original hebreo."

4. See discussion in Felix Albrecht, *Psalmi Salomonis*, SVTG 12.3 (Göttingen: Vandenhoeck & Ruprecht, 2018), 181–82.

5. See Bons, "Philosophical Vocabulary," 57–58.

vocabulary—are a decisive counterargument against the hypothesis that the Psalms of Solomon were originally written in Hebrew.

The aim of the following sections is to explore the specific background of Pss. Sol. 16.10, especially the idea of controlling human anger. In a first stage, it is necessary to gain an overview on how biblical texts speak of human anger and if the idea of control of anger is attested in the Old Testament, both in Greek and Hebrew language. Of course, we should not rule out the possibility that the authors of the Psalms of Solomon had knowledge of both textual traditions. In a second stage I will address the question of how to explain the idea of "unreasoning wrath" against the background of Greek literature. To the best of my knowledge, this issue has not been dealt with in past research on the Psalms of Solomon.[6] Finally, some conclusions will be drawn as to better understand the quotation ὀργὴν καὶ θυμὸν ἄλογον μακρὰν ποίησον ἀπ' ἐμοῦ, taking into consideration its biblical and nonbiblical roots.

2. Human Anger in the Old Testament: A Brief Overview

To begin with, it is interesting to note that in the Old Testament the attestations of human anger are far less frequent than those dealing with divine anger. More than five hundred passages allude to divine anger whereas around two hundred mention human anger.[7] Anyway, as for this latter category, one might conclude that in the Old Testament narratives human anger normally is not judged negatively. Not one of the protagonists of the narratives exhorts another person to calm down or to control his anger. In order to illustrate this idea, it might suffice to quote two examples:

(1) After having instigated her son Jacob to take away his father's blessing to the detriment of his firstborn son, Esau, Rebekah fears for Jacob's life because the news of Esau's anger had reached her. However, instead

---

6. See already Joseph Viteau, *Les Psaumes de Salomon: Introduction, texte grec et traduction, avec les principales variantes de la version syriaque par François Martin*, Documents pour l'étude de la Bible (Paris: Letouzey et Ané, 1911), 132, who quotes the adjective ἄλογος in a list of words of the Psalms of Solomon that have an interesting meaning ("offrent un sens intéressant," 126).

7. For the *status quaestionis* see, e.g., Stefan H. Wälchli, *Gottes Zorn in den Psalmen: Eine Studie zur Rede vom Zorn Gottes in den Psalmen im Kontext des Alten Testaments und des Alten Orients*, OBO 244 (Göttingen: Vandenhoeck & Ruprecht, 2012), 1–33; Wälchli, "Zorn (AT)," in the online lexicon Wibilex (https://www.bibelwissenschaft.de/stichwort/35502/).

of calming down Esau, Rebekah gives Jacob the following advice: "Now therefore, my son, obey my voice; flee at once to my brother Laban in Haran, and stay with him a while, until your brother's fury turns away" (Gen 27:43–44 NRSV). In other words, Esau's anger is considered to be the most natural thing of the world that comes and goes. Therefore, Rebekah does not confront Esau but is only concerned about Jacob although he had wronged his brother with her support.[8]

(2) Another example is Saul's anger against his antagonist David. In the dialogue between Jonathan and David in 1 Sam 20, David fears Saul's wrath, which means that his life is in danger. However, neither Jonathan, Saul's son, nor David know the king's real attitude, although they have to reckon with Saul's anger (vv. 9–10). But what will happen if this would be the case? Once more, and just like in the case of Esau's anger, the solution does not lie in calming down and appeasing Saul—a task that Jonathan would be expected to undertake—but in sending away David so that he is safe (v. 13).[9]

Needless to say, in these two texts human anger, whether justified or not, is not at all condemned, and no measures aimed at achieving a balance between the interested parties are taken. The only response is to prevent violent confrontation by suggesting to the person in danger that they escape.

Another attitude towards human anger becomes evident in nonnarrative Old Testament texts, in particular in wisdom literature. As before, it might suffice to quote some examples.

In Prov 16:32 the wisdom teacher pleads for bridling human anger: טוב ארך אפים מגבור ומשל ברוחו מלכד עיר, "one who is slow to anger is better than the mighty, and one whose temper is controlled than one who captures a city" (NRSV). In contrast to its immediate context,[10] verse 32 con-

---

8. For a careful analysis of Gen 27, see, e.g., Irmtraud Fischer, *Women Who Wrestled with God: Biblical Stories of Israel's Beginnings* (Collegeville, MN: Liturgical Press, 2005), 63, who comments on Rebekah's reaction as follows: "Rebecca is aware of Esau's justified, helpless rage. She does not speak a word of judgment against him. To prevent anything bad from happening, her beloved son must leave, while Esau can remain."

9. For this detail, see also P. Kyle McCarter Jr., *I Samuel: A New Translation with Introduction, Notes and Commentary*, AB 8 (Garden City, NY: Doubleday, 1980), 345: "David does not act alone in his decision not to return to Gibeah; rather he does so with the assistance and the counsel of Jonathan. Moreover he does not go willingly but is forced to flee by Saul's animosity."

10. For further details, see the commentaries of the book of Proverbs, e.g. Arndt Meinhold, *Sprüche Kapitel 16–31*, vol. 2 of *Die Sprüche*, Zürcher Bibelkommentare

fronts two human behaviors: military audacity, on the one hand, and the capacity of restraining anger, on the other. Obviously, self-control is not first and foremost recommended to the king or his high officials whose good or bad behavior could have serious consequences for their subordinates, but everybody seems to be invited to bridle his anger.[11] Interestingly, the MT uses the phrase ארך אפים, which is elsewhere employed for describing God himself (Exod 34:6, etc.). The LXX translates the verse as follows: κρείσσων ἀνὴρ μακρόθυμος ἰσχυροῦ, ὁ δὲ κρατῶν ὀργῆς κρείσσων καταλαμβανομένου πόλιν, "a man who is slow to anger is better than the mighty, and he who controls his temper better than one who captures[12] a city" (NETS). It goes without saying that the LXX does not diverge considerably from its Hebrew *Vorlage*, for example, by introducing significant additions or by changing the meaning of the text fundamentally. Yet, the LXX borrows the adjective μακρόθυμος as a rendering of ארך אפים from the Pentateuch (especially Exod 34:6), even though Prov 16:32 deals with human rather than divine anger.[13] However, the LXX slightly modifies the text. Thus, three observations can be made: (1) The Greek translation introduces the noun ἀνήρ, filling a gap in the Hebrew text. Hence, there is no doubt that the advice of verse 32 is given each man and not only kings or nobles. (2) The noun רוח is rendered by ὀργή, probably for "greater specificity."[14] (3) The Greek translation underlines the parallelism between the two lines of the verse by the double κρείσσων.[15] Thus, the second κρείσσων forms an alliteration with κρατῶν. It

---

(Zürich: Theologischer Verlag, 1991), 280; Magne Sæbø, *Sprüche*, Das Alte Testament Deutsch (Göttingen: Vandenhoeck & Ruprecht, 2012), 229.

11. See also Meinhold, *Sprüche Kapitel 16–31*, 280.

12. The use of καταλαμβάνω in the meaning "to conquer" (a city or its parts) is attested both in Greek literature (e.g. Herodotus, *Hist.* 5.72; Thucydides, *Hist.* 3.72) and in the LXX (e.g., Num 21:32). For the use of this verb in the LXX Proverbs, cf. Johann Cook, *The Septuagint of Proverbs—Jewish and/or Hellenistic Proverbs? Concerning the Hellenistic Colouring of LXX Proverbs*, VTSup 69 (Leiden: Brill, 1997), 73.

13. For these phenomena see, e.g., Emanuel Tov, "The Impact of the LXX Translation of the Pentateuch on the Translation of the Other Books," in *The Greek and Hebrew Bible: Collected Essays on the Septuagint*, ed. Emanuel Tov, VTSup 77 (Leiden: Brill, 1999), 183–94.

14. Thus Michael V. Fox, *Proverbs: An Eclectic Edition with Introduction and Textual Commentary*, HBCE (Atlanta: SBL Press, 2015), 253.

15. For a broader study of this phenomenon see Gerhard Tauberschmidt, *Secondary Parallelism: A Study of Translation Technique in LXX Proverbs*, AcBib 15 (Atlanta: Society of Biblical Literature, 2004).

should be underlined that the verb κρατέω governing the genitive ὀργῆς is not a specific biblical expression but is attested in non-Jewish literature, for example, in Menander's *Sent.* 22: Ἄνθρωπος ὢν γίνωσκε τῆς ὀργῆς κρατεῖν,[16] "as a human, be determined to restrain anger."

In another quotation (Prov 29:11) it is in particular the fool to whom the attitude of giving free *rein to his anger* is attributed: כל־רוחו יוציא כסיל וחכם באחור ישבחנה, "a fool gives full vent to anger, but the wise quietly holds it back" (NRSV). Interestingly, the verb of the second line, שבח, is elsewhere used for calming the sea (Pss 65:8; 89:10). Hence, the wise is supposed to be capable of self-control, unlike the fool who, literally, "makes go out all his anger." The disadvantage of this latter attitude for society is evident.[17] Once again, the LXX offers a translation that differs slightly from the MT: ὅλον τὸν θυμὸν αὐτοῦ ἐκφέρει ἄφρων, σοφὸς δὲ ταμιεύεται κατὰ μέρος, "a fool declares his whole anger, but the wise reserves it in part" (NETS). Whether the LXX requires another Hebrew verb than שבח, for example, חשב ("to consider, to esteem") or חשך ("to withhold, to spare")[18] might be left undecided. Be this as it may, the LXX clearly underlines the idea that the fool lacks self-control while the wise is supposed to restrain his anger, at least in part (κατὰ μέρος). However, the syntagm κατὰ μέρος is hardly a literal translation of באחור but appears to be a quite free translation. Perhaps it can be explained by the translator's wish to create a contrast between the attitude of the fool who declares his *whole* anger, on the one hand, and the conduct of the wise who is able to control—thus the meaning of ταμιεύομαι—his anger, at least *partially*.[19]

This brief overview could be completed by an analysis of other biblical texts dealing with human anger, for example, Eccl 7:9 where anger (MT: כעס—LXX: θυμός) is said to settle in the bosom of fools, or Prov 29:8 where the wise who turn away anger (MT: ישיבו אף—LXX: ἀπέστρεψαν ὀργήν) are contrasted with people who put the city in turmoil. These pas-

---

16. Quoted according to Carlo Pernigotti, *Menandri Sententiae*, Studi e testi per il Corpus dei papiri filosofici greci e latini 15 (Florence: Olschki, 2008), 186.

17. See also Sæbø, *Sprüche*, 350.

18. For this debate, see, e.g., the critical apparatus of the *BHQ* and Fox, *Proverbs*, 373.

19. For this interpretation, see Hans-Winfried Jüngling, Hermann von Lips, and Ruth Scoralick, "Paroimiai/Proverbia/Sprichwörter/Sprüche Salomos," in *Psalmen bis Daniel*, vol. 2 of *Septuaginta Deutsch: Erläuterungen und Kommentare zum griechischen Alten Testament*, ed. Martin Karrer et al. (Stuttgart: Deutsche Bibelgesellschaft, 2011), 1998. For ταμιεύομαι, see also David-Marc d'Hamonville, *Les Proverbes: Traduction du texte grec de la Septante, Introduction et notes*, BA 17 (Paris: Cerf, 2000), 334.

sages certainly testify to the awareness that anger could be dangerous both for the individual and for society. Nevertheless, it should be highlighted that an explicit warning of anger is missing in these texts. Thus, one cannot but conclude that all in all the Old Testament evidence concerning control of anger is more than meager. As for the LXX, one should bear in mind that the two favorite words for "anger" are θυμός and ὀργή, just like in Pss. Sol. 16.10 and in the LXX Psalter (e.g. Pss 77:38; 84:4 LXX).[20]

3. Some Considerations on the Greek Background of Pss. Sol. 16.10

The purpose of this paragraph is to provide some clues of interpretation of the last line of Pss. Sol. 16.10: ὀργὴν καὶ θυμὸν ἄλογον μακρὰν ποίησον ἀπ' ἐμοῦ.[21] Obviously, it appears impossible to explain this line in the light of the scarce evidence of biblical texts dealing with control of anger. As for the so-called pseudepigrapha, explicit warnings of anger are rare, for example, Pseudo-Phocylides, *Sent.* 57: μὴ προπετὴς ἐς χεῖρα, χαλίνου δ' ἄγριον ὀργήν, "Do not be rash with [your] hands, but bridle your wild anger." However, the vocabulary of this quotation differs largely from Pss. Sol. 16.10,[22] which lacks the metaphor of "bridling." The same holds true for other quotations dealing with control of anger, e.g. Philo, *Leg.* 3.147; *Deus* 71; 4 Macc 2:16–20.

As for the vocabulary of the last line of Pss. Sol. 16.10, it has already been noted that the word pair θυμός and ὀργή are favorite words of the LXX. *Mutatis mutandis* biblical examples of the phrase μακρὰν ποίησον ἀπ' ἐμοῦ are not missing, although they are less frequent, for example, Prov 2:16; 5:8; 30:8. In Prov 30:8 LXX, Agur prays to God to remove far from him falsehood and lying (μάταιον λόγον καὶ ψευδῆ μακράν μου ποίησον).

---

20. See also Takamitsu Muraoka, "Pairs of Synonyms in the Septuagint Psalter," in *The Old Greek Psalter: Studies in Honour of Albert Pietersma*, ed. Robert J. V. Hiebert, Claude E. Cox, and Peter J. Gentry, JSOTSup 332 (Sheffield: Sheffield Academic, 2001), 36–43 at 37–39; Dorota Hartman, *Emozioni nella Bibbia: Lessico e passaggi semantici fra Bibbia ebraica e LXX*, Archivio di Studi ebraici 9 (Naples: Centro di Studi ebraici, 2017), 113.

21. Text-critical variants are not attested, see the recent critical edition of the Psalms of Solomon: Albrecht, *Psalmi Salomonis*, 353.

22. For the Greek background of this quotation, see, e.g., Pieter Willem van der Horst, *The Sentences of Pseudo-Phocylides: With Introduction and Commentary*, SVTP 4 (Leiden: Brill, 1978), 152–53.

But what about the adjective ἄλογος, a rare word in the LXX? In the LXX texts originally written in Greek, ἄλογος refers to unreasoning animals (Wis 11:15; 4 Macc 14:14, 18), which is in line with Greek use of the word (e.g., Plato, *Prot.* 321b), or to persons supposed to be unreasonable (3 Macc 5:40). In the translated books the adjective appears only twice:

(1) In Exod 6:12 Moses is worried about not being able to persuade Pharaoh to let the Israelites leave Egypt. Whereas in the MT Moses complains of being uncircumcised of lips (ערל שפתים), the LXX renders this phrase freely: ἐγὼ δὲ ἄλογός εἰμι.[23]

(2) In Num 6:12 the same adjective is used in the context of laws concerning the defilement of Nazirites. If a Nazirite defiles himself by proximity to a dead body he is expected to renew his vow, and the previous days of his vow do not count (MT: יפלו): αἱ ἡμέραι αἱ πρότεραι ἄλογοι ἔσονται.[24]

But why is human anger qualified as ἄλογος in Pss. Sol. 16.10? This idea appears to be unparalleled in biblical writings. Therefore, it is necessary to search for parallels elsewhere in order to better explain the quotation. Without any claim to completeness, the idea that anger is unreasoning can be illustrated in the light of the following examples taken from non-Jewish Greek literature:[25]

(1) In the first book, chapter 10, of his *Rhetoric*, Aristotle deals with the different motives which prompt people to act unjustly. Within the scope of the present essay, only the aspects of Aristotle's theory of human action that are important for a better understanding of the idea of "unrea-

---

23. For this translation, see Roger Le Déaut, "La Septante, un Targum?," in *Études sur le judaïsme hellénistique: Congrès de Strasbourg (1983)*, ed. R. Kuntzmann, J. Schlosser, LD 119 (Paris: Cerf, 1984), 149: "A Ex 6,12 traduire 'incirconcis des lèvres' par *alogos eimi* est aussi acceptable que de rendre *Do not enter* par *Sens interdit*." For the presentation of Moses in this verse and in its context, see also Amy Balogh, "Negotiating Moses's Divine-Human Identity in LXX Exodus," *JSCS* 52 (2019): 91–101, in particular 97–101.

24. For an explanation of this translation, see, e.g., Gilles Dorival, *Les Nombres: Traduction du texte grec de la Septante, Introduction et notes*, BA 4 (Paris: Cerf, 1994), 247; for a detailed interpretation of the prescription and the meaning of its last element, see also Innocenzo Cardellini, *Numeri 1,1–10,10: Nuova versione, introduzione e commento*, I libri biblici 4 (Milan: Paoline, 2013), 221–22, 270.

25. For overviews of this topic in non-Jewish Greek literature, see e.g., William V. Harris, *Restraining Rage: The Ideology of Anger Control in Classical Antiquity* (Cambridge, MA: Harvard University Press, 2001); Kostas Kalimtzis, *Taming Anger: The Hellenic Approach to the Limitations of Reason* (London: Bloomsbury, 2014).

soning anger" are highlighted.²⁶ First and foremost, Aristotle distinguishes between two categories of human actions: those which are the result of one's own effort and those which are instead due to chance or necessity (1368b33–35). As for the first category, Aristotle introduces a further distinction: some human actions are the result of habit, others the result of longing (ὄρεξις), which could be rational or irrational (1369a1–2: τὰ μὲν δι'ἔθος τὰ δὲ δι'ὄρεξιν, τὰ μὲν διὰ λογιστικὴν ὄρεξιν τὰ δὲ δι' ἄλογον). As for the irrational longings, Aristotle mentions two in particular, anger and desire (1369a4): ἄλογοι δ' ὀρέξεις ὀργὴ καὶ ἐπιθυμία.²⁷ Hence, anger and desire are not influenced by reason but of irrational nature, the adjective ἄλογος denoting what is not rational (see also 1370a19).²⁸

(2) About one century after Aristotle, the Greek historian Polybius attests to the idea of unreasoning anger, albeit in the context of historical and political reflections. Two sections deserve further attention. First, in a sort of *excursus* on the virtues and vices of a military leader, in this instance Hannibal, Polybius points out the consequences of his behavior for his subordinates. In this context, the historian mentions the θυμὸς ἄλογος, among the possible moral deficiencies of a general that could ultimately play into the hands of the enemy (*Hist.* 3.81.9).²⁹ Second, the term ὀργὴ ἄλογος appears once more in a general consideration on the function of religion in society. Comparing the Romans and their moral values with the other neighboring peoples, Polybius is convinced that religion plays a paramount role for social cohesion and individual morality, especially in the Roman commonwealth, because he claims that "every multitude is volatile, full of lawless desires, unreasoning anger, and violent wrath" (*Hist.* 6.56.11: πᾶν πλῆθός ἐστιν ἐλαφρὸν καὶ πλῆρες ἐπιθυμιῶν παρανόμων, ὀργῆς ἀλόγου, θυμοῦ βιαίου). Therefore, it can be

---

26. For an in-depth analysis of the passage in its context, see, e.g., Gisela Striker, "Emotions in Context," in *Essays on Aristotle's Rhetoric*, ed. Amélie Oksenberg Rorty (Berkeley: University of California Press, 1996), 286–302.

27. The idea that especially desire (ἐπιθυμία) is to be considered an irrational longing (ὄρεξις ἄλογος) is known to Philo, *Leg.* 3.115.

28. For some basic definitions of the philosophical meanings of the adjective ἄλογος, see, e.g., Christoph Horn and Christof Rapp, eds., *Wörterbuch der antiken Philosophie* (Munich: Beck, 2002), 35.

29. For a more detailed interpretation of this passage, see e.g. Arthur M. Eckstein, *Moral Vision in The Histories of Polybius* (Berkeley: University of California Press, 1995), 162.

concluded that according to Polybius "the effect of religion in restraining the masses is highly beneficial."[30]

Whereas Polybius condemns the serious consequences of unreasoning anger, another Greek author, Menander, explicitly stresses the necessity of self-control. The context of the fragment has not been handed down to us. Nevertheless, the text in itself is sufficiently clear: ὀργῆς γὰρ ἀλογίστου κρατεῖν ἐν ταῖς ταραχαῖς μάλιστα τὸν φρονοῦντα δεῖ, "for the wise man should above all in the midst of troubles keep under control unreasoning anger."[31] Of course, the adjective used in this quotation is not identical with ἄλογος but an etymological cognate whose meaning is close to ἄλογος. Anyway, there is no doubt that Menander formulates in a general manner (δεῖ) that the wise is called upon to restrain unreasoning anger.

4. Conclusion: How to Explain Pss. Sol. 16.10?

At the end of this essay it is time to return to the questions raised in the introduction. In particular, three observations can be made.

(1) The vocabulary of the quotation at issue is without any doubt influenced by the language of the LXX. This holds true for the terminology of anger, θυμός and ὀργή, as well as for the phrase μακρὰν ποίησον ἀπ᾽ ἐμοῦ. Thus, the author of Pss. Sol. 16 appears to be deeply indebted to biblical prayer language. However, an exact parallel is missing, both in the LXX Psalms and in the LXX Proverbs.

(2) Concerning the biblical background, there is only scarce evidence for the idea of self-control and of restraining anger. The examples quoted above have in common with Pss. Sol. 16.10 the vocabulary—respectively θυμός and ὀργή—and the idea that anger ought to be controlled. However, they are formulated as wisdom sayings and not as an element of prayer addressed to God.

(3) The idea that anger is unreasoning or irrational is not attested elsewhere in biblical writings. Therefore, compared with the other LXX occurrences of the adjective ἄλογος, its use in Pss. Sol. 16.10 is not easy to explain against its biblical background. This situation changes if Greek

---

30. Eckstein, *Moral Vision*, 137.

31. The fragment is quoted according to Rudolf Kassel and Colin Austin, eds., *Menander: Testimonia et Fragmenta apud scriptores servata*, vol. 6.2 of *Poetae comici graeci* (Berlin: de Gruyter, 1998), 361. In this edition, the text has the number 742. In older editions, however, e.g., LCL 132, 498, the fragment has the number 574K.

literature is taken into consideration. As the examples quoted above can illustrate, anger was considered a sort of behavior held for ἄλογος, an idea that goes back to Aristotle. Admittedly, we cannot take for granted that the author of Pss. Sol. 16 was familiar with the works of Aristotle or Polybius. But we should not rule out the hypothesis that he had come into contact with the Greek philosophical ideas he alludes to, albeit indirectly. The fact that Philo is familiar with such ideas (see *Leg.* 3.116) shows that they were widespread.

To conclude, the author of Pss. Sol. 16 does not formulate a further *mashal* (proverb) warning against anger and exhorting a person to control oneself but clothes his idea in a prayer: that God helps him to put far from him unreasoning anger.

Changing Contexts: Psalms of Solomon 11 and Its Parallel in Baruch 4:5–5:9

Johanna Erzberger

1. Introduction

Psalms of Solomon 11 has repeatedly been judged as unique among the psalms of the corpus for reasons of form as well as of content.[1] In contrast to one significant subset of the psalms, Pss. Sol. 11 shows no focus on the individual. In contrast to another group of the psalms, which are, like Pss. Sol. 11 itself, dedicated to Jerusalem and to the nation, it lacks any

---

1. Pss. Sol. 11 is not listed under any of Claus Westermann's categories of different text genres attributed to the Psalms of Solomon (*Lob und Klage in den Psalmen* [Göttingen: Vandenhoeck & Ruprecht, 1977]). It is also not classified by Otto Eissfeldt, who distinguishes between different types of language (hymn, lamentation, thanksgiving, didactic poem) (*The Old Testament: An Introduction*, trans. P. R. Ackroyd [New York: Harper & Row, 1965], 611–13). Pss. Sol. 11 is, however, considered a hymn among complaint and thanksgiving psalms by Svend Holm-Nielsen ("The Importance of Late Jewish Psalmody for the Understanding of the Old Testament Psalmodic Tradition," *ST* 14 [1960]: 1–54). For an overview of earlier categorizations, see Paul N. Franklyn, "The Cultic and Pious Climax of Eschatology in the Psalms of Solomon," *JSJ* 18 (1987): 2. Concerning the psalm's characterization as a hymn, see Marinus de Jonge, "The Expectation of the Future in the Psalms of Solomon," in *Jewish Eschatology, Early Christian Christology and the Testaments of the Twelve Patriarchs*, ed Marinus de Jonge, NovTSup 63 (Leiden: Brill, 1991), 3–27. George W. E. Nickelsburg counts it under the poems focusing on the people's destiny as distinct from the individual's (*Jewish Literature between the Bible and the Mishnah: A Historical and Literary Introduction* [Minneapolis: Fortress, 2011], 238, 241). For an overview of more recent discussions, see André Kabasele Mukenge, *L'unité littéraire du livre de Baruch*, Etudes bibliques 38 (Paris: Gabalda, 1998), 333–34.

references to identifiable historical events.[2] Moreover, because Pss. Sol. 11 concentrates on Jerusalem's triumph by watching her children return and avoids any explicit allusions to a negative perspective, this psalm, as Svend Holm-Nielsen has put it, "really is the only polite one of the bunch."[3]

Psalms of Solomon 11 shares several textual features with Bar 4:5–5:9, the most obvious of which concern Pss. Sol. 11.2-7a and Bar 5:5-8. However, the relationship between the two texts is highly controversial.

---

2. Kabasele Mukenge, *L'unité*, 334-35, 342. For a discussion of references to historical events in other psalms, see Kabasele Mukenge, *L'unité*, 338. There is a broad consensus on understanding Pss. Sol. 2 and 8 as referring to Pompey (see Joseph L. Trafton, "The Bible, the *Psalms of Solomon*, and Qumran," in *The Dead Sea Scrolls and the Qumran Community*, vol. 2 of *The Bible and the Dead Sea Scrolls*, ed. James H. Charlesworth [Waco, TX: Baylor University Press, 2006], 427). Kenneth Atkinson and Benedikt Eckhardt have argued that Pss. Sol. 17 refers to the siege of Jerusalem by Herod the Great. See Kenneth Atkinson, "Herod the Great, Sosius, and the siege of Jerusalem (37 B.C.E.) in Psalm of Solomon 17," *NovT* 38 (1996): 313-23; Atkinson, "Toward a Redating of the *Psalms of Solomon*: Implications for Understanding the *Sitz im Leben* of an unknown Jewish sect," *JSP* 17 (1998): 85-112; Atkinson, "On the Herodian Origin of Militant Davidic Messianism at Qumran: New Light from *Psalm of Solomon 17*," *JBL* 118 (1999): 435-60; Benedikt Eckhardt, "Pss. Sol. 17, die Hasmonäer und der Herodompeius," *JSJ* 40 (2009): 465-92. In their view, 17.5-6 refers to the Hasmonean dynasty and 17.7-9 to its imminent end. It is Herod, not Pompey, who ends the Hasmonean line. Herod is thus to be identified with the ἄνθρωπον ἀλλότριον γένους ἡμῶν of 17.7 according to Atkinson and Eckhardt. Atkinson posits that Herod is also the πάροικος of 17.28, while the Roman general Sosius is to be identified with the ἀλλογενής ("Herodian Origin," 441; "Herod the Great," 321). According to Eckhardt, the ἄνομος of 17.11 is Pompey; according to Atkinson, he is Herod ("Redating of the *Psalms of Solomon*," 106). Moses Aberbach understands Pss. Sol. 11 as commenting on the liberation of Palestine by the Parthians from Herod's rule ("The Historical Allusions of Chapters IV, XI, and XIII of the Psalms of Solomon," *JQR* 41 [1950]: 379-396). Cf. Johannes Tromp, "The Sinners and the Lawless in Psalm of Solomon 17," *NovT* 35 (1993): 360-61, with regard to Pss. Sol. 17. There is, however, no explicit link to the Parthians or Herod. Samuel Rocca discusses Pss. Sol. 11 as referring to the extension of the Temple Mount by Herod ("Josephus and the Psalms of Solomon on Herod's Messianic Aspirations: An Interpretation," in *Making History: Josephus and Historical Method*, ed. Zuleika Rodgers, JSJSup 110 [Leiden: Brill, 2007], 325). In identifying the messianic figure in Pss. Sol. 17 as Herod, however, Rocca stands alone. The flattening of the high mountains clearly reprises a biblical motif used elsewhere.

3. Cf. Franklyn, "Cultic and Pious Climax," 14. Pss. Sol. 11 is also not marked by any of the ideological elements that have been said to be characteristic of the *Psalms of Solomon*, such as the distinction between sinners and the righteous (Kabasele Mukenge, *L'unité*, 338).

After a short analysis of each text separately, this essay proposes a fresh view on both texts' interdependencies with the goal of further elucidating the ways in which the material shared by Pss. Sol. 11.2–7a and Bar 5:5–8 is integrated into its respective contexts. While Bar 5:5–8 is more obviously linked to its larger context by several verbal references that pertain to issues characteristic of 4:5–5:8, the links between Pss. Sol. 11.2–7a and the full corpus of the Psalms of Solomon are limited to common motifs that appear in varying forms and thus render any direct dependence improbable. The psalm's integration into the corpus is constituted by several literary references between Pss. Sol. 11.1, 7b–9 and individual psalms of the corpus. This essay will argue that the ways in which the common material is integrated into the respective contexts of Baruch and the Psalms of Solomon serve specific ideas of divine involvement in history.

2. Psalms of Solomon 11

¹ τῷ Σαλωμων εἰς προσδοκίαν σαλπίσατε ἐν Σιων ἐν σάλπιγγι σημασίας ἁγίων κηρύξατε ἐν Ιερουσαλημ φωνὴν εὐαγγελιζομένου ὅτι ἠλέησεν ὁ θεὸς Ισραηλ ἐν τῇ ἐπισκοπῇ αὐτῶν
² στῆθι Ιερουσαλημ ἐφ' ὑψηλοῦ καὶ ἰδὲ τὰ τέκνα σου ἀπὸ ἀνατολῶν καὶ δυσμῶν συνηγμένα εἰς ἅπαξ ὑπὸ κυρίου
³ ἀπὸ βορρᾶ ἔρχονται τῇ εὐφροσύνῃ τοῦ θεοῦ αὐτῶν ἐκ νήσων μακρόθεν συνήγαγεν αὐτοὺς ὁ θεός (cf. Bar 5:5)
⁴ ὄρη ὑψηλὰ ἐταπείνωσεν εἰς ὁμαλισμὸν αὐτοῖς οἱ βουνοὶ ἐφύγοσαν ἀπὸ εἰσόδου αὐτῶν
⁵ οἱ δρυμοὶ ἐσκίασαν αὐτοῖς ἐν τῇ παρόδῳ αὐτῶν πᾶν ξύλον εὐωδίας ἀνέτειλεν αὐτοῖς ὁ θεός
⁶ ἵνα παρέλθῃ Ισραηλ ἐν ἐπισκοπῇ δόξης θεοῦ αὐτῶν (cf. Bar 5:7–8)
⁷ ἔνδυσαι Ιερουσαλημ τὰ ἱμάτια τῆς δόξης σου ἑτοίμασον τὴν στολὴν τοῦ ἁγιάσματός σου (Bar 5:1)
ὅτι ὁ θεὸς ἐλάλησεν ἀγαθὰ Ισραηλ εἰς τὸν αἰῶνα καὶ ἔτι
⁸ ποιήσαι κύριος ἃ ἐλάλησεν ἐπὶ Ισραηλ καὶ Ιερουσαλημ ἀναστῆσαι κύριος τὸν Ισραηλ ἐν ὀνόματι δόξης αὐτοῦ
⁹ τοῦ κυρίου τὸ ἔλεος ἐπὶ τὸν Ισραηλ εἰς τὸν αἰῶνα καὶ ἔτι

Psalms of Solomon 11 exhibits a clear structure. The introductory verse (11:1), which imagines an unidentified addressee, and the threefold ending in verses 7b, 8, 9 both speak about Israel and Jerusalem in the third person and frame the central part that directly addresses Jerusalem. This central part, verses 2–7, can be further divided into verses 2–3, 4–6, and 7a according to changes in subject matter. Verse 1 starts with two imperatives (σαλπίσατε, κηρύξατε) that commemorate God's mercy on Israel—to sound the trumpet in Zion and to proclaim the voice of the one who brings good news in Jerusalem. Verses 2–3, which have a close parallel in Bar 5:5–6, start with another imperative (στῆθι), a direct to Jerusalem, telling her to stand upon the heights in order to see her children return from every direction. Verses 4–6, which has its own close parallel in Bar 5:7–8, depicts a transformation of nature that facilitates the aforementioned return. Verse 7a also starts with an imperative (ἔνδυσαι), which again addresses Jerusalem by telling her to put on the clothes of her glory. Though verse 7a recalls Bar 5:1, the parallel is not as close as those just mentioned.

To this point in the psalm, then, we have seen two motifs that focus on the personified city (Pss. Sol. 11.2–3, 7a) frame a motif focusing on the people (vv. 4–6).[4] This motif continues in verse 7b which justifies Jerusalem's triumphant gesture of donning her glorious clothing with the fact that God has proclaimed good things for eternity. Verse 8 changes the addressee and turns to God, asking him to fulfill his promise concerning Israel and Jerusalem and to raise Israel. The final verse proclaims God's mercy over Israel through the use of formulaic language.[5]

There is an obvious break between verse 1 and verse 2 in terms of their addressees. While the unknown addressee of verse 1 is supposed to announce the good news in Zion—a designation that is not adopted again in the following verses—Jerusalem is the addressee of verses 2–3. Although verses 4–6 continue the speech addressing Jerusalem, there is a shift in terminology due to a change in the motif applied to those who return: verse 2, referring to Jerusalem's personification as mother, has τὰ τέκνα, while verse 6, concentrating on Israel's return, has Ισραηλ. Verse 7b, which states God's proclamation of something good for all eternity, would have constituted an ending on its own.[6] In talking about Jerusalem and Israel, verse 8 explicitly names both protagonists.[7] In asking God to fulfill

---

4. Cf. Kabasele Mukenge, *L'unité*, 343.

5. According to Kabasele Mukenge, v. 1 and vv. 8–9 provide a liturgical frame for the prophetic nucleus of vv. 2–7 (*L'unité*, 339–40). His liturgical understanding builds heavily on the interpretation of σαλπίζω, and its relation to תרועה, which is considered to be the Hebrew word translated by σαλπίζω in Pss. Sol. 11.1.

6. Cf. Kabasele Mukenge, *L'unité*, 344.

7. The mention of Jerusalem in v. 8 seems superfluous in light of Israel having

his promise, verse 8 presupposes that it has not yet been fulfilled, thus standing in tension with verse 7b.

3. Baruch 4:5–5:9

Baruch 4:5–5:9 can be divided into subsections according to changes in speaker and addressee.[8] Two main subsections (4:5–29; 4:30–5:9) each start with θαρσεῖτε. In the first main subsection (4:5–29) the speaker, presumably the prophet, addresses Israel. In the second main subsection (4:30–5:9), the speaker addresses Jerusalem. The first main subsection (4:5–29) can be further divided into three paragraphs: in 4:5–9a the prophet addresses Israel; in 4:9b–16 he quotes Jerusalem addressing her neighbors; and in 4:17–29 he quotes Jerusalem addressing her children. Baruch 5:5–9, which displays parallels with Pss. Sol. 11, is part of the second main subsection, announcing Israel's future while addressing Jerusalem.

A first closing is supplied by 5:4. Here, Jerusalem, receiving a new name from God, reprises Jerusalem being named by God in 4:5. These two verses together thus constitute a frame.

θαρσεῖτε λαός μου μνημόσυνον Ισραηλ (Bar 4:5)

κληθήσεται γάρ σου τὸ ὄνομα παρὰ τοῦ θεοῦ εἰς τὸν αἰῶνα εἰρήνη δικαιοσύνης καὶ δόξα θεοσεβείας (Bar 5:4)

---

been mentioned twice (Kabasele Mukenge, *L'unité*, 344), but it establishes a connection with the Jerusalem theme of the preceding verses.

8. In research up to this point, 4:5–5:9 has been divided into a varying number of strophes with imperatives or vocatives taken as markers. See, e.g., Carey A. Moore, *Daniel, Esther, and Jeremiah: The Additions: A New Translation with Introduction and Commentary*, AB 44 (New York: Doubleday, 2007), 305–8, 316. For an overview, see Sean A. Adams, *Baruch and the Epistle of Jeremiah: A Commentary Based on the Texts in Codex Vaticanus*, Septuagint Commentary Series (Leiden: Brill, 2014), 119. Recently a division made according to changes in speaker and audience has been prevalent. See Odil Hannes Steck, *Das apokryphe Baruchbuch: Studien zu Rezeption und Konzentration 'kanonischer' Überlieferung*, FRLANT 160 (Göttingen: Vandenhoeck & Ruprecht, 1993), 177–85; Ruth Henderson, *Second Temple Songs of Zion: A Literary and Generic Analysis of the Apostrophe to Zion (11QPs^a XXII 1–15), Tobit 13:9–18 and 1 Baruch 4:30–5:9*, DCLS 17 (Berlin: de Gruyter, 2014), 184; Adams, *Baruch*, 119.

The separation between the subsections closed by 5:4 and begun by 5:5 is underlined by 5:5, where the call to rise, to stand, and to look toward the east recalls and condenses 4:36-37.

³⁶ περίβλεψαι πρὸς ἀνατολάς Ιερουσαλημ καὶ ἰδὲ τὴν εὐφροσύνην τὴν παρὰ τοῦ θεοῦ σοι ἐρχομένην ³⁷ ἰδοὺ ἔρχονται οἱ υἱοί σου οὓς ἐξαπέστειλας ἔρχονται συνηγμένοι ἀπ' ἀνατολῶν ἕως δυσμῶν τῷ ῥήματι τοῦ ἁγίου χαίροντες τῇ τοῦ θεοῦ δόξῃ (Bar 4:36-37)

ἀνάστηθι Ιερουσαλημ καὶ στῆθι ἐπὶ τοῦ ὑψηλοῦ καὶ περίβλεψαι ρὸς ἀνατολὰς καὶ ἰδέ σου συνηγμένα τὰ τέκνα ἀπὸ ἡλίου δυσμῶν ἕως ἀνατολῶν τῷ ῥήματι τοῦ ἁγίου χαίροντας τῇ τοῦ θεοῦ μνείᾳ (Bar 5:5)

Baruch 5:5-8, consisting of a call for Jerusalem to watch her children return (vv. 5-6, paralleling Pss. Sol. 11.2-3) and a description of changes in the natural world that facilitate their return (vv. 7-8, paralleling Pss. Sol. 11.4-5) has been considered by some to be a later edition along with the closing verse, Bar 5:9.[9]

Notwithstanding 5:5-9 representing a later addition, 5:5-9 does not comprise a uniform text. Not only does it combine two motifs that are attested independently of each other in other biblical texts,[10] but some details connected with these motifs do not work well with each other. While 5:6 introduces the idea of Jerusalem's children being carried, the motif of the transformation of nature in 5:7-8 presupposes that they are walking.

4. Baruch 5 and Psalms of Solomon 11

Eduard Ephraem Geiger was the first to discover similarities between Pss. Sol. 11 and Bar 4:5-5:9.[11] Since then, all possible dependencies between

---

9. While Steck defends the unity of the poem on the basis of content (*Baruchbuch*, 200-5) and Adams on the basis of the manuscripts, which nowhere attest a shorter version of the poem (*Baruch*, 142), the possibility of an independent origin and a later addition of 4:30-5:4, expanded by 5:5-9, has been raised again recently by Henderson (*Second Temple Songs*, 255-56).

10. The motif of Jerusalem seeing the return of her children and the motif of the transformation of nature are attested separately in other biblical texts. In both of the texts at hand, the distinct origin of these motifs is still clearly visible.

11. P. Eduard Ephraem Geiger, *Der Psalter Salomo's, Herausgegeben und Erklärt* (Augsburg: Wolff, 1871). Cf. Kabasele Mukenge, *L'unité*, 330.

the texts have been discussed. A majority opinion supporting the priority of Bar 4:5–5:9 (Pesch, Goldstein, Steck) has gradually replaced the majority opinion that Bar 4:5–5:9 was dependent on Pss. Sol. 11 (Moore).[12] While those who have argued for the dependency of Bar 5:5–9 (or even 5:1–9, including the motif of Jerusalem changing her clothes) on Pss. Sol. 11 propose that Pss. Sol. 11 represented a shorter and more well-structured text, those who have argued for a dependency of Pss. Sol. 11 on Bar 5:5–9 (or 5:1–9) maintain that the passages that create intertextual links between the two texts are better integrated into their broader context.[13] Meanwhile, others have argued that the similarities are more convincingly explained by a hitherto unknown common source.[14] In the history of research, this question of textual dependency is tied up with the dating of both texts and with the question of their original languages.

4.1. Excursus: Original Languages

The original language of Bar 4:5–5:9 has been thoroughly discussed. Most scholars tend to assume that Bar 4:5–5:9 is based on a Hebrew text.[15] Hebraisms, however, are less evident in the poetic than in the prose parts of the book. One of the main arguments for Bar 4:5–5:9 having been written in Hebrew is the parallels between Bar 5:5–8 and Pss. Sol. 11, building on the broad consensus that the Psalms of Solomon was written in Hebrew.[16] Lately, however, this consensus has been questioned.[17] In fact, the most obvious parallels between Bar 4:5–5:9 and Pss. Sol. 11 indicate an interdependency of the Greek versions rather than independent

---

12. Wilhelm Pesch, "Die Abhangigkeit des 11. Salomonische Psalms vom letzten Kapitel des Buches Baruch," *ZAW* 67 (1955): 251–63; Jonathan A. Goldstein, "The Apocryphal Book of I Baruch," *PAAJR* 47 (1980): 191–92; Steck, *Baruchbuch*, 240–42; Moore, *Daniel, Esther, and Jeremiah*, 315–16.

13. Cf. Kabasele Mukenge, *L'unité*, 346, 348–49. For the second argument cf. already Pesch, "Abhängigkeit."

14. Johann Jakob Kneucker, *Das Buch Baruch: Geschichte und Kritik, Übersetzung und Erklärung auf Grund des wiederhergestellten hebräischen Urtextes mit einem Anhang über den pseudepigraphischen Baruch* (Leipzig: Brockhaus, 1879), 43–44; Henderson, *Second Temple Songs*, 266, 272.

15. Cf. Kabasele Mukenge, *L'unité*, 364.

16. Cf. Kabasele Mukenge, *L'unité*, 337.

17. See discussion in Felix Albrecht, *Psalmi Salomonis*, SVTG 12.3 (Göttingen: Vandenhoeck & Ruprecht, 2018), 181–82.

translations from a Hebrew text. Deviations in wording can be explained as adjustments to the wording of a larger context or to significant intertexts. It might, therefore, also be worth reconsidering the question of the original language of Bar 4:5–5:9.

4.2. Pss. Sol. 11.2–3 // Bar 5:5

² στῆθι Ιερουσαλημ ἐφ' ὑψηλοῦ καὶ ἰδὲ τὰ τέκνα σου ἀπὸ ἀνατολῶν καὶ δυσμῶν συνηγμένα εἰς ἅπαξ ὑπὸ κυρίου ³ ἀπὸ βορρᾶ ἔρχονται τῇ εὐφροσύνῃ τοῦ θεοῦ αὐτῶν ἐκ νήσων μακρόθεν συνήγαγεν αὐτοὺς ὁ θεός (Pss. Sol. 11.2–3)

⁵ ἀνάστηθι Ιερουσαλημ καὶ στῆθι ἐπὶ τοῦ ὑψηλοῦ καὶ <u>περίβλεψαι ρὸς ἀνατολὰς</u> καὶ ἰδέ σου <u>συνηγμένα τὰ τέκνα</u> ἀπὸ <u>ἡλίου</u> δυσμῶν ἕως ἀνατολῶν <u>τῷ ῥήματι τοῦ ἁγίου χαίροντας τῇ τοῦ θεοῦ</u> μνείᾳ ⁶ ἐξῆλθον γὰρ παρὰ σοῦ πεζοὶ ἀγόμενοι ὑπὸ ἐχθρῶν εἰσάγει δὲ αὐτοὺς ὁ θεὸς πρὸς σὲ αἰρομένους μετὰ δόξης ὡς θρόνον βασιλείας (Bar 5:5–6)

³⁶ <u>περίβλεψαι πρὸς ἀνατολάς</u> Ιερουσαλημ καὶ ἰδὲ τὴν εὐφροσύνην τὴν παρὰ τοῦ θεοῦ σοι ἐρχομένην ³⁷ ἰδοὺ ἔρχονται <u>οἱ υἱοί</u> σου οὓς ἐξαπέστειλας ἔρχονται <u>συνηγμένοι</u> ἀπ' ἀνατολῶν ἕως δυσμῶν <u>τῷ ῥήματι τοῦ ἁγίου χαίροντες τῇ τοῦ θεοῦ</u> δόξῃ (Bar 4:36–37)

Psalms of Solomon 11.2 and Bar 5:5 exhibit nearly identical wording containing an imperative telling Jerusalem to stand upon the heights (Pss. Sol. 11.2: στῆθι Ιερουσαλημ ἐφ' ὑψηλοῦ; Bar 5:5: ἀνάστηθι Ιερουσαλημ καὶ στῆθι ἐπὶ τοῦ ὑψηλοῦ) and see her children being gathered (Pss. Sol. 11.2: καὶ ἰδὲ τὰ τέκνα σου … συνηγμένα; Bar 5:5: καὶ ἰδέ σου συνηγμένα τὰ τέκνα). However, while they are gathered from the east to the west (ἀπὸ ἡλίου δυσμῶν ἕως ἀνατολῶν) according to Bar 5:5, they are gathered from west and east (ἀπὸ ἀνατολῶν καὶ δυσμῶν) according to Pss. Sol. 11.2. These directions are further supplemented by the north and the remote islands in Pss. Sol. 11.3. Baruch 5:5 and Pss. Sol. 11.2–3 both attribute the gathering of the children to God, but this attribution is expressed in significantly different ways (Bar 5:5: τῷ ῥήματι τοῦ ἁγίου; Pss. Sol. 11.2: ὑπὸ κυρίου). Another imprecise parallel, which lacks lexical coherence, is the motif of the children returning in joy (Bar 4:37: χαίροντες τῇ τοῦ θεοῦ δόξῃ; Pss. Sol. 11.3: τῇ εὐφροσύνῃ τοῦ θεοῦ αὐτῶν).

Most of Bar 5:5 represents a shortened version of Bar 4:36–37. Compared to Bar 4:36–37, Bar 5:5 lacks several textual elements that are not strictly connected with the motif of the returning children. These elements do, however, create a link to the preceding parts of the poem and integrate the motif of the return of the children into its broader context. Thus, οὓς ἐξαπέστειλας ἔρχονται in 4:37 echoes ἐξαπέστειλα δὲ μετὰ κλαυθμοῦ καὶ πένθους in 4:11 and, less literally, ἐξέπεμψα γὰρ ὑμᾶς μετὰ πένθους καὶ κλαυθμοῦ in 4:23, according to which Zion has actively sent her children away.[18] The wording [καὶ ἰδὲ] τὴν εὐφροσύνην τὴν παρὰ τοῦ θεοῦ σοι ἐρχομένην in 4:36 reprises one of the poem's key words (εὐφροσύνη), which is used in verses 11, 23 in the immediate context of elements that verse 37 refers to. This word εὐφροσύνη also occurs in 4:29 and 5:9. Apart from the command to Jerusalem to stand upon the heights (Pss. Sol. 11.2: στῆθι Ιερουσαλημ ἐφ' ὑψηλοῦ; Bar 5:5: ἐπὶ τοῦ ὑψηλοῦ), all the elements shared by Pss. Sol. 11.2–3 and Bar 5:5 also appear in Bar 4:36–37.

Neither the initial imperative ἀνάστηθι nor περίβλεψαι πρὸς ἀνατολὰς nor τῷ ῥήματι τοῦ ἁγίου χαίροντας τῇ τοῦ θεοῦ μνείᾳ in Bar 5:5 have any analog in Pss. Sol. 11.2. The command περίβλεψαι πρὸς ἀνατολὰς in Bar 5:5 reprises Bar 4:36 and also mirrors the following imperative ἰδέ, which is represented not only in Bar 5:5 but also in Pss. Sol. 11.2.[19] The word ἀνάστηθι, which has parallels in Isa 52:2; 61:17, might have been introduced as a parallel to the synonymous imperative, στῆθι, which follows it in Bar 5:5 and is shared with Pss. Sol. 11.2.[20] Such a doubling would follow the example of περίβλεψαι and ἰδέ. Moreover, τῷ ῥήματι τοῦ ἁγίου χαίροντας τῇ τοῦ θεοῦ μνείᾳ reprises its counterpart in Bar 4:37 almost word-for-word.

Several textual elements shared by both Bar 5:5 and 4:36–37 comprise variations. The directions of the gathering of the children in Bar 5:5 (ἀπὸ ἡλίου δυσμῶν ἕως ἀνατολῶν) constitute a variation not only with respect to Pss. Sol. 11.2–3, but also with respect to Bar 4:37, since 5:5 reverses the directions given there (ἀπ' ἀνατολῶν ἕως δυσμῶν). The word μνείᾳ in τῷ ῥήματι τοῦ ἁγίου χαίροντες τῇ τοῦ θεοῦ μνείᾳ (Bar 5:5), which has no equivalent in Pss. Sol. 11.2, replaces δόξῃ in its otherwise word-for-word

---

18. Cf. Johanna Erzberger, "One Author's Polyphony: Zion and God Parallelized (Bar 4:5–5:9)," in *Studies on Baruch: Composition, Literary Relations, and Reception*, ed. Sean A. Adams (Berlin: de Gruyter, 2016), 79–96.

19. The word ἰδέ is equally represented by Bar 4:36, having τὴν εὐφροσύνην as its object.

20. Kabasele Mukenge, *L'unité*, 350. The addition of ἀνάστηθι fully explains the change in the word order of the following phrase vis-à-vis Pss. Sol. 11.2.

parallel in Bar 4:36–37. Additionally, instead of υἱοί, Bar 5:5 has τέκνα (as does Pss. Sol. 11.2).

By replacing δόξῃ (Bar 4:37: τῷ ῥήματι τοῦ ἁγίου χαίροντες τῇ τοῦ θεοῦ δόξῃ) with μνείᾳ (Bar 5:5: τῷ ῥήματι τοῦ ἁγίου χαίροντας τῇ τοῦ θεοῦ μνείᾳ), Bar 5:5 reinforces the link not only to Bar 4:36–37, but also to other preceding passages such as Bar 4:5, 27, which it echoes.[21]

The verbatim parallels between Bar 5:5 and 4:36, on the one hand, and Bar 5:5 and Pss. Sol. 11.2, on the other, can be explained as Bar 5:5 reworking a shortened version of Bar 4:36–37 by means of adding the motif of standing on the heights—either independently or based on another source text. This source text could either be Pss. Sol. 11 itself or a common source.[22] The theory that Bar 5:5 is based on Pss. Sol. 11 or a common source could also explain the motivation for changing υἱοί to τέκνα since συνηγμένα τὰ τέκνα in Bar 5:5 and Pss. Sol. 11.2 is not a verbatim equivalent to οἱ υἱοί συνηγμένοι in Bar 4:37. If, alternatively, Pss. Sol. 11 was dependent on Bar 5:5, the literary implementations would have to be considered to be limited to the motif of Jerusalem standing on the heights, which is most likely secondary in Bar 5:5.[23] However, the existing parallels between Pss. Sol. 11.2–3 and Bar 4:36–37 argue for a longer history of textual interaction.

4.3. Excursus: Bar 5:6

Baruch 5:6, which is missing from Pss. Sol. 11, introduces an antithetical parallelism. Those who have been led away by the enemies on foot are carried back on God's initiative. In offering a retrospective to the time when Jerusalem's children left, its first colon creates a link to the preceding passages of the poem. But this image of the children being carried creates a tension with the motif that follows. Its inclusion might, however, have been motivated by several imprecise parallels to other biblical texts.

---

21. In addition, Kabasele Mukenge observes more detached language in Bar 5:5, which would correspond to similar tendencies elsewhere in Bar 5:5–9. He reads εὐφροσύνη in Pss. Sol. 11.3 as indicating God's εὐφροσύνη (*L'unité*, 351–52). It might, however, just as easily be read as a *genetivus objectivus*.

22. The phrase ἐπὶ τοῦ ὑψηλοῦ does not easily fit its context. It is primarily the watchman, not the personified city, who stands up on the height in order to keep watch all around.

23. Cf. Henderson, who considers ἐπὶ τοῦ ὑψηλοῦ to originate from a common source text (*Second Temple Songs*, 269).

4.4. Pss. Sol. 11.4–5 // Bar 5:7–8

⁴ ὄρη ὑψηλὰ ἐταπείνωσεν εἰς ὁμαλισμὸν αὐτοῖς οἱ βουνοὶ ἐφύγοσαν ἀπὸ εἰσόδου αὐτῶν ⁵ οἱ δρυμοὶ ἐσκίασαν αὐτοῖς ἐν τῇ παρόδῳ αὐτῶν πᾶν ξύλον εὐωδίας ἀνέτειλεν αὐτοῖς ὁ θεός (Pss. Sol. 11.4–5)

⁷ συνέταξεν γὰρ ὁ θεὸς ταπεινοῦσθαι πᾶν ὄρος ὑψηλὸν καὶ θῖνας ἀενάους καὶ <u>φάραγγας πληροῦσθαι</u> εἰς ὁμαλισμὸν τῆς γῆς ἵνα βαδίσῃ Ισραηλ ἀσφαλῶς τῇ τοῦ θεοῦ δόξῃ ⁸ ἐσκίασαν δὲ καὶ οἱ δρυμοὶ καὶ πᾶν ξύλον εὐωδίας τῷ Ισραηλ προστάγματι τοῦ θεοῦ (Bar 5:7–8)

⁴ <u>πᾶσα φάραγξ πληρωθήσεται</u> καὶ πᾶν ὄρος καὶ βουνὸς ταπεινωθήσεται καὶ ἔσται πάντα τὰ σκολιὰ εἰς εὐθεῖαν καὶ ἡ τραχεῖα εἰς πεδία ⁵ καὶ ὀφθήσεται ἡ δόξα κυρίου (Isa 40:4–5a)

Psalms of Solomon 11.4–5 consists of four individual motifs (the lowering of mountains, the lowering of hills, the shading thickets, and the fragrant tree) that are all likewise components of Bar 5:7–8. In Bar 5:7, these four motifs are complemented by a fifth, the filling up of the valleys. Psalms of Solomon 11.4 and Bar 5:7 have a close parallel in Isa 40:4, which consists of three of these motifs, whose order is changed (as the filling up of the valleys precedes the lowering of the mountains and hills in Isa 40:4).

Notwithstanding the common general motif and common textual elements, the structure of the two sections differs. Baruch 5:7–8 is made up of two phrases. God, who is the grammatical subject of the first phrase, orders (συνέταξεν γὰρ ὁ θεὸς) the leveling of mountains and hills and the filling up of the valleys.[24] At God's command (προστάγματι τοῦ θεοῦ), which constitutes the final adverbial of the second phrase, the woods and every fragrant tree give shade to Israel. Neither συνέταξεν γὰρ ὁ θεὸς at the beginning of Bar 5:7 nor προστάγματι τοῦ θεοῦ at the end of Bar 5:8 has an equivalent in Pss. Sol. 11.4–5 or Isa 40:4.

Psalms of Solomon 11.4–5, on the other hand, exhibits a chiastic structure.[25] While God is the subject of the two framing actions, insofar as he lowers the mountains and causes the fragrant tree to grow, the fleeing

---

24. The infinitive ταπεινοῦσθαι in Bar 5:7, which differs from the finite verb form ἐταπείνωσεν in Pss. Sol. 11.4, can be explained as depending on the initial συνέταξεν ὁ θεὸς, which is one of the textual elements restricted to and structuring Bar 5:7–8.

25. Kabasele Mukenge, *L'unité*, 343–44.

of the hills and the shading of the thickets are not explicitly attributed to God (even if the framing does so implicitly).²⁶

The phrase εἰς ὁμαλισμὸν, which is shared by Bar 5:7 and Pss. Sol. 11.4, is placed differently according to the particular structure of its respective immediate contexts. While εἰς ὁμαλισμὸν is an adverbial modifier of ἐταπείνωσεν in Pss. Sol. 11.4 (ὄρη ὑψηλὰ ἐταπείνωσεν), in Bar 5:7 it refers to all three of the elements constituting the first phrase (ταπεινοῦσθαι πᾶν ὄρος ὑψηλὸν καὶ θῖνας ἀενάους καὶ φάραγγας πληροῦσθαι).

Baruch 5:7 is closer to Isa 40:4 than to Pss. Sol. 11.4. This observation is based on the representation of the fifth element of the filling up of the valleys as well as other details. While Isa 40:4 presents valley, mountain, and hill in the singular in conjunction with πᾶς, Pss. Sol. 11.4 uses the plural for mountains and hills. Baruch 5:7 goes partly with one, partly with the other version: πᾶν ὄρος ὑψηλὸν in Bar 5:7 (vis-à-vis ὄρη ὑψηλὰ in Pss. Sol. 11.4) corresponds with πᾶν ὄρος (without ὑψηλὸν) in Isa 40:4. The plural θῖνας in Bar 5:7 differs from the singular βουνός in Isa 40:4, not only as a vocabulary item but also in number. Though differently contextualized, it echoes the plural οἱ βουνοὶ in Pss. Sol. 11.4. The language of filling up the valleys (καὶ φάραγγας πληροῦσθαι) in Bar 5:7, which has an almost word-for-word parallel in Isa 40:4 (πᾶσα φάραγξ πληρωθήσεται) but no equivalent in Pss. Sol. 11, changes πᾶσα φάραγξ. This would have corresponded to the use of the singular (in conjunction with πᾶς), to which Bar 5:7 seems to adapt, in using πᾶν ὄρος, to φάραγγας πληροῦσθαι. The plural οἱ βουνοὶ corresponds to the plural θῖνας, which now precedes οἱ βουνοὶ in Bar 5:4.

While in Isa 40:4 and Bar 5:7 the hills are part of a parallelism, according to which the hills are lowered like the mountains, οἱ βουνοὶ ἐφύγοσαν ἀπὸ εἰσόδου αὐτῶν in Pss. Sol. 11.4 breaks the parallelism in accordance with the chiastic structure described above. Psalms of Solomon 11.4 might be inspired by Ps 113 [114]:3–4 (which also has βουνοί).²⁷ This chiastic structure reinterprets a key word (βουνοί; Isa 40:4: θίς; Bar 5:7) that is part

---

26. Another difference concerns the tenses. In Isa 40:4 the changes in the natural world are described with a passive form (a *niphal* in the Hebrew). While Isa 40:4 has future forms and Pss. Sol. has aorist forms throughout, Bar 5:7–8 has aorist forms for the finite verbs. Both ταπεινοῦσθαι and πληροῦσθαι are infinitive present forms. The abrupt change in Bar 5:7–8 to the past tense has often been observed (Moore, *Daniel, Esther, and Jeremiah*, 315; Henderson, *Second Temple Songs*, 266).

27. Kabasele Mukenge, *L'unité*, 343; Henderson, *Second Temple Songs*, 270. The use of psalmic language underlines the literary genre of the text.

of this motif in parallel texts while sacrificing the parallelism between the cola in favor of the above described chiastic structure and quoting another source. Therefore, this chiastic structure as it appears in Pss. Sol. 11.4 (or its source) is most likely secondary with respect to Bar 5:7–8 or an earlier form of the motif as represented by both Bar 5:7–8 and Isa 40:4. The word βουνός, which is used in both Isa 40:4 and Pss. Sol. 11.4, is the more common term, while θίς, which is used in Bar 5:5, appears only four times in the Septuagint (Gen 49:26; Deut 12:2; Job 15:7; Bar 5:7). A change of the Greek term in Bar 5:7 from βουνὸς to θίς might have been inspired by Gen 49:26.[28]

Baruch 5:8 and Pss. Sol. 11.5, having no parallel in Isa 40, share the phrase οἱ δρυμοὶ ἐσκίασαν (though with variation in word order) and the expression πᾶν ξύλον εὐωδίας. While ἐσκίασαν in Bar 5:7 has two subjects, οἱ δρυμοὶ καὶ πᾶν ξύλον εὐωδίας, in Pss. Sol. 11.4 it has only one subject, δρυμοί. The phrase ἐν τῇ παρόδῳ αὐτῶν (which has no equivalent in Bar 5:7), separates the two elements, the second of which is made the object of God's gardening activity. This allows one to read the Psalms of Solomon in such a way that the trees offer fragrance instead of shade, which results in a more coherent picture.[29]

The woods that provide shade (Bar 5:8: ἐσκίασαν δὲ καὶ οἱ δρυμοί; Pss. Sol. 11.5: οἱ δρυμοὶ ἐσκίασαν) for the returning exiles and the fragrant tree (πᾶν ξύλον εὐωδίας) both appear in Bar 5:8 and Pss. Sol. 11.5. Notably, these images have no model in any known biblical or nonbiblical intertext. The idiosyncrasy of the fragrant tree strongly suggests that Bar 5:5–8 and Pss. Sol. 11.4–5 are either interdependent or building on a common (and unknown) source.[30]

Baruch 5:7–8 and Isa 40:4–5a share features that have no equivalent in Pss. Sol. 11.4–6. These include the motif of the valleys being filled, the parallel lowering of the mountains and hills, the singular ὄρος by contrast

---

28. See also Kabasele Mukenge (*L'unité*, 347), who considers θίς to be more pretentious. More elevated language is also represented by the verb βαδίζω instead of ἀσφαλῶς in Bar 4:7, which, however, can be explained by the occurrence of the same word elsewhere in the poem.

29. Kabasele Mukenge, *L'unité*, 354.

30. Goldstein considers the motif of the shade-giving trees to be based on Isa 41:19–20 ("Apocryphal Book," 191–92). Henderson (*Second Temple Songs*, 269) follows his argument. The parallel, however, remains vague. There is no verbatim parallel that would justify considering Isa 41:19–20 as a common source.

to the plural in Pss. Sol. 11.4, and the position of the announcement of God's glory. At the same time, Bar 5:7–8 and Pss. Sol. 11.4–5 share features that have no equivalent in Isa 40:4–5a such as εἰς ὁμαλισμὸν, the plural of θῖνας and οἱ βουνοὶ versus the singular βουνὸς in Isa 40:4, and the relative closeness of the formulation of the announcement of God's glory. However, Pss. Sol. 11.4–5 and Isa 40:4–5a share no common features that are absent from Bar 5:7 other than βουνος/βουνοὶ (versus θίς in Bar 5:7, which can be explained by θίς being inspired by Gen 49:26). It is, therefore, more likely that there is some interdependence between Baruch and Isaiah, as well as between the Psalms of Solomon and Baruch, rather than between the Psalms of Solomon and Isaiah.

Baruch 5:5–8 might be understood as building on Isa 40:4 and a text containing the motif of the fragrant tree. The differing position of the lowering of the valleys argues for Bar 5:5–8 modifying another *Vorlage* according to Isa 40:4 rather than primarily depending on it.

Although Pss. Sol. 11.4–5, which lacks the motif of the valleys being filled, might be considered to have limited its choice of material from Bar 5:7–8 to whatever was necessary to create a chiastic structure, the mixture of plural and singular for nouns in Bar 5:7 argues for Bar 5:7 being based on Pss. Sol. 11.4 rather than Pss. Sol. 11.4 being based on Bar 5:7.

4.5. Pss. Sol. 11.6 // Bar 5:7b

ἵνα παρέλθῃ Ισραηλ ἐν ἐπισκοπῇ δόξης θεοῦ αὐτῶν (Pss. Sol. 11.6)

ἵνα βαδίσῃ Ισραηλ ἀσφαλῶς τῇ τοῦ θεοῦ δόξῃ (Bar 5:7b)

The clause ἵνα βαδίσῃ Ισραηλ ἀσφαλῶς τῇ τοῦ θεοῦ δόξῃ in Bar 5:7 has a close, but not word-for-word parallel in ἵνα παρέλθῃ Ισραηλ ἐν ἐπισκοπῇ δόξης θεοῦ αὐτῶν in Pss. Sol. 11.6. It has frequently been observed that the phrase makes more sense in its context in the Psalms of Solomon.[31] It has less often been remarked that the parallel in Isa 40:4 likewise closes with an announcement of the Lord's glory. While the announcement of Israel's protection by God's glory in Bar 5:7 and the announcement of the appearance of God's glory in Isa 40:5 are similarly positioned in context, the wording of Bar 5:7 is closer to Pss. Sol. 11.6.

---

31. Cf. already Pesch, "Abhängigkeit," 262.

The differences between Bar 5:7 and Pss. Sol. 11.6 concern the verb βαδίζω in Bar 5:7 versus παρέρχομαι in Pss. Sol. 11.6 (the verbs are synonyms) and ἐν ἐπισκοπῇ in Pss. Sol. 11.6 versus ἀσφαλῶς in Bar 5:7. The phrase ἐν ἐπισκοπῇ creates a link with Pss. Sol. 11.1.[32] The verb βαδίζω, which has appeared twice in Bar 4:19, might have been chosen in order to establish a link with this passage, where βαδίζω is used to describe the movement, that is, Jerusalem's children not returning.[33] The reinterpretation and more logical relocation of the announcement of God's glory might have been due to Pss. Sol. 11 as well as to its *Vorlage*. Alternatively, Bar 5:7 might have relocated the announcement under the influence of Isa 40:4.

4.6. Excursus: Pss. Sol. 11.7a and Bar 5:1

> ἔνδυσαι Ιερουσαλημ τὰ ἱμάτια τῆς δόξης σου ἑτοίμασον τὴν στολὴν τοῦ ἁγιάσματός σου ὅτι ὁ θεὸς ἐλάλησεν ἀγαθὰ Ισραηλ εἰς τὸν αἰῶνα καὶ ἔτι (Pss. Sol. 11.7)

> [20] περιεζώσατο σάκκον ἀντὶ ἐνδύματος εὐπρεπείας σχοινίον περὶ τὴν κεφαλὴν αὐτῆς ἀντὶ στεφάνου [21] περιείλατο μίτραν δόξης ἣν περιέθηκεν αὐτῇ ὁ θεός ἐν ἀτιμίᾳ τὸ κάλλος αὐτῆς ἀπερρίφη ἐπὶ τὴν γῆν (Pss. Sol. 2:20–21)

> ἐξεδυσάμην τὴν στολὴν τῆς εἰρήνης ἐνεδυσάμην δὲ σάκκον τῆς δεήσεώς μου κεκράξομαι πρὸς τὸν αἰώνιον ἐν ταῖς ἡμέραις μου (Bar 4:20)

> ἔκδυσαι Ιερουσαλημ τὴν στολὴν τοῦ πένθους καὶ τῆς κακώσεώς σου καὶ ἔνδυσαι τὴν εὐπρέπειαν τῆς παρὰ τοῦ θεοῦ δόξης εἰς τὸν αἰῶνα [2] περιβαλοῦ τὴν διπλοΐδα τῆς παρὰ τοῦ θεοῦ δικαιοσύνης ἐπίθου τὴν μίτραν ἐπὶ τὴν κεφαλήν σου τῆς δόξης τοῦ αἰωνίου (Bar 5:1–2)

The motif of Jerusalem changing her clothes appears once again in the broader contexts of both Pss. Sol. 11.7 and Bar 5:1 (see Pss. Sol. 2.20–21; Bar 4:20). Psalms of Solomon 2.20–21; 11.7 and Bar 4:20; 5:1 are marked by similar structural patterns, namely, by paired pieces of clothing that

---

32. Kabasele Mukenge, *L'unité*, 353; Henderson, *Second Temple Songs*, 272.
33. Henderson, *Second Temple Songs*, 272.

symbolize Jerusalem's grief and triumph respectively. This pattern depicts a piece of clothing either by the juxtaposition of a piece of clothing and an abstract noun in a genitive construction (cf. Isa 61:10) or occasionally by an abstract noun that metaphorically replaces the piece of clothing altogether (Bar 5:1: τὴν εὐπρέπειαν τῆς παρὰ τοῦ θεοῦ δόξης; cf. Pss. Sol. 2.21).[34] The presence of common words such as στολή (Bar 4:20; 5:1; Pss. Sol. 11.7) or σάκκος (Bar 4:20; Pss. Sol. 2.20) might be due to the motif in general and does not justify the assumption of direct dependence.

Baruch 5:2 and Pss. Sol. 2.20–21; 11.7 show an interrelation based on δόξα, which is a key word of the larger contexts of all three passages (Bar 4:24, 37; 5:1, 2, 4, 6, 7, 9; Pss. Sol. 2.5, 19, 21, 31; 11.6, 8). They are interrelated even more tightly by a combination of μίτρα and δόξα in Bar 5:2 (τὴν μίτραν ἐπὶ τὴν κεφαλήν σου τῆς δόξης τοῦ αἰωνίου) and Pss. Sol. 2.21 (μίτραν δόξης). The complex construction τὴν μίτραν ἐπὶ τὴν κεφαλήν σου τῆς δόξης τοῦ αἰωνίου (Bar 5:2), which has attracted attention, represents a development of the idea represented by Pss. Sol. 2.20–21.[35]

While the evidence does not suffice to prove direct dependence between the versions of the motif of Jerusalem changing her clothes in Baruch and the Psalms of Solomon,[36] the usage of δόξα in each is marked by an important difference that characterizes the respective ideologies of the texts: while it is the δόξα of Jerusalem according to Pss. Sol. 2.21; 11.7, it is the δόξα of God according to Bar 5:1–2.

5. The Adaptation of the Common Material in Baruch

A common *Vorlage* that would be closer to Pss. Sol. 11.2–6 (without v. 3) than to Bar 5:5–8 seems to be the most convincing solution concerning the question of interdependency. The fact of the common material being more obviously adapted to its current context in Bar 4:5–5:9 touches on several characteristic issues of Bar 4:5–5:9.

---

34. In a similar way δόξα replaces a piece of garment in Isa 52:1 LXX, especially vis-à-vis the Hebrew original.

35. If there is any kind of a direct dependence to be assumed, it would consist in Bar 5:2 building on Pss. Sol. 2.20–21. Direct dependence is, however, not necessary. Bar 5:2 could be building on a common motif.

36. The placement of the motif in these two texts can therefore not be used as an argument for the direction of dependency between the parallels in Bar 5:1–9 and Pss. Sol. 11, as is discussed by Kabasele Mukenge (*L'unité*, 256) and Henderson (*Second Temple Songs*, 270).

5.1. God Acting by His Word

The motif of God acting by means of his word (Bar 5:7: συνέταξεν γὰρ ὁ θεὸς; 5:8: προστάγματι τοῦ θεοῦ) establishes the organizing structure of Bar 5:7–8. That constitutes one of the major differences between Bar 5:7–8 and its parallels. It also reprises a motif that has already been a point of distinction between Bar 5:5 (which itself reprises Bar 4:36–37) and Pss. Sol. 11.2 in the preceding subsection. According to Bar 5:5, Jerusalem's children are gathered by the Holy One's word (τῷ ῥήματι τοῦ ἁγίου), rather than by the Lord (ὑπὸ κυρίου) as in Pss. Sol. 11.2. Just as Bar 5:5 reprises 4:36–37, 5:7–8 here inscribes itself into and reinforces an ideological or theological feature of the larger context of 4:5–5:9.

5.2. The Directions of Return

In the context of the fictional setting of Baruch, the imperative περίβλεψαι πρὸς ἀνατολάς, which Bar 4:36 and 5:4 have in common, calls to mind the Babylonian exile. The verses that follow 4:36, according to which the children are gathered from the east to the west, correspond to the fictional setting.[37] The verses that follow 5:4 (ἀπ' ἀνατολῶν ἕως δυσμῶν), while reversing the order of the given directions, remain connected to the wording of 4:36. If read against the background of the function of the motif of the Babylonian exile in Baruch, according to which the Babylonian exile is applicable to the situation of the diaspora in later times, the reversing of the order of the directions opens up the metaphor for later returns while highlighting the connection to the original metaphor.[38]

---

37. The imagery of the east does not fit with the well-known metaphor of the enemy from the north, which is well attested in the book of Jeremiah, where it refers to the Babylonians. Christian-Bernard Amphoux and Arnaud Serandour ("La date de la forme courte de Jérémie," in *Eukarpa: Études sur la Bible et ses exégètes*, ed. Mireille Loubet and Didier Pralon [Paris: Cerf, 2011], 28) have pointed out that the Babylonians were actually situated in the east and understands the north in Jeremiah as enigmatically referring to Alexander or his Seleucid successors, not to the Babylonians. Without discussing the meaning of the metaphor in Jeremiah, the east makes good sense as referring to the Babylonians in the context of the book of Baruch.

38. *Pace* Steck, *Baruchbuch*, 227. It is not necessary to identify Bar 4:36 and 5:4 with two distinct movements of return.

6. The Recontextualization of the Common Material in Pss. Sol. 11 and in the Corpus of the Psalms of Solomon

6.1. Pss. Sol. 11.2–7a (the Common Material) in the Corpus of the Psalms of Solomon and the Motif of the Directions of Return in Pss. Sol. 11

Psalms of Solomon 11.2–7a makes use of motifs that echo other psalms in the corpus: the characterization of Jerusalem as mother, the return of the exiled, and Jerusalem changing her clothes, all of which are equally attested in other biblical texts.[39] While parallels between Bar 5:5–9 and Pss. Sol. 11.2–6 are close enough to suggest a common *Vorlage* that has already combined originally independent motifs, any links between Pss. Sol. 11.2–7a and the entire corpus of the Psalms of Solomon (links that are limited to these common motifs) remain weak. Their different forms render direct dependence unlikely, however.

There are, on the other hand, no indications of the common material having been reworked in order to fit the corpus. The motif of the directions of return might serve as a cross check. Psalms of Solomon 11.2 offers the same elements as Bar 5:4, following the order of Bar 4:36, which more genuinely seems to be connected with the original motif. However, it reinterprets them by turning the giving of directions into the first part of a list, which is supplemented by verse 3, which itself has no equivalent in Bar 4:37. The north and the islands complete the directions given in Pss. Sol. 11.2. The islands in Pss. Sol. 11.3 would have to be located in the west, not in the south as they would be if the list of directions is considered to be complete. The west already being part of a more original version of the motif as it is represented by Bar 4:37 might explain its substituting for another direction. In biblical texts islands often indicate

---

39. The otherwise unidentified speaker of Pss. Sol. 1, who refers to his or her children, might be identified with Jerusalem (Kabasele Mukenge, *L'unité*, 342). Pss. Sol. 2 presents Jerusalem as mother of her children. Pss. Sol. 17 features the return of Jerusalem's children. Parallels between Pss. Sol. 8.17 and 11.4 (8.17: ὁμαλίζω; 11.4: ὁμαλισμός; 8.17 and 11.4: ἀπὸ εἰσόδου αὐτῶν) (Kabasele Mukenge, *L'unité*, 341) are due to the fact that Pss. Sol. 8 refers to images that usually (in Pss. Sol. 11 as in other biblical texts) signify the return of the exiles in order, instead, to describe the foolish welcome of a foreign ruler. The precisely parallel wording of 8.17 and 11.4 (ἀπὸ εἰσόδου αὐτῶν), however, is interesting as it applies to a textual element in Pss. Sol. 11, where the text differs from its parallel in Bar 5.

remote places.⁴⁰ The children will finally return from all sides, including from remote places.

Although the motif of the directions from which the children return in Pss. Sol. 11.2–3 is most likely secondary to the more original version of the motif in Bar 4:37 (v. 3 constitutes a secondary addition), it seems not to be related to motifs of direction in other psalms in the corpus. In Pss. Sol. 8.15 the enemy arrives ἀπ' ἐσχάτου τῆς γῆς. According to Pss. Sol. 17.12 the inhabitants of Jerusalem are sent ἕως ἐπὶ δυσμῶν. Both examples have been read as references to historical events. Psalms of Solomon 11.2–3, however, clearly does not refer to any historical reference point.

The common material has clearly been reworked to suit its larger context in Baruch and has less obviously been reworked for that purpose in Pss. Sol. 11. Therefore, Pss. Sol. 11.2–7a is most likely building on a common *Vorlage* that is closer to Pss. Sol. 11.2–6 (with the exception of Pss. Sol. 11.3) than to Bar 5:5–9.

6.2. Pss. Sol. 11.1, 7b–9 (the Frame) and the Corpus of the Psalms of Solomon

Intertextual references between Pss. Sol. 11 and Bar 5 do not concern the poem's frame in 11.1, 7b–9, which can be shown to have word-to-word correspondences with other parts of the corpus instead. Psalms of Solomon 11.1 has a close parallel in Joel 2:1 LXX and might have been influenced by it.⁴¹ The sound of the trumpet in Pss. Sol. 11.1 (σαλπίσατε ... ἐν σάλπιγγι), which announces God's mercy to Israel, reprises Pss. Sol. 8.1 (φωνὴν σάλπιγγος), which announces war. While Pss. Sol. 8 asks for the gathering of Israel, 11.2 announces it as already accomplished. The key words φωνὴ [εὐαγγελιζομένου] and ἐλεέω in the first verse of Pss. Sol. 11 reprises key words of Pss. Sol. 8 (v. 1: φωνὴν [πολέμου]; vv. 27, 28: ἔλεος).⁴² The phrases φωνὴν πολέμου and φωνὴ εὐαγγελιζομένου once again create

---

40. E.g., Ps 72:10; Isa 49:1; 60:9, 19; Jer 38:10, Cf. especially the LXX of Sir 47:16; Isa 49:22; Jer 50[27]:39.

41. Joel 2:1 LXX: σαλπίσατε σάλπιγγι ἐν Σιων κηρύξατε ἐν ὄρει ἁγίῳ μου καὶ συγχυθήτωσαν πάντες οἱ κατοικοῦντες τὴν γῆν διότι πάρεστιν ἡμέρα κυρίου ὅτι ἐγγύς (Sound the trumpet in Sion, make a proclamation in my holy mountain, and let all the inhabitants of the land be confounded: for the day of the Lord is near). Pesch, "Abhängigkeit," 257.

42. Kabasele Mukenge, *L'unité*, 341.

an inexact correspondence. In 11.1 the sound of the trumpet is identified with the call of the saints (ἅγιοι), which has no equivalent in Joel. The word ἅγιοι in Pss. Sol. 17.32, 43 and λαὸς ἅγιος in 17.27 designate the righteous. In 11.1, ἅγιοι might foreshadow this terminology. The announcement of the day of the Lord is replaced by the good news, which is to be told as described in 11.1b.

The phrasing ὅτι ὁ θεὸς ἐλάλησεν ἀγαθὰ Ισραηλ εἰς τὸν αἰῶνα καὶ ἔτι, which in Pss. Sol. 11.7b follows the motif of the changing of clothes, is unconnected with the preceding motif and has no equivalent in any other parallel text using it. In the context of Pss. Sol. 11, it constitutes a first closing. The phrase εἰς τὸν αἰῶνα has close parallels in the final verses of Pss. Sol. 8, 9, and 12 (comprising variations of εἰς τὸν αἰῶνα) and in εἰς εὐφροσύνην αἰώνιον in 10.8. Psalms of Solomon 11.7b might therefore have been intended not only to constitute an earlier ending to the psalm but also to link the psalm to the rest of the corpus.

The tension between verse 7 and verses 8, 9 might be an indication that verse 9 constitutes a later ending as well, characterizing the proclaimed good thing as not yet arrived. The final formula of verse 9 (τοῦ κυρίου τὸ ἔλεος ἐπὶ τὸν Ισραηλ εἰς τὸν αἰῶνα καὶ ἔτι) equally echoes the final verses of the surrounding psalms (8.43; 9.11; 10.8; 12.6).[43] The substantive ἔλεος is unique to the final formula in 11.9. In Pss. Sol. 11, the substabtive ἔλεος in verse 9 refers to the word ἐλεέω in v.1 and thus constitutes a frame.

6.3. Pss. Sol. 11: The Common Material and the Frame

Divergences between the core (Pss. Sol. 11.2–7a) and the frame (11.1, 7b–9) have already been mentioned. They are reinforced by different kinds of links to different intertexts, which characterize Pss. Sol. 11.2–7a on the one hand and 11.1, 7b–9 on the other. While Pss. Sol. 11.2–7a echoes similar motifs in other psalms of the corpus, the frame of Pss. Sol. 11.2–7a is characterized by several direct references to other psalms.

Psalms of Solomon 11.2–7a is most easily explained as building on older material from a common source that 11.2–6 shares with Bar 5:5–8; this source has been less reworked in the Psalms of Solomon than in the context of Baruch. The framing verses' links to other psalms in the corpus suggest that the frame was created in order to embed the psalm in the

---

43. Cf. already Pesch, "Abhängigkeit," 257.

corpus and argue against an independent existence of Pss. Sol. 11 as a whole before its inclusion into the corpus.[44]

7. Understanding Pss. Sol. 11 in the Context of the Corpus of the Psalms of Solomon

The corpus of the Psalms of Solomon is framed by Pss. Sol. 1 and 18,[45] which offer a general perspective, and by the interrelated Pss. Sol. 2 and 17, which focus on Jerusalem. Within this frame Pss. Sol. 11 is placed at the end of a block of psalms dedicated to Jerusalem and the nation (chs. 7–10) and before another block dedicated to the individual (chs. 12–16).[46] It, therefore, occupies a significant position within the corpus. It is particularly Pss. Sol. 2, 8, and 17 that Pss. Sol. 11 reprises, both by the exact references contained in the frame as well as by shared motifs. In contrast to Pss. Sol. 2, 8, and 17, which refer to historical events, the salvation announced in Pss. Sol. 11 is not associated with any discernable or even imagined historical context.

Baruch, the full corpus of the Psalms of Solomon, and Pss. Sol. 11 in particular offer three different modes of understanding divine action in history. In contrast to both Bar 5:5–8, which follows the general idea of Baruch in using the Babylonian exile as a code applicable to later historical events, and to those psalms of the corpus of the Psalms of Solomon that

---

44. Cf. Kabasele Mukenge, *L'unité*, 333. In the light of the history of the passage that I have outlined in this essay, the wording ἐν τῇ ἐπισκοπῇ in Pss. Sol. 11.1 (which is reprised by ἐν ἐπισκοπῇ in Pss. Sol. 11.6 [Kabasele Mukenge, *L'unité*, 353; Henderson, *Second Temple Songs*, 272]), would have been chosen to fit the latter rather than the latter constituting an adaption to Pss. Sol. 11.1.

45. Cf. Franklyn, "Cultic and Pious Climax"; Otto Kaiser, *Gott, Mensch und Geschichte: Studien zum Verstandnis des Menschen und seiner Geschichte* (Berlin: de Gruyter, 2010), 11. Pss. Sol. 17 was created as a counterpart of Pss. Sol. 2 (Kaiser, *Gott, Mensch und Geschichte*, 118). Kabasele Mukenge argues for intertextual links only between Pss. Sol. 1 and 17 and considers Pss. Sol. 2–16, which he considers to be older, to be randomly distributed in this frame. Pss. Sol. 18 is supposed to be of a later date.

46. According to Franklyn, the framed corpus might be divided into three blocks of psalms, Pss. Sol. 3–6; 12–16 focusing on the individual, Pss. Sol. 7–10 focusing on Jerusalem and the nation ("Cultic and Pious Climax," 3–4). Also, according to Kaiser, Pss. Sol. 11 is followed by a group of psalms (Pss. Sol. 12–16) that focus on the individual (*Gott, Mensch und Geschichte*, 111).

depict God acting in the authors' contemporary history, Pss. Sol. 11 forgoes all historical references and places God's act of final salvation in the eschatological future.[47] One major change that Pss. Sol. 11 introduces into the common material shared with Pss. Sol. 5.5–9, the delimitation of the directions of return in 11.3, functions to disconnect the psalm both from specific historical events as well as from metaphors that refer to them. The fact that Pss. Sol. 11 is intertextually linked to Pss. Sol. 2 and 17 while its message lacks any association with historical references offers commentary on a corpus that would already have been framed by these psalms that refer to God acting in the authors' or redactors' contemporary history.

Psalms of Solomon 11 comments on those psalms that understand God to be the actor behind historical events of the reader's time by using material echoing topics already present in other psalms, by adding a frame that creates a more precise link to some of them, and by dissociating the announced salvation from history.

---

47. In contrast to Pss. Sol. 17, it is not a messianic figure but God himself who enables Jerusalem's children to return (de Jonge, "Expectation," 101). God, however, is marked as the agent behind the messianic figure in the introductory and final verses of Pss. Sol. 17.

Understanding the History, Theology, and Community of the Psalms of Solomon in Light of the Dead Sea Scrolls

Kenneth Atkinson

1. Introduction

The eighteen Psalms of Solomon constitute a significant witness to Second Temple Jewish theology, liturgy, and history.[1] It is the most detailed extant pre-Christian witness to Jewish messianic thought.[2] As a poetic composition, the Psalms of Solomon is also among the earliest Jewish prayer books to have survived from antiquity. Its documentation of the 63 BCE Roman conquest of Jerusalem makes it a rare contemporary historical witness to events of the late Hasmonean period. However, considerable debate surrounds this collection of poems. The identity of their authors is unknown; the community that likely produced and preserved them is uncertain; and the manner of their composition, collection, and redaction, are all disputed.[3] What could possibly shed light on these and many other questions surrounding the Psalms of Solomon is the contemporary collection of Second Temple Jewish documents known as the Dead Sea Scrolls.

This study seeks to go beyond a superficial recounting of verbal parallels to explore what the Dead Sea Scrolls may tell us about the Psalms of

---

1. For the contents and historical background of the Psalms of Solomon, see further Kenneth Atkinson, *I Cried to the Lord: A Study of the Psalms of Solomon's Historical Background and Social Setting*, JSJSup 84 (Leiden: Brill, 2004), esp. 2–14, 211–22.

2. See further Atkinson, *I Cried to the Lord*, 129–79.

3. The Psalms of Solomon was likely written by multiple authors and collected together in its present form at some unknown date. For scholarship on this issue and the proposed authors of these poems, see further Kenneth Atkinson, *An Intertextual Study of the Psalms of Solomon* (Lewiston, NY: Mellen, 2001), 395–429.

Solomon's historical and theological background as well as the community that produced them. The poetic and prayer texts from the Dead Sea Scrolls are an ideal collection for comparison with the Psalms of Solomon since there is near universal scholarly agreement that a large percentage of the Dead Sea Scrolls did not emanate from the Qumran sect but were brought to the site and used by the community there.[4] I am particularly interested in determining whether any patterns emerge between prayers and poetic works regarded as sectarian and nonsectarian that could shed light on the Psalms of Solomon. Because much scholarly literature has focused on the Hodayot, I will mainly concentrate on other lesser-known Qumran texts.[5] I will begin with a little background about prayers and poetry in the Dead Sea Scrolls that is helpful for understanding the Psalms of Solomon before comparing these poems with the materials from Qumran.

---

4. Much of the debate over the relationship between the site of Qumran and the Dead Sea Scrolls is based on the differing definitions of what constitutes a sectarian text and how to determine which documents were produced at the site rather than brought there and how all these were used together. For a discussion of these issues, which seeks to overturn much conventional wisdom of the accepted Qumran paradigm, see further Gwynned de Looijer, *The Qumran Paradigm: A Critical Evaluation of Some Foundational Hypotheses in the Construction of the Qumran Sect*, EJL 43 (Atlanta: SBL Press, 2015), esp. 1–87. Despite this criticism of the traditional view, there is an overwhelming amount of evidence to connect the Dead Sea Scrolls with the site of Qumran and also with the Essenes as described by Josephus. For these issues, see further Kenneth Atkinson and Jodi Magness, "Josephus's Essenes and the Qumran Community," *JBL* 129 (2010): 317–42; Florentino García Martínez, "Reconsidering the Cave 1 Texts Sixty Years After Their Discovery: An Overview," in *Qumran Cave 1 Revisited*, ed. Daniel K. Falk et al., STDJ 91 (Leiden: Brill, 2010), 1–13.

5. Although the Dead Sea Scrolls are often associated with a sectarian community, which is commonly identified as the Essenes, the prayers from this collection are less sectarian than the other writings from this corpus. They contain the same forms and contents as other Second Temple prayers. See further Bilhah Nitzan, *Qumran Prayer and Religious Poetry*, trans. Jonathan Chipman, STDJ 12 (Leiden: Brill, 1994), esp. 5–8, 40–45. For literature on the Hodayot, see Eileen M. Schuller and Lorenzo DiTommaso, "A Bibliography of the Hodayot, 1948–1996," *DSD* 4 (1997): 55–101; Schuller, "Recent Scholarship on the Hodayot 1993–2010," *CurBR* 19 (2011): 119–62.

2. The Poetic Dead Sea Scrolls: Identifying the Corpus

Studying prayers in the Dead Sea Scrolls is difficult since there are many definitions of what constitutes a prayer.[6] For the purpose of this study, I am adopting a broad definition that includes works addressed to God either by an individual or group. I include various types of prayers, such as praise, thanksgiving, supplication, or repentance used by individuals or groups. Because poetry is often used for liturgical purposes, I am not making any distinction between prayer and poetry since both were typically written for liturgical use in antiquity.

Determining the exact number of prayers in the Dead Sea Scrolls is difficult since most of these documents survive in fragments. Joins between pieces are often uncertain and frequently hypothetical. The number of fragments from Cave 4 is estimated at 15,000, and the total number of scroll fragments is estimated between 10,000 to 100,000. The most recent count identifies 931 manuscripts in the collection of Dead Sea Scrolls. If we assume that the average scroll consists of forty fragments, this comes to some 37,000 fragments that make up 931 manuscripts. Excluding those documents that are represented in multiple copies, then 445 individual works were found at Qumran. However, this figure is not identical with the number of compositions since many are represented in multiple copies. If the duplicates are subtracted from this number, then there are approximately 350 independent compositions in the Dead Sea Scrolls.[7]

---

6. See further, Esther G. Chazon, "Psalms, Hymns, and Prayers," *EDSS* 2:710–15; Jeremy Penner, *Patterns of Daily Prayer in Second Temple Judaism*, STDJ 104 (Leiden: Brill, 2014), 1–34.

7. For these figures, see Emanuel Tov, *Textual Criticism of the Hebrew Bible, Qumran, Septuagint: Collected Essays*, VTSup 3 (Leiden: Brill, 2015), 267–88; Tov, foreword to *The Meaning of the Dead Sea Scrolls: Their Significance for Understanding the Bible, Judaism, Jesus, and Christianity*, ed. James C. VanderKam and Peter W. Flint (San Francisco: HarperSanFrancisco, 2002), ix–x. See further the comprehensive listing of the Dead Sea Scrolls in Emanuel Tov, ed., *The Texts from the Judaean Desert: Indices and an Introduction to the Discoveries in the Judaean Desert Series*, DJD 39 (Oxford: Clarendon, 2002). Hanan Eshel provides slightly different figures and states that more than 16,000 fragments from some six hundred scrolls and three hundred literary works were found in Cave 4a. Because scholars classify fragments differently, and sometimes combine them, there is no exact consensus concerning the exact number of scrolls or fragments found in Cave 4 or the other Qumran caves. See Hanan Eshel,

The index to the Discoveries in the Judaean Desert (DJD) series adopts a very broad definition of prayer. It lists fifty-seven individual documents under the heading "Poetic and Liturgical Texts."[8] Many of these are extant in multiple copies. These scrolls are quite diverse and include two scrolls of daily prayers (4Q503; 4Q504; 4Q506); three collections of liturgical texts for festivals (1Q34+34bis; 4Q409; 4Q502; 4Q505; 4Q507–508); collections concerned with the Sabbath Sacrifice (4Q400–407; 11Q17); three works used in covenantal ceremonies (4Q255–257; 4Q262; 5Q11; 1Q28b; 4Q286–290); two purification rituals (4Q284; 4Q414; 4Q512); five exorcisms (4Q444; 4Q510–511; 6Q18; 8Q5; 11Q11); and one liturgical text that is also classified as a calendrical text (4Q334).[9] Related nonliturgical poetic texts include the following works: the Hodayot and six similar or related texts (1QH^{a-b}; 4QH^{a-f}; 4Q433; 4Q433a; 4Q434–440; 4Q440a); two scrolls of laments (4Q179; 4Q455); three collections of psalms (4Q87; 4Q380–381; 4Q392+393); one sapiential poetic text (4Q411); and three documents labelled as various poetic texts (4Q448; 4Q215a; 4Q471b). The DJD index also lists twenty-four works under the general heading "Fragmentary Poetic or Liturgical Texts."[10] It is difficult to determine what to include among the poetic and liturgical texts since sectarian documents such as the Serek and the War Scroll also contain prayers. The Serek even

---

"The Fate of the Scrolls and Fragments: A Survey from 1946 to the Present," in *Gleanings from the Caves*, ed. Torleif Elgvin (London: Bloomsbury T&T Clark, 2016), 35.

8. Armin Lange with Ulrike Mittmann-Richert, "Annotated List of the Texts from the Judaean Desert Classified," in Tov, *Texts from The Judaean Desert*, 136–39.

9. Falk adapts this list as follows: seventeen collections of liturgical prayers or songs for calendrical occasions (blessings for days of the month [4Q503]; two copies prayers for days of the week [4Q504, 4Q506]; four copies of festival prayers [1Q34+34bis, 4Q507, 4Q508, 4Q509+505]; liturgical prayers likely written for festivals [4Q502]; nine copies of the Songs of the Sabbath Sacrifice [4Q400–407 and 11Q17]); two lists of songs and prayers and days of the month (4Q334) and festivals of the year (4Q409); nineteen collections of prayers or songs for ritual occasions (three for purification [4Q284, 4Q414, 4Q512]; nine blessing and cursing rituals [4Q286–290, 1Q28b, 4Q275, 4Q280, 5Q14]; seven apotropaic hymns [4Q444, 4Q510–511, 6Q18], and exorcism incantations [4Q560, 8Q5, 11Q11]). Daniel K. Falk, "Material Aspects of Prayer Manuscripts at Qumran," in *Literature or Liturgy? Early Christian Hymns and Prayers in Their Literary and Liturgical Context in Antiquity*, ed. Clemns Leonhard and Hermut Löhr, WUNT 363 (Tübingen: Mohr Siebeck, 2014), 41.

10. Lange with Mittmann-Richert, "Annotated List," 139. This list includes the following: 1Q36; 1Q39; 3Q6; 4Q280; 4Q291–293; 4Q441–443; 4Q446; 4Q449–451; 4Q456; 4Q457b; 4Q471c; 4Q499–501; 4Q528; 6Q16; 11Q15–16.

regulates times of prayer (1QS IX, 26b–XI, 22) while the War Scroll lists the instances when prayers should be recited before battle (1QM X, 8–XII, 18; XVIII, 5–XIX, 8).[11] If we include these texts, then the total is approximately 91 scrolls that contain prayers. But there are many more.

The DJD index lists nearly four additional pages of texts under the heading "Unclassified Manuscripts."[12] A large number of these are clearly prayers, hymns, liturgical works, and documents relevant to our discussion. Not included in this listing are the prayers in the Aramaic corpus found in the Dead Sea Scrolls, such as the Genesis Apocryphon, the Book of Giants, the Aramaic Levi Document, and the Prayer of Nabonidus. If we count the large number of prayers found among the Dead Sea Scrolls in the biblical texts, this, when added to the unclassified prayer fragments and Aramaic texts, would substantially increase the number of prayers at Qumran. Prayers were clearly of great important to those who produced, copied, and preserved the Dead Sea Scrolls. They constitute a significant portion of the texts found at Qumran. Many of these reflect similar prayer traditions found in the Psalms of Solomon.

3. The Dead Sea Scrolls and the Psalms of Solomon: Penitential Prayer

The Psalms of Solomon in their use of Scripture reflect the penitential prayer tradition inspired by the Deuteronomic cycle of national rewards and punishments.[13] Rodney Werline classifies penitential prayer as a "direct address to God in which an individual, group, or individual on behalf of the group confesses sins and petitions for forgiveness as an act of repentance."[14] The Psalms of Solomon is most similar to those petitionary prayers in the Dead

---

11. Seven collections (4Q503–504; 4Q505?; 4Q506; 4Q400–407; 11Q17; 1Q34+34bis; 4Q507–509) explicitly attest to the performance of prayer at regular fixed times during the day, for Sabbaths, and for festivals. See further, Jeremy Penner, "Mapping Fixed Prayers from the Dead Sea Scrolls onto Second Temple Period Judaism," *DSD* 21 (2014): 39.

12. Lange with Mittmann-Richert, "Annotated List," 145–49.

13. For the theological perspective in these poems, see further Kenneth Atkinson "Theodicy in the Psalms of Solomon," in *Theodicy in the World of the Bible*, ed. Antti Laato and Johannes C. de Moor (Leiden: Brill, 2003), 546–75.

14. See Rodney A. Werline, "Defining Penitential Prayer," in *The Origins of Penitential Prayer in Second Temple Judaism*, vol. 1 of *Seeking the Favor of God*, ed. Mark J. Boda, Daniel K. Falk, and Rodney A. Werline, EJL 21 (Atlanta: Society of Biblical Literature, 2006), xv.

Sea Scrolls that blend together Deuteronomistic traditions of repentance and restitution that also recount Israel's history as marred by sin.[15] The nonsectarian liturgical document the Words of the Luminaries (4Q504–506), which contains a collection of penitential prayers in a set liturgical pattern, is one of the best examples of this type of prayer from the Dead Sea Scrolls.

The Words of the Luminaries uses penitential prayer in alignment with the Deuteronomistic cycle of sin-punishment-restoration to explain current events. Like the Psalms of Solomon, this Qumran document is motivated by historical recollections. The author regards his present distress, and persecution by his enemies, as God's punishment for the nation's sins (4Q504 1–2 V–VI). As with the Psalms of Solomon, the Words of the Luminaries regard confession and supplication as part of the process of repentance.[16] In one passage the author pleads: "look upon our af[fliction] and our suffering and our oppression; deliver your people Isra[el] from all] the lands, near and far to wh[ich you have exiled them]" (4Q504 1–2 VI, 11–14). This verse is reminiscent of many passages in the Psalms of Solomon (Pss. Sol. 5.8; 7.8; 8.27, 30; 9.8; 10.8; 18.2). The writer's hope for a return of the diaspora community is similar to Pss. Sol. 11 and 8.28. The absence of any distinctive sectarian terminology or ideas in the Words of the Luminaries indicates that it is of non-Qumranic origin and likely inherited from some earlier Jewish community.[17] Yet, it was also an important text at Qumran since it is extant in three manuscripts that were copied over the entire course of the Qumran community's nearly two-hundred-year history.[18]

---

15. See further, Kenneth Atkinson, "Enduring the Lord's Discipline: Soteriology in the *Psalms of Solomon*," in *This World and the World to Come: Soteriology in Early Judaism*, ed. Daniel M. Gurtner (London: T&T Clark, 2011), 145–66.

16. This composition connects penitential prayers with a set liturgical pattern. See further, Esther G. Chazon, "The *Words of the Luminaries* and Penitential Prayer in Second Temple Times," in *The Development and Impact of Penitential Prayer in Second Temple Judaism*, vol. 2 of *Seeking the Favor of God*, ed. Mark J. Boda, Daniel K. Falk, and Rodney A. Werline, EJL 22 (Atlanta: Society of Biblical Literature, 2007), 177–86.

17. See further Esther G. Chazon, "Is *Diveri ha-me'orot* a Sectarian Prayer," in *The Dead Sea Scrolls: Forty Years of Research*, ed. Devorah Dimant and Urial Rappaport, STDJ 10 (Leiden: Brill, 1992), 3–17.

18. The script of 4Q504 is dated around 150 BCE and 4Q505 sometime in the later Hasmonean period, possibly between 70–60 BCE. See Brian Webster,

The Words of the Luminaries is similar to two other prayer collections from Qumran. The first is 4Q503 Daily Prayers. It, and the Words of the Luminaries, are the only two collections explicitly written for daily recital discovered at Qumran.[19] Like the Words of the Luminaries, the Daily Prayers contains no explicit sectarian features and is likely non-Qumranic in origin.[20] The Words of the Luminaries is also similar to the composition known as Festival Prayers (1Q34+34bis; 4Q505?; 4Q507–4Q509), which is a collection of prayers for annual festivals.[21] Festival Prayers is also regarded as a nonsectarian composition.[22] The author (1Q34+34bis 1–3) espouses a dualism between the righteous and the wicked that is reminiscent of several passages in the Psalms of Solomon. This similarity is significant since the words "sinner" and "righteous" occur thirty-five times each in the Psalms of Solomon. In comparison, the word "sinner" is used in the much lengthier canonical Psalter only seventy times and approximately forty times in Sirach, while the word "righteous" is found only fifty times in the biblical Psalter and some one hundred times in Proverbs.[23] This suggests that the distinction between the righteous and the sinner

---

"Chronological Index of the Texts from the Judaean Desert," in Tov, *Texts from the Judaean Desert*, 381, 394.

19. Daniel K. Falk, *Daily, Sabbath, and Festival Prayers in the Dead Sea Scrolls*, STDJ 27 (Leiden: Brill, 1998), 95.

20. Chazon, "Psalms," 710; Falk, *Daily, Sabbath, and Festival Prayers*, 22–29. The text is dated between 100–70 BCE. See Webster, "Chronological Index," 390.

21. Penner, "Mapping Fixed Prayers," 58. The dates of the four different copies of the text are: 4Q509 (ca. 70–60 BCE); 1Q34–1Q34^{bis} (ca. 50–25 BCE); 4Q507 (ca. 15 CE), and 4Q508 (ca. 1–30 CE). See James H. Charlesworth and Dennis T. Olson, "Prayers for Festivals (1Q34–1Q34^{bis}; 4Q507–509)," in *The Dead Sea Scrolls: Hebrew, Aramaic, and Greek Texts with English Translations; Pseudepigraphic and Non-Masoretic Psalms and Prayers*, ed. James H. Charlesworth and Henry W. L. Rietz, PTSDSSP 4A (Louisville: Westminster John Knox, 1997), 47; Webster, "Chronological Index," 394, 422. The document 4Q505 (ca. 70–60 BCE), often included among the copies of this text, consists of so many fragments that it is impossible to arrange them in any certain order. See Webster, "Chronological Index," 394.

22. Carol A. Newsom, "'Sectually Explicit' Literature from Qumran," in *The Hebrew Bible and Its Interpreters*, ed. William H. Propp, Baruch Halpern, and David Noel Freedman (Winona Lake: Eisenbrauns, 1990), 177; Falk, *Daily, Sabbath, and Festival Prayers*, 155–94.

23. For these statistics, see Mikael Winninge, *Sinners and the Righteous: A Comparative Study of the Psalms of Solomon and Paul's Letters*, ConBNT 26 (Stockholm: Almqvist & Wiksell, 1995), 3.

was of particular importance to the authors of the Psalms of Solomon and Festival Prayers.

Although there are many similarities between the Psalms of Solomon and Festival Prayers, there are some notable differences. Psalms of Solomon 5.4 expresses a belief in predestination in which the word "judgments," τὸ κρίμα, likely translates an original Hebrew חוק, with the meaning "what has been prescribed."[24] In contrast, the dualism of the Festival Prayers is closer to the dualism of the "Treatise on the Two Spirits" incorporated into columns III–IV of the Serek. The use of "lot" in Festival Prayers (1Q34–1Q34^{bis} 1–3 I, 2) is reminiscent of the use of the words "lot" and "light" in Pss. Sol. 3.12, and these images are also contained in the Treatise on the Two Spirits.[25] In one passage, the author of Festival Prayers appears to echo several apocalyptic writings found at Qumran with the proclamation, "but you know the things hidden and the thing[s] revea]led" (4Q508 2 4; cf. 4Q509 212 1).

Festival Prayers, like the Words of the Luminaries and the Psalms of Solomon, emphasizes the importance of remembrance, the admission of guilt, and petitions for forgiveness. Its description of the author's community as "poor and needy" (1Q34–1Q34^{bis} 3–5 II, 9) is reminiscent of many passages in the Psalms of Solomon where the community is referred to as "poor" (Pss. Sol. 5.2, 11; 10.6; 15.1; 18.2).[26] Because one copy of Festival Prayers appears on the back of a copy of the War Scroll, which is universally recognized as a sectarian composition, this would seem to indicate that these prayers were written as a liturgical proclamation of the Qumran sect's distinctive deterministic theology. However, the back of another copy of the War Scroll contains a copy of the nonsectarian Words of the

---

24. George B. Gray, "The Psalms of Solomon," *APOT* 2:637.

25. Charlesworth and Olson, "Prayers for Festivals," 48. 1QS 1–4 is missing in 4QS^{d,e} and is different in its theology, style, and terminology with other Dead Sea Scrolls and likely originated from an earlier source. See further Armin Lange, *Weisheit und Prädestination. Weisheitliche Urordnung und Prädestination in den Textfunden von Qumran*, STDJ 18 (Leiden: Brill, 1995), 121–32.

26. These similarities have even been used to propose that the word "poor" is a religious word in the Psalms of Solomon like in the Dead Sea Scrolls. For this thesis, see Pierre Prigent, "Psaumes de Salomon," in *La Bible: Écrits intertestamentaires*, ed. Andre Dupont-Sommer, Marc Philonenko, and Daniel A. Bertrand, Bibliothèque de la Pléiade (Paris: Gallimard, 1987), 959. For rebuttals of this interpretation, see Atkinson, *I Cried to the Lord*, 185–86; Winninge, *Sinners and the Righteous*, 113. For additional discussion, see G. Anthony Keddie's contribution in this volume.

Luminaries that teaches the opposing doctrine.[27] These two scrolls show that the Qumran sect recited prayers that espoused both predestination and free will. The Psalms of Solomon also contains the same theological contradiction. The disavowal of free will in Pss. Sol. 5.4 would appear to endorse the predestination of Festival Prayers and the Treatise on the Two Spirits while the declaration of freewill in Pss. Sol. 9.5 embraces the opposing teaching.[28] Yet, both beliefs appear together in the same collection of poems. Even the Serek, despite its clear determinism and predestination, states that humans are responsible for their decision to repent and join the community (e.g., 1QS I, 11; III, 8; V, 13–14).

The presence of petitionary prayers within a sect characterized by determinism should not be surprising since the members of the Qumran community were not modern systematic theologians, and no theological system is entirely consistent. This is especially true of religious determinism, which cannot systematically account for all the difficulties of human existence. The Dead Sea Scroll prayer texts are quite diverse and espouse conflicting theologies. What has been overlooked in much Qumran scholarship is the possibility that nonsectarian texts took on new meanings there, especially when read alongside sectarian texts. One example is the collection of hymns of praise known as Barkhi Nafshi (4Q434–438).[29] These hymns are very similar to the Psalms of Solomon and speak of a righteous group (4Q437 2 I, 12), the poor (4Q434 1 I, 1), the helpless (4Q434 1 I, 2; 4Q436 1 I, 1), the humble (4Q434 1 I, 2–3) and the chosen ones (4Q438 3 2). They all thank God for his past actions in history. Barkhi Nafshi contains many references to parts of the body that are reminiscent of the Psalms of Solomon (Pss. Sol. 1.3; 2.15; 3.2; 4.1, 19; 6.1, 4; 8.1, 3, 5; 12.3; 13.4; 14.8; 15.3, 6, 11; 17.13, 25).[30] Barkhi Nafshi is not considered a

---

27. The earliest copy of Festival Prayers (4Q509) is found on the sixth exemplar of the War Scrolls (4Q496) on the backside of fragments 1–119. The third exemplar of the Words of the Luminaries (4Q506) is found on the back of fragments 131–132 of 4Q509. See Charlesworth and Olson, "Prayers for Festivals," 47; Stephen J. Pfann, "List of the Texts from the Judaean Desert," in Tov, *Texts from the Judaean Desert,"* 70–71.

28. See further Atkinson, *I Cried to the Lord*, 185–86, 191–93.

29. The copies of this text have been dated as follows: 4Q434 (1–30 BCE); 4Q435–4Q437 (30 BCE–68 CE); 4Q438 (50–25 BCE). See further Webster, "Chronological Index," 405, 421, 422, 424

30. See further George J. Brooke, "Body Parts in Barkhi Nafshi and the Qualifications for Membership of the Worshipping Community," in *Sapiential, Liturgical and Poetical Texts from Qumran: Proceedings of the Third Meeting of the International*

sectarian text.[31] However, it is easy to imagine how the Qumran community could have reinterpreted its references to body parts to show how the eschatological worshiping community was reflected in each individual's physical composition. Although the same cannot be said of the Psalms of Solomon since there is no evidence that it was used at Qumran, the many verbal and theological parallels between it and the Dead Sea Scrolls may still be indicative of some relationship. If so, this should be sought in a place other than Qumran.

Although the Dead Sea Scrolls were discovered and used at Qumran, many of these documents emanated elsewhere and were brought to the site at different times.[32] Because several Scrolls describe events in Jerusalem, some were certainly produced there. Although several other locations have been proposed as the location where the Psalms of Solomon was written, because of their focus on this city in Pss. Sol. 1, 2, 4, 8, 11, and 17, the majority of scholars accept a Jerusalem provenance for the entire collection.[33] Because the Psalms of Solomon and many Dead Sea Scrolls likely share the same geographical origin, a look at how they portray Jerusalem may tell us something about their authors.

The noun "Zion" occurs only in Pss. Sol. 11.1. It appears approximately thirty-seven times in twenty-three different Dead Sea Scrolls.[34] Of these, the following are nonbiblical poetic compositions: 4QCatena A (4Q177); 4QApocryphal Lamentations A (4Q179); 4QAges of Creation A (4Q180); 4QNoncanonical Psalms A (4Q380); 4QApocryphal Psalm and

---

Organization for Qumran Studies, Published in Memory of Maurice Baillet, ed. Daniel K. Falk, Florentino García Martínez, and Eileen Schuller, STDJ 35 (Leiden: Brill, 2000), 79–94.

31. See Brooke, "Body Parts," 79. Some prominent scholars consider this text sectarian. See, for example, Mika S. Pajunen, "From Poetic Structure to Historical Setting: Exploring the Background of the *Barkhi Nafshi* Hymns," in *Prayer and Poetry in the Dead Sea Scrolls and Related Literature: Essays in Honor of Eileen Schuller on the Occasion of Her Sixty-Fifth Birthday*, ed. Jeremy Penner, Ken M. Penner, and Cecilia Wassen, STDJ 98 (Leiden; Brill, 2012), 355–76.

32. John J. Collins, *Beyond the Qumran Community* (Grand Rapids: Eerdmans, 2010), 52–87.

33. See further Atkinson, *Intertextual Study*, 397–98.

34. Martin G. Abegg Jr., "Concordance of Proper Nouns in the Non-biblical Texts from Qumran," in Tov, *Texts from the Judaean Desert*, 279–80; Abegg, with James E. Bowley and Edward M. Cook, *The Non-biblical Texts from Qumran*, vol. 1.2 of *The Dead Sea Scrolls Concordance* (Leiden: Brill, 2003), 637.

Prayer (4Q448); 4QRenewed Earth (4Q475); 4QWords of the Luminaries[a] (4Q504), and Apostrophe to Zion (4Q88; 11Q5). Two of these texts, 4QCatena A and 4QAges of Creation A (4Q180), contain many theological concepts and vocabulary common in the sectarian scrolls such as determinism (4QAges of Creation A [4Q180] 1 2; 2–4 II, 10) and the *yaḥad* (4Q177 3 4–6).[35] The image of Zion in the Psalms of Solomon is perhaps closest to the Apostrophe to Zion (4Q88 VII, 14–VIII, 15; 11Q5 XXII, 1–10).[36] This Qumran composition is preserved in its entirety among the non-Masoretic Psalms in the Cave 11 Psalms Scroll (11Q5; 11QPs[a]). It is partially preserved in 4Q88 (4QPs[f]), which contains some different readings. The fragment 11Q6 also preserves a few words of the composition.

The Apostrophe to Zion is a poem that is reminiscent of the personification of Zion as a mother in Pss. Sol. 1 and 11.[37] Both texts depart from the traditional portrayal of Jerusalem as a daughter, barren female, young woman, or young girl about to be wed.[38] Instead, they depict Zion in concrete terms in the future, which is envisioned as a restoration of its glorious past. These works all use Isa 66:10–11 to emphasize that God has not forgotten Zion. Psalms of Solomon 11 is closely connected with Bar 4:36–5:9. However, there are some notable differences. The author of Baruch, like the writer of Ben Sira, correlates wisdom and torah. Ben Sira also combines the teaching of Proverbs that life is fulfilled through children with the Deuteronomic view of life as the survival of the covenant people.[39] Although the noun "wisdom" appears five times in the Psalms of Solomon (Pss. Sol. 4.9; 17.23, 29, 35; 18.7), it is not used with this understanding. Rather the Psalms of Solomon associates wisdom with God's

---

35. Martin G. Abegg Jr., "The Time of Righteousness (4Q251a): A Time of War or a Time of Peace?," in Penner, Penner, and Wassen, *Prayer and Poetry in the Dead Sea Scrolls*, 6, 9; Daniel K. Falk, "Petition and Ideology in the Dead Sea Scrolls," in Penner, Penner, and Wassen, *Prayer and Poetry in the Dead Sea Scrolls*, 153–54.

36. 11Q5 is dated to the first half of the first century CE while 4Q88 is dated to 50 BCE. See Webster, "Chronological Index," 399, 430.

37. See further, Ruth Henderson, "Structure and Allusion in the *Apostrophe Zion* (11QPs[a] 22:1–15)," *DSD* 20 (2013): 51–70.

38. See Eric D. Reymond, *New Idioms within Old: Poetry and Parallelism in the Non-Masoretic Poems of 11Q5 (=11QPs[a])*, EJL 31 (Atlanta: Society of Biblical Literature, 2011), 140–43.

39. Shannon Burkes, "Wisdom and Law: Choosing Life in Ben Sira and Baruch," *JSJ* 30 (1999): 260–67.

judgment (Pss. Sol. 2.10, 15-18; 32-35; 3.3; 4.8; 5.1-4; 8.7-8, 23-25, 32; 9.5; 10.5; 15.8, 12; 17.3, 10; 18.3).

There are no discernible connections between the concept of Zion personified in the Psalms of Solomon and the Dead Sea Scrolls that use this image. Rather, because they are all poetic texts influenced by Scripture, it is not surprising that they contain many verbal parallels. However, the Apostrophe to Zion may bear one interesting similarity with the Psalms of Solomon. It appears in different places in two scrolls. In the Cave 11 Psalms Scroll it occurs with several biblical Psalms alongside several non-Masoretic psalms and a prose description of David's literary production influenced by the solar calendar of 364 days.[40] In this manuscript it also precedes a plea for deliverance that is reminiscent of the Hodayot and the Psalms of Solomon. It is also preceded by a wisdom text known as the "Hymn to the Creator" whose description of the cosmos is similar to that found in Pss. Sol. 18.10-12. Several psalms in the Cave 11 Psalms Scroll, like the Psalms of Solomon, are also extant in Syriac (Pss 151A; 154; 155). In another manuscript the Apostrophe to Zion is preceded by canonical Pss 107 to 109, in that order, followed by an "Apostrophe to Judah" and an "Eschatological Hymn."[41] Although the short length of the Apostrophe to Zion and its frequent allusions to Scripture make it difficult to comment upon, it appears that the scroll 11Q5 that contains this text is of non-Qumranic origin.[42]

The Apostrophe to Zion contains some interesting similarities with Pss. Sol. 11 and 17. These texts do not petition for what has already been realized. Rather, they all ask for perfection of character, the destruction of their enemies, the ingathering of the exiles, and the renewal of the true kingdom and glory of Jerusalem. Because these features are found in other prayers from Qumran and writings of the Second Temple period, the verbal parallels between them should not be regarded as indicative of any

---

40. In this text (11QPs^a XXVII, 2-11) the author not only writes that David composed the entire scroll but also states that he spoke it through prophecy and portrays him as a sage like Ben Sira. See further James A. Sanders, *The Psalms Scroll of Qumran Cave 11 (11QPs^a)*, DJD 4 (Oxford: Clarendon, 1965), 91-93.

41. The Apostrophe to Zion is found in 11Q5, 4Q88, and 11Q6. Only the first copy is complete.

42. James A. Sanders, "Psalm 154 Revisited," in *Biblische Theologie und gesellschaftlicher Wandel: Für Norbert Lohfink*, ed. Georg Braulik, Walter Gross, and Sean McEvenue (Freiburg: Herder, 1993), 301.

relationship between the Psalms of Solomon and the Dead Sea Scrolls. Rather, differences between the two collections of texts are quite profound.

Michael Stone has commented that the axis of history for the Qumran movement is primarily based on the narratives of Enoch and Noah and their accounts of supernatural origins of evil.[43] This would account for the apocalyptic worldview of some Qumran prayers that overtly display a sectarian outlook. However, the prayers in the Aramaic scrolls—all widely held to predate Qumran—are linked with primordial sin and fallen angels. In these texts Israel's ancestors have no need to repent or confess.[44] In contrast, other prayers at Qumran stress the Deuteronomistic worldview and reject apocalyptic revelation.[45] The use of the personification of Zion and the Deuteronomistic worldview to explain Israel's suffering in the Psalms of Solomon is most similar to the nonsectarian prayer texts, suggesting that the community behind this collection of pseudepigraphical poems should not be associated with the Qumran sect.

The Psalms of Solomon is unlike the thirty Aramaic Dead Sea Scroll prayers. All these Qumran texts are contextualized within a narrative and placed in the mouths of specific individuals or groups and are generally connected with primordial sin and fallen angels. In these Aramaic works

---

43. Michael Stone, *Ancient Judaism: New Visions and Views* (Grand Rapids: Eerdmans, 2011), 31–58.

44. Daniel A. Machiela, "The Aramaic Dead Sea Scrolls: Coherence and Context in the Library of Qumran," in *The Dead Sea Scrolls at Qumran and the Concept of a Library*, ed. Sidnie White Crawford and Cecilia Wassen, STDJ 116 (Leiden: Brill, 2016), 244–58. Machiela notes that approximately 130 (14.4 percent) of the 900+ Qumran texts are in Aramaic. This figure excludes legal documents and receipts from Cave 4. Aramaic texts were found in 7 of the 11 caves (Caves 1–6 and 11). For the "apocalyptic construction of reality" in these and the Hebrew sectarian texts, see further George W. E. Nickelsburg, "Social Aspects of Palestinian Jewish Apocalypticism," in *Apocalypticism in the Mediterranean World and the Near East: Proceedings of the International Colloquium on Apocalypticism, Uppsala, August 12–17, 1979*, ed. David Hellholm (Tübingen: Mohr Siebeck, 1983), 641–54.

45. For this debate between the penitential prayer tradition and the apocalyptic worldview, see Lorenzo DiTommaso, "Penitential Prayer and Apocalyptic Eschatology in Second Temple Judaism," in Penner, Penner, and Wasen, *Prayer and Poetry in the Dead Sea Scrolls*, 115–33. See also the discussion and literature cited in Lorenzo DiTommaso, "The Development of Apocalyptic Historiography in Light of the Dead Sea Scrolls," in *Celebrating the Dead Sea Scrolls: A Canadian Collection*, ed. Peter W. Flint, Jean Duhaime, and Kyung S. Baek, EJL 30 (Atlanta: Society of Biblical Literature, 2011), 497–522.

Israel's ancestors have no need to repent or confess: penitential prayer is rejected in favor of apocalyptic revelation.[46] In contrast, Hebrew prayers at Qumran, such as the Words of the Luminaries, like the Psalms of Solomon, stress the Deuteronomistic worldview and reject apocalyptic revelation.[47] The use of the personification of Zion and the Deuteronomistic worldview to explain Israel's suffering in the Psalms of Solomon is most similar to the non-sectarian Qumran prayer texts. Because it is unlikely that the Aramaic Dead Sea Scrolls with their apocalyptic worldview were written by the same circles that composed the Qumran penitential prayers, any passages in the Dead Sea Scroll prayers that reflect the cosmology of the Aramaic scrolls does not indicate a common origin. Rather, the small use of apocalyptic imagery in other works suggests that such traditions were widely known, but largely rejected by the writers of penitential prayers. Because only Pss. Sol. 18.10–12 reflects a cosmological worldview, the Psalms of Solomon should not be connected with the Qumran sect and its related communities. However, there are other important similarities between the two that shed some important light on Second Temple prayers, namely, our extant manuscripts.

4. The Shape of the Manuscripts

The Psalms of Solomon is similar in appearance to many Dead Sea Scroll prayer texts, especially the Cave 11 Psalms Scroll and the Hodayot. Printed editions of the scrolls and the Greek and Syriac texts of the Psalms of Solomon are often arranged according to poetic units. Because none of our extant manuscripts of the composition are written stichometrically, it is often uncertain where verses and paragraphs end. Nevertheless, the Psalms of Solomon most easily divides into poetic units like many of the poetic

---

46. See further Daniel A. Machiela, "Prayer in the Aramaic Dead Sea Scrolls: Catalogue and Overview," in Penner, Penner, and Wassen, *Prayer and Poetry in the Dead Sea Scrolls*, 292–93; Penner, "Mapping Fixed Prayers," 59–61.

47. For this theme, with a focus on memory in the Psalms of Solomon, see further Matthew E. Gordley, "Creating Meaning in the Present by Reviewing the Past: Communal Memory in the Psalms of Solomon," *JAJ* 5 (2014): 368–92; William Horbury, "The Remembrance of God in the Psalms of Solomon," in *Memory in the Bible and Antiquity: The Fifth Durham-Tübingen Research Symposium (Durham, September 2004)*, ed. Steven C. Barton, Loren T. Stuckenbruck, and Benjamin G. Wold. WUNT 212 (Tübingen: Mohr Siebeck, 2007), 111–28. See also the contribution by Rodney Werline in this volume.

Dead Sea Scrolls.[48] Although we do not possess any Jewish manuscripts of the Psalms of Solomon, given the composition's length, we can assume the collection was originally written on animal skin like the majority of Qumran texts. Because papyrus was not very durable, it was less suitable for liturgical works that would have been in constant use. It is, therefore, not surprising that only 10 percent of the Dead Sea Scrolls are written on papyrus.[49] However, these may tell us something about the importance and use of prayer books like the Psalms of Solomon in antiquity. This is particularly true of opisthographs.

The majority of opisthographs at Qumran are on papyrus. Most are prayer texts and were written by the same scribe on both sides of the papyrus.[50] The bulk of papyrus documents appear to be personal copies.[51] Some of these contain both prayers and excerpts from rule books like the Serek, which show that they were used together.[52] This, and the large number of prayer texts and sectarian rulebooks in the Dead Sea Scrolls, indicates that there was a close association between the two genres. Some prayers at Qumran were apparently delivered to bring about the lifestyle envisioned in the sectarian texts. Sectarian texts, moreover, often include prayers that appear to have been recited. These texts, however, were not copied on the same side of a scroll. Rather, the Qumran scrolls almost always contain a single literary composition and no scroll contains a compilation of different literary works on one side.[53] The bulk of prayer texts appear on

---

48. This is most visible in the critical edition of Wright, which presents an arrangement of each psalm like the canonical psalter to give some idea of the collection's original appearance. Robert B. Wright, *The Psalms of Solomon: A Critical Edition of the Greek Text*, Jewish and Christian Text in Contexts and Related Studies 1 (London: T&T Clark, 2007).

49. For a complete inventory, see Emanuel Tov, "Lists of Specific Groups of Texts from the Judaean Desert," in Tov, *Texts from the Judaean Desert*, 204–8.

50. For a complete inventory, see Tov, "Lists," 211–13. For an analysis of these texts that also shows that the compositions written on the same papyrus such as the War Scroll reflect the same orthography often associated with the Qumran sect, see George J. Brooke, "Between Scroll and Codex: Reconsidering the Qumran Opisthographs," in *On Stone and Scroll: Essays in Honour of Grahm Ivor Davies*, ed. J. K. Aitken, Katharine J. Dell, and Brian A. Mastin, BZAW 420 (Berlin: De Gruyter, 2011), 123–38.

51. Michael O. Wise, *Thunder in Gemini and Other Essays on the History, Language and Literature of Second Temple Palestine*, JSPSup 15 (Sheffield: JSOT Press, 1994), 129–30.

52. Falk, "Material Aspects," 40–56.

53. Falk, "Material Aspects," 40–75.

quite short scrolls. This is undoubtedly because of their liturgical character, which dictated the use of small scrolls for ease of use.

The Psalms of Solomon bear some hallmarks of liturgical usage similar to that found in Qumran sectarian prayers and other scrolls. The Psalms of Solomon is not excessively long as is true of most of the Qumran liturgical texts. Like these compositions, the Psalms of Solomon stresses the practice of regular prayer (Pss. Sol. 3.3; 5.1; 6.1–2; 7.6–7; 15.1). Like the Dead Sea Scrolls, it is difficult to classify the eighteen Psalms of Solomon because they contain several classic psalm-types.[54] These include laments (Pss. Sol. 4; 5; 7; 8; 9; 12; 17), thanksgiving psalms (Pss. Sol. 2; 13; 15; 16), and hymns (Pss. Sol. 3; 6; 10; 11; 14; 18). All these genres are common in prayer texts from Qumran, which often, like the Cave 11 Psalms Scroll, contain diverse types of prayers in a single scroll. These writings all make ample use of intertextuality.[55] This feature is common in Second Temple prayer texts and should not be regarded as mere imitation or an inferior style. Rather, it was the custom to show fluency in biblical idioms. Second Temple prayers were not written to replace Scripture, but to accompany it.[56] This feature is also a hallmark of liturgical texts and shows the high regard that the communities of the Scrolls and the Psalms of Solomon had for those works they regarded as Scripture.

The Psalms of Solomon bear one important similarity with those Dead Sea Scrolls that exist in multiple copies, namely, that they have undergone a considerable process of alternation whose extent is unknown. The presence of words that are rare in the LXX in the Psalms of Solomon suggests that our present Greek edition is rather late, which should make us cautious in our efforts to reconstruct the original text.[57] The Greek manuscripts contain many substitutions, changes in word order, omissions, and alterations likely inserted by later scribes to improve the text. Some

---

54. See further, Atkinson, "Theodicy," 6–8.

55. Atkinson, *Intertextual Study*, 402–4; Carol A. Newsom, *The Self as Symbolic Space: Constructing Identity and Community at Qumran*, STDJ 52 (Leiden: Brill, 2004), 1–21.

56. See further Hindy Najman, *Seconding Sinai: The Development of Mosaic Discourse in Second Temple Judaism*, JSJSup 77 (Leiden; Brill, 2003), 44–69.

57. Examples of these features in the Psalms of Solomon include: ἐκλογή (18.5); ὑποκρίνομαι (4.22); καταφορά (16.1; cf. Aquila's translation of Gen 2:21); μήνισις (2.23); ἀναπτέρωσις (4.12); αὐτάρκεια (5.16); ἀνάξις (18.5).

of these changes appear to reflect tenth century CE Greek revisions.[58] The Greek text also appears to have undergone some later theological updating. Several scholars have noted that the problematic passage in 9.4 does not reflect a Semitic text. Rather, as Eberhard Bons convincingly demonstrated, the use of ἐκλογή in this verse (cf. 18.5) reflects Greek philosophy, particularly Stoicism, and not Semitic thought.[59] The many changes in the Greek manuscripts suggest that the Psalms of Solomon, like many Dead Sea Scrolls, remained a living text.[60] These changes, found in Christian manuscripts of the Psalms of Solomon, suggest that Christians used the collection for liturgical purposes long after its date of composition and continued to update it according to their needs.

There is another important similarity between the Psalms of Solomon and many of the poetic Dead Sea Scrolls. The Psalms of Solomon appears in different places in the manuscript tradition alongside other texts that are indicative of their later uses. The Syriac provides some valuable clues concerning the later use of the Psalms of Solomon. It was appended in two manuscripts to the Christian collection of hymns known as the Odes of

---

58. The manuscript groups 260 (MSS 260, 149, 471, 606, 3004) and 629 (MSS 629, 769) contain many substitutions, changes in word order, omissions, and changes likely inserted by later scribes to improve the text (e.g., MS 655: 15.8d and 17.11; MS 659: 9.8h; 11.6; MSS 655 and 659: 4.12b; 8.19c, 8.20a; 9.1b). Datives were replaced with accusatives (MSS 336 and 769), which was common by the tenth century CE. The replacement of the sigmatic -σαν ending with -εν for the third-person plural aorist optative also occurs in the MS 253 group and in MS 336 at 4.8a. Several of the lexical impossibilities preserved in Wright's critical edition should be considered itacisms and likely attributed to Byzantine scribes—for example, ἐλογήσωμαι (15.5); διηρπάζωσαν (8.11); κληρονομίσαισαν (12.6). None of the eleven Greek manuscripts, or the five witnesses to the Syriac text, predate the tenth century CE. For the manuscripts and grammatical features disused in this section, see further Kenneth Atkinson, "Psalms of Solomon: Greek," in *Deutero-Canonical Scriptures*, vol. 2 of *The Textual History of the Bible*, ed. Matthias Henze (Leiden: Brill, 2019); Atkinson, "Psalms of Solomon: Syriac," in Henze, *Textual History of the Bible*.

59. Eberhard Bons, "Philosophical Vocabulary in the Psalms of Solomon: The Case of Ps. Sol. 9:4," in *The Psalms of Solomon: Language, History, Theology*, ed. Eberhard Bons and Patrick Pouchelle, EJL 40 (Atlanta: SBL Press, 2015), 49–78.

60. Like the Qumran texts, the different manuscripts of the Psalms of Solomon show minor changes, indicating that they were made at the time the text was recopied and not inserted into an existing manuscript. For this phenomenon in the Dead Sea Scrolls, see further Emanuel Tov, "The Writing of Early Scrolls and the Literary Analysis of Hebrew Scripture," *DSD* 13 (2003): 339–47.

Solomon, incorporated into Christian prayers in two other manuscripts, and included as a marginal note translated from the Greek into Syriac in one manuscript of the Hymns of Severus. The Odes and Psalms of Solomon are listed in Pseudo-Athanasius's *Synopsis Scripturae Sacrae* and the ninth-century CE *Stichometria* of Patriarch Nicephorus among "those of the Old (Testament) that are spoken against and not accepted by the church."[61] These references likely attest to the circulation of the two compositions in Greek, but it is unknown when they were placed together. Their combination in two manuscripts shows that Syriac-speaking Christians used both texts in their liturgy. These and other features in the compositions suggest that Jews earlier used the Psalms of Solomon in a similar manner. Reworking, reuse, and updating appears to have been a common feature of prayer texts from Qumran as well as the Psalms of Solomon. One additional example may shed some additional light on the Psalms of Solomon.

5. The Dead Sea Scrolls and the Psalms of Solomon: The Pesharim

Another genre of Dead Sea Scrolls bears some relationship with the Psalms of Solomon, namely, the pesharim. Several studies have examined historical similarities between these texts.[62] However, I will restrict my comments to a largely overlooked pesher that has some relationship both to the Psalms of Solomon and Qumran poetry, namely, the exegesis of canonical Ps 37 in the Psalms Pesher (4Q171).[63]

The Psalms Pesher is clearly a sectarian text that describes the conflict between the Teacher of Righteousness and the Wicked Priest.[64] However,

---

61. For the manuscript tradition, see further Atkinson, "Psalms of Solomon: Greek"; Atkinson, "Psalms of Solomon: Syriac."

62. Atkinson, *I Cried to the Lord*, esp. 45–46, 165–66, Shani L. Berrin [Tzoref], "*Pesher Nahum, Psalms of Solomon* and Pompey," in *Reworking the Bible: Apocryphal and Related Texts at Qumran*, ed. Esther G. Chazon, Devorah Dimant, and Ruth A. Clements, STDJ 58 (Leiden: Brill, 2005), 65–84.

63. The text is written in the same script as 4Q166 (4QpHos^a) and may have been produced by the same scribe. See Maurya P. Horgan, "Psalm Pesher 1 (4Q171=4QpPs^a =4QpPs37 and 45)," in *The Dead Sea Scrolls: Hebrew, Aramaic, and Greek Texts with English Translation: Pesharim, Other Commentaries, and Related Documents*, ed. James H. Charlesworth, PTSDSSP 6B (Louisville: Westminster John Knox, 1997), 6.

64. For this incident, see 1QpHab XI, 6–8; 4Q171 1–10 IV, 8. There is some uncertainty as to the meaning of the verbs in the 1QpHab XI clause and whether the Teacher of Righteousness is the object in the 4Q171 clause. Loren Stuckenbruck

the author introduces some new elements into the biblical text. The writer emphasizes the "piety of the poor" in canonical Ps 37 to describe his righteous group whose piety was torah-centered (4Q171 II, 2, 15). He also inserts an allusion to Deuteronomistic theology to warn of the consequence of failing to follow the Torah (4Q171 II, 2b–5a). Like the Psalms of Solomon (Pss. Sol. 3.4; 7.3, 9; 8.26, 29; 10.1–4; 13.7, 10; 16.4, 11–15), the author believes that salvation is accomplished through affliction (1–10 II, 9–14). This concept as expressed in the Psalms Pesher is similar to a passage in the Word of the Luminaries where the same teaching is found (4Q504 1–2 VI, 11; 1–2 VI, 6–7).

More than any other sectarian scroll, the Psalms Pesher associates the elect status of its members with poverty. It also describes the "period of humiliation" (4Q171 II, 9–12). Like the Psalms of Solomon, the author of the Psalms Pesher believed the righteous who suffer and patiently endure their affliction will be on the right side with God. This teaching regarding the poor and affliction is closest to the Hodayot (1QH^a VI, 3–4; IX, 36; X, 31–35; XI, 25; XIII, 16, 18, 21, 22), which also repudiates the rich. In her study of wealth in the Dead Sea Scrolls, Catherine Murphy argues that although the Hodayot uses the word poverty for actual economic hardship, the poems do not merely praise poverty. Rather, they emphasize the priority of the righteous poor over the wealthy.[65] The Hodayot also makes a connection between the poor and the time of humiliation and purification. The terminological links between the Hodayot and the Psalms Pesher in this regard are striking. The similarities between the Psalms Pesher, the Words of the Luminaries (1–10 II, 1–3; 4Q504 1–2 VI, 6–7, 11), and Festival Prayers (4Q508 2 3; 4Q509 16 3) may suggest that many teachings found in the Qumran poetic texts, especially the Hodayot (4Q171 II, 9–12;

---

notes that the Wicked Priest's retribution is expressed with the perfect in 1QpHab 11 whereas 4Q171 1–10 IV, 9–10 has the imperfect. Loren T. Stuckenbruck, "Temporal Shifts from Text to Interpretation: Concerning the Use of the Perfect and Imperfect in the *Habakkuk Pesher* (1QpHab)," in *Qumran Studies: New Approaches, New Questions*, ed. Michael Thomas Davis and Brent A. Strawn (Grand Rapids: Eerdmans, 2007), 143–44. For these issues, see further, Kenneth Atkinson, "The Identification of the 'Wicked Priest' Reconsidered: The Case for Hyrcanus II," in *Sibyls, Scriptures, and Scrolls: John Collins at Seventy*, ed. Joel Baden, Hindy Najman, and Eibert Tigchelaar (Leiden: Brill, 2017), 93–10.

65. Catherine M. Murphy, *Wealth in the Dead Sea Scrolls and in the Qumran Community*, STDJ 40 (Leiden: Brill, 2002), 243–50.

1QH^a XI, 25–29), influenced the sectarian writer of the Psalms Pesher.[66] Although the Psalms Pesher contains no identifiable historical allusions that can be dated, its similarity with the other pesharim suggests a fairly late date of composition. This is important since several of the pesharim, especially the Nahum Pesher (4Q169), describe events reflected in the Psalms of Solomon.[67]

6. Implications for the Study of Second Temple Judaism

The presence of sectarian and nonsectarian prayers in the Dead Sea Scrolls, and the evidence that the Qumran community used both in its liturgy, suggests that the sect incorporated several preexisting Jewish prayer books in their worship. We may have evidence that something similar occurred in the Psalms of Solomon, whose authors may have been influenced by prayer traditions that circulated in antiquity. A look at the dates of the Qumran prayers is quite illustrative. Works such as the Words of the Heavenly Luminaries, Songs of the Sabbath Sacrifice, Daily Prayers, and Festival Prayers, all have been dated to the pre-Maccabean period.[68] This suggests that regular formulaic prayer developed alongside temple worship and not in reaction to its destruction. It also shows that Judaism was theologically diverse in the pre-Maccabean period.

Many of the similarities between the Dead Sea Scrolls and the Psalms of Solomon likely have their origin in prayer traditions that developed in the pre-Maccabean period and that were constantly reused by various Jewish communities. Several passages in the Psalms of Solomon provide

---

66. See further, Jutta Jokiranta, *Social Identity and Sectarianism in the Qumran Movement*, STDJ 105 (Leiden: Brill, 2013), 138–42.

67. Unlike the Psalms of Solomon and the Dead Sea Scrolls prayer and liturgical texts, the pesharim are rather late and reflect events from approximately 100 to 40 BCE and refer to the Romans. See further James H. Charlesworth, *The Pesharim and Qumran History: Chaos or Consensus?* (Grand Rapids: Eerdmans, 2002), 77–118.

68. See further, Eileen M. Schuller, "Prayers and Psalms from the Pre-Maccabean Period," *DSD* 13 (2006): 306–18. Although paleography cannot determine whether a Qumran text is an autograph or a revision of an earlier document, the prayer texts all reflect early dates in contrast to historical Dead Sea Scrolls that date considerably later. For the importance of this issue, see further Kenneth Atkinson, "Representations of History in 4Q331 (4QpapHistorical Text C), 4Q332 (4QHistorical Text D), 4Q333 (4QHistorical Text E), and 4Q468e (4QHistorical Text F): An Annalistic Calendar Documenting Portentous Events?," *DSD* 14 (2007): 125–51.

some evidence of this feature. The list of vices in Pss. Sol. 8.10–12 is similar to CD IV, 15–18, which suggests it is an ancient exegetical tradition critical of the temple priests that influenced both the Psalms of Solomon and the Qumran sect.[69] However, the Psalms of Solomon lack the apocalyptic outlook of the Qumran community. Although the Psalms of Solomon contain some cosmological elements in 18.10–12, they differ from the cosmology of a prayer book such as Festival Prayers that appears to have developed in close connection with the apocalyptic cosmology of books such 1 Enoch.

Rather than seeking to connect the Psalms of Solomon with the Qumran community, it is more appropriate to ask how both groups used, adapted, and incorporated earlier pre-Maccabean texts and concepts into their liturgies and lifestyles. The pre-Maccabean prayer texts are all influenced by Scripture. The style of poetry in these texts is closer to that of the biblical psalms than to the expansive style of the Hodayot. These pre-Maccabean prayers make ample use of intertexuality and creatively rework already existing materials in new and creative ways. These are all features evident in the Psalms of Solomon. But there is one overlooked difference between the Psalms of Solomon and the Dead Sea Scrolls: only the community of the former work rejected the sacrificial system.

The community of the Psalms of Solomon developed a unique theological practice. Confident in their belief that the temple had become defiled, they rejected both its priests and the sacrificial system as a means to atone for sins (Pss. Sol. 1.8; 2.3–4; 8.11–13). Rather, they maintained their covenant relationship through prayer (Pss. Sol. 3.3; 5.1; 6.1–2; 7.6–7; 15.1) and fasting (Pss. Sol. 3.7–8a), but not temple worship and sacrifice. The righteous atoned for sin through confession, penance, and enduring God's discipline.[70] But, contrary to popular belief, the same was not true of the members of the Qumran community who both used earlier pre-Maccabean prayers in their worship and who also wrote original liturgical works. This sect also maintained its own sacrificial system.

The rise in prayer literature at Qumran is often connected with the community's loss of the sacrificial cult in which worship in the form of prayer takes on a new importance. It is assumed that the Qumran sectar-

---

69. For this issue and the priests in the Psalms of Solomon and selected Qumran texts, see further Kenneth Atkinson, "Perceptions of the Temple Priests in the Psalms of Solomon," in Bons and Pouchelle, *Psalms of Solomon*, 79–86.

70. See further Atkinson, "Theodicy," 26–29; Atkinson, "Enduring the Lord's Discipline," 155–60.

ians viewed their settlement as a spiritual substitute for the temple and, like the community of the Psalms of Solomon, rejected the sacrificial system.[71] In an insightful suggestion in their study of Festival Prayers, James H. Charlesworth and Dennis Olson raise the possibility that the frequent mention of offerings in this text may indicate that these prayers were accompanied by rituals of nonanimal offerings or sacrifices such as meal offerings of grain, new wine, and oil. They suggest that sacrifice may not have been totally replaced by prayer at Qumran.[72] The presence of numerous buried animal bones and ash throughout the settlement of Qumran and an altar at the site shows that such rituals took place there.[73]

A structure located in L135, and the enclosure to the north of the secondary building at Qumran (L130-135), has been identified as a sacrificial courtyard in the late first century BCE. Jean-Baptiste Humbert proposed that the square stone feature protruding from the eastern corner of this area is the remains of an altar.[74] This unhewn altar is made of earth similar to the description of Exod 20:24-25. Robert Donceel's full publication of the plans, drawings, and photographs of this locus from Roland de Vaux's excavation provides additional evidence showing that sacrifice

---

71. For selected examples of this common belief, see Gary A. Anderson, "The Praise of God as a Cultic Event," in *Priesthood and Cult in Ancient Israel*, ed. Gary A. Anderson and Saul M. Olyan, JSOTSup 125 (Sheffield: JSOT Press, 1991), 15-33; Esther G. Chazon, "The Function of the Qumran Prayer Texts: An Analysis of the Daily Prayers (4Q503)," in *The Dead Sea Scrolls Fifty Years after Their Discovery: Proceedings of the Jerusalem Congress, July 20-25, 1997*, ed. Lawrence H. Schiffman, Emanuel Tov, and James C. Vanderkam (Jerusalem: Israel Exploration Society, 2000), 217-25; James L. Kugel, "Topics in the History of the Spirituality of the Psalms," in *Jewish Spirituality: From the Bible through the Middle Ages*, ed. Arthur Green (New York: Crossroads, 1986), 1:122-23; Bilhah Nitzan, *Qumran Prayer and Religious Poetry*, trans. Jonathan Chapman, STDJ 12 (Leiden: Brill, 1994), 31, 111-15; Lawrence H. Schiffman, "The Dead Sea Scrolls and the Early History of Jewish Liturgy," in *The Synagogue in Late Antiquity*, ed. Lee I. Levine (Pittsburgh: American Schools of Oriental Research, 1987), 42; Schiffman, "Sacrifice in the Dead Sea Scrolls," in *The Actuality of Sacrifice: Past and Present*, ed. Alberdina Houtman et al., Jewish and Christian Perspectives Series 28 (Leiden: Brill, 2014), 89-106; Shemaryahu Talmon, *The World of Qumran from Within: Collected Studies* (Jerusalem: Magnes, 1989), 200-25.

72. Charlesworth and Olson, "Prayers for Festivals," 49.

73. Jodi Magness, "Were Sacrifices Offered at Qumran? The Animal Bone Deposits Reconsidered," *JAJ* 7 (2016): 5-34.

74. Jean-Baptiste Humbert, "L'espace sacré a Qumrân. Propositions pour l'archéologie," *RB* 191 (1994): 161-214.

was conducted on a large scale at Qumran as is evident from the extensive ash deposits discovered throughout the settlement.[75] The presence of this altar has two important implications. First, it demonstrates that the rise in Second Temple prayer literature did not emerge as a result of the loss of the sacrificial cult. Because the Qumran community engaged in sacrifice and used both earlier pre-Maccabean prayers alongside their original compositions, this shows that the Dead Sea Scrolls prayer texts were used in conjunction with sacrifices just like mainstream Jews used similar prayers in the Jerusalem temple liturgy.[76] Second, the community of the Psalms of Solomon was truly unique: its members rejected the sacrificial system and engaged in prayer and fasting to atone for sins.

7. Conclusion

Although there are many verbal and theological similarities between the Psalms of Solomon and the Dead Sea Scrolls, there is no discernible evidence to connect the communities behind the two compositions. Most of the verbal parallels regarded by some as indicative of a relationship should largely be attributed to intertextuality.[77] The Psalms of Solomon and the Qumran writings contain many similar statements of praise using ברוך, such as the Cave 11 Psalms Scroll, the thanksgiving hymns of the War Scroll, the Hodayot, Daily Blessings, and Festival Prayers. The requests for forgiveness found in all these texts appear to have been a common feature of Second Temple period prayer. Unlike their biblical parallels, the existential troubles of the authors of the Psalms of Solomon and these Qumran prayers were different. The temple had been rebuilt, the cult had been renewed, and Judea had survived, but the redemption foretold by the prophets had not occurred.

---

75. See Robert Donceel, *Khirbet Qumrân (Palestine): Le Locus 101 et ses vestiges d'activité artisanale*, QC 17 (Cracow: Enigma, 2005), 22–24, 54–57, 130–34.

76. The importance of this observation is beyond the limits of the present study and will be expanded upon in a future published version of my recent conference presentation on the topic: Kenneth Atkinson, "Biblical 'Land' Texts in the Dead Sea Scrolls: The Wilderness Experience Revived at Qumran" (paper presented at the Annual Meeting of the Society of Biblical Literature, Atlanta, GA, 21 November 2015).

77. See further George J. Brooke, "Aspects of the Theological Significance of Prayer and Worship in the Qumran Scrolls," in Penner, Penner, and Wassen, *Prayer and Poetry in the Dead Sea Scrolls*, 35–54.

For the writers of the Psalms of Solomon, such as the author of Pss. Sol. 11.8, the focus of their petitions is for God to fulfill what he has spoken to Israel and Jerusalem. Such hopes appear to have begun in the pre-Maccabean period and were adopted by the Qumran community and the writers of the Psalms of Solomon. Rather than attempting to connect them with the Qumran sect, the Psalms of Solomon should be viewed as another witness to Jewish frustrations of the Second Temple period that their prayers had yet to be answered. The writers of the Psalms of Solomon and the Qumran community both believed that the only way to bring about the period of redemption was to perfect one's character so as to be worthy of redemption. What makes the Psalms of Solomon unique is that later generations of Christians found the testimony of these poems so compelling and continued to use and preserve them for centuries. This Christian appropriation of the Psalms of Solomon makes it among the most amazing noncanonical documents to have survived from the Second Temple period and provides us with a window into the theological diversity of both ancient Judaism and Christianity.

Poverty and Exploitation in the Psalms of Solomon: At the Intersection of Sapiential and Apocalyptic Discourses

G. Anthony Keddie

"The Psalms of Solomon is literature of crisis."[1] With these words, Robert Wright articulates a pervasive assumption about these poems, which are saturated with images of war, exploitation, and impoverishment. Just as historians have tended to view apocalyptic texts as literature of the poor and oppressed or more recently as literature of resistance against empire,[2]

I want to thank the participants in the Second International Meeting on the Psalms of Solomon for their insightful comments and suggestions on this paper. I am especially grateful to Patrick Pouchelle for organizing the meeting and for his generous hospitality. Thanks also to Jonathan Kaplan, who offered helpful feedback on a draft of this paper.

1. Robert B. Wright, "Psalms of Solomon," *OTP* 2:643. This section of Wright's introduction lists V. Schwartz as second author.
2. Literature of the poor and oppressed: e.g., David Hellholm, "The Problem of Apocalyptic Genre and the Apocalypse of John," *Semeia* 36 (1986): 13–64; E. P. Sanders, "The Genre of Palestinian Jewish Apocalypses," in *Apocalypticism in the Mediterranean World and the Near East: Proceedings of the International Colloquium on Apocalypticism, Uppsala, August 12–17, 1979*, ed. David Hellholm (Tübingen: Mohr Siebeck, 1983), 447–59. Literature of resistance: e.g., Richard A. Horsley, *Revolt of the Scribes: Resistance and Apocalyptic Origins* (Minneapolis: Fortress, 2010); Anathea Portier-Young, *Apocalypse against Empire: Theologies of Resistance in Early Judaism* (Grand Rapids: Eerdmans, 2011); Portier-Young, "Jewish Apocalyptic Literature as Resistance Literature," in *The Oxford Handbook of Apocalyptic Literature*, ed. John J. Collins (Oxford: Oxford University Press, 2014), 145–62. For a critique of this paradigm, see G. Anthony Keddie, "Judaean Apocalypticism and the Unmasking of Ideology: Foreign and National Rulers in the Testament of Moses," *JSJ* 44 (2013): 301–4; Keddie, *Revelations of Ideology: Apocalyptic Class Politics in Early Roman Palestine*, JSJSup 189 (Leiden: Brill, 2018).

specialists on the Psalms of Solomon have often linked their language of poverty and oppression with the real historical situation of their authors and original audiences. Scholars frequently assert on the basis of the psalms' language of poverty and exploitation that they more-or-less accurately reflect a situation of widespread deprivation caused by the inception of Roman sovereignty in Judea and were written to give hope to those suffering from the crises of the mid-first century BCE.[3]

Despite an implicit consensus in scholarship that poverty and oppression are a significant theme in this text and are crucial for understanding its historical and social contexts, to my knowledge no one has yet endeavored to examine systematically poverty and exploitation in the Psalms of Solomon.[4] This paper makes inroads into this topic by examining the language of impoverishment in this text in relation to contemporaneous literature as well as the changing socioeconomic situation in Judea in the period from Pompey's conquest through the early part of Herod's reign.

I begin by laying out some theoretical and historical tenets for studying the interface of religion and socioeconomic inequality in early Roman Judea. Next, I identify broadly apocalyptic and sapiential discourses on poverty and exploitation in the Judean literature of the Hellenistic and

---

3. In addition to Robert Wright, see, among others, Kenneth Atkinson, *I Cried to the Lord: A Study of the Psalms of Solomon's Historical Background and Social Setting*, JSJSup 84 (Leiden: Brill, 2004), 219–20; Atkinson, "Theodicy in the Psalms of Solomon," in *Theodicy in the World of the Bible*, ed. Antti Laato and Johannes C. de Moor (Leiden: Brill, 2003), 546–75; Rodney A. Werline, "The *Psalms of Solomon* and the Ideology of Rule," in *Conflicted Boundaries in Wisdom and Apocalypticism*, ed. Lawrence M. Wills and Benjamin G. Wright, SymS 35 (Atlanta: Society of Biblical Literature, 2005), 69–87; Werline, "The Experience of God's *Paideia* in the *Psalms of Solomon*," in *Linking Text and Experience*, vol. 2 of *Experientia*, ed. Colleen Shantz and Rodney A. Werline, EJL 35 (Atlanta: Society of Biblical Literature, 2012), 17–44; Brad Embry, "The *Psalms of Solomon* and the New Testament: Intertextuality and the Need for a Re-evaluation," *JSP* 13 (2002): 101. Cf. Nadav Sharon, "Between Opposition to the Hasmoneans and Resistance to Rome: The *Psalms of Solomon* and the Dead Sea Scrolls," in *Reactions to Empire: Sacred Texts in Their Socio-political Contexts*, ed. John A. Dunne and Dan Batovici, WUNT 372 (Tübingen: Mohr Siebeck, 2014), 41–54.

4. It is also striking that the Psalms of Solomon are conspicuously absent in two important books on socioeconomic ethics in Second Temple Judea: Mark D. Mathews, *Riches, Poverty, and the Faithful: Perspectives on Wealth in the Second Temple Period and the Apocalypse of John*, SNTSMS 154 (Cambridge: Cambridge University Press, 2013); Samuel L. Adams, *Social and Economic Life in Second Temple Judea* (Louisville: Westminster John Knox, 2014).

early Roman periods before turning to an analysis of pertinent passages in the Psalms of Solomon. I argue that the Psalms of Solomon mediate sapiential and apocalyptic discourses on inequality, generating a class subjectivity that awkwardly construes poverty positively as self-sufficiency, yet attributes the cause of poverty to unjust sociopolitical authorities and allows for prayer as the only form of agency through which humans can ameliorate it. I further propose that the discourse on inequality in the Psalms of Solomon offers a refracted view of the socioeconomic impact of the Roman tribute from the vantage point of the early Herodian age.

1. Religious Discourse and Socioeconomic Inequality in Early Roman Judea

In the wake of Moses Finley's influential works on the ancient economy, the study of class in antiquity is often met with disdain.[5] For many, Finley cogently demonstrated that the category of class was not operative in antiquity, claiming that it is better to speak of the Roman *ordines* or status categories such as patron and client; slave, freedperson, and free; or other social, civic, and military distinctions. However, while Finley's rejoinder that ancient economies did not divide society into a bourgeoisie and proletariat is correct, his status categories fail to explain the inequalities of wealth that were rampant in the late-Hellenistic and Roman periods.[6]

---

5. Finley's best-known treatment is *The Ancient Economy* (Berkeley: University of California Press, 1973). On Finley's influence on the study of the ancient economy, see Jean Andreau, "Twenty Years after Moses I. Finley's *The Ancient Economy*," in *The Ancient Economy*, ed. Walter Scheidel and Sitta von Reden (Edinburgh: Edinburgh University Press, 2002), 33–52; Richard P. Saller, "Framing the Debate over Growth in the Ancient Economy," in *The Ancient Economy: Evidence and Models*, ed. J. G. Manning and Ian Morris (Stanford: Stanford University Press, 2005), 251–69.

6. See William V. Harris, "On the Applicability of the Concept of Class in Roman History," in *Forms of Control and Subordination in Antiquity*, ed. Tōru Yuge and Masaoki Doi (Leiden: Brill, 1988), 598–610; Harris, *Rome's Imperial Economy: Twelve Essays* (Oxford: Oxford University Press, 2011); Neville Morley, *Theories, Models, and Concepts in Ancient History* (London: Routledge, 2004), 66–81; Ernst Emanuel Mayer, *The Ancient Middle Classes: Urban Life and Aesthetics in the Roman Empire 100 BCE–250 CE* (Cambridge: Harvard University Press, 2012); Hans van Wees and Nick Fisher, "The Trouble with 'Aristocracy,'" in *"Aristocracy" in Antiquity: Redefining Greek and Roman Elites*, ed. Nick Fisher and Hans van Wees (Swansea: Classical Press of Wales, 2015), 1–58.

In recent years, social historians have reconsidered the matter of class in the ancient world. Keith Hopkins, for instance, proposed an influential "tax-and-trade" model that makes sense of inequality as a function of exploitation.[7] Between 200 BCE and 300 CE, Rome bolstered its economy through the exploitation of its provincial subjects. The collection of monetary taxes by the government through its *publicani* (tax farmers) and the collection of rents by landowners increased the wealth of provincial and imperial elites, resulted in the pooling of wealth in Rome, and supported the integration of the Roman economy.[8] Such a disparity in the distribution of resources and income caused by this interdependent system of taxes, rents, and trade has led some scholars to posit a rigid binary in Roman society: the 99 percent who were poor workers and the 1 percent who owned the means of production.[9] Walter Scheidel and Steven Friesen, among others, have called for a more precise stratification.[10] They argue that about 3 percent of the population were elites with considerable wealth, 6–12 percent were middlers, and the rest of the population congregated near or below subsistence level. While the number of middlers may

---

7. Keith Hopkins, "Rome, Taxes, Rents and Trade," in *The Ancient Economy*, ed. Walter Scheidel and Sitta von Reden (Edinburgh: Edinburgh University Press, 2002), 190–232.

8. William V. Harris, "The Late Republic," in *The Cambridge Economic History of the Greco-Roman World*, ed. Walter Scheidel, Ian Morris, and Richard P. Saller (Cambridge: Cambridge University Press, 2013), 520.

9. E.g., Justin J. Meggitt, *Paul, Poverty and Survival*, SNTW (Edinburgh: T&T Clark, 1998).

10. Walter Scheidel and Steven J. Friesen, "The Size of the Economy and the Distribution of Income in the Roman Empire," *JRS* 99 (2009): 69–91; Steven J. Friesen, "Poverty in Pauline Studies: Beyond the So-Called New Consensus," *JSNT* 26 (2004): 323–61. The Scheidel/Friesen economic scale focuses particularly on the empire at its demographic peak (mid-second century CE) and therefore might not fit the late Republic neatly. However, as Hopkins has shown, provincial incorporation in the late Republic is precisely what generated the systemic inequalities of wealth that defined the imperial economy. Thus, while further work needs to be done on socioeconomic stratification in early Roman Judea, we may provisionally envision a similar breadth of inequality, perhaps with a lower percentage of middlers for the early part of the period. For an important recent attempt to quantify the economy of early Roman Judea, see Hayim Lapin, "Temple, Cult, and Consumption in Second Temple Jerusalem," in *Expressions of Cult in the Southern Levant in the Greco-Roman Period: Manifestations in Text and Material Culture*, ed. Oren Tal and Zeev Weiss, Contextualizing the Sacred 6 (Turnhout: Brepols, 2017), 241–53.

have varied more or less considerably, it is significant that the overwhelming majority of the population felt the daily pressures of subsistence, which was threatened by war and drought.[11]

In these discussions, poverty is a slippery term whose conceptual power is often lost in the interstices of history and rhetoric. The crux of the problem is that poverty is malleable in connotation and subjective in terms of identity. Those attempting to ford this impasse have profitably applied Pierre Bourdieu's social theory in order to underscore the unconscious social and cultural production of class, as opposed to its economic determination.[12] Like the freedman Trimalchio in Petronius's *Satyricon*, one can have considerable wealth and high-class aspirations but still be deemed low-class by other social actors. Class has both individual and collective dimensions. It is a variable of social existence constrained, but not determined, by access to economic resources.[13] Cultural and social affinity deriving from the subjective class dispositions of individuals may support collective action but not necessarily.[14]

---

11. See Peter Garnsey, *Famine and Food Supply in the Graeco-Roman World: Responses to Risk and Crisis* (Cambridge: Cambridge University Press, 1988).

12. Pierre Bourdieu, *Distinction: A Social Critique of the Judgement of Taste*, trans. R. Nice (Cambridge: Harvard University Press, 1984). For sociological applications of Bourdieu's theory to class analysis, see Mike Savage, *Class Analysis and Social Transformation* (Philadelphia: Open University Press, 2000); Beverly Skeggs, *Class, Self, Culture* (London: Routledge, 2004); Klaus Eder, *The New Politics of Class: Social Movements and Cultural Dynamics in Advanced Societies* (London: Sage, 1993). For an application to social dynamics in Herodian Judea, see Andrea M. Berlin, "Herod the Tastemaker," *NEA* 77 (2014): 108–19.

13. I prefer to speak of class as a dynamic socioeconomic variable and take each text's construction of its class identity on its own. Because class dispositions vary so much, I abstain from producing a universal definition of "poor" or "rich." Rather, I emphasize that each text has a distinct perception of their community's class identity and the class identity of their opponents. This class discourse is often politically powerful as a statement defining the causes of, and solutions to, socioeconomic inequality. I disagree with Bruce J. Malina's Finley-influenced conception of "poor" and "rich" as simply status categories, although social status is surely at stake. As Paul W. Hollenbach has noted, these class constructions also address, even if very unrealistically by historical standards, economic structures. See Malina, "Wealth and Poverty in the New Testament and Its World," *Int* 41 (1987): 354–67; Hollenbach, "Defining Rich and Poor Using the Social Sciences," *Society of Biblical Literature 1987 Seminar Papers*, SBLSP 26 (Atlanta: Scholars, 1987), 30–63.

14. Eder, *New Politics of Class*.

An approach to class, and concomitantly to poverty, as a "socially habituated subjectivity" dovetails with recent work on the intersection of religious discourse and class in religious studies.[15] For instance, Sean McCloud shows through ethnographic work on two American Pentecostal churches that, despite having nearly identical socioeconomic demographics, their assemblies generated differing class subjectivities through their dress, bodily practices during worship, and sermons. McCloud further highlights the influence of religious discourse on understandings of class. He identifies two prominent "class theologies" widespread in American Protestantism as "Economic Arminianism," which claims that every human has the freewill to "pull themselves up by the bootstraps" in religious and economic endeavors, and "Divine Hierarchies," which posits that all socioeconomic states are divinely determined.[16] Religious discourses, whether oral or textual, often propagate particular perspectives on socioeconomic structures and human agency that affect class dispositions and social relations in material landscapes.

Such a revised understanding of the relationship between religious discourse and class is useful for evaluating the rhetoric of poverty and exploitation in the Psalms of Solomon. In the meager work on inequality in Judean texts from this period, poverty is deemed either metaphorical and theological or as reflecting material deprivation.[17] Robert Hann took a middle road in his important work on the Psalms of Solomon. He argued that the first generation of the community that produced the text was probably not poor but voluntarily entered a state of poverty and an ideology of poverty that would have attracted subsequent converts to the sect from

---

15. Sean McCloud, *Divine Hierarchies: Class in American Religion and Religious Studies* (Chapel Hill: University of North Carolina Press, 2007); Sean McCloud and William A. Mirola, eds., *Religion and Class in America: Culture, History, and Politics*, International Studies in Religion and Society 7 (Leiden: Brill, 2009).

16. McCloud, *Divine Hierarchies*, 105–34.

17. For poverty as usually indicative of material deprivation, see Catherine M. Murphy, *Wealth in the Dead Sea Scrolls and in the Qumran Community*, STDJ 40 (Leiden: Brill, 2002). For poverty as metaphorical and theological, see Mathews, *Riches, Poverty, and the Faithful*. For poverty in the Psalms of Solomon as merely religious language, see Pierre Prigent, "Psaumes de Salomon," in *La Bible: Écrits intertestamentaires*, ed. André Dupont-Sommer, Marc Philonenko, and Daniel A. Bertrand, Bibliothèque de la Pléiade (Paris: Gallimard, 1987), 959.

the lower classes of society.[18] He also noted that the language of relative deprivation in the psalms likely enhanced the reality of the community's poverty.[19] While agreeing with Hann's points about the rhetorical manipulation of poverty in the text, I contend that his strong emphasis on the Psalms of Solomon community as sectarian obscures the political function of this text in social scenes and supposes material deprivation in the community that has no basis other than the language of poverty in the text. As I argue in what follows, the psalms do not reflect real material conditions but refract them with a political lens. In this way, the text was a resource used by its producers in an attempt to obtain power by delegitimizing opponents and objectifying socioeconomic structures as exploitative.

A few words are in order about socioeconomic structures in the world of the Psalms of Solomon. First, by *structure* I mean a set of rules and resources that facilitate the reproduction of particular social relations.[20] Structures do not exist on their own, but only through the action of humans. Transformation of structures occurs when actors, in their contestation over resources, gain knowledge of the rules of these structures and attempt to transpose or subvert them. Texts can play an important role in this process of transformation. In Judea in the early Roman period, I identify three major socioeconomic structures that generated and sustained inequalities of wealth: taxation, tithing, and land tenancy. To these one might add war, access to local markets, and

---

18. Robert R. Hann, "The Community of the Pious: The Social Setting of the Psalms of Solomon," *SR* 17 (1988): 169–89.

19. Hann, "Community of the Pious," esp. 175–77; Kenneth Atkinson has develovoped aspects of this theory, arguing that the poverty language in the Psalms of Solomon is indicative of the real poverty that this community "deliberately adopted" after becoming disaffected with the temple leadership. See Atkinson, *An Intertextual Study of the Psalms of Solomon* (Lewiston, NY: Mellen, 2000), esp. 104–7; Atkinson, *I Cried to the Lord*, 185–86; Atkinson, "Enduring the Lord's Discipline: Soteriology in the Psalms of Solomon," in *This World and the World to Come: Soteriology in Early Judaism*, ed. Daniel M. Gurtner (London: T&T Clark, 2011), 149; Atkinson, "Perceptions of the Temple Priests in the Psalms of Solomon," in *The Psalms of Solomon: Language, History, Theology*, ed. Eberhard Bons and Patrick Pouchelle, EJL 40 (Atlanta: SBL Press, 2015), 86. See also Atkinson's contribution in this volume.

20. I am adapting social theory from William H. Sewell, *Logics of History: Social Theory and Social Transformation* (Chicago: University of Chicago Press, 2005), 124–51. Sewell's theory represents an attempt to combine the social theories of Pierre Bourdieu and Anthony Giddens.

environmental factors, but these were not constants. Between the Ptolemaic and Roman periods in Judea, these structures changed far less than is often assumed.[21]

Nevertheless, the mid-first century BCE did witness some notable shifts of these socioeconomic structures. Foremost among these was the imposition of the Roman tribute, which must have increased taxation considerably.[22] According to Cicero, after Pompey made Judea tributary (cf. Josephus, *A.J.* 14.74), the tribute was first collected there by *publicani*, elite tax farmers whose own wealth derived from siphoning taxes they exacted beyond what was required by the Roman authorities making the contracts for tax collection. Nearly a decade later, the Syrian governor Gabinius divided Judea into five taxation districts managed by respective συνέδρια ("councils") in 56 BCE, thereby arrogating the role of tax farmers to Judean elites.[23] A tactic typical

---

21. The continuity of socioeconomic structures between the Hellenistic and early Roman periods has rightly been stressed in some recent scholarship: e.g., E. P. Sanders, *Judaism: Practice and Belief, 63 B.C.E.-66 C.E.* (London: SCM, 1992), 146–69; Jack Pastor, *Land and Economy in Ancient Palestine* (London: Routledge, 1997); Samuel Rocca, *Herod's Judaea: A Mediterranean State in the Classical World*, TSAJ 122 (Tübingen: Mohr Siebeck, 2008); Adams, *Social and Economic Life*. Structural continuity, or "path dependence" (to borrow a term from New Institutional Economics), has also been stressed in recent studies of provincial transformation in Roman Egypt: J. G. Manning, *Land and Power in Ptolemaic Egypt: The Structure of Land Tenure* (Cambridge: Cambridge University Press, 2003); Andrew Monson, *From the Ptolemies to the Romans: Political and Economic Change in Egypt* (Cambridge: Cambridge University Press, 2012); cf. the essays in Walter Scheidel, Ian Morris, and Richard P. Saller, eds., *The Cambridge Economic History of the Greco-Roman World* (Cambridge: Cambridge University Press, 2007). The points that I briefly address in this section are the subject of much more extensive analysis in my *Class and Power in Roman Palestine: The Socioeconomic Setting of Judaism and Christian Origins* (Cambridge: Cambridge University Press, 2019).

22. See Fabian E. Udoh, *To Caesar What Is Caesar's: Tribute, Taxes, and Imperial Administration in Early Roman Palestine, 63 B.C.E.-70 C.E.*, BJS 343 (Providence: Brown Judaic Studies, 2005); Sanders, *Judaism*, 146–69; Rocca, *Herod's Judaea*, 203–12. While we lack substantial evidence to definitively determine the costs of tribute and other forms of taxation in early Roman Judea, it is clear that these varied with political changes.

23. Cicero, *Prov. cons.* 5.10. Cf. Cicero, *Pis.* 41, 48; *Sest.* 43.63; *Flac.* 28.69; Dio Cassius, *Hist. rom.* 39.56, 59; Josephus, *B.J.* 1.170; *A.J.* 14.91. See further, Nadav Sharon, "Setting the Stage: The Effects of the Roman Conquest and the Loss of Sovereignty," in *Was 70 CE a Watershed in Jewish History? On Jews and Judaism before and after the*

of Roman provincialization,[24] Gabinius endowed Judean elites with political and economic power, which was later reaffirmed and regulated by Julius Caesar.[25] Under Pompey, the Syrian governors, Caesar, Antony, and Herod, tributes were exacted from Judeans in differing ways and at differing rates. Fabian Udoh has argued, however, that as client-king, Herod probably was not required to collect tribute for Rome.[26] This important proposal has merit, but only for the Augustan period of Herod's reign, after 31 BCE.[27] Under Antony's sway, it seems that Herod exacted some form of tribute from his subjects, even if it was irregular.[28] The tribute in its various forms would have caused an increasing number of people to contract loans from elites, probably with interest, and if they were unable to repay these, they risked losing their property. Even after the tribute was likely relieved in 31 BCE, other forms of taxation would still have threatened the means of those living near subsistence.

In sum, the most significant changes to the structures that sustained inequalities of wealth in the period between Pompey's conquest and Actium were the imposition of the tribute and the concomitant formation of συνέδρια managed by Jewish elites. The collection of the tribute widened the gap between elites and nonelites, and the effects of war on trade, the land, and the people must have further induced this inequality.

Destruction of the Second Temple, ed. Daniel R. Schwartz, Zeev Weiss, and Ruth A. Clements, AJEC 78 (Leiden: Brill, 2012), 415–46.

24. On Judea's provincialization in its broader Roman context, see Martin Goodman, *The Ruling Class of Judaea: The Origins of the Jewish Revolt against Rome A.D. 66-70* (Cambridge: Cambridge University Press, 1987), 231–51; Warwick Ball, *Rome in the East: The Transformation of an Empire* (London: Routledge, 2000); Maurice Sartre, *The Middle East under Rome*, trans. Catherine Porter and Elizabeth Rawlings (Cambridge: Harvard University Press, 2005); Kevin Butcher, *Roman Syria and the Near East* (London: British Museum Press, 2003).

25. Josephus, *A.J.* 14.200–206; Appian, *Bell. civ.* 5.4. See further Udoh, *To Caesar What Is Caesar's*, 31–99.

26. Udoh, *To Caesar What Is Caesar's*, 137–59. Cf. Pastor, *Land and Economy in Ancient Palestine*, 109–10.

27. Rocca (*Herod's Judaea*, 197–239) argues that we should split Herod's economic record into two parts, 37–31 BCE under Antony and 31–4 BCE under Augustus.

28. Udoh has shown that the relevant passage in Appian (*Bell. civ.* 5.75) is fraught with problems (*To Caesar What Is Caesar's*, 137–43), but I contend that it nevertheless shows that Antony imposed the tribute on Herod.

2. Explanations of Inequality in Contemporaneous Judean Literature

To address the contingencies of this changing socioeconomic situation in early Roman Judea, the producers of the Psalms of Solomon reworked received traditions about poverty and exploitation. Other Judean texts of the Hellenistic and Roman eras did similarly. A brief survey of late-Second Temple Judean explanations of inequality is useful for situating the strategies of the Psalms of Solomon.

The most prominent source for socioeconomic ethics in Second Temple texts is Deuteronomy.[29] As Deut 8:17–18 stipulates,

ואמרת בלבבך כחי ועצם ידי עשה לי את־החיל הזה
וזכרת את־יהוה אלהיך כי הוא הנתן לך כח לעשות חיל למען הקים
את־בריתו

Do not say to yourself, "My power and the might of my own hand has gotten me this wealth." But remember the Lord your God, for it is he who gives you power to get wealth so that he may confirm his covenant.

With this exhortation, Deuteronomy attributes the power to change socioeconomic states—to transcend poverty—to God, rather than human action alone. Humans are dependent on God for the production of wealth. What is not stated clearly here is whether poverty is also God's will. Deuteronomy assumes that the poor and rich coexist and advances a set of ethics in support of the poor: those who lend or give to the poor whatever they need will receive divine blessing while those who do not will incur guilt (15:7–11). While not quite promoting an institution of charity, Deuteronomy does encourage protection of the poor.[30]

---

29. Mathews, *Riches, Poverty, and the Faithful*, 36–37 and passim.

30. As Gary Anderson explains, with the tithe for the poor in Deuteronomy (26:12–16), "we see the beginnings of the sacralization of gifts to the poor" (*Charity: The Place of the Poor in the Biblical Tradition* [New Haven: Yale University Press, 2013], 28). While the biblical influence on charity should not be overlooked, institutions of organized charity separate from biblical tithing and Greco-Roman euergetism (e.g., *tamhui* and *quppa*) did not crystallize until the rabbinic period. See Gregg Gardner, *The Origins of Organized Charity in Rabbinic Judaism* (Cambridge: Cambridge University Press, 2015), 10–21.

As Samuel Adams has shown, out of Deuteronomic socioeconomic ethics, two distinctive discourses on poverty emerged in the Second Temple era: one sapiential and one apocalyptic.[31] Most texts fall on a spectrum between the two. In general, sapiential discourses view wealth as a sign of virtue and divine blessing while warning about the danger of obsession with it. Inequality is natural, if not explicitly God's will. Some scribes even considered inequality opportune, since it enables the rich to support the poor, thereby proving their virtue and ensuring divine rewards, despite perpetuating socioeconomic inequality.[32] Wealth is a this-worldly reward for a virtuous life.

The book of Ben Sira is a good example of the sapiential discourse. Writing in the early second century BCE for an audience of elites, Ben Sira developed several Deuteronomic ideas. In 11:21, he urges his readers, "Trust in the Lord and continue in your labor, for it is easy in the eyes of the Lord to make the poor rich [πλουτίσαι πένητα] suddenly, in an instant." Here the sage contends that human labor alone does not produce wealth unless it is God's will. Moreover, Ben Sira uses the language of poverty to describe those who have work as well as shelter and sustenance (29:21–22) and therefore are near subsistence level, not destitute.[33] Inequality is unproblematic for Ben Sira, who further states in 13:24 that "wealth [עשיר/πλοῦτος] is good if it is free from sin, and poverty [עוני/πτωχεία] is evil only in the opinion of the ungodly." Poverty is naturalized by this statement, which encourages elites not to belittle the poor. The text portrays wealth positively but with hesitation.[34] Ben Sira elsewhere

---

31. Adams, *Social and Economic Life*, 183–205. My division between sapiential and apocalyptic discourses is imprecise and does not necessarily correspond to distinctions of genre. While it is unlikely that ancient Judeans would have always perceived or been concerned about the contradictions between present-oriented sapiential ethics and future-oriented apocalyptic ethics, I isolate these in order to demonstrate the impact of apocalyptic eschatology on socioeconomic ethics.

32. On the ethical problem that practices of charity tend to sustain and validate the relations of dependence and inequality of wealth for which charity is an intended solution, see Gardner, *Origins of Organized Charity*, 1–5; Steven J. Friesen, "Injustice or God's Will? Early Christian Explanations of Poverty," in *Wealth and Poverty in Early Church and Society*, ed. Susan R. Holman (Grand Rapids: Baker, 2008), 17–36.

33. Benjamin G. Wright III and Claudia V. Camp, "Who Has Been Tested by Gold and Found Perfect? Ben Sira's Discourse of Riches and Poverty," *Henoch* 23 (2001): 160–62.

34. See Sir 11:17, 22; 14:14–17; 40:25–26; 41:1–3; 44:6–7, 10–15.

cautions that anxiety over wealth can cause sleeplessness (31:1–11 NETS). While wealth is good, the love and pursuit of it can lead to sin. The rich must remember God as the source of their wealth. The sage makes this point by recasting Deut 8:17 in 5:1:[35]

(MS A) אל תשען על חילך ואל תאמר יש לאל ידי
Do not rely on your wealth and do not say, "I have power in my hand."
μὴ ἔπεχε ἐπὶ τοῖς χρήμασίν σου καὶ μὴ εἴπῃς αὐτάρκη μοί ἐστιν.

Notably, the grandson's Greek translation uses the loaded term αὐτάρκη ("self-sufficiency") here, eschewing that quality of human autonomy sought after by Stoics and Cynics because such a claim does not acknowledge God's role. Inequality for Ben Sira was not a problem but an opportunity. The elites for whom he writes can prove righteousness and atone for sin through almsgiving and cautiously standing surety for neighbors in need but not at the risk of impoverishing oneself.[36] In this sapiential discourse, inequality is natural and not the consequence of injustice.

Apocalyptic discourses, on the other hand, often categorically reject wealth and economic interactions as evil or unjust. Inequality is not natural or divinely ordained, but it is the consequence of injustice. Apocalyptic texts usually excoriate the rich and/or rulers as the cause of inequality and invert the sapiential approach to wealth by sanctifying poverty as a divine blessing. They expect relief for the poor by God in an eschatological age, when socioeconomic states will be equalized, rather than by humans in the present.

A paradigmatic example of the apocalyptic discourse on poverty is the second-century BCE Epistle of Enoch (1 En. 92–105), which heralds the imminent judgment of the rich. This text categorically rejects wealth, condemning the rich as sinners and their victims as the righteous, pious, or wise, though never using the language of poverty.[37] The rich (Eth. *be'ulān*)

---

35. Mathews, *Riches, Poverty, and the Faithful*, 72.
36. On almsgiving: Sir 3:30; 17:22; 29:12; 40:17, 24. On cautiously standing surety: 8:13; 29:14–20. Ben Sira's insistence on these practices is probably based on Deut 15:7–11. See further, Adams, *Social and Economic Life*, 194; Wright and Camp, "Tested by Gold," 158.
37. There is, however, in 1 En. 96.5 a singular description of the community as "the lowly" (Mathews, *Riches, Poverty, and the Faithful*, 54). See further, George W. E. Nickelsburg, "Revisiting the Rich and Poor in 1 Enoch 92–105 and the Gospel accord-

are unidentified perpetrators of injustice, who have disregarded Deuteronomy's injunction about wealth:[38]

> Woe to you, rich, for in your riches you have trusted; from your riches you will depart, because you have not remembered the Most High in the days of your riches. (94.8)[39]

Unlike Ben Sira, who urges the poor to "continue in your labor," the Epistle of Enoch explains that human labor has proven unable to change socioeconomic states. The sentiment that "we labored [Eth. ṣāmawna] and worked and were not masters of our labor [Eth. ṣāmāna]" (103.11), and similar statements condemning the exploitation of labor by the rich throughout the text, connects the Epistle of Enoch's opponents with the Giants of the Book of the Watchers (1 En. 7.3), who devoured the labor (Eth. ṣāmā) of the sons of men.[40] Retribution for this labor will not occur in the present age, but the righteous will receive vindication at judgment. The producers of this text identify labor as a sphere of exploitation but do not connect this labor to socioeconomic structures as other texts do. The mid-first century BCE Parables of Enoch (1 En. 37–71), for instance, agrees with the Epistle of Enoch that "everything that [the righteous] labor over [Eth. yeṣāmewu], the sinners lawlessly devour" (53.2) but identifies these wealthy sinners as the kings, the mighty, the exalted, and the landowners (Eth. 'ella ye'exxazéwwā la-medr or -yabs, and variants).[41] By calling out landowners, the Parables of Enoch implicates land tenancy as a mode of exploitation obviating upward mobility.[42] Unlike sapiential discourses,

---

ing to Luke," *NTS* 25 (1978–1979): 324–44; Richard A. Horsley, "Social Relations and Social Conflict in the Epistle of Enoch," in *For a Later Generation: The Transformation of Tradition in Israel, Early Judaism, and Early Christianity*, ed. R. A. Argall, Beverly Bow, and Rodney A. Werline (Harrisburg, PA: Trinity, 2000), 100–15.

38. Mathews, *Riches, Poverty, and the Faithful*, 52–53.

39. Translations of 1 Enoch are based on George W. E. Nickelsburg and James C. VanderKam, *1 Enoch: A New Translation*, 2 vols. (Minneapolis: Fortress, 2004, 2012).

40. Loren T. Stuckenbruck, *1 Enoch 91–108*, CEJL (Berlin: de Gruyter, 2007), 554–55; George W. E. Nickelsburg in Nickelsburg and VanderKam, *1 Enoch*, 2:196.

41. See Pierluigi Piovanelli, "'A Testimony for the Kings and the Mighty Who Possess the Earth': The Thirst for Justice and Peace in the Parables of Enoch," in *Enoch and the Messiah Son of Man: Revisiting the Book of Parables*, ed. Gabriele Boccaccini (Grand Rapids: Eerdmans, 2007), 363–79.

42. It is also possible that 1 En. 53.1 is a subversive critique of the imperial collection of tributes: "There my eyes saw a deep valley, and its mouth was open, and all

apocalyptic discourses more typically critique, or at least allude to, structures of inequality.

Most Second Temple explanations of inequality fall somewhere between the sapiential and apocalyptic poles. For instance, the late second-century BCE nonsectarian work 1Q/4QInstruction is interpenetrated by sapiential and apocalyptic traditions on inequality.[43] Like sapiential discourses, the work explains that God is responsible for lifting people out of poverty (4Q416 2 III, 11–12). Contra Ben Sira (29:14–20), however, the text discourages the practice of surety.[44] Those who accept a loan are as much in peril as those who provide it, for the debtor will lose sleep from anxiety over its repayment (4Q417 2 I, 19–22). Like apocalyptic discourses, however, 1Q/4QInstruction envisions wealth (הון) as a corrupting influence and distraction from the ultimate goal of the faithful, the pursuit of the רז נהיה ("the mystery that is to be"). Along with its dismissal of surety, the extant text does not clearly expound human solutions to inequality such as almsgiving. While one elusive section of the text appears to encourage the pooling of economic surpluses within the community, this seems to be an unregulated practice of exchanging one kind of resource for another rather than a communal institution of relief for the poor.[45] Furthermore, the text describes its addressee, the *mebin* ("discerning one"), as poor (עני) despite his presumed ability to provide loans.[46] Ultimately, 1Q/4QInstruction naturalizes, and even sanctifies,

---

who dwell on the land and the sea and the islands will bring its gifts and presents and tributes, but that deep valley will not become full." However, I hesitate to draw this conclusion based on the Geʿez text, whose language (Eth. ʾammexā, ʾasteʿā, and gādā) indicates the transmission of contributions or gifts rather than taxes (Eth. gebr, qaraṣ, ṣabbāḥt, etc.) per se. Moreover, the depiction of kings bringing tributes to God here appears to be based on Ps 72 (Matthew Black, *The Book of Enoch, or, I Enoch: A New English Edition with Commentary and Textual Notes*, SVTP 7 [Leiden: Brill, 1985], 217; Nickelsburg and VanderKam, *1 Enoch*, 2:195).

43. For 1Q/4QInstruction as nonsectarian, see Eibert Tigchelaar, *To Increase Learning for the Understanding Ones*, STDJ 44 (Leiden: Brill, 2001), 247–48.

44. In discouraging surety, 1Q/4QInstruction is in agreement with Proverbs (6:1–5; 11:15; 17:18; 20:16; 22:26–27). Cf. Adams, *Social and Economic Life*, 114–21.

45. Murphy, *Wealth in the Dead Sea Scrolls*, 179.

46. 4Q415 VI, 2; 4Q416 2 II, 20; III, 2, 8, 12, 19; 4Q418 177 5. On poverty as different than destitution in this text, see Benjamin G. Wright III, "The Categories of Rich and Poor in the Qumran Sapiential Literature," in *Sapiential Perspectives: Wisdom Literature in Light of the Dead Sea Scrolls*, ed. John J. Collins, Gregory E. Sterling, and Ruth A. Clements, STDJ 51 (Leiden: Brill, 2001), 112–13; Mathews, *Riches*,

poverty while discouraging typical human solutions to inequality. More clearly sectarian-oriented texts, such as the Damascus Document, Community Rule, and Hodayot also tend to combine the sapiential emphasis on human agency in alleviating poverty with the apocalyptic critique of injustice as the cause of inequality. The result, however, is less awkward because the emphasis in these texts is on the community as a mechanism for economic justice.

In Second Temple texts that address socioeconomic inequality, then, one finds an array of perspectives. Sapiential discourses show little concern for structures of inequality, but urge human agency as a means to mitigate the plight of the poor. Apocalyptic discourses often invoke socioeconomic structures of inequality as a function of polemics against their opponents, but they tend to present divine intervention in history as the only recourse for the eradication of socioeconomic inequality. Texts operating at the intersection of sapiential and apocalyptic ethics contain an ideological contradiction by modern epistemological standards. Is socioeconomic inequality God's will or the result of human injustice? Who resolves socioeconomic inequality, God or humans?

3. Poverty and Exploitation in the Psalms of Solomon

Before assessing the explanation of inequality in the Psalms of Solomon, it is useful to consider their socioeconomic vocabulary. As Kenneth Atkinson has noted, "the poor" is a positive communal self-description in the Psalms

---

Poverty, and the Faithful, 83. There is a long-standing debate over whether poverty in 1Q/4QInstruction is metaphorical or real. Benjamin G. Wold ("Metaphorical Poverty in *Musar leMevin*," *JJS* 58 [2007]: 140–53) and Mathews (*Riches, Poverty, and the Faithful*, 85–90) claim that it is wholly or mostly metaphorical, while Murphy (*Wealth in the Dead Sea Scrolls*, 171–74), Adams (*Social and Economic Life*, 198), Wright ("Categories of Rich and Poor," 112), and Matthew Goff (*The Worldly and Heavenly Wisdom of 4QInstruction*, STDJ 59 [Leiden: Brill, 2003], 129), among others, view poverty in the text as wholly or mostly indicating an actual state of deprivation. I suggest that the simple dichotomy of metaphorical vs. real does not do justice to the subjective quality of class discourse and its implications on social life and economic practice. It is clear from the text that poverty is not akin to destitution for those who produced this text, but it is integral to their self-understanding in relation to outsiders, angels, God, and other members of their community. In this sense, poverty is neither metaphorical nor real, or both at the same time.

of Solomon along with "the righteous" and "the pious."[47] The Greek text's positive term for the poor is πτωχός, which appears five times, all in reference to God: God is the "refuge of the poor" in 5.2; "the help of the poor and needy" in 5.11; and the "refuge of the poor" in 15.1. He has mercy on the poor in 10.6 and hears the prayers of the poor in 18.2. The term πένης ("needy," "destitute") appears alongside the poor in 5.2 and its cognate πενία ("need," "destitution") is wished upon opponents in 4.6 and 4.15 and considered an affliction by which God tests people in 16.13, 14. Both πτωχός and πένης in the LXX translate the distinct Hebrew terms אביון, דל, עני, רש, and מסכן, without consistent discrimination.[48] Most frequently, however, πτωχός corresponds to עני ("poor," "oppressed," "dependent"), and πένης to אביון ("needy," "destitute").[49] The Greek Psalms of Solomon follow this Septuagintal usage, ambiguously presenting the πτωχός as poor but better off than the πένης, who is in urgent need of assistance to survive. This language often echoes Psalms LXX, and Ps 37[36] in particular, which condemns unjust wealthy men for oppressing the "poor and needy" (πτωχὸν καὶ πένητα, 36:14 LXX).[50]

Other notable terms that imply poverty in the Psalms of Solomon are ταπεινός ("low," "humble") and ταπείνωσις ("humiliation") (2.35; 3.8; 5.12), as well as ὑστερέω ("to be wanting," "to lack," "to need") (18.2). Language of wealth is less frequent in the Psalms of Solomon, occurring on three occasions: once with the noun πλοῦτος, "wealth" or "riches," to describe human wealth (1.4), and twice using the adjective πλούσιος in reference to God's gift (5.14; 18.1).[51] The psalms also imply wealth using ὑπερπλεονάζω ("to

---

47. Atkinson, "Enduring the Lord's Discipline," 149.

48. A useful discussion of the vocabulary of poverty in ancient Jewish literature is Gildas Hamel, *Poverty and Charity in Roman Palestine* (Berkeley: University of California Press, 1990), 164–211. References to the relevant lexica can be found there. Cf. Timothy J. M. Ling, *The Judaean Poor and the Fourth Gospel*, SNTSMS 136 (Cambridge: Cambridge University Press, 2006), 98–145.

49. As Hamel (*Poverty and Charity*, 167–70) explains, this Septuagintal usage is paradoxical because, in classical Greek literature, the πτωχός is the more needy individual, the destitute or beggar. The πένης, though also looked down upon by elites, was usually an agricultural laborer or craftsman who had work, but was dependent on others for commerce. Though not identical in meaning, πένης is much more similar to the עני of the Hebrew Bible than the אביון.

50. Cf. Pss 40:17; 70:5; 72:4; 72:12; 74:21; 86:1; 109:16, 22; 113:7; 140:12.

51. Πλούσιον in Pss. Sol. 5.14 may be a corruption of πλούτου (Joseph L. Trafton, *The Syriac Version of the Psalms of Solomon: A Critical Evaluation*, SCS 11 [Atlanta: Scholars, 1985], 78 n. 38).

abound exceedingly") in 5.16 and the expression ἐν ἀγαθοῖς ("in goods," "in possessions") in 1.6 and 5.18. In addition to these terminological loci, however, portraits of inequality and exploitation abound. In what follows, I examine some of the most pertinent passages.

3.1. Psalms of Solomon 4

As John Collins points out, the Psalms of Solomon "repeatedly castigate the arrogance of the rich."[52] Psalms of Solomon 4, a denunciation of people-pleasers, one of whom illegitimately sits "in the council of the holy," provides some insights into the identity of these rich. I quote here following the Greek tradition:[53]

> [10] He uses deceitful words, so that he may carry out his unjust desire.
> He does not give up until he prevails in scattering them as orphans.
> [11] He devastates a house on account of his unlawful desire.
> He deceives with words, because he thinks there is no one who sees or judges.
> [12] He gorges himself with unlawful acts at one place,
> and then his eyes focus on another house,
> to destroy it with clamorous words
> [13] With all this, his appetite, like Sheol, is not satisfied.
> [14] Lord, may his portion be in dishonor before you.
> May he go out groaning and come back cursing.
> [15] Lord, may his life be lived in pain, destitution [πενίᾳ], and anxiety;
> may he sleep with pains and wake with anxiety.
> [16] May sleep be taken away from his temples at night
> May he fail disgracefully in every work of his hands.
> [17] May he return to his house empty-handed,

---

52. John J. Collins, *The Apocalyptic Imagination: An Introduction to Jewish Apocalyptic Literature*, 3rd ed. (Grand Rapids: Eerdmans, 2016), 176.

53. All translations of the Psalms of Solomon are my adaptations based on Robert B. Wright, *The Psalms of Solomon: A Critical Edition of the Greek Text*, Jewish and Christian Texts in Contexts (London: T&T Clark, 2007); and Kenneth Atkinson, "Psalms of Solomon," in *A New English Translation of the Septuagint*, ed. Albert Pietersma and Benjamin G. Wright III (Oxford: Oxford University Press, 2007), 763–76.

may his house lack everything, with which he would satisfy himself;
¹⁸ May his old age be spent alone and childless, until he is taken away.
¹⁹ Let wild animals tear apart the flesh of the people-pleasers, and may the bones of the unlawful ones disgracefully bleach out in the sun.
²⁰ May crows peck out the eyes of these hypocrites, because they disgracefully seized so many people's houses, and greedily scattered them.

This psalm depicts powerful people-pleasers who use deception to consume the property of others. The presence of at least one of these people-pleasers in the council, the συνέδριον in 4.1 ("Ἵνα τί σύ βέβηλε κάθησαι ἐν συνεδρίῳ ὁσίων), has suggested to most commentators that this psalm excoriates the institution of the Sanhedrin.⁵⁴ Atkinson, however, convincingly remarks that the council is still described as holy; it is certain parties within it who are denounced.⁵⁵ Since Julius Wellhausen, scholars have tended to identify these people-pleasers in the συνέδριον as Sadducees and some have further attempted to pinpoint the profane man (βέβηλε in 4.1) as Aristobulus II, whom Josephus says was supported by Sadducees (A.J. 13.416–447).⁵⁶ If this psalm reflects a time

---

54. Most manuscripts have ἐν συνεδρίῳ ὁσίων, but some just have ἐν συνεδρίῳ and others have ἐν συνεδρίῳ ὁσίῳ (R. Wright, *Psalms of Solomon: Critical Edition*, 82–83). The latter suggests that at least some ancient scribes transmitting the Psalms of Solomon understood this as a reference to the institution of the Sanhedrin. For arguments in favor of a reference to the Jerusalem council in this psalm, see Herbert E. Ryle and Montague R. James, *Psalms of the Pharisees, Commonly Called the Psalms of Solomon* (Cambridge: Cambridge University Press, 1891), 40–41; Mikael Winninge, *Sinners and the Righteous: A Comparative Study of the Psalms of Solomon and Paul's Letters* (Stockholm: Almqvist & Wiksell, 1995), 50–54; Atkinson, *I Cried to the Lord*, 92–96. Atkinson cogently argues that the description of this council as holy, powerful, and corrupt makes it an unlikely description of a small local council.

55. Atkinson, *I Cried to the Lord*, 95. For an evaluation of the influence of Gabinius's formation of συνέδρια on the political institutions of Judea and their perception, see, among others, Sharon, "Setting the Stage," 415–46. For an important revisionist understanding of the Jerusalem συνέδριον as a more-or-less ad hoc advisory council of Judean elites, see David M. Goodblatt, *The Monarchic Principle: Studies in Jewish Self-Government in Antiquity*, TSAJ 38 (Tübingen: Mohr Siebeck, 1994), 77–130, esp. 109.

56. On the opponents as Sadducees, see Julius Wellhausen, *Die Pharisäer und die Sadduzäer: Eine Untersuchung zur innerin jüdischen Geschichte* (Griefswald: Bamberg,

in which Aristobulus II had some political power, it must refer to the period between 66 and 63 BCE in which he was high priest and king.[57] It is noteworthy, then, that the text portrays this person as neither priestly nor royal but as an authority within the συνέδριον. Moreover, the people-pleasers bear a striking resemblance to polemical descriptions of the Pharisees.[58] The "seekers after smooth things" (דורשי החלקות) of Pesher Nahum and some of the other Dead Sea Scrolls are castigated as flatterers and hypocrites just like the people-pleasers of this psalm.[59] The Pharisees are at least as likely of a candidate for the people-pleasers

---

1874), 146–47. On the opponents as Sadducees and the profaner as Aristobulus II, see Ryle and James, *Psalms of the Pharisees*, 38–41; Winninge, *Sinners and the Righteous*, 55–56; Atkinson, *I Cried to the Lord*, 101–4. For analysis of these polemical descriptions, see Patrick Pouchelle, "Flatterers, Whisperers, and Other Hypocrites: New Denominations for Sinners in the Writings of the Second Temple Period," in *New Vistas on Early Judaism and Christianity*, ed. Lorenzo DiTommaso and Gerbern Oegema, Jewish and Christian Texts in Contexts and Related Studies 22 (London: T&T Clark, 2016), 234–50.

57. Winninge, *Sinners and the Righteous*, 55; Atkinson, *I Cried to the Lord*, 100–4.

58. The ἀνθρωπάρεσκοι of Pss. Sol. 4 are based on Ps 53 LXX [52]. See Pouchelle's contribution in this volume. While not conclusive, a growing pool of linguistic evidence suggests that either the original language of parts of the Psalms of Solomon was Greek or the originally Hebrew psalms were translated loosely into Greek at an early stage in their transmission. On the language of the text, see further Eberhard Bons, "Philosophical Vocabulary in the Psalms of Solomon: The Case of Pss. Sol. 9:4," in Bons and Pouchelle, *Psalms of Solomon*, 49–58; Kenneth Atkinson, "Psalms and Odes of Solomon: Psalms of Solomon," in *Deutero-Canonical Scriptures*, vol. 2 of *Textual History of the Bible*, ed. Matthias Henze and Frank Feder (Leiden: Brill, 2019), 332–50.

59. Among other references in the Dead Sea Scrolls, see 1QH[a] X, 14–16; XII, 7–14. On this sobriquet, see Shani L. Berrin [Tzoref], *The Pesher Nahum Scroll from Qumran: An Exegetical Study of 4Q169*, STDJ 53 (Leiden: Brill, 2004), 91–99. Tzoref has made a convincing case for the Psalms of Solomon and 4QpNah sharing a common historical perspective. However, I am not as quick to conclude that while 4QpNah critiques the Pharisees, and to some degree the Sadducees, the Psalms of Solomon is a Pharisaic indictment of the Hasmoneans. I propose, instead, that Pss. Sol. 4 may also condemn the Pharisees and thus that the similarity between 4QpNah and the psalms is even greater than Tzoref has argued. See Berrin [Tzoref], "*Pesher Nahum*, Psalms of Solomon and Pompey," in *Reworking the Bible: Apocryphal and Related Texts at Qumran*, ed. Esther G. Chazon, Devorah Dimant, and Ruth A. Clements, STDJ 58 (Leiden: Brill, 2005), 65–84.

as the Sadducees, perhaps more if we disabuse this psalm of a pre-Pompeian dating.⁶⁰

If we consider the text a product of the early Herodian period, as is increasingly typical in recent scholarhip, it makes most sense that the people-pleasers are Hyrcanus II and his supporters, many of whom may have been Pharisees.⁶¹ After Pompey's conquest, Gabinius's reorganization of the economic infrastructure in Palestine set Judean elites in the Jerusalem συνέδριον in control of exacting the tribute. Hyrcanus II was placed at the head of the Jerusalem συνέδριον, where he maintained authority until his exile during the reign of Antigonus, before being reestablished as a public figure in Jerusalem by Herod in 36 BCE (Josephus, *A.J.* 15.11–21). Between 36 and 30 BCE, a likely period for the compilation of the Psalms of Solomon in my judgment, Hyrcanus was a relic of Hasmonean political authority closely supervised by Herod.

If this proposal holds weight, it is noteworthy that the text blames neither Pompey nor Herod for the impoverishment of the masses, but rather Hyrcanus II and his supporters. As the head of the Jerusalem συνέδριον, Hyrcanus was the face of tax collection during much of the period between Pompey and Herod, at which time Judea came under the Roman tribute.⁶²

---

60. The reasoning of Winninge (*Sinners and the Righteous*, 55) and Atkinson (*I Cried to the Lord*, 96) that Pss. Sol. 4 must be pre-Pompeian because it does not allude to Pompey's conquest cannot be substantiated.

61. See Benedikt Eckhardt, "PsSal 17, die Hasmonäer und der Herodompeius," *JSJ* 40 (2009): 465–92; Eckhardt, "The Psalms of Solomon as a Historical Source for the Late Hasmonean Period," in Bons and Pouchelle, *Psalms of Solomon*, 7–30; Johannes Tromp, "The Sinners and the Lawless in Psalm of Solomon 17," *NovT* 35 (1993): 344–61; Kenneth Atkinson, "Herod the Great, Sosius, and the Siege of Jerusalem (37 B.C.E.) in Psalm of Solomon 17," *NovT* 38 (1996): 313–22; Atkinson, "On the Herodian Origin of Militant Davidic Messianism at Qumran: New Light from Psalm of Solomon 17," *JBL* 118 (1999): 435–60; Werline, "*Psalms of Solomon* and the Ideology of Rule," 70; Horsley, *Revolt of the Scribes*, 152–54; Samuel Rocca, "Josephus and the Psalms of Solomon on Herod's Messianic Aspirations: An Interpretation," in *Making History: Josephus and Historical Method*, ed. Zuleika Rodgers, JSJSup 110 (Leiden: Brill, 2007), 313–33. See also Pouchelle's contribution in this volume. Because Hyrcanus II shared Salome Alexandra's politics, it is likely that he had Pharisaic support (Josephus, *B.J.* 1.107–112; *A.J.* 13.405–409). I am unaware of any prior argument for Hyrcanus II being the profaner of Pss. Sol. 4, although see Atkinson's remarks on this possibility in *I Cried to the Lord*, 100–101.

62. Tithes to Hyrcanus II and the tribute are suggestively conflated in Caesar's decree in Josephus, *A.J.* 14.203.

Yet, this psalm does not depict poverty from the standpoint of agrarian laborers or the destitute. The focus of this polemic is eviction and the seizing of houses as a consequence of the hypocrisy of the people-pleasers (4.5, 9, 11, 12, 17, 20). Throughout the Psalms of Solomon, a person's house is a locus of piety, as exemplified by the image of the righteous one always searching his house in 3.6–8.[63] Psalms of Solomon 4 similarly suggests that the righteous have houses but have lost them due to interactions with the people-pleasers. This might be a reference to taxation impeding subsistence, but the particular emphasis on breaking contracts (4.4) seems to allude to foreclosures caused by exploitative loan practices on the part of Judean elites. Unlike the lawless deceivers of Pss. Sol. 12, the people-pleasers are denounced for socioeconomic injustice.

There are several other noteworthy elements in this psalm's discourse on inequality. First, the injustice of the people-pleasers is related to a lack of virtue. In 4.3, lack of self-control (ἀκρασία) emerges as one of their abuses of wealth, and the image of their ruthless seizure of property supports this. Second, 4.21 explains that in all of their acts, "they have not remembered God," which invokes the admonition of Deut 8:17 to remember God as the source of one's power to gain wealth much like the Epistle of Enoch.[64] Third, unlike Ben Sira, but similar to 1Q/4QInstruction, 4.15–16 links sleeplessness and pain with poverty and wishes it on those with wealth.[65] Finally, the claim that the people-pleasers scattered the pious as orphans

---

63. Cf. the different uses of οἶκος, which can mean house/home, household, or both simultaneously, in Pss. Sol. 6.5; 7.10; 8.18; 9.5, 11; 10.8; 12.3, 5; 15.11; 17.42.

64. On remembrance of God in the Psalms of Solomon, see William Horbury, "The Remembrance of God in the Psalms of Solomon," in *Memory in the Bible and Antiquity: The Fifth Durham-Tübingen Research Symposium (Durham, September 2004)*, ed. Steven C. Barton, Loren T. Stuckenbruck, and Benjamin G. Wold, WUNT 212 (Tübingen: Mohr Siebeck, 2007), 111–28. See also Rodney Werline's contribution to this volume.

65. On the meanings of sleep (ὕπνος) in the Psalms of Solomon, see Sven Behnke, "Die Rede vom Schlaf in den Psalmen Salomos und ihr traditions-geschichtlicher Hintergrund," in Bons and Pouchelle, *Psalms of Solomon*, esp. 99 on Pss. Sol. 4. Aside from its theological valences, it is worth noting that the effects of the pursuit of wealth on sleep are a common theme in ancient discussions of socioeconomic ethics. Not only does it appear in these Judean texts, but also in the mid-first century BCE Philodemus of Gadara critiqued Xenophon for arguing that the best property managers are those who wake before their servants and go to sleep after them. For Philodemus, losing sleep in order to gain wealth interferes with the philosopher's pursuit of wisdom, which ultimately results in superior property management practices. See

through their deceptive interactions (4.10, 20) does not relate dislocation to military action. Rather, it invokes the socioeconomic process through which new taxation pressures caused those near subsistence level to seek out loans from elites, probably through contracts that placed interest on those loans. Due to those interest rates, however, as well as continued war conditions and environmental pressures, they are sometimes unable to repay those loans and face eviction.[66]

In sum, the polemic of Pss. Sol. 4 has an economic subtext that makes sense as a reaction against Herod's ostensible reempowerment of Hyrcanus II in the mid-30s BCE. Simultaneously a critique of Hyrcanus II and his supporters and the tax-gathering and loan practices of Jewish elites in the συνέδριον, this psalm attributes the cause of socioeconomic inequality to human injustice and offers no human solution to it. In this way, the psalm resembles the apocalyptic reception of Deuteronomic ethics, as Rodney Werline has argued from a different angle.[67] The psalm, however, does not call for divine judgment of the people-pleasers in an eschatological age, but in an impending messianic era.

3.2. Psalms of Solomon 5

Whereas Pss. Sol. 4 generates a class portrait that attributes inequality to systemic human injustice and offers no human solution, Pss. Sol. 5 casts God as the maker of inequality and supports a form of human action as a means to alleviate poverty.

This first-person psalm begins by praising God for his merciful and just judgments and asserting his control over human wealth. It uses an economic metaphor in 5.4: "for a human and their portion are before you on the balance [σταθμῷ]; one cannot add in order to increase [πλεονάσαι] against your judgment, O God." In spite of this rigid acclamation of God's

---

Voula Tsouna, *Philodemus, On Property Management*, WGRW 33 (Atlanta: Society of Biblical Literature, 2012).

66. Environmental pressures are reported at several points in the text but most clearly in a reference at Pss. Sol. 17.18 to a drought causing the scattering of people much like the people-pleasers do in Pss. Sol. 4 (Ryle and James, *Psalms of the Pharisees*, xliii). Because these conditions were recurring (if irregular), such allusions cannot be connected to a particular instance with certainty. Nevertheless, the famine during Herod's seige in 17.18 fits nicely with Josephus's description of a famine at this time (*A.J.* 14.475), as Atkinson observes ("Herod the Great," 320).

67. Werline, "*Psalms of Solomon* and the Ideology of Rule," 84–85.

control over human economic fortune, the next verse acknowledges, in Deuteronomic fashion, human intercession as a prerequisite for divine action: "When we are persecuted, we call on you for help and you will not turn away our prayer" (5.5). God justifies economic states, then, but only in response to human prayers and righteousness. Humans begin the process. Verse 8 continues: "For if I am hungry, I will cry out to you, O God, and you will give me something." The subsequent verses affirm that God provides for all living things, and for kings, rulers, and peoples, petitioning also that he will provide for the "poor and needy" (5.10–14).

What exactly the psalm means by "poor and needy" comes into question in verses 16–17:

> Happy is the one whom God remembers with a proportionate self-sufficiency [ἐν συμμετρίᾳ αὐταρκείας]. If one abounds excessively [ὑπερπλεονάσῃ], they sin. Moderate wealth [τὸ μέτριον] with righteousness is sufficient [ἱκανὸν], for this comes with the Lord's blessing: to be satisfied with righteousness.

With these statements, Pss. Sol. 5 converges with the sapiential discourse on socioeconomic ethics. Patrick Pouchelle has demonstrated that 5.16–17 alludes to the sapiential ethics of Prov 30:8 LXX:[68]

> πλοῦτον δὲ καὶ πενίαν μή μοι δῷς σύνταξον δέ μοι τὰ δέοντα καὶ τὰ αὐτάρκη.
> Give me neither wealth nor destitution, but appoint what is necessary and sufficient to me.

Despite their positive self-identification as poor, the producers of Pss. Sol. 5 do not reject wealth. Instead, they expect that righteousness and prayer will provoke God to provide humans "with a proportionate self-sufficiency" (ἐν συμμετρίᾳ αὐταρκείας). In addition to the allusion to Prov 30:8 LXX, Pss. Sol. 5.16 may also invoke Deut 8:17 in the same way as Ben Sira. In light of αὐτάρκη μοί ἐστιν functioning as a loose

---

68. Patrick Pouchelle, "The Simple Bare Necessities: Is Pss. Sol. 5 a Wisdom Prayer?," in *Tracing Sapiential Traditions in Ancient Judaism*, ed. Hindy Najman, Jean-Sébastien Rey, and Eibert J. C. Tigchelaar, JSJSup 174 (Leiden: Brill, 2016), 138–54. Cf. G. Buchanan Gray, "The Psalms of Solomon," APOT 2:637 n. 6; Ryle and James, *Psalms of the Pharisees*, 61.

translation of ידי לאל יש in Sir 5:1, it stands to reason that the use of αὐτάρκεια in Pss. Sol. 5.16 also draws a link to the Deuteronomic admonition. Like Prov LXX and Ben Sira, Pss. Sol. 5 views self-sufficiency as a positive attribute that is not simply the result of human agency, but also divine agency. The use of αὐτάρκεια, then, is not as impressive evidence of a Greek original text as Eberhard Bons has suggested.[69] Regardless, the attribution of human self-sufficiency and moderate wealth to God in these lines concurs with the sapiential reception of Deuteronomic ethics. Abundance beyond self-sufficiency leads to sin, as Pss. Sol. 4 claimed, while moderate wealth is sufficient.

Self-sufficiency is not poverty by most standards, especially at a time when the majority of the population lived near or below subsistence level. It is surprising that the psalm enshrines self-sufficiency as an ideal while poverty appears almost akin to righteousness elsewhere. Perhaps it is for this reason that the Syriac translators revised these verses:

> Blessed is the man whom the Lord remembers in poverty [ܒܡܣܟܢܘܬܐ], for a man will exceed his sufficiency [ܣܦܩܬܐ] so that he sins because of it; advantageous is poverty [ܒܡܣܟܢܘܬܐ] with righteousness. (Syr. Pss. Sol. 5.18–20)[70]

In this tradition, poverty has replaced self-sufficiency as a positive ideal while merely exceeding self-sufficiency supplants having excessive wealth as its sinful foil. At the same time that this translation betrays the ascetic ideals of late antique Syriac Christianity,[71] it highlights the incongruity between the socioeconomic ideals of this passage and the poverty language in the other psalms.

This psalm is confusing for several additional reasons. The affirmation of God's control over socioeconomic mobility is at tension with the emphasis on prayer provoking God to action. Psalms of Solomon 9.4–7

---

69. Bons, "Philosophical Vocabulary," 51. Additionally, Pouchelle notes that αὐτάρκησεν occurs in Deut 32:10 LXX ("Simple Bare Necessities").

70. Translation from Trafton, *Syriac Version*, 73.

71. On the significance of poverty in Syriac Christianity, see further Susan Ashbrook Harvey, "The Holy and the Poor: Models from Early Syriac Christianity," in *Through the Eye of a Needle: Judeo-Christian Roots of Social Welfare*, ed. Emily Albu Hanawalt and Carter Lindberg (Kirksville: Thomas Jefferson University Press, 1994), 43–66.

further connects prayer to human free will. From the perspective of the producers of the Psalms of Solomon, prayer and other attributes of righteousness are forms of human agency, of free will, that cooperate with divine action.[72] A critical approach to the assertion of human agency in the determination of socioeconomic states, however, must identify prayer as impotent to relieve poverty in social practice.

Psalms of Solomon 5 is very different than Pss. Sol. 4. On the one hand, Pss. Sol. 4, like apocalyptic discourses, attributes inequality to human injustice, alludes to structures that facilitate injustice, and does not mention human agency as a means to overcome poverty. On the other hand, Pss. Sol. 5, like sapiential discourses, attributes inequality to divine justice, does not allude to structures hindering mobility, and stresses prayer as a form of human agency. Nevertheless, both psalms are silent about social practices that might relieve poverty, whether extra- or intracommunal.

3.3. Other Psalms of Solomon

In addition to Pss. Sol. 4 and 5, there are three other references to poverty and exploitation that merit attention.

First, Pss. Sol. 8.10–12 castigates the temple priests of the late Hasmonean period for the same failures the Damascus Document labels the "three nets of Belial": fornication, wealth, and defilement of the sanctuary (CD IV, 12–19).[73] Where the Damascus Document simply has

---

72. As Ryle and James (*Psalms of the Pharisees*, l) argue, the combined belief in divine providence and human free will here is akin to the philosophy attributed to the Pharisees (Josephus, *B.J.* 2.14, 163; *A.J.* 18.3; cf. m. 'Abot 3:16). The complications of the Josephan passages are judiciously addressed in Jonathan Klawans, *Josephus and the Theologies of Ancient Judaism* (Oxford: Oxford University Press, 2012), 44–91. The concurrence of the Psalms of Solomon with Josephus's view of Pharisaic philosophy is indeed striking, but the Josephan portrait is also heavily biased towards the author's own philosophy as well as his prerogative of coloring the Pharisees as Stoics. Although important evidence that the psalms may have come from a Pharisaic community, it is equally possible that the psalms came from some other community with a compatibilist theology.

73. In IV, 17, the manuscript has הזהין ("arrogance"), but most scholars emend this to הזנון. As Murphy (*Wealth in the Dead Sea Scrolls*, 37–40) remarks, however, even if this common emendation is not accepted, there can be little doubt that the producers of the Damascus Document indict the temple priests for their arrogance and their wealth. Cf. CD VI, 14–17; 1QpHab VIII, 3–IX, 7. For the connection, see Robert B.

wealth, however, Pss. Sol. 8.11 elaborates that "they plundered the sanctuary of God, as if there were no redeeming heir."[74] The priests' wealth is sinful because it derived from the exploitation of the people through the temple apparatus. Elsewhere the Psalms of Solomon explicate that the temple is Israel's inheritance from God (7.2); thus, the priests have exploited the rightful heirs of the sanctuary. The temple tax, and perhaps also tithes and offerings, are in view here.[75] Psalms of Solomon 8's deprecation of the temple priests shares with Pss. Sol. 4 an apocalyptic critique of wealth.[76] Human injustice involves structural economic exploitation, which can only be overcome by God's action, not eschatologically, but in their present age.

A very different reference to poverty occurs in Pss. Sol. 16. Verses 12–15 petition God as such:

> Support me with approval and happiness,
> > when you strengthen me.
> > > Whatever you will give is good enough for me.
> Because if ever you fail to give us strength,
> > who can endure discipline in need [πενία]?
> When people are tested by means of their mortality,
> > you are examining them in their flesh and in the affliction of need [θλίψει πενίας]:
> The righteous endures these things;
> > he will receive mercy from the Lord.

Although these lines agree with Pss. Sol. 5 that God provides sustenance, they do not glorify self-sufficiency. Rather, they render destitute poverty (πενία) as an opportunity to show righteousness. This type of poverty is associated with the survival of bare life, which requires far less than

---

Wright, "The *Psalms of Solomon*: The Pharisees and the Essenes," in *1972 Proceedings of the International Organization for Septuagint and Cognate Studies and the Society of Biblical Literature Pseudepigrapha Seminar*, ed. Robert A. Kraft, SCS 2 (Missoula: Society of Biblical Literature, 1972), 144–45; Atkinson, "Temple Priests," 88.

74. Horsley (*Revolt of the Scribes*, 153) notes similar language in 1QpHab IX, 4–7, but here the temple priests plunder the nations, not the sanctuary.

75. Cf. Sanders, *Judaism*, 160.

76. This psalm also contains the most distinctive revelatory language in the collection. See Sharon, "Opposition to the Hasmoneans," 50; Atkinson, "Temple Priests," 88–89.

self-sufficiency. The righteous person endures this undesirable state of destitution by placing their hope in God in return for his mercy and support. Like sapiential discourses, these lines ascribe socioeconomic mobility to God but admit a human part in the process. Insufficient human action results in poverty, which people can only overcome with divine support. Psalms of Solomon 16, then, has a sapiential bent, but also places an apocalyptic emphasis on divine mercy as the reward for endurance and mobility.

The final psalm worthy of inclusion here is Pss. Sol. 17, which details the messiah's judgment and destruction. Like apocalyptic discourses, this psalm envisages the dawning of a messianic kingdom that rectifies what the psalmists consider the social ills of the present age. On the topic of poverty and exploitation, two lines are apt. The first involves land distribution: "He will distribute them upon the land according to their tribes" (17.28). As a reversal of the unjust redistribution implied by Pss. Sol. 4, this line expects that the messiah will assure a just allotment of land, presumably in which each person owns their own land without threat of eviction. The second line involves taxation, asserting that the messiah will not "need to accumulate gold and silver for war" (17.33). Apophatically, taxation surfaces here as a form of exploitation that will not prevail in the messianic age. Likely alluding to the imposition of the tribute after Pompey's conquest and its continued, if irregular, collection through the early part of Herod's reign, this statement points to the changes to the structure of taxation as perceived in the early Herodian age.

With these three additional comments on inequality, then, it appears that sapiential and apocalyptic perspectives on inequality converge in differing ways throughout the collection. This results in an inconsistent discourse on inequality whose most constant threads are the connection between excessive wealth and sin and a striking disinterest in social solutions to poverty.

4. Conclusions

By situating the Psalms of Solomon's class rhetoric in its literary and historical contexts, I have proposed that the psalms' particular conflation of apocalyptic and sapiential perspectives on inequality distinguishes this text from most literature of its time. While the Damascus Document, Community Rule, and Q source also operate at the intersection of these discourses, they nevertheless convey from the sapiential discourse some platform for social justice in the interim before divine intervention. The

Psalms of Solomon do not. In this way, the class subjectivity the text generates most closely resembles that of 1Q/4QInstruction, but even the latter elucidates better and worse economic interactions. No other surviving text from this time has so much to say about poverty, but so little about its avoidance and eradication. What does this tell us about the circle that produced the Psalms of Solomon, their historical setting, and the function of the text?

The widespread understanding of the Psalms of Solomon as crisis literature with the primary function of giving hope to the poor and oppressed needs to be complicated. Most significantly, it is critical to justify the language of poverty in the text against its indications of socioeconomic situation. For instance, the text consistently identifies homes and congregations as spaces occupied by those identified as poor. This implies that the intended audience of the psalms consisted of homeowners associated with a community with some form of organization, probably with some relation to prayerhalls or synagogues (Pss. Sol. 10.7; 17.16).[77] In comparison to the Damascus Document and Q source, for instance, the text also contains little agrarian language, signifying an urban context. This fits with Atkinson's conclusion that the producers of the text resided in or around Jerusalem and may have been disenfranchised from the temple cult.[78] Yet, even if Atkinson is right that some form of downward mobility instigated the production of the Psalms of Solomon, this could have been a sociopolitical demotion but not an economic one. Alternatively, the producers of the text may not have experienced any sort of downgrade but simply found in the changing socioeconomic structures of their times an opportunity to attract support for their own political ideology and community. That the producers of these psalms were learned scribes concerned for houses and congregations suggests a socioeconomic location above subsistence level, probably considerably.[79]

---

77. See Atkinson, *I Cried to the Lord*, 211–20.

78. Atkinson, "Temple Priests."

79. On the relatively high socioeconomic levels of scribal circles, see Karel van der Toorn, *Scribal Culture and the Making of the Hebrew Bible* (Cambridge: Harvard University Press, 2007). On scribes as subelites (or elites, I would add) in Hellenistic-Roman Palestine, see Giovanni Bazzana, *Kingdom of Bureaucracy: The Political Theology of Village Scribes in the Sayings Gospel Q*, BETL 274 (Leuven: Peeters, 2015); Bazzana, "Galilean Village Scribes as the Authors of the Sayings Gospel Q," in *Q in Context II*, ed. Markus Tiwald, BBB 173 (Göttingen: Vandenhoeck & Ruprecht, 2015),

The foregoing analysis of the language of poverty is corroborative. Poverty for the producers of this text is akin to self-sufficiency—to relative comfort and security with some resources, but not excessive wealth. This type of poverty (πτωχεία) is different than destitution (πενία), which is an undesirable state. Thus, poverty in the Psalms of Solomon is rhetorical and metaphoric—a literary and theological construct—in one sense, yet more than that. The class discourse in the Psalms of Solomon would have had concrete social implications that were likely enhanced in their use and performance through other indications of class distinction. Just as Werline has argued that the text uses the language of discipline to affect a certain type of subject-formation,[80] I propose that the Psalms of Solomon generates a class subjectivity with significant effects—namely, aversion to the Hasmoneans, Herod, and certain elites associated with the Jerusalem συνέδριον and temple as exploitative creators of inequality and discouragement of the human role in social transformation.

This text's class rhetoric inculcates subjects with distinct views on the relation of structure and agency. While the psalms point to persons and structures as causes of inequality, they also allow for some agency in the determination of socioeconomic states. Prayer, in particular, appears as a mechanism through which people can call on God to relieve their poverty and oppression. While this is agency,[81] and likely a source of hope for the audience of the text, it is devoid of social power to affect resistance on the

---

133–48. See also Chris Keith, *Jesus against the Scribal Elite: The Origins of the Conflict* (Grand Rapids: Baker, 2014).

80. Rodney A. Werline, "The Formation of the Pious Person in the Psalms of Solomon," in Bons and Pouchelle, *Psalms of Solomon*, 133–54. Cf. Angela Kim Harkins, *Reading with an "I" to the Heavens: Looking at the Qumran Hodayot through the Lens of Visionary Traditions*, Ekstasis 3 (Berlin: de Gruyter, 2012).

81. Saba Mahmood explains that a critical study of agency must attend to its meaning "within the grammar of concepts within which it resides" (*Politics of Piety: The Islamic Revival and the Feminist Subject* [Princeton: Princeton University Press, 2005], 34). This agency, however, is also "a product of the historically contingent discursive traditions in which they are located" (32). Prayer in the Psalms of Solomon is a form of agency against economic exploitation generated at the intersection of sapiential and apocalyptic socioeconomic discourses. What I have not been able to consider here, and will have to return to in an additional study, is the particular ways that prayer functions as a source of social cohesion and communal identity formation within particular communities (see, e.g., Jerome H. Neyrey, *Give God the Glory: Ancient Prayer and Worship in Cultural Perspective* [Grand Rapids: Eerdmans, 2007]).

ground. In fact, the Psalms of Solomon interpellates subjects with class dispositions that discourage them from attempting to change their socioeconomic positions aside from through prayer.

The Same Scholarly Fate?
A Short Comparison between the Psalms of Solomon and the Assumption of Moses

Patrick Pouchelle

1. Introduction

The so-called Assumption of Moses or Testament of Moses was edited by Antonio M. Ceriani in 1861 from a single Latin manuscript, a palimpsest.[1] The text is incomplete and often difficult to read, especially after the chemical treatments it suffered in an attempt to reveal its text.[2] Accordingly, the most recent edition by Johannes Tromp is based on the preceding edition of Ceriani and that of Carl Clemen, as well as old photographs of the manuscript.[3]

---

1. Antonio M. Ceriani, *Monumenta Sacra et profana ex codicibus praesertim Bibliothecae Ambrosianae*, 5 vols. (Milan: Bibliotheca Ambrosiana, 1861–1868), 1:55–62. Nevertheless, the text was known before the discovery of Ceriani. Johann Albert Fabricius had collected some quotations of this text by Gelasius of Cyzicus in his *Codex Pseudepigraphus Veteris Testamenti collectus, castigatus, testimoniisque, censuris et animadversionibus illustratus*, 2 vols. (Hamburg: Felginer, 1722–1723). The manuscript edited by Ceriani was also partially edited by Peyron in 1824. For more details, see Johannes Tromp, *The Assumption of Moses: A Critical Edition with Commentary*, SVTP 10 (Leiden: Brill, 1993), 87–92. For the problematic title of this work, see Fiona Grierson, "The Testament of Moses" *JSP* 17 (2008): 265–80, esp. 266–74.

2. See Tromp, *Assumption of Moses*, 91.

3. Carl Clemen, *Die Himmelfahrt des Mose*, KlT 10 (Bonn: Marcus & Weber, 1904). The manuscript was unavailable at the time Tromp produced his commentary (*Assumption of Moses*, 1). Hopefully, the current project directed by Todd Hanneken, "The Jubilees Palimpsest Project" (jubilees.stmarytx.edu), will soon provide better photographs so that a new critical edition would become possible.

Even though it was identified by Ceriani as the Assumption of Moses, this text belongs to the literary genre of the testament, and some scholars have suggested that it should be called the Testament of Moses.[4] Indeed, this text presents Moses as giving his last will and commandments to Joshua. These last words are mainly prophetic in the sense that they predict what will happen to Israel. Understood as *ex eventu* prophecy, it is generally assumed that the Assumption of Moses alludes to the war of Varus that follows the death of Herod.[5]

The Psalms of Solomon is a collection of eighteen prayers,[6] preserved in eleven Greek manuscripts and five Syriac manuscripts. They imitate canonical psalms. They allude to a siege of Jerusalem, generally identified as the one made by Pompey in 63 BCE. They also develop an interest in the concept of παιδεία, which is understood as a pedagogical means of God. God corrects his devout owing to their sins, whereas the wicked are left alone until the time of divine judgment.[7]

At first sight, differences between the texts are obvious. For instance, Moses and Joshua are not mentioned by the Psalms of Solomon. Moreover, the Assumption of Moses is not a messianic text like Pss. Sol. 17.[8] Unlike the Psalms of Solomon,[9] the Assumption of Moses presents a clear

---

4. See Tromp, *Assumption of Moses*, 115–16.

5. See below.

6. The most recent critical edition is Felix Albrecht, *Psalmi Salomonis*, SVTG 12.3 (Göttingen: Vandenhoeck & Ruprecht, 2018). The current numbering of the Psalms of Solomon was established by Oscar von Gebhardt, *Die Psalmen Salomo's zum ersten Male mit Benutzung der Athoshandschriften und des Codex Casanatensis*, TUGAL 13.2 (Leipzig: Hinrichs, 1895). For the sake of understandability, I have altered the numbering of authors writing before von Gebhardt to adapt it to current usage.

7. See Patrick Pouchelle, "Prayers for Being Disciplined: Notes on παιδεύω and παιδεία in the Psalms of Solomon," in *The Psalms of Solomon: Language, History, Theology*, ed. Eberhard Bons and Patrick Pouchelle, EJL 40 (Atlanta: SBL Press, 2015), 115–32.

8. The Psalms of Solomon describes a Messiah (17.32; 18.5, 7). In the Assumption of Moses, the mysterious Taxo who tries to resist the prince of the nations could be understood as a messiah, but he is never qualified as such. See Johannes Tromp, "Taxo, the Messenger of the Lord," *JSJ* 21 (1990): 200–209; Kenneth Atkinson, "Taxo's Martyrdom and the Role of the *Nuntius* in the '*Testament of Moses*': Implications for Understanding the Role of Other Intermediary Figures," *JBL* 125 (2006): 453–76. Atkinson noticed that the messiah in the Pss. Sol. 17.32 is "pure from sin" like Taxo (As. Mos. 9.3–7).

9. The degree to which the Psalms of Solomon are apocalyptic, if at all, is debated.

apocalyptic section (As. Mos. 10), in which God, described as the Heavenly One, will come out of his holy palace and act for his children.

These differences might explain why scholarship has never produced a thorough and detailed comparison of these two texts.[10] Adolf Hilgenfeld compares our two texts once, to emphasize that the messianic king expected by the Psalms of Solomon is not similar to the messianic Levite Taxo.[11] Frequently a commentator of one text uses the other text, as one among other pseudepigrapha, to illustrate some specificities. The first commentators on the Assumption of Moses to use the Psalms of Solomon extensively in this way were Moriz Schmidt and Adalbert Merx.[12] R. H.

There is no description of two realms, one terrestrial and one heavenly. Cf. Martin Karrer, *Der Gesalbte, die Grundlagen des Christustitels*, FRLANT 151 (Göttingen: Vandenhoeck & Ruprecht, 1991), 254; Young S. Chae, *Jesus as the Eschatological Davidic Shepherd*, WUNT 2/216 (Tübingen: Mohr Siebeck, 2006), 117-18. Albert-Marie Denis sees some "apocalyptic notations" although the "work isn't apocalyptic" (*Introduction à la littérature religieuse judéo-hellénistique*, 2 volumes [Turnhout: Brepols, 2000], 1:508 n. 6). Raija Sollamo interprets Pss. Sol. 17 as apocalyptic because this psalm describes the irruption of God's action in human history ("Messianism and the 'Branch of David' Isaiah 11,1-5 and Genesis 49,8-12," in *The Septuagint and Messianism*, ed. Michael A. Knibb, BETL 195 [Leuven: Peeters, 2006], 367). See also Kenneth E. Pomykala, *The Davidic Dynasty Tradition in Early Judaism, Its History and Significance for Messianism*, EJL 7 (Atlanta: Scholars, 1995), 169.

10. The first edition of the Psalms of Solomon was made earlier by Juan Luis de la Cerda, *Adversaria Sacra* (Lyon: Louis Prost, 1626). See the introduction of the present book.

11. Adolf Hilgenfeld, *Messias Judaeorum, Libris eorum Paulo ante et Paulo post Christum natum conscriptis illustratus* (Leipzig: Fues, 1869), lxxv-lxxvi. The only other comparison is in Hilgenfeld's "Nachträge zu den Psalmen Salomo's und der Himmelfahrt des Moses," ZWT 11 (1868): 353, where he compares *profectionis Fynicis* (which he retroverted to πορεία Φοινίκος) with the attestation of πορεία in Pss. Sol. 18.10. Hilgenfeld edited the Assumption of Moses in his "Mosis Assumptionis, quae supersunt nunc primum edita et illustrata," *Novum Testamentum extra canonem receptum* (Leipzig: Weigel, 1866), 93-116 and offers a Greek retroversion in "Die Psalmen Salomo's und die Himmelfahrt des Moses, griechisch hergestellt und erklärt," ZWT 11 (1868): 273-309; Hilgenfeld, *Messias Judaeorum*, 435-68. He offers an edition of the Psalms of Solomon twice: "Die Psalmen Salomo's," 134-68; Hilgenfeld, *Messias Judaeorum*, 1-33.

12. Moriz Schmidt and Adalbert Merx, "Die Assumptio Mosis mit Einleitung und erklärenden Anmerkungen," *Archiv für wissenschaftliche Erforschung des Alten Testaments* 1 (1869): 111-52. Gustav Volkmar, *Mose Prophetie und Himmelfahrt: Eine Quelle für das Neue Testament zum ersten Male deutsch herausgegeben, im zusammenhang der Apokrypha und der Christologie überhaupt*, Handbuch der Apocryphen 3

Charles's influential book identifies the author of the Assumption of Moses as a quietist Pharisee and presents the Psalms of Solomon as an example of another text that originated from the same milieu.[13] Similarly, the famous commentators of the Psalms of Solomon, Herbert Edward Ryle and Montague Rhodes James, as well as Joseph Viteau,[14] compared the Psalms of Solomon with other pseudepigrapha systematically. They observed some parallels with the Assumption of Moses but did not conclude that there was any relationship between the two texts.

During the period of scholarship that Tromp called a "waning of interest,"[15] which both texts suffered from the beginning of the twentieth century to the 1970s, nothing noteworthy was produced. Moreover, the recent resurgence of interest which touched the Assumption of Moses and the Psalms of Solomon, as well as many other pseudepigrapha, does not provide further insight into their comparison.[16] Tromp uses the Psalms of Solomon in his edition and commentary on the Assumption of Moses but

---

(Leipzig: Fues, 1867), 124 uses the Psalms of Solomon once when dealing with the dating of the Assumption of Moses.

13. R. H. Charles, *The Assumption of Moses Translated from the Latin Sixth Century MS., the Unemended Text of which Is Published Herewith, Together with the Text in Its Restored and Critically Emended Form* (London: Adam & Charles Black, 1897), li–liii. He sometimes referenced the Psalms of Solomon, particularly in his discussion of As. Mos. 7 (Charles, *Assumption of Moses*, 25–28), as well as to observe a shift towards nationalistic interests (34).

14. Herbert Edward Ryle and Montague Rhodes James, *Psalms of the Pharisees Commonly Called the Psalms of Solomon* (Cambridge: University Press, 1891), lxx; Joseph Viteau, *Les Psaumes de Salomon: Introduction, texte grec et traduction par J. Viteau, avec les principales variantes de la version syriaque par François Martin*, Documents pour l'étude de la Bible (Paris: Letouzey et Ané, 1911), 163–64.

15. Tromp, *Assumption of Moses*, 103.

16. Tromp dates the renewal of interest in the Assumption of Moses to the publication of the French translation and commentary by Ernest-Marie Laperrousaz, *Le Testament de Moïse (généralement appelé 'Assomption de Moïse'). Traduction avec introduction et notes*, Semitica 10 (Paris: Adrien-Maisonneuve, 1970). We could date the renewal of interest in the Psalms of Solomon to the article of Robert B. Wright: "The Psalms of Solomon: the Pharisees and the Essenes," in *1972 Proceedings for the International Organization for Septuagint and Cognate studies*, ed. Robert A. Kraft, SCS 2 (Atlanta: Society of Biblical Literature, 1972), 136–54. Wright worked throughout his career on a critical edition, which was published in 2007 (see above). The German contribution to this renewal should also be mentioned: Svend Holm-Nielsen, "Die Psalmen Salomos," *JSHRZ* 4:51–112; Joachim Schüpphaus, *Die Psalmen Salomos: Ein Zeugnis Jerusalemer Theologie und Frömmigkeit in der Mitte des vorchristlichen Jahr-*

without analyzing the two texts together. The most recent analysis of the two texts remains the one done by Norbert Johannes Hofmann, who dedicated one paragraph to it.[17] Hofmann concluded that there is not a literary dependence but mainly borrowing from a common tradition. Kenneth Atkinson in his commentary on the Psalms of Solomon does not compare our two texts.[18] More recently, however, he published two articles on the Assumption of Moses.[19] In the latest one, he compared the pacifist attitude of Taxo to the violent nature of the Davidic messiah in Pss. Sol. 17.[20]

With the publication of the entire Dead Sea Scrolls, scholars, like Atkinson, are now able to do research on the Psalms of Solomon, as well as on the Assumption of Moses, in comparison with the scrolls. R. Steven Notley and William Horbury, for instance, have detected some similarities in the use of Scripture in As. Mos. 10.2, Pss. Sol. 11.1, and 11Q13 II, 4–23, when these texts deal with the messenger in charge of announcing an eschatological period by combining Isa 52:7 and Lev 25:8–12.[21]

The aim of this essay is to show that, despite this lack of mutual interest, scholarship on the Assumption of Moses and on the Psalms of Solomon followed similar paths, at least on three different topics, namely, the question of language, the question of dating, and the question of provenance. By presenting these similarities, I will also introduce some other parallels that could be of some interest. I do not intend to prove that the Assumption of Moses originated from the same language, at the same time, and from the same community as the Psalms of Solomon, but rather

---

hunderts, ALGHJ 7 (Leiden: Brill, 1977). The renewal of interest in pseudepigrapha more generally culminated with the publication of *OTP*.

17. Norbert Johannes Hofmann, *Die Assumptio Mosis: Studien zur Rezeption massgültiger Überlieferung*, JSJSup 67 (Leiden: Brill, 2000), 257–60.

18. Kenneth Atkinson, *I Cried to the Lord: A Study of the Psalms of Solomon's Historical Background and Social Setting*, JSJSup 84 (Leiden: Brill, 2004).

19. Atkinson, "Taxo's Martyrdom," 453–76; Atkinson, "Herod the Great as *Antiochus Redivivus*: Reading the Testament of Moses as an Anti-Herodian Composition," in *Of Scribes and Sages: Ancient Versions and Traditions*, ed. Craig A. Evans, 2 vols. (London: T&T Clark, 2004), 1:134–49.

20. Atkinson, "Herod the Great," 147–48 n. 48.

21. See R. Steven Notley, "The Kingdom of Heaven Forcefully Advances," in *The Interpretation of Scripture in Early Judaism and Christianity*, ed. Craig A. Evans, JSPSup 33 (Sheffield: Sheffield Academic, 2000), 279–311; William Horbury, "'Gospel' in Herodian Judaea," in *Herodian Judaism and New Testament Study*, WUNT 193 (Tübingen: Mohr Siebeck, 2006), 97–99.

that both texts puzzled scholars similarly owing to the fact that they offer a unique view on a complex period in Second Temple Judaism. Therefore, further comparative studies should be undertaken so as to delve deeper into this crucial period.

2. The Question of Language

Hilgenfeld suggested that both texts were written in Greek.[22] His argument was based on the proximity of these texts with the translated Septuagint and the Wisdom of Solomon. These arguments have been refuted: the proximity with the Septuagint could not help us to detect the original language as it is precisely a translated text, and the closeness detected by Hilgenfeld with the Wisdom of Solomon was assessed as too weak.[23] Moreover, some Semitisms detected in both works led to the conclusion of a Hebrew or Aramaic original.[24]

The nineteenth- and early twentieth-century scholars were biased. They assumed that Greek was not spoken and written in Palestine. Even if they accepted that Greek could be present in Palestine, they denied that it was used to write religious texts.[25] We know today that this view was wrong.[26]

Tromp challenged the theory of a Hebrew original defended by Charles. He begins to refute Charles's argument by noting that the alleged Hebraisms could occur in a text genuinely written in Greek.[27]

---

22. Hilgenfeld, *Messias Judaeorum*, xvi–xviii (Psalms of Solomon), lxxiii (Assumption of Moses).

23. For the Assumption of Moses, see Charles, *Assumption of Moses*, xxxviii–xxxix; for the Psalms of Solomon, see Ryle and James, *Psalms of the Pharisees*, lxxxiv–lxxxvi.

24. Charles, *Assumption of Moses*, xxxviii–xlv, and Ryle and James, *Psalms of the Pharisees*, lxxvii–lxxxvii. For the Assumption of Moses, Charles debated between Aramaic and Hebrew as the original language and concluded for a Hebrew original. His assumption of a Semitic original was so strong that when David H. Wallace refuted Charles's arguments ("The Semitic Origin of the Assumption of Moses," *TZ* 5 [1955]: 321–28), he simply concludes that we could not assess whether the original language was Hebrew or Aramaic. Laperrousaz follows this line of argument (*Le Testament de Moïse*, 17).

25. E.g., Ryle and James, *Psalms of the Pharisees*, lxxvii–lxviii.

26. See, for instance, the discussion in Catherine Hezser, *Jewish Literacy in Roman Palestine*, TSAJ 81 (Tübingen: Mohr Siebeck, 2001), 231–36.

27. Tromp, *Assumption of Moses*, 83–85, 117–18. For instance, *in respectu quo respiciet* (As. Mos. 1.8) could be based on Gen 50:24 LXX (ἐπισκοπῇ δὲ ἐπισκέψεται)

Thereafter, he positively presents three arguments for a Greek original. First, he notes the use of rare words or expressions with no or very few attestations in the Vulgate (e.g., *incomprehensibilis* in 11.16).[28] Second, he presents the use of the proper name *Fynicis* (1.3) as a transliteration of Φοινίκη to denote Canaan. Although attested a few times (Exod 6:15; 16:35; Josh 5:12; Job 40:30), this rendering is infrequent in the LXX relative to the literal transliteration Χανάαν.[29] Third, he noticed a remarkable frequency of the verb *habere* for denoting possession, whereas the Hebrew does not have such construction[30] and the LXX prefers to render the Hebrew idiom more literally instead of with this more classical way. Tromp concludes that the hypothesis of a genuine Greek original has more weight. Although he does not prove this hypothesis, he suggests that scholars should not take a Hebrew or Aramaic original for granted any longer.[31]

The consensus about the original language of the Psalms of Solomon has recently been challenged.[32] For instance, some philosophical vocabulary found in Pss. Sol. 9 may suggest that a Hebrew *Vorlage* is improbable.[33] Similarly, the LXX is sometimes used by the Psalms of Solomon in a way that could not be explained by a Hebrew *Vorlage*.[34]

An example is the presence of the word ἀνθρωπάρεσκος in Pss. Sol. 4.19 referring to Ps 53[52]:6 LXX, which has a completely different text in the MT.[35] I would suggest that in As. Mos. 7.4, the word ἀνθρωπάρεσκος may also be hidden:

---

and *tribus sanctitatis* (As. Mos. 2.4) could be a Hebraism of a genuine Greek text; see, for example, Rom 1:4 for a similar construction: κατὰ πνεῦμα ἁγιωσύνης.

28. To be completely convincing, this kind of argumentation should also take into account the *Vetus Latina*. Nevertheless, a critical edition is still lacking for many of the books of the Old Testament.

29. This argument was also presented by Hilgenfeld, along with the use of the expression *in libro deuteronomio* (*Messias Judaeorum*, lxxiii).

30. Hebrew uses the *lamed* construction.

31. See also Grierson, "Testament of Moses," 274.

32. See the discussion in Albrecht, *Psalmi Salomonis*, 181–82.

33. Eberhard Bons, "Philosophical Vocabulary in the Psalms of Solomon: The Case of Ps Sol 9:4," in Bons and Pouchelle, *Psalms of Solomon*, 49–58.

34. Albrecht, *Psalmi Salomonis*, 182.

35. See G. Anthony Keddie, *Revelations of Ideology: Apocalyptic Class Politics in Early Roman Palestine*, JSJSup189 (Leiden: Brill, 2018), 91 n. 10 and the scholarship cited there.

Qui erunt homines dolosi, sibi placentes, ficti in omnibus sui, et omni hora diei amantes convivia, devoratores, gulae....
They will be deceitful men, self-complacent, hypocrites in all their dealings, and who love to debauch each hour of the day, devourers, gluttons....

For *sibi placentes*, Tromp suggests φίλαυτος as a Greek *Vorlage*.[36] This is an insightful suggestion as this word occurs in 2 Tim 3:2 in a similar context:

ἔσονται γὰρ οἱ ἄνθρωποι φίλαυτοι φιλάργυροι ἀλαζόνες ὑπερήφανοι βλάσφημοι, γονεῦσιν ἀπειθεῖς, ἀχάριστοι ἀνόσιοι....
For people will be lovers of themselves, lovers of money, boasters, arrogant, abusive, disobedient to their parents, ungrateful, unholy.... (NRSV)

In the Vulgate, as well as in the *Vetus Latina*, φίλαυτος is rendered as *homines seipsos amantes* or *homines sui amatores* but once by *homines sibi placentes* as quoted by Cyprian.[37] Should this Greek *Vorlage* for φίλαυτος be correct, then we could infer that the translator knew the version of Cyprian and was therefore a Christian whose textual tradition is close to what Hermann J. Frede defined as the "African Text."[38] In commentaries, scholars frequently allude to the usage of φίλαυτος in Aristotle, but here, the author of the Pastoral Epistles may well borrow from Philo.[39] In fact,

---

36. Tromp, *Assumption of Moses*, 211.

37. Cyprian, *Unit. eccl.* 16(14) supplies this in a quotation with other original renderings (e.g., *parentibus indictoaudientes* ["heedless of their parents"] for γονεῦσιν ἀπειθεῖς, whereas other witnesses have *non aubaudientes*, *non obsequentes*, or *inoboedienties*. See Hermann J. Frede, *Epistulae ad Thessalonicenses Timotheum, Titum, Philemonem, Hebraeos*, VL 25.1 (Freiburg: Herder, 1975–1982), 755; Maurice Bévenot, "An 'Old Latin' Quotation (II Tim. 3,2), and Its Adventures in the MSS. of St. Cyprian's *De unitate ecclesiae* Chap. 16," in *Papers Presented to the Second International Conference on Patristic Studies Held at Christ Church, Oxford, 1955*, ed. Kurt Aland and Frank Leslie Cross, StPatr 1-1, TUGAL 63 (Berlin: Akademie, 1957), 249–52.

38. For the definition of this type of text, see Frede, *Epistulae ad Thessalonicenses*, 145–47.

39. In Philo, φίλαυτος is always negative. See especially the list of vices in *Sacr.* 32 and *Ios.* 143. But see also *Leg.* 1.49; 3.231; *Cher.* 74; *Fug.* 81; *Mut.* 221; *Somn.* 2.219; *Spec.* 1.344; once for women in *Hypoth.* 11.14, dealing with Essenes but more often with Cain: *Sacr.* 3, 52; *Det.* 32, 68, 78; *Post.* 21. For connections to Aristotle, see Martin

in the Hebrew Bible, there is no a word for describing this kind of vice. The unique occurrence of what might have been a Hebrew *Vorlage* for φίλαυτος, that is, אהב נפש in Prov 19:18, is quite positive.[40] It is therefore reasonable to see in φίλαυτος a Greek word that originated from Hellenistic Judaism and had no Hebrew *Vorlage*.

Nevertheless, Cyprian's reading is unusual, and Augustine may have seen it as an interpretation of *seipsos amantes* (*Enarrat. Ps.* 106.14. Cf. *Civ.* 14.13). Michael A. Fahey suggests two other occurrences of this expression in Cyprian's letters,[41] with less textual contact with 2 Tim 3:2. In fact, the expression *sibi placentes* belongs to the *Vetus Latina*, in Ps 53[52]:6, in the same textual tradition as the one witnessed by Cyprian.[42] Indeed, in a few manuscripts, the *Vetus Latina* reads *Deus dissipavit ossa hominum sibi placentium*.[43] The expression *hominum sibi placentium* corresponds to the compound ἀνθρωπάρεσκος in Ps 53[52]:6 LXX where it corresponds to a difficult Hebrew word with completely different meaning ("to encamp"). The word ἀνθρωπάρεσκος normally means "to please men," as it is also used in Col 3:22 and Eph 6:6. Accordingly, Jerome translated the Hebrew of Ps 53[52]:6 by *Deus dispersit ossa circumdantium*, a reading close to the MT, whereas the so-called Gallican psalter offers *Deus dissipavit ossa eorum qui hominibus placent*, a rendering close to the LXX.

For the few attestations of *hominum sibi placentium* in the *Vetus Latina*, we could assume αὐτάρεσκος as a corruption of ἀνθρωπάρεσκος as a different *Vorlage*. In this case, the Latin translator added *hominum* to

---

Dibelius and Hans Conzelmann, *The Pastoral Epistles*, ed. Helmut Koester, trans. Philip Buttolph and Adela Yarbro, Hermeneia (Philadelphia: Fortress, 1973), 116; Luke Timothy Johnson, *The First and Second Letters to Timothy*, AB 35A (New York: Doubleday, 2001), 404.

40. LXX: ἀγαπᾷ ἑαυτόν. See also T. Benj. 4.5, speaking of God.

41. On Cyprian, *Ep.* 3.3; 11.1, see Michael A. Fahey, *Cyprian and the Bible: A Study in Third-Century Exegesis*, BGBH 9 (Tübingen: Mohr Siebeck, 1971), 515–16.

42. The so-called Western text, see Alfred Rahlfs, *Psalmi cum Odis*, Septuaginta Societatis Scientiarum Gottingensis Auctoritate 10 (Göttingen: Vandenhoeck & Ruprecht, 1931), §5.14, p. 42. Even if Cyprian himself quoted Ps 53[52]:6 with a wording close to the Vulgate.

43. The first manuscript is a Greek-Latin psalter. One column has the Greek transcription in Latin letters (here *anthroparescon*) while the second column has the Latin translation (*hominum placentium sibi*). See Giuseppe Bianchini, *Vindiciae Canonicarum Scripturarum Vulgatae Latinae Editionis* (Rome: S. Michaelis, 1740), 86. This book mentioned two other witnesses of *hominum sibi placentium*.

smooth the text. Another possibility is that he understood ἀνθρωπάρεσκος as meaning a "man who pleases man" (i.e., himself or one another). A similar nuance may be conveyed in 2 Clem 13.1.[44]

As presented below, the presence of ἀνθρωπάρεσκος in Pss. Sol. 4.19 could show that the Psalms of Solomon were written in Greek. The same could also be said about αὐτάρεσκος and cognates, which hardly appeared in any Jewish literature,[45] apart from αὐταρέσκεια corresponding to נפש in the translation of Qoh 6:9 by Symmachus. Therefore, whatever the Greek *Vorlage* of *sibi placentes* would be, it has no clear Hebrew *Vorlage* or points toward a reading specific to the LXX. It is thus easier to conceive of a Greek original than a Hebrew.

As a conclusion, scholarship of both texts followed the same academic path. Hilgenfeld assumed that the original text was in Greek. He was refuted and the Hebrew (or Aramaic) origin was taken for granted. Recently, the Greek hypothesis has reappeared as a result of a better assessment of the dependency of these texts on the LXX, especially when the LXX diverges from the MT, when this divergence is better explained by the translator than by a different *Vorlage*, and when the Assumption of Moses or Psalms of Solomon uses this allusion in a different way than the LXX. This last criterion shows that our texts had cut the lexical link with the Hebrew.

3. The Question of Dating

Both texts are often dated to the early Roman period. Attempts to attribute them to Christian authors are not well accepted.[46] Moreover, those who

---

44. See 2 Clem 13.1: καὶ μὴ γινώμεθα ἀνθρωπάρεσκοι· μηδὲ θέλωμεν μόνον ἑαυτοῖς ἀρέσκειν ("And let us not be found men-pleasers. Neither let us desire to please one another only" [trans. Lightfoot]).

45. The earliest attestation seems Ignatius, *Ep.* 11.9 *recensio longior*.

46. Joshua Efron asserted that the Psalms of Solomon were written by Christians ("The Psalms of Solomon, the Hasmonean Decline and Christianity," in *Studies on the Hasmonean Period*, SJLA 39 [Leiden: Brill, 1987], 219–86). This was not well-accepted; see John J. Collins, review of *Studies on the Hasmonean Period* by Joshua Efron, *CBQ* 52 (1990): 372. Interestingly, the Jewish attribution of the Assumption of Moses has also been challenged by Edna Israeli: "'Taxo' and the Origin of the 'Assumption of Moses,'" *JBL* 128 (2009): 735–57. According to Israeli, the Assumption of Moses should have been written by a Christian because Taxo is similar to a Christian messiah according to some Christian commentators. This identification may give a clue to the understanding of the name Taxo as an abbreviation for Christ. These arguments are questionable

deny the use of these texts as historical sources[47] do not really refute their attribution to this period but only assert that these texts are of no help in shedding light on it.

The dating of the Assumption of Moses is complicated by a possible incoherence in the text. Since Charles, the dating of the text was believed to be relatively clear: in 6.6 it is said that the "petulant" king has ruled thirty-four years, and this is precisely the length of the reign of Herod the Great.[48] Following this, the text alludes to his descendants who ruled for less time than he. Herod had three children who served as rulers: Archelaus, Antipas, and Philip. The latter two did not rule over Judea, but their reigns lasted more than that of their father. On the contrary, Archelaus reigned less than ten years over Jerusalem. We can conclude that the Assumption of Moses was probably written shortly after 6 CE, the date after which Archelaus was exiled in Vienna (in Gaul).[49] Another possibil-

---

since it is not because some Christian commentators compare Taxo to Christ that the Assumption of Moses should have been written by a Christian person. This view fails to produce real proof and overlooks the Jewish origins of Christianity. I agree that since all these pseudepigrapha have been preserved in Christian tradition, their Jewish origin may be questioned. Some more rigorous criteria should be built; see James R. Davila, *The Provenance of the Pseudepigrapha: Jewish, Christian, or Other?*, JSJSup 105 (Leiden: Brill, 2005), and its use by Grierson, "Testament of Moses," 277.

47. In 2013, Benedikt Eckhardt opened the First Meeting on the Psalms of Solomon by stating how this identification was biased by the anti-Semitism and orientalism of German scholars in the nineteenth century ("The Psalms of Solomon as a Historical Source for the Late Hasmonean Period," in Bons and Pouchelle, *Psalms of Solomon*, 23–24). Eckhardt's essay concludes by denying the Psalms of Solomon any value as a historical source. Van Henten thinks that it is not possible to identify precisely which king is alluded to by the "petulant" king in As. Mos. 6.6 (Jan Wilhelm van Henten, "Moses about Herod, Herod about Moses? *Assumptio Mosis* and Josephus' *Antiquities* 15.136," Pretoria, 27 August 2012, Thessaloniki, 25 April 2013). The mention of 34 for the length of the reign of the king could be an allusion to the stay in Egypt and then a corruption for 430 years. A similar argument is used by William Loader, "Herod or Alexander Janneus? A New Approach to the *Testament of Moses*," *JSJ* 46 (2015): 28–43 to assert that the Assumption of Moses alludes to the reign of Alexander Janneus. See also Anathea Portier-Young, "Theologies of Resistance in Daniel, The Apocalypse of Weeks, the Book of Dreams, and the Testament of Moses" (PhD diss., Duke University 2004).

48. Charles, *Assumption of Moses*, lv–lviii. See also Tromp, *Assumption of Moses*, 116. However, Josephus says thirty-seven years (*A.J.* 17.190).

49. Laperrousaz, *Le Testament de Moïse*, 96–99; Grierson, "Testament of Moses," 275–77; G. Anthony Keddie, "Judaean Apocalypticism and the Unmasking of Ideology: Foreign and National Rulers in the Testament of Moses," *JSJ* 44 (2013): 301–33.

ity is to assume that the author of the Assumption of Moses does not really care about Antipas and Philip. In this case, he may also take Agrippa I into account, as he ruled only from 41 to 44 CE.[50]

Finally, the text alludes to "a mighty king from the West" who "will burn part of their temple with fire" (As. Mos. 6.8). This allusion is thought as fitting well with the so-called war of Varus. Gustav Hölscher has refuted this identification as Varus came not from the West but from the North (Antioch), as he was not a king, but a delegate of Rome, and as the temple was not burnt by Varus but by Sabinus, his procurator.[51] For Atkinson, there arguments are not convincing since we cannot expect the author of the Assumption of Moses to be a precise historian. A mighty king coming from the west should be understood as a mighty Roman, and the fact that only part of the temple burnt suggests the war of Varus, even if the author does not make any difference between Varus and Sabinus.[52]

However, after alluding to the king who may be identified as Varus, the text seems to break its own narrative through an evocation of the Maccabean revolt. Charles attempted to fix this issue by considering chapters 8–9 to be out of place and relocating them between chapters 5 and 6.[53] This view has been refuted by Jacob Licht.[54] Should the unity of the text be preserved, then the evocation occurring from chapter 7 onward should be an eschatological expectation. John J. Collins suggests that Taxo is an idealized Mattathias Maccabee in an anti-Hasmonean polemic. Taxo will succeed where Mattathias and his sons failed: to keep the law of God.[55] This explains the closeness of As. Mos. 8–9 to the Antiochian persecution. In a similar way, Atkinson reinterprets these chapters as denoting Herod as an "*Antiochus redivivus.*"[56]

---

50. Charles, *Assumption of Moses*, xxv–xxvi.

51. Gustav Hölscher, "Über die Entstehungszeit der 'Himmelfahrt Moses,'" *ZNW* 17 (1916): 108–27, 149–58. Tromp takes this refutation as granted (Tromp, *Assumption of Moses*, 117). Hanan Eshel, "Publius Quinctilius Varus in Jewish Sources," *JJS* 59 (2008): 112–19, esp. 114–15.

52. Atkinson, "Herod the Great," 139–41.

53. Charles, *Assumption of Moses*, 28–30.

54. Jacob Licht, "Taxo and the Apocalyptic Doctrine of Vengeance," *JJS* 12 (1961): 95–103.

55. John J. Collins, "The Date and Provenance of the Testament of Moses," in *Studies on the Testament of Moses*, ed. George W. E. Nickelsburg, SCS 4 (Cambridge: Society of Biblical Literature, 1973), 27–29.

56. Atkinson, "Herod the Great," 134–49.

On the contrary, George W. Nickelsburg asserted that the Assumption of Moses was a composite work.⁵⁷ Chapter 6 is a later interpolation. For him, the sinners described in chapter 5 are not clearly punished by the "petulant king." This issue of genre raised by Nickelsburg disappears if these chapters immediately follow chapter 5, relating how the Antiochian king punished sinners.⁵⁸

The debate between Collins and Nickelsburg was resolved when the latter acknowledged that "a revised version of [the Testament of Moses] could have been intended to serve the purpose suggested by Collins."⁵⁹ Collins subsequently conceded "that the use of Antiochian material as an eschatological tableau in the present form of [the Testament of Moses] is more easily explained if it figured in its proper historical sequence in an earlier form of the book."⁶⁰ Otherwise said, Nickelsburg may be correct in asserting an earlier stage of production, whereas Collins is also right in putting the emphasis on the fact that the text as received dates back from the war of Varus.

It is striking that Atkinson offers a similar debate with himself as regarding the dating of Pss. Sol. 17. Virtually all scholars agree in dating the Psalms of Solomon after the Pompeian siege of Jerusalem. This identification was first established by Franz Karl Movers.⁶¹ Yet, the Pompeian identification raises some textual and historical questions, especially in Pss. Sol. 17. Even Movers admitted that the Herodian period should be the historical setting of this psalm. The problem involves the interpretation of a few verses. The allusion behind 17.6 is usually believed to allude to Hasmonean kings:

ἐν δόξῃ ἔθεντο βασίλειον ἀντὶ ὕψους αὐτῶν, ἠρήμωσαν τὸν θρόνον Δαυιδ ἐν ὑπερηφανίᾳ ἀλλάγματος (or ἀλαλάγματος).

---

57. George W. E. Nickelsburg "An Antiochian Date for the Testament of Moses," in Nickelsburg, *Studies on the Testament of Moses*, 33–37.

58. Tromp, *Assumption of Moses*, 120–23. See also Magen Broshi and Esther Eshel, "The Greek King Is Antiochus IV (4QHistorical Text = 4Q248)," *JJS* 48 (1997): 120–29 for the reconstruction and the identification of a Qumran fragment to the Antiochian period.

59. Nickelsburg, "Antiochian Date," 37.

60. John J. Collins, "Some Remaining Traditio-Historical Problems in the Testament of Moses," in Nickelsburg, *Studies on the Testament of Moses*, 39.

61. Franz Karl Movers, "Apokryphen-Literatur," *Kirchen-Lexikon oder Encyclopädie der Katholischen Theologie und ihrer Hilfswissenschaften* 1 (1847): 339–41.

They set up in glory a palace (or a kingdom) because of their arrogance, they laid waste to the throne of David in arrogant substitution (or: "in arrogant shout of war").

Beyond the textual issue of ἀλλάγματος or ἀλαλάγματος,[62] the verse explains that kings usurp the throne of David, that is, the Hasmoneans who did not belong to the tribe of Judah. This identification is generally well-accepted,[63] even if it lacks a clear reference to the high-priesthood (unlike As. Mos. 6.1). Indeed, the Pharisees, who are often the suggested sectarian affiliation of the Psalms of Solomon, rebuked the Hasmonean kings for their mixture of being kings and high priests.[64] A bigger problem comes from the identification of the man who attacks them and is "foreign to our race" (17.7):

Καὶ σύ, ὁ θεός, καταβαλεῖς αὐτοὺς καὶ ἀρεῖς τὸ σπέρμα αὐτῶν ἀπὸ τῆς γῆς ἐν τῷ ἐπαναστῆναι αὐτοῖς ἄνθρωπον ἀλλότριον γένους ἡμῶν.
And you, God, will reject them and remove their seed from the land when you have lifted up against them a man foreign to our race.

It seems improbable that this man is Pompey as he does not annihilate the Hasmonean dynasty, unless this is a wish expressed by the psalmist.[65] The

---

62. There is a textual issue here as some manuscripts suggest ἀλαλάγματος ("shout") instead of ἀλλάγματος ("exchange"). Scholars are divided regarding the choice of the best reading. Atkinson implicitly accepts ἀλαλάγματος, interpreting it as "tumultuous," but by giving to ἀλαλαγμός its basic meaning of "shout of war" (e.g., Josh 6:20) (*I Cried to the Lord*, 130; NETS). Ryle and James suggest "with a tumultuous shout of triumph" (*Psalms of Pharisees*, 131). Wright prefers ἀλλάγματος: "Their arrogant substitution desolated David's throne" (*Psalms of Solomon*, 178). The Syriac version agrees with ἀλλάγματος. Whatever the chosen reading, this part of the verse remains obscure.

63. But see Johannes Tromp, who identifies the power that contested the Romans as the Parthians ("Sinners and the Lawless in Psalm of Solomon 17," *NovT* 35 [1993]: 360–61).

64. See for instance Vasile Babota, *The Institution of the Hasmonean High Priesthood*, JSJSup 165 (Leiden: Brill, 2014), 277–79. The historicity of this polemic has been questioned by Eckhardt, "Psalms of Solomon as a Historical Source," 21–22.

65. The presence of the future tense for καταβαλεῖς and ἀρεῖς here is intriguing and led some scholars to alter them in their translations as they interpreted them as erroneous translations of Hebrew imperfects. But, the tense could fit the context, as

one who actually murdered the last Hasmoneans was Herod. Moreover, Herod, as an Idumean, was only a "half-Jew,"[66] as the Idumeans were converted to Judaism very recently (see Josephus, *A.J.* 13.257–58) and were thus possibly still considered as foreigners.

The identification of Herod with the "man foreign to our race" is also not without problems. Indeed, from verse 11 onward, the "lawless one," who devasted the land and expelled people to the west could not be Herod but should be Pompey, who exiled Aristobulus.[67] So here we may have a strange chronological structure, which hardly makes historical sense: first, the Hasmonean kings; second, Herod; and, third, Pompey.

These difficulties are clearly exemplified by the evolution of Atkinson's thought. In an early article, he suggests that the lawless one may refer to Sosius, the Roman who besieged Jerusalem with Herod.[68] In 2000, he attributes the allusions Pss. Sol. 17.6–14 to Herod alone.[69] In his later commentary, he suggests a purely Pompeian identification.[70] When I asked Atkinson very recently about the evolution of his thinking, he replied that, in fact, he would suggest that Pss. Sol. 17 is composite, or, was edited at least twice—once to commemorate the siege by Pompey and once to commemorate the siege of Sosius.[71]

---

the psalmist may wish that the "Hasmoneans" will be overthrown. The shift to the aorist in v. 9 denotes the irrevocable judgment of God (see Atkinson, *I Cried to the Lord*, 136–37).

66. Benedikt Eckhardt, "'An Idumean, That Is, a Half-Jew': Hasmoneans and Herodians between Ancestry and Merit," in *Jewish Identity and Politics between the Maccabees and Bar Kokhba: Groups, Normativity, and Rituals*, ed. Benedikt Eckhardt, JSJSup 155 (Leiden: Brill, 2012), 91–115.

67. See Ernest-Marie Laperrousaz, "Le milieu d'origine du 17e des psaumes (apocryphes) de Salomon," *REJ* 150 (1991): 557–64.

68. Kenneth Atkinson, "Herod the Great, Sosius, and the Siege of Jerusalem (37 B.C.E.) in Psalm of Solomon 17," *NovT* 38 (1996): 313–22. André Caquot asserted a similar view in "Les Hasmonéens, les Romains et Hérode: Observations sur Ps Sal 17," in *Hellenica et Judaïca, Hommage à Nikiprowetzky*, ed. André Caquot, Mireille Hadas-Lebel, and Jean Riaud, Collection de la Revue des Études Juives 3 (Leuven: Peeters, 1986), 213–18.

69. Kenneth Atkinson, *An Intertextual Study of The Psalms of Solomon* (Lewiston: Mellen, 2000), 358–68.

70. Atkinson, *I Cried to the Lord*, 135–39.

71. See also H. Daniel Zacharias, "The Son of David in Psalms of Solomon 17," in *"Non-canonical" Religious Texts in Early Judaism and Early Christianity*, ed. Lee

For the Assumption of Moses as well as for Pss. Sol. 17, the dating issues revolve around literary-critical interpretations. This reveals a similar structure of the two texts that could be summarized by the following table:

	Psalms of Solomon	Assumption of Moses
Illegitimate kings	17.5–6	6.1
Punished by someone	A man foreign to our race 17.7–8	A petulant king 6.2–7
Followed by the intervention of a foreigner who exiles people,	Pompey? Herod? Sosius? 17.11–14	Varus 6.8–9
and by the general corruption of Israel,	17.15–20	7–9
a terrible catastrophe,	The revolt of nature 17.18–19 (not in place)	The intervention of an Antiochian-like king 8
and the flight of the righteous	The flight to the wilderness 17.16–17 (not in place)	The flight of Taxo to a cave 9
Ending with a messianic or eschatological expectation	A Davidic king 17.21–46	A divine intervention announced by a messenger 10.1–10

Obviously, this structure remains artificial in regards to certain historical and textual difficulties. For instance, whereas Herod kills young and old in the Assumption of Moses, the same image serves to describe the lawless one in Pss. Sol. 17.11.[72] Moreover, the corruption of Israel leads to the revolt of the earth in the Psalms of Solomon but to the intervention of another foreign king in the Assumption of Moses. Finally, this catastrophe

---

Martin McDonald and James H. Charlesworth, Jewish and Christian Texts in Contexts and Related Studies 14 (London: T&T Clark, 2012), 73–87.

72. This is a biblical topos (e.g., Ezek 9:6; Lam 2:21).

is described after the flight of the righteous in the Psalms of Solomon and before it in the Assumption of Moses. Yet the flight of "those who loved the synagogues of the devout" in Pss. Sol. 17.16 may well correlate with the will of Taxo to be hidden in a cave.[73] The expectation is different in Pss. Sol. 17, which is clearly messianic, whereas the Assumption of Moses is not so clearly messianic.

For both texts, this structure fits well with the historical setting of the war of Varus. It is probably not a pure coincidence that Josephus relates many messianic movements at that time. After the death of Herod, having experienced the ineptitude of Archelaus and the war of Varus, some movements may have expected a divine intervention, whatever form it could take, with a Messiah or not.

To my knowledge, nobody has suggested Varus as the lawless one in Pss. Sol. 17.11. However, when compared to Josephus, we could find some similarities:

- Varus devasted the land, killed many people and reduced other to slavery (Josephus, *B.J.* 2.66–71; *A.J.* 17.286–291)
- Flights of people (*B.J.* 2.72; *A.J.* 17.292)
- Varus exiled some rulers away to the west (*B.J.* 2.77–78; *A.J.* 17.297)
- Could we compare the rulers exposed to derision to the crucifixion ordained by Varus (*B.J.* 2.75; *A.J.* 17.295)?

It is also striking that some scholars have suggested identifying the community of the Psalms of Solomon with the antimonarchic delegation that met Pompey since such a delegation is also described by Josephus just after the war of Varus.[74] Moreover, the account of Pss. Sol. 8.17–19, which describes the foreigner entering Jerusalem as a father in the house of his son, could fit Varus as well as Pompey (see Josephus, *A.J.* 17.73). However,

---

73. Atkinson recalls that Josephus relates a similar story in *A.J.* 14.429–430 ("Herod the Great," 145). See also Mark F. Whitters, "Taxo and His Seven Sons in the Cave (Assumption of Moses 9–10)," *CBQ* 72 (2010): 718–31, esp. 724–29.

74. See Josephus, *A.J.* 14.41–45; 17.301, 304–314; *B.J.* 2.84–93. Cf. Israël Lévi, "Les Dix-huit bénédictions et les Psaumes de Salomon," *REJ* 32 (1896): 173; Brad J. Embry, "The *Psalms of Solomon* and the New Testament: Intertextuality and the Need for a Reevaluation," *JSP* 13 (2002): 118. However, Eckhardt doubts that this delegation ever existed ("Psalms of Solomon as a Historical Source," 23–24).

Josephus and the Psalms of Solomon clearly do not depend each other. Nothing in the account of Josephus allows us to determine why Varus could have been perceived as a lawless one who did something infamous against God in Jerusalem (Pss. Sol. 17.14).

Therefore, these similarities could be owing to the use of common topoi. Indeed, if Nickelsburg was right in seeing revisions in our texts from a first attempt to express the idea that foreign kings are "instruments of God's judgement"—and "they will attack Israel, and ignorant of His purpose, they will suppose that they can destroy her"[75]—then we could detect such beliefs in Pss. Sol. 2.1-3, 25-29. In fact, many events could confirm this belief, which interprets new events with the eyes of the past. Such topoi were confirmed or used by historians like the authors of the books of Maccabees or Josephus and obviously by historical events too. The list of foreign mighty persons who enter arrogantly into Jerusalem and suffered a severe punishment is extensive: Apollonios (1 Macc 1:30-32), Heliodorus (2 Macc 3:9), Antiochius IV (1 Macc 6:16-17; 2 Macc 9:5-6), Ptolemy (3 Macc 1:8-11), Pompey (Pss. Sol. 2.1-3, 25-29; 8.16-18; 4Q386;[76] Josephus, *B.J.* 1.142-143), Crassus (Josephus, *B.J.* 1.169; *A.J.* 14.53-57), Pacorus (Josephus, *B.J.* 1.253-255), Varus (Josephus, *B.J.* 2.72-75),[77] and even Vespasian and Titus.[78]

There were at least two exceptions. First, the fate of Sabinus is unknown (see Josephus, *B.J.* 2.74; *A.J.* 17.294), but he may have been considered as only a cameo. More importantly, the siege of Jerusalem by Herod and Sosius was not followed by divine wrath against them. Herod ruled over Judea more than thirty years and Sosius lived at least until 17 BCE, if we

---

75. Nickelsburg, "Antiochian Date," 37.

76. According to Hanan Eshel, "4Q386: An Allusion to the Death of Pompey in 48 BCE?" [Hebrew], *Shnaton* 14 (2004): 195-203.

77. This is the same Varus who was defeated in the famous Battle of the Teutoburg Forest (9 CE). Eshel suggests that this fate was unknown to Josephus and more generally to Jews ("Publius Quinctilius Varus," 112-13, 115-19). As for Josephus, the great pain suffered by Romans after the disaster of Teutoburg might be the reason why Josephus did not mention that his death was owing to the anger of God. His Roman readers might not have been receptive to this. Similarly, he does not link the death of Pompey or that of Crassus to their sacrilege.

78. See Israël Lévi, "La mort de Titus," *REJ* 15 (1887): 62-69; Mireille Hadas-Lebel, *Jerusalem against Rome*, Interdisciplinary Studies in Ancient Culture and Religion 7 (Leuven: Peeters, 2006), 148-50.

could identify him with the person called Sosius who attends the secular games in this year.[79]

Accordingly, this succession of sieges of Jerusalem may explain why some communities may read these events as cycles with the same typological analysis based in the Antiochian crisis:[80]

- People of Jerusalem have sinned.
- A foreign leader is called by God to besiege Jerusalem.
- Arrogantly he overrides what God requests him to do.
- God intervenes against him.

Yet, Herod somewhat broke these cycles. This might have been an impetus for some communities to alter their texts to take this fact into account. Whereas Pompey's intervention could be interpreted as a new Antiochus who defiled the temple, Herod could not be interpreted in such a way.[81] This led the revisors of both texts to introduce the idea that Herod punished the Hasmoneans (Psalms of Solomon) or succeeded them (Assumption of Moses), whereas the general corruption of the people will be dealt with later, probably at the time of the last edition of these texts, after the war of Varus and possibly after the exile of Archelaus.

These are my tentative ideas as to a possible way to explain the difficulties detected in both texts. We should remain extremely cautious, however, since the tumultuous history of Israel between 63 BCE and 70 CE complicates the interpretation of both texts. Indeed, these texts might have helped their communities as they suffer any of the Jerusalem sieges from Pompey onward. Conversely, any specificity noticed during a siege might have been digested and reintroduce in the text even at the price of the loss of coherency. It is probably an illusion to think that we could reach the original versions of these texts, to identify them with precise historical events, and to reconstruct all of their developments.

---

79. Jens Bartels and Werner Eck, "Sosius," *BNP* A13 (2008): 660–62.
80. Atkinson, "Herod the Great,"148–49; Hilgenfeld, "Die Psalmen Salomo's," 305. Cf. Tromp, *Assumption of Moses*, 110 n. 1.
81. *Pace* Atkinson, "Herod the Great."

4. The Question of Provenance

Scholarship on the Psalms of Solomon and Assumption of Moses has witnessed similar trends. During an initial period of different scholarly attributions, the enemies polemically described in As. Mos. 7 and Pss. Sol. 4.12 were generally understood as the Pharisees.[82] However, a couple of eminent scholars argued instead for a Pharisaic origin for both the Assumption of Moses and the Psalms of Solomon—Charles and Julius Wellhausen, respectively[83]—and these views gained some adherents. Thereafter, the discovery of the Dead Sea Scrolls led some scholars to challenge the theory of Pharisaic origins for each text and instead suggest an origin among the Essenes.[84] This connection was supported by some parallels between our texts and the Dead Sea Scrolls, even though neither the Psalms of Solomon nor the Assumption of Moses was found among the Dead Sea Scrolls. Finally, this Essene hypothesis was refuted due to a greater appreciation of the differences between the sectarian Dead Sea Scrolls and both texts. Moreover, the biases of the arguments have also come under examination. Indeed, all of these older identifications were based on the description of the four sects or parties by Josephus: scholars proved that the texts could not belong to three of the four parties and then concluded that the last one should be the best candidate.[85]

---

82. Among other attributions for the Assumption of Moses, this leads Schmidt and Merx, "Die Assumptio Mosis," 121–22 to suggest an Essene attribution, and many others to see a Zealot as an author (see Charles, *Assumption of Moses*, xxi–xxviii for a detailed survey of the different hypotheses). For the Psalms of Solomon: notably to the Sadducees, see Viteau, *Les Psaumes de Salomon*, 196–203, for a detailed survey until Wellhausen.

83. Charles, *Assumption of Moses*, li–liv; Julius Wellhausen, *Die Pharisäer und die Sadducäer: Eine Untersuchung zur inneren jüdischen Geschichte* (Greifswald: Bamberg, 1874), 112–64.

84. For the Assumption of Moses, see Laperrousaz, *Le Testament de Moïse*, 88–95. For the Psalms of Solomon, see Wright, "Psalms of Solomon, the Pharisees and the Essenes," 136–54; Wright, "Psalms of Solomon," *OTP* 2 (1985): 639–70, esp. 641–42; Pierre Prigent, "Psaumes de Salomon," in *La Bible: Ecrits intertestamentaires*, ed. Andrei Dupont-Sommer, Marc Philonenko, and Daniel A. Bertrand, Bibliothèque de la Pléiade 337 (Paris: Gallimard, 1987), 986 nn. 16–17.

85. Particularly interesting here is the correction made by James Charlesworth to the contribution of Wright in *OTP*: "it is unwise to force these psalms into any model of the Pharisees or Essenes" (Wright, "Psalms of Solomon," 2:642).

Owing to this short history of modern exegesis, one could raise the following question: as it is difficult to identify the community behind each work and as the research followed exactly the same path, could it be possible that both texts originated from the same community, whatever this community might have been? This question has never been addressed by scholars; they usually noticed the parallels either without making firm conclusions as to the identification of the two communities or by implicitly affirming their common identity.[86]

This kind of naïve question is probably impossible to solve owing to at least three issues:

(1) Apart from a few Greek quotations, the Assumption of Moses is only known to us in Latin, translated from the Greek.[87] Any retroversion of the Assumption of Moses into Greek for comparing with the Psalms of Solomon is ultimately a speculation.[88] The use of the *Vetus Latina*, in addition to the Vulgate, may strengthen a lexical proximity. However, as the LXX should be used cautiously to determine its *Vorlage*, so the *Vetus Latina* should also be used cautiously, being also aware that scholarship is far from having the same efficient tools as for the LXX.

(2) Once a direct link is established between the Assumption of Moses and the Psalms of Solomon, we should assess whether or not this proves that the authors originated from the same community. Indeed, both texts could derive from a common source, namely, the LXX.[89] Most of the similarities noticed so far by scholars may be understood in this way.

(3) Lastly, we know very little about the ways communities identified themselves (*idem*) or defined themselves against other communities (*ipse*). This could lead to a misuse of parallels. On the one hand, different communities may well have shared some common characteristics; on the other hand, did ancient communities share our modern concerns over coherency? Do two different sayings always require that two different communities wrote the texts or that an evolution occurred within the same community?[90] Otherwise said, what criteria should be given for assessing

---

86. For instance, Charles takes for granted that the Psalms of Solomon were of Pharisaic origin (*Assumption of Moses*, 34).
87. See John Priest, "Testament of Moses," *OTP* 1 (1983): 920.
88. Hilgenfeld attempted such a Greek retroversion; see above.
89. See Priest, "Testament of Moses," 1:924.
90. For instance, Pss. Sol. 17 is messianic, whereas Pss. Sol. 11 expects the intervention of God alone. Does this prove that Pss. Sol. 11 was not written by the same

whether similar sayings originated from the same community or different sayings from different communities?

Let us have a look at some examples. One of the famous examples of proximity between the Psalms of Solomon and the Assumption of Moses is the exaltation to the stars. In Pss. Sol. 1.5, sinners are described as thinking that they are exalted to the stars so that they will never fall, whereas in As. Mos. 10.9, it is God who with his wings exalts his people to the stars. In fact, both passages may well independently refer to Isa 14:13, where the king of Babylon considers himself as a star within the stars but nevertheless fell down suddenly: "I will ascend to heaven; I will raise my throne above the stars [Heb. כוכב] of God" (NRSV).[91] A similar thought can be found in Jer 51[28]:9 LXX:

ἐξῆρεν ἕως τῶν ἄστρων [Heb. שחקים, "clouds"[
[her judgment] rose up even to the stars (NETS)

In the MT, the text says that the judgment against Babylon is so great that it is unforgivable, unhealable. By using the word "star," it is possible that the LXX of Jeremiah suggests a discrete and probable allusion to Isa 14:13. The judgment against Babylon is as high as was her arrogance.[92] This metaphor is also used once in the Dead Sea Scrolls:

למזורות יבקעו אפעה ושוא (1QH[a] X, 27–28)
Right up to the stars[93] burst | emptiness and deceit…. (DSSSE)

These lines describe the sinners belonging to the assembly of Belial, possibly identified with Babylon; their fate will be the same (see 1QH[a] X, 29). In Pss. Sol. 1.5, the same Isaianic metaphor is used in a different way. These were the children of Jerusalem who burst themselves up to the stars:

---

community as Pss. Sol. 17 or was written before or after Pss. Sol. 17? Or does the expectation of a Davidic messiah not preclude the expectation of divine intervention at the same time?

91. Atkinson also considers an allusion to Jer 51:9 (*Intertexual Study*, 8).

92. See also Dan[OG] 8:10, describing an apocalyptic horn, an impudent king (cf. 8:23): καὶ ὑψώθη ἕως τῶν ἀστέρων τοῦ οὐρανοῦ ("And it was raised unto the stars of the sky").

93. Here, the Hebrew word (מזרות) is not the same as in Isa 14:13. This word occurs in Job 38:32, transliterated in the Old Greek: μαζουρωθ. It probably denotes some constellations (see *HAL*, 2:566, s.v. "מַזָּרוֹת"; or *DCH*, 5:211, s.v. "מַזָּרוֹת").

ὑψώθησαν ἕως τῶν ἄστρων, εἶπαν Οὐ μὴ πέσωσιν.
They [the children of Jerusalem; see v. 3] were exalted to the stars; they said they would not fall.

This may be a mixture of Isa 3:16[94] and Isa 14:13. Interestingly enough, As. Mos. 10.8–9 also speaks of this metaphor applied to the inhabitants of Israel:

Et ascendes supra cervices et alas aquilae, et inplebuntur, et altavit te Deus, et faciet te herere caelo stellarum, loco habitationis ejus.[95]
And you will mount on the neck and the wings of an eagle, and they will be filled, and God will exalt you, and make you live in the heaven of the stars, the place of his habitation.

There can be little doubt that As. Mos. 10.8–9 is an interpretation of Exod 19:4:

You have seen what I did to the Egyptians, and how I bore you on eagles' wings and brought you to myself. (Exod 19:4 NRSV)

In this case, the promised land (or the wilderness), which is the probable allusion in Exod 19:4, is replaced by heaven (see also Isa 63:9). It would be too tempting to see in the Psalms of Solomon a response to a community's pretension that may have been the same as in the Assumption of Moses: one community thinking they will be exalted by God, the other reproaching it to glorify itself. In fact, the Assumption of Moses and the Psalms of Solomon come from two lines of traditions. The former focuses on the exaltation of the people by God, joining this idea with Exod 19:4, leading them to hope to be members of the celestial and divine court. The latter joins the self-exaltation of the children of Jerusalem (see Isa 3:16) with the self-exaltation of Babylon. A textual dependency is difficult to prove.

A more promising proximity lies in the fact that the altar has been trampled or defiled according to both As. Mos. 5.4[96] and Pss. Sol. 8.12:

---

94. Ἀνθ' ὧν ὑψώθησαν αἱ θυγατέρες Σιων ("Because the daughters of Sion were exalted"—i.e., they were boastful).

95. A conjecture accepted by Tromp, *Assumption of Moses*, 20 n. 164. The Latin here has *eorum* (their habitation).

96. See also As. Mos. 8.5, possibly referring to the building of an idolatrous altar on the temple's altar (1 Macc 1:54; see Tromp, *Assumption of Moses*, 221–22).

Sed quidam altarium inquinabunt[97] *de muneribus quae imponent Domino.*
Some people will defile the altar with the offerings they will bring to the Lord. (Tromp)

ἐπατοῦσαν τὸ θυσιαστήριον κυρίου ἀπὸ πάσης ἀκαθαρσίας καὶ ἐν ἀφέδρῳ αἵματος ἐμίαναν τὰς θυσίας ὡς κρέα βέβηλα.
They trampled the altar of the Lord [coming] from all kinds of uncleanness and with menstrual blood, they defiled the sacrifices as though they [were] common meat. (see also Pss. Sol. 2.2)

One should not be confused by the fact that many times in the Hebrew Bible the sacrifice is said to be denied or refused by God (e.g., Isa 1:11; Amos 5:21; Hos 6:6). It is rarely said that an altar was defiled by profane offerings. For instance, in Mal 1:7–10, the Lord reproaches his priests that they despise his name by offering polluted meals. He rejects the sacrifice. This is deemed a vain sacrifice; however, nothing is said about the defilement of the altar. It seems that this originality has been neglected by commentators.[98]

Implicitly, such "defilement" or "profanation" could be detected in the ritual of the purification of the altar during the Day of Atonement (Lev 16:19).[99] Conversely, a direct defilement could be found in three passages only. In the covenant code (Exod 20:25 LXX: μιαίνω; *Vetus Latina: polluo* or *maculo*), an altar made of stone could be profaned if these stones had been hewn by a chisel. This defilement, however, occurs at the setting up of the altar, not during a sacrifice.

The profanation of the altar of Bethel could be the nearest example in the Hebrew Bible. In 2 Kgs 23:16, Josias not only destroyed the temple of Bethel but profaned (LXX: μιαίνω; *Vetus Latina: sacrilegus*) its altar by offering humans bones, which were the bodies of the dead priests of this temple. This act was so important that the biblical narrative foretold it in 1 Kgs 13:1–10. The altar was profaned because it had been set up by Jeroboam, while erecting two golden calves intended to deter his people

---

97. The verb used by the Assumption of Moses to denote defilement is *inquino*, which is notably used in the *Vetus Latina* of Wis 7:25 to translate μιαίνω.

98. See, for instance, Tromp, *Assumption of Moses*, 193–94; Hofmann, *Die Assumptio Mosis*, 258; Laperroussaz, *Le Testament de Moïse*, 118.

99. See Jacob Milgrom, *Leviticus 1–16*, AB 3A (New York: Yale University Press, 1998).

from going up to the temple of Jerusalem. This altar was the symbol of the misdeed of the northern kingdom. Interestingly, the LXX translates "altar" with θυσιαστήριον, leading one to think that Josias really polluted an altar dedicated to the true God, even though it was illegitimately established (see notably Amos 2:8; 3:14).

The most important altar defilement is the one related by 1 Maccabees. Antiochus IV constructed a "desolating sacrilege" on the altar consisting, at least, of a new illegitimate and idolatrous altar (βωμός) on the true altar (θυσιαστήριον) as described in 1 Macc 1:59. Later, when Judas conquered Jerusalem and purified the temple, the issue was what to do with the profaned altar (1 Macc 4:45 LXX: βεβηλόω; Vetus Latina: *profano*). It was decided to demolish it and to replace it.

These two latter narratives describe the major and definitive defilement of altars. In As. Mos. 5.4 and Pss. Sol. 2.2; 8.12, the altar is grievously profaned. If we combine As. Mos. 5.4 with the description of the ritual of the Day of Atonement, we could infer that the altar is defiled by people who pretended to be priests but were not.[100] In this case, the Day of Atonement ritual will be no longer effective, and the altar will remain defiled until true priests come.

The collocation found in the Psalms of Solomon is quite unusual. Whereas in Pss. Sol. 2.2 the altar is trampled because people walked upon it (καταπατέω is used with a more concrete meaning), in the Pss. Sol. 8.12 the altar is trampled "from all kinds of uncleanness and with menstrual blood." The verb πατέω[101] is here used as a synonym of μιαίνω. It is tempting to interpret this wording as an allusion to Zech 12:3: θήσομαι τὴν Ιερουσαλημ λίθον καταπατούμενον πᾶσιν τοῖς ἔθνεσιν ("I will set Jerusalem as a trampled stone by all nations") (see also Pss. Sol. 2.20). This allusion points toward an eschatological explanation of both texts.

---

100. See also CD XI, 17–21, which conceives that impure hands could pollute the altar, probably alluding to the impure priests who rule the current temple. See David Hamidović, *L'écrit de Damas, le manifeste essénien*, Collection de la revue des études juives (Leuven: Peeters, 2011), 151 n. 29. This does not imply that this defilement is the sign of an eschatological period but could rather be a hope for an actual return of the community to the temple. See Charlotte Hempel, *The Laws of the Damascus Document: Sources, Tradition and Redaction*, STDJ 29 (Leiden: Brill, 1998), 37–38.

101. More usually, the temple is trampled by gentiles (1 Macc 3:45, 51; 4:60) or by impious people (2 Macc 8:2), this could explain the variant of the Syriac here: the "temple."

Indeed, Notley and Horbury have compared Pss. Sol. 11.1, As. Mos. 10.2, and 11Q13 in their use of the one who brings good news (εὐαγγελιζόμενος; *nuntius*; מבשר). They have shown that these three texts combine Isa 52:7[102] with Lev 25:9–10. The Isaianic messenger is also the one who proclaims the Jubilee at the Day of Atonement. Otherwise said, this is the day on which the altar is purified. The defilement of the altar is therefore an element of their eschatological expectation: the altar is defiled so that it could be purified when the eschatological era occurs.

Should this interpretation hold true, then the Psalms of Solomon, Assumption of Moses, and 11Q13 share the same general eschatological pattern. Although they may have originated from the same community, we should not overlook the difference as well. The messenger in 11Q13 is Melchizdek, a king and high priest. In the Assumption of Moses, the messenger remains anonymous; it could be an angel, Taxo, or Moses, but seems not to be a king.[103] In the Psalms of Solomon, the messenger remains anonymous. It would be wiser to assert that each of these texts shares the same expectation but does not interpret it in exactly the same way.

5. Conclusion

Our comparative study has shown that the language of these two texts was probably Greek. The recent rehabilitation of a Greek original for both texts require further attention, for the implicit conception of a Palestinian Judaism not willing to produce Greek texts during this period has proved to be false.

---

102. In Hebrew: מבשר; in LXX: εὐαγγελιζόμενος; the *Vetus Latina* is more difficult: *qui annuntiant* (main variants of African texts [C]), *euangelizantium* (the older shape of *Vetus Latina* [X]), or *euangelizantis* (European texts [E]). According to Jerome, the LXX of Origen should be translated as *euangelizans* (text type O), the Vulgate as *adnuntiantis*. See Roger Gryson, *Esaias*, 2 vols., VL 12 (Freiburg: Herder, 1987–1997), 2:1255; for the text types, see 1:15–19.

103. Angel: see Tromp, *Assumption of Moses*, 229–30. Taxo: e.g., Tromp, "Taxo, the Messenger of the Lord," 200–209; Tromp, *Assumption of Moses*, 230–31. Moses: E.g., William Horbury, "Moses and the Covenant in the Assumption of Moses and the Pentateuch," in *Covenant as Context: Essays in Honour of E. W. Nicholson*, ed. Andrew D. H. Mayes and Robert B. Salter (Oxford: Oxford University Press, 2003), 191–208. This messenger is not a high priest either, although he is probably associated with priesthood (Tromp, *Assumption of Moses*, 230).

Moreover, the Assumption of Moses and the Psalms of Solomon share roughly the same historical setting: the different sieges of Jerusalem, from the one of Pompey onward to at least the war of Varus, analyzed through a typology that dates back to the Hasmonean revolt. The historical development of these texts is complex. They were probably revised throughout this period by reassessing the events when they occurred and trying to make sense of the long reign of Herod.

It is difficult to determine that the community behind the Assumption of Moses is the same as the Psalms of Solomon. The two communities evidently shared some common preoccupations, but they did not answer to the challenges of their times in the same way, even if they both interpret events from a somewhat Deuteronomistic perspective. These views may well have been accepted by several Jewish communities.

Before the discoveries of the Dead Sea Scrolls, scholars analyzed these texts against their own religious backgrounds and scientific knowledge of this period. This led to two major errors: (1) the assumption that Greek was not used as a language to produce religious texts in Palestine; and (2) there were only four sects or parties that could have written these texts. On the one hand, we now know that a process of revision of the LXX was in progress during the first century BCE. These two ideas has been proved false.

Further research is therefore needed and should delve deeper into this comparison. The aim of such investigation, to which we shall add the Dead Sea Scrolls, is not to identify precisely by whom, when, and where these texts were written but more broadly to realize that studying common features and issues may help us to understand this early Roman period better.

Violators of the Law and the Curse of the Law: The Perception of the Torah in the Psalms of Solomon and in Paul's Letter to the Galatians

Stefan Schreiber

The Psalms of Solomon criticize violators of the law with a striking frequency. The genesis of this corpus of psalms probably lies in Jerusalem in the period after the occupation by Pompey in 63 BCE and more precisely after Pompey's death in Egypt in 48 BCE, to which Pss. Sol. 2.26 alludes.[1] It is in this situation, where the influence of Roman politics and of Hellenistic culture has increased, that the Psalms of Solomon elaborate their understanding of the torah. The situation of Paul, on the other hand, when he writes the Letter to the Galatians almost four generations later, is marked by the new conviction that Jesus is the Christ. This fundamentally changes his view of the torah. This essay seeks to contrast the two ways of looking at the torah in order to bring out their profiles more clearly. I begin with the Psalms of Solomon.

1. The Psalms of Solomon and the Torah

At first sight, the torah does not appear to play any great role in the theology of the Psalms of Solomon, since the νόμος is mentioned positively only in Pss. Sol. 10.14 and 14.2. We do, however, encounter the semantic field around νόμος with negative connotations: the use of this concept is dominated by talk about lawlessness, breaches of the law, and lawbreakers. Our investigation will show that this is not based on a general understanding

---

1. See Svend Holm-Nielsen, "Die Psalmen Salomos," *JSHRZ* 4: 58–59; Kenneth Atkinson, *I Cried to the Lord: A Study of the Psalms of Solomon's Historical Background and Social Setting*, JSJSup 84 (Leiden: Brill, 2004), 135–39.

of law (in the sense that someone does not keep to the laws and conventions of society) but refers to the torah of Israel, which offers the criterion for judging whether a person is righteous as God understands this. It is precisely the picture of the lawbreaker that makes it clear how important obedience to the torah is for the life of Israel.

1.1. The Wrong Understanding of the Torah

Especially in Pss. Sol. 4, 8, and 12, we are given a picture of persons who do not keep the torah or else who interpret it falsely and thus lead others into error. The "unholy" one at the beginning of Pss. Sol. 4 is the one who makes the God of Israel angry through "breaches of the law" (παρανομίαι).[2] He is described polemically as a hypocrite, since he insists that sinners should be condemned before the court, although he himself is entangled in a multitude of sins (4.2–3); he sins by night and in secret (4.5). According to 4.6, one who behaves in this manner lives "in hypocrisy" (ἐν ὑποκρίσει, cf. 4.20, 22). In concrete terms, his sin consists of sexual desire and lies: he actively desires several women[3] and makes contracts under oath with no intention of observing them (4.4–5).

The Psalms of Solomon see a very grave problem in the behavior of the ungodly Jewish persons who embody the unholy, namely, that they have a negative influence on other households, which were the basic societal

---

2. Robert B. Wright (*The Psalms of Solomon: A Critical Edition of the Greek Text*, Jewish and Christian Texts in Contexts and Related Studies 1 [London: T&T Clark, 2007], 83) translates the noun too unspecifically as "rotten behavior." The reference to the torah cannot be overlooked here. Psalms of Solomon 4.1 specifies as context ἐν συνεδρίῳ, which is surely a reference to the Sanhedrin in Jerusalem. The standard edition of the Psalms of Solomon remains that by Oscar von Gebhardt (*Die Psalmen Salomo's zum ersten Male mit Benutzung der Athoshandschriften und des Codex Casanatensis*, TUGAL 13.2 [Leipzig: Hinrichs, 1895]), which was included in Alfred Rahlfs's concise edition of the Septuagint (1935); see now Alfred Rahlfs and Robert Hanhart, eds, *Septuaginta* (Stuttgart: Deutsche Bibelgesellschaft, 2006), 471–89. Wright, *Psalms of Solomon*, presents a new edition, but see the criticism in Felix Albrecht, "Zur Notwendigkeit einer Neuedition der Psalmen Salomos," in *Die Septuaginta—Text, Wirkung, Rezeption*, ed. Wolfgang Kraus and Siegfried Kreuzer, WUNT 325 (Tübingen: Mohr Siebeck, 2014), 110–23.

3. The androcentric perspective reflects the societal circumstances in first century Jerusalem. The one who prays in Pss. Sol. 16.17–18, on the other hand, asks to be preserved "from every evil woman" and from "the beauty of a lawbreaking woman" (κάλλος γυναικὸς παρανομούσης) who deceives him (ἀπατάω).

units in the ancient world. Through their false teachings and their false exposition of the torah, they lead other houses (which are the nuclei of Jewish tradition and piety) into error and corrupt them. The unholy cultivates conduct with other houses, apparently without any evil intention ("cheerfully as though without guile," 4.5). But in reality, he is guided by a destructive intention because his eyes are directed "to the house of the man who is in security" (ἐν εὐσταθείᾳ)—that is to say, a house anchored in the Jewish tradition—in order "to destroy each other's wisdom with transgressors' [παράνομοι] words" (4.9). He wishes to seduce other persons to practice "unrighteous desire" (4.10), and 4.11-12 states that he lays waste a house for the sake of a lawless desire (ἕνεκεν ἐπιθυμίας παρανόμου) and deceives people with his words. He destroys the next house with seductive speeches. This is called παρανομία (a "breach of the law"). Psalms of Solomon 4.20 reaffirms that the hypocrites "have laid waste the houses of many men in dishonor and have scattered them in their lust." Lust, as the central cause of immoral or sinful conduct, designates the selfish desire to possess in both the Hellenistic-Roman world and the early Jewish world.[4]

It is characteristic of the unholy that he seeks to please humans (ἀνθρωπάρεσκος, 4.7, 19). At 4.8, this craving is linked to one particular exposition of the torah: λαλοῦντα νόμον μετὰ δόλου ("He speaks the Torah with deceit").[5] We do not know what authority entitles the unholy people to expound the torah. The expression λαλεῖν νόμον ("to speak the torah") signals a pejorative evaluation of this exposition, since λαλεῖν can also mean "to talk nonsense." This means that the text focuses on disputed questions of the correct exposition of the torah. The reference to a craving for admiration may indicate an exposition of the torah that was more open vis-à-vis the Hellenistic culture. The ethical behavior of the others, which is evil from the perspective of Psalms of Solomon, is called their "deeds" (ἔργα) at 4.7.[6]

---

4. For material, see Stefan Schreiber, *Der erste Brief an die Thessalonicher*, ÖTK 13.1. (Gütersloh: Gütersloher, 2014), 208–9.

5. See the translation by Wright, *Psalms of Solomon*, 87: "who deceitfully quotes the Torah." The reference to the torah is lost in Wolfgang Kraus and Martin Karrer, eds, *Septuaginta Deutsch: Das griechische Alte Testament in deutscher Übersetzung* (Stuttgart: Deutsche Bibelgesellschaft, 2009), 919: "indem er Recht spricht mit Trug." The three best manuscripts offers a different wording: λαλοῦντα μόνον μετὰ δούλου ("He speaks alone with slave"); see Felix Albrecht, *Psalmi Salomonis*, SVTG 12.3 (Göttingen: Vandenhoeck & Ruprecht, 2018), 337.

6. Cf. the ἔργα of the human with a negative connotation also in Pss. Sol. 4.16; 17.8 (parallel to "sins"); in 6.2, the "deeds" succeed because they are protected by

This picture of the "lawbreakers" (παράνομοι, 4.19, 23) is contrasted with the righteousness of God, which can remove unrighteousness (4.24). The positive antithesis to the lawbreakers appears in 4.23, 25: "those who fear the Lord in their innocence" and "love" him.

Psalms of Solomon 8.9 also speaks, with particular reference to the Jewish priests in Jerusalem, of "breakings of the law" (παρανομίαι), which provoke God's wrath. It illustrates this by means of the following crimes (8.9–12): incest, adultery, plundering of God's sanctuary, and polluting the altar of sacrifice (θυσιαστήριον) and the sacrifices.[7] It is first and foremost the priests in the temple who are defamed here, and it appears that the cult is ultimately made impossible by such pollution. Psalms of Solomon 8.13 underlines the gravity of these sins by saying that they surpass even the gentiles (ὑπὲρ τὰ ἔθνη).

The association with the sinful conduct of the peoples is interesting because this may be a further indication of the intention with which the lawbreakers interpret the torah: in the eyes of Psalms of Solomon, they are conforming to the lifestyle of the Hellenistic world. This is also indicated by the context in 8.14–22, which interprets the incursion of the gentiles into Jerusalem as God's reaction to the sinful behavior of the upper classes in Jerusalem: these persons were willing to make the invasion possible (see 2.1–5, 11–14; 17.11–18). This is an allusion to the incursion of Pompey into Jerusalem in 63 BCE and to the opening of the city by the Hasmonaean Hyrcanus II and his adherents.[8]

God, and in 18.8, the messiah guides human beings "in deeds of righteousness in the fear of God"; in 9.4 and 16.9, the "deeds" are open for both righteous and unrighteous conduct.

7. The sacrifices are made impure by the "flow of blood," that is to say, by contact with menstrual blood: the priests are accused of having sexual contacts with impure women, with the result that the cult becomes impure. See Kenneth Atkinson, "Enduring the Lord's Discipline: Soteriology in the *Psalms of Solomon*," in *This World and the World to Come: Soteriology in Early Judaism*, ed. Daniel M. Gurtner (London: T&T Clark, 2011), 158; Moyna McGlynn, "Authority and Sacred Space: Concepts of the Jerusalem Temple in Aristeas, Wisdom, and Josephus," *BN* 161 (2014): 124–26.

8. The Romans intervened thereby in the power struggle between Hyrcanus II and Aristobulus II, who had holed up in the temple precincts; see Josephus, *B.J.* 1.131–132, 142–147; *A.J.* 14.58–63. On the background, see Holm-Nielsen, "Die Psalmen Solomos," 79–80; Mikael Winninge, *Sinners and the Righteous: A Comparative Study of the Psalms of Solomon and Paul's Letters*, ConBNT 26 (Stockholm: Almqvist & Wiksell, 1995), 64–65; Atkinson, *I Cried to the Lord*, 21–36, 60–64, 135–39; Atkinson,

Psalms of Solomon 12 takes the form of a prayer to be saved from the lawbreakers. The image of the enemy sketched in this psalm is that of a "lawbreaking [παράνομος] and wicked man" whose speech is dismissed as lawless and slanderous, mendacious and deceitful (12.1). The actions of these "lawbreakers" (παράνομοι) are once again described at 12.3-4 as the strife and rupture that they bring about in the "houses," that is to say, in the Jewish families. The positive antithesis appears at 12.5 in "the man who makes peace in the home"—it is clear that the ideal meant here is unity of the people. The basis for this peace is not stated explicitly, but it is the understanding of the torah held by the group that stands behind the Psalms of Solomon. The problem that smolders in the background is the contentious behavior vis-à-vis the torah. This becomes visible in the polemic against the lawless persons.

1.2. The Permanent Election of Israel

Psalms of Solomon 9.2 laments the "lawlessnesses" (ἀνομίαι) of Israel, which have led, thanks to God's righteous judgment, to the "dispersion" (διασπορά). But even though Israel has behaved wrongly, this is not the end, since the punishment of Jerusalem makes possible a conversion to God (9.6-7). Psalms of Solomon 9.8-11 holds fast to the permanent election by God that is deeply rooted in Israel's history: he is God for his people Israel, which he loves, which belongs to him, and which is permitted to ask for his mercy (9.8). The covenant formula (Lev 26:12; Jer 11:4) is echoed in the formulation: "You are God, and we are a people whom you have loved, ... we are yours." Psalms of Solomon 9.9 emphasizes the election of Israel as the seed of Abraham (see 18.3) over against (παρά) all the gentiles. God has set his name upon Israel, and the election is irrevocable: God will not cast his people off. Psalms of Solomon 9.10 summarizes this salvific action of God upon Israel in the theology of the covenant: God has made a covenant with the fathers that makes hope and conversion possible

---

"Enduring the Lord's Discipline," 147. See also Pss. Sol. 17.4-7, sinful rulers from Israel. It is possible that "the godless man" at 13.5 refers to Aristobulus II. Nadav Sharon underlines the anti-Roman attitude of the Psalms of Solomon in "Between Opposition to the Hasmoneans and Resistance to Rome: The *Psalms of Solomon* and the Dead Sea Scrolls," in *Reactions to Empire: Sacred Texts in Their Socio-political Contexts*, ed. John A. Dunne and Dan Batovici, WUNT 372 (Tübingen: Mohr Siebeck, 2014), 41-54.

for Israel. In all eternity, therefore, God's mercy remains upon the house of Israel (9.11).[9] The covenant forms the basis upon which Israel can lead a godly life.

Naturally, the contemporary situation posed the urgent question of how the conquest of Israel by the foreign political power of Rome could be compatible with the conviction that Israel was God's chosen people. The Psalms of Solomon apply a paradigm from the theology of history here: the sins of the people are seen as provoking the intervention of God, whose instrument is the foreign power (1.7–8; 2.11–13; 8.9–14, 22; 17.5–8, 19–20). This interpretation bears the mark of the Deuteronomic historical scheme that is established in Deut 28–32 and that frequently occurs in early Jewish literature:[10] Israel has sinned against the Sinai covenant and the torah, has been punished by God, but after Israel turns anew to God, it experiences his blessing. The prayer of the pious man in Pss. Sol. 8.25–34 expresses this conversion to God (within the covenant). This makes it clear that Israel has not been abandoned or rejected by God. Israel has been punished, and now God's mercy can come into its own once again (7.3–10; 9.9–11).[11]

However, not everyone in Israel follows God's instruction, since some are walking along the paths of the gentiles. This is why the Psalms of Solomon are pervaded by the contrast between the role models of the righteous and the sinners.[12] After the history of the Roman invasion in 63 BCE has been recapitulated in Pss. Sol. 2, Pss. Sol. 3–7 characterize the life of the righteous and sinners in this historical framework. Psalms of Solomon

---

9. Cf. the bestowal of eternal salvation in 7.8; 11.7; 14.3–5; 17.4.

10. See George W. E. Nickelsburg, "Torah and the Deuteronomic Scheme in the Apocrypha and Pseudepigrapha: Variations on a Theme and Some Noteworthy Examples of Its Absence," in *Das Gesetz im frühen Judentum und im Neuen Testament: Festschrift C. Burchard*, ed. Dieter Sänger and Matthias Konradt, NTOA 57 (Göttingen: Vandenhoeck & Ruprecht, 2006), 222–35.

11. See Joseph L. Trafton, "The Bible, the *Psalms of Solomon*, and Qumran," in *The Dead Sea Scrolls and the Qumran Community*, vol. 2 of *The Bible and the Dead Sea Scrolls*, ed. James H. Charlesworth (Waco, TX: Baylor University Press, 2006), 435; cf. Atkinson, "Enduring the Lord's Discipline," 154.

12. See Winninge, *Sinners and the Righteous*, esp. 125–36; Stefan Schreiber, "Can Wisdom Be Prayer? Form and Function of the Psalms of Solomon," in *Literature or Liturgy? Early Christian Hymns and Prayers in their Literary and Liturgical Context in Antiquity*, ed. Clemens Leonhard and Hermut Löhr, WUNT 363 (Tübingen: Mohr Siebeck, 2014), 89–106.

3.3–12 posits a direct opposition between the two groups. Psalms of Solomon 4.1 then begins by addressing an "unholy" man (βέβηλε),[13] who sits "in the council of the holy" although his heart is far away from the Lord. It then sketches a critical picture of the godless man. In Pss. Sol. 12–16, the righteous and the sinners are contrasted in an eschatological perspective. The righteous are promised deliverance, but the sinners are threatened with destruction.

This opposition reveals the frontline between two different cultural models, since the sinners are not only the gentiles (although they too are sinners, cf. Pss. Sol. 2.1–2), but, even more so, the Jews who are open to the influence of the Roman-Hellenistic culture and therefore risk hollowing out their own identity from within. The distinction between the righteous and the sinners becomes an existential question for the group behind the Psalms of Solomon, who are influenced by early Jewish wisdom, but also by the theology of Deuteronomy. Within Israel, there arises a core group of those who remain faithful to their God and are therefore righteous.[14] It is vital to perceive who is in fact a sinner, that is to say, one who has assimilated to the Hellenistic culture.[15] One must keep strictly apart from such persons in order not to betray one's own identity.

1.3. The Torah as Testimony to God's Mercy

Psalms of Solomon 10.1–3 begins with a beatitude on the one who accepts God's reproof, education, and—to keep to the image—"blows from the whip," and lets himself be changed thereby. The motif of education

---

13. The adjective βέβηλος basically means "accessible" because not closed off by holiness or consecration, and hence "profane." See Franz Passow, *Handwörterbuch der Griechischen Sprache*, 4 vols, 5th ed (repr. Darmstadt: Wissenschaftliche Buchgesellschaft, 2008), 1.1:499.

14. Jens Schröter, "Gerechtigkeit und Barmherzigkeit: Das Gottesbild der Psalmen Salomos in seinem Verhältnis zu Qumran und Paulus," *NTS* 44 (1998): 568. Udo Schnelle ("Gerechtigkeit in den Psalmen Salomos und bei Paulus," in *Jüdische Schriften in ihrem antik-jüdischen und urchristlichen Kontext*, ed. Hermann Lichtenberger and Gerbern S. Oegema, JSHRZ Studien 1 [Gütersloh: Gütersloher, 2002], 368) speaks of the "true Israel," but this term is not used by the Psalms of Solomon.

15. Cf. the merely *putative* righteousness of Jerusalem in Pss. Sol. 1 and the comparison of the "sinners" with the "gentiles" (1.8; cf. 8.3). The terms "lawbreakers" (4.23; 1.1–6), "impurity" (8.22), and "lawlessness" (e.g., 15.8, 10) point to the distance from the tradition of Israel; this is expressly formulated in Pss. Sol. 17.14–15.

describes God's salvific action with regard to the righteous in order that he may bring them back to the right path again and again, provided that they accept his education (10.3, "those who love him in truth").

In the Psalms of Solomon, God's παιδεία is a central factor of what he does for the righteous in Israel: God "judges Israel with education" (κρίνων τὸν Ἰσραὴλ ἐν παιδείᾳ, 8.26), and God is the "educator" (παιδευτής) of Israel (8.29). Psalms of Solomon 13.6–11 contrasts the destruction of the sinner with the "education" (παιδεία) of the righteous man, whose "transgressions" (παραπτώματα) have occurred without an evil intention, in ignorance (13.7; cf. 3.8; 18.4). The use of the concept of παραπτώματα is in itself an indication that no intentional sinning is meant here (cf. 3.7).[16] God exhorts the righteous man like a beloved son and educates him like a first-born (13.9). Against the social-historical background of the appreciation of the eldest son in classical antiquity, this expresses a very special devotion on the part of the father and the prospect of having the position of the preferential heir. God extinguishes the transgressions of the righteous through his education (13.10), and the chastisement purifies from sins (10.1–2). This presupposes that the righteous also sin but that they repent again and again and turn to God in faithfulness (3.6–8; 9.6–7). This is why there is a difference between the sinfully righteous[17] and notorious sinners, so that 17.5 can state: "But in our sins there rose up sinners against us."

God's motivation is called his "mercy" (ἔλεος). Psalms of Solomon 10.4 takes up the theme of God's mercy to his servants and links it—and thus the entire motif complex of education—to the torah: the testimony (μαρτυρία) to God's merciful action is "in the law of the everlasting covenant" (ἐν νόμῳ διαθήκης αἰωνίου).[18] This appeals to the torah in its positive function of attesting and presenting God's salvific will, and the torah can do this in the framework of the covenant that God has made with Israel. God's mercy appears as the general thrust of the torah. All the cultic and ethical demands that the torah makes of Israel are borne by this mercy, or they assist human beings to live out of this mercy.[19] The torah shows the

---

16. See Winninge, *Sinners and the Righteous*, 133.

17. This is the category in Winninge, *Sinners and the Righteous*, 131–34. Schnelle ("Gerechtigkeit," 368) calls being righteous "a status concept."

18. The "eternal covenant" recalls the covenant with Abraham in Gen 17:13, 19. See Pss. Sol. 9.9.

19. The assertion by Winninge (*Sinners and the Righteous*, 206) that "the Torah also has a 'negative' disciplinary task" fails to do justice to this insight. Pss. Sol. 7.9

path to understand God's education and offers orientation for one's concrete behavior. In other words, the torah itself has an educational function. This is why the testimony is also found on the paths of human beings who are under God's "supervision"[20]—that is, those who live in fellowship with God. Logically, therefore, the reference to the testimony in torah to God's mercy flows into Israel's praise of its God in 10.5-7.

God's mercy and compassion is a leitmotif of the picture of God in the Psalms of Solomon.[21] This shows that God does not expect perfection of his righteous ones but is always ready to forgive their sins if they repent and turn back to him. Despite their sins, the righteous are blessed (not punished) by God in 9.7, and God's kindness turns to them when they have sinned and then repent. Ultimately, mercy corresponds to the "righteousness" (δικαιοσύνη) of God, of which the Psalms of Solomon frequently speak, for example, in 4.2-5: God's righteousness means the implementation of his salvific will and of his teachings (which are written in the law, 10.4; 14.2). It can have a negative effect in the judgement against the sinners and a positive effect in the education of the pious.[22] God's loving action toward Israel in the covenant, through which he initiated his saving relationship to Israel, was always the basis for the implementation of his righteousness.[23] Humans can correspond to God's righteousness when they understand and shape their entire lives in their

---

draws a parallel between "yoke" (ζυγός) and "education." If one hears in the concept of ζυγός the following of the torah, then the educational function of the torah is implied here too. Ζυγός is related to the torah in Jer 2:20 LXX, 5:5 LXX; Gal 5:1; 2 Cor 6:14; Matt 11:28-30; Acts 15:10; 2 En. 34.1; 48.9; 2 Bar. 41.3, and in rabbinic literature (e.g., m. 'Abot 3:5); this use could have been transmitted via sapiential traditions that call Wisdom ζυγός (Sir 6:30; 51:26).

20. "Supervision" (ἐπισκοπή) refers here to God's present-day activity, not to the eschaton (cf. 11.6). Atkinson ("Enduring the Lord's Discipline," 161) takes a different position.

21. Ἔλεος or ἐλεημοσύνη in Psalms of Solomon: 4.25; 9.8, 11; 10.3-4, 6-7; 11.1, 9; 13.12; 15.13, 16.3, 6, 15; 17.3, 34, 45; 18.3, 5, 9; cf. the entire promise of salvation in 11.1-9. This, as George Steins ("Die Psalmen Salomos—ein Oratorium über die Barmherzigkeit Gottes und die Rettung Jerusalems," in *Laetare Jerusalem*, ed. Nikodemus C. Schnabel, Jerusalemer theologisches Forum 10 [Münster: Aschendorff, 2006], 137) states, is clear evidence that the Psalms of Solomon cannot be seen "als jüdische Kronzeugen der 'Werkgerechtigkeit.'"

22. Cf. Pss. Sol. 2.15; 4.24; 8.24-26 ("the God of righteousness, who judges Israel with education").

23. See Schröter, "Gerechtigkeit," 566.

relationship to God. Accordingly, righteousness is the principle of right conduct in 9.4–5; its antithesis is to do wrong. The pious can perform righteous deeds (9.3), but this line of thought ends in the rhetorical question in 9.6, "To whom will you show kindness, O God, if not to those who call upon the Lord?"

1.4. The Torah as Guideline

Psalms of Solomon 14.1 begins with an assurance to the righteous: "Faithful is the Lord to those who love him in truth, to those who endure his education." This is then made more precise in 14.2, "those who walk in the righteousness of his ordinances [προστάγματα], in the law [νόμος] which he commanded us that we might live [εἰς ζωὴν ἡμῶν]." A positive picture is painted of the Jewish law in the framework of God's relationship to Israel. It contains instructions for a successful life with God that continues to exist even beyond death: "they will live in it (the law) forever" (ζήσονται ἐν αὐτῷ εἰς τὸν αἰῶνα, 14.3). The torah, which offers the guiding principle for Israel's life, has a saving and educative function (cf. 10.1–4). At the same time, it is the basis of the identity of the righteous ones in Israel, who may hope for eternal life.

Psalms of Solomon 14.2–3 contains an allusion to Lev 18:4–5 LXX, which demands that all the instructions and legal decisions of God be preserved and put into action: it is through these that a human being will live. The allusion picks up the concepts of πορεύομαι ("to walk") and προστάγματα ("instructions"), as well as the future form ζήσονται (Lev 18:5: ζήσεται) with the specification ἐν αὐτῷ (Lev 18:5: ἐν αὐτοῖς). Psalms of Solomon 14.3 expands the affirmation "they will live in it" with "forever" (εἰς τὸν αἰῶνα), thereby placing the accent on the future, eschatological life with God. Life according to the torah is motivated by the prospect of eternal life. This, however, must not be misunderstood as a soteriological achievement on the part of the human being.[24]

---

24. This, however, is the position taken by Simon J. Gathercole in "Torah, Life, and Salvation: Leviticus 18:5 in Early Judaism and the New Testament," in *From Prophecy to Testament: The Function of the Old Testament in the New*, ed. Craig A. Evans (Peabody: Hendrickson, 2004), 133: "doing Torah is the precondition of a future life"; "it is dependent on obedience to the Torah." Cf. Eric Ottenheijm, "'Which If a Man Do Them He Shall Live by Them': Jewish and Christian Discourse on Lev 18:5," in *The Scriptures of Israel in Jewish and Christian Tradition: Essays in Honour of*

The psalm goes on to promise the pious an eternal, paradisiac life with God (14.3-5, 10), but their antithesis, the "sinners and lawbreakers [παράνομοι]" who followed their sin and their desire (ἐπιθυμία), will end in the realm of the dead and in destruction (14.6-9). One who keeps to God's instructions—the torah—lives in his righteousness, that is, in a positive correspondence to God's salvific will. Righteousness thus also concerns the behavior of the *human being* with regard to the torah: one who lives according to the torah acts in righteousness and thus has a share in God's righteousness (cf. 5.17). This, however, does not mean that he *merits* this share.[25] God's saving action cannot be merited, since it has already taken place in the covenantal election, and can be lost only through a conscious and consistent turning away from God. E. P. Sanders has described the connection between the covenant and the torah in early Judaism by means of the concept of covenantal nomism. This means that

> one's place in God's plan is established on the basis of the covenant and that the covenant requires as the proper response of man his obedience to its commandments, while providing means of atonement for transgression.... Obedience maintains one's position in the covenant, but it does not earn God's grace as such.[26]

Maarten J. J. Menken, ed. Bart J. Koet, Steve Moyise, and Joseph Verheyden, NovTSup 148 (Leiden: Brill, 2013), 305. On the relevance of the "deeds" to salvation, see also Schnelle, "Gerechtigkeit," 373. James D. G. Dunn (*The Theology of Paul the Apostle* [Grand Rapids: Eerdmans, 1998], 152-53), on the other hand, understands "life" in Lev 18:5 as "a way of life, and not of a life yet to be achieved or attained" (153); it is "the way life is lived within and by ... the covenant people" (152).

25. Winninge, *Sinners*, 133 (on 5.17) goes too far when he asserts "that righteousness is a positive achievement of the pious Jew." On the contrary, it is a question of a *correspondence* to the righteousness of God. See Andreas Lindemann, "Paulus—Pharisäer und Apostel," in *Paulus und Johannes: Exegetische Studien zur paulinischen und johanneischen Theologie und Literatur*, ed. Dieter Sänger and Ulrich Mell, WUNT 198 (Tübingen: Mohr Siebeck, 2006), 333, 336, but the statement that this "jenen Status und jenes Selbstverständnis des Menschen, den Paulus als ἰδία δικαιοσύνη bezeichnet" (333), devalues the intention of the Psalms of Solomon excessively, and leads to an insufficiently differentiated position.

26. E. P. Sanders, *Paul and Palestinian Judaism: A Comparison of Patterns of Religion* (Philadelphia: Fortress, 1977), 75; cf. 319-20, 420, 426, 544. Cf. Martin G. Abegg Jr. "4QMMT, Paul and 'Works of the Law,'" in *The Bible at Qumran: Texts, Shape, and Interpretation*, ed. Peter W. Flint and James C. VanderKam (Grand Rapids: Eerdmans, 2001), 203-16; Atkinson, "Enduring the Lord's Discipline," 151-53. For a lively discussion of Sanders's theses, see Donald A. Carson, Peter T. O'Brien, and Mark A.

God's saving will and the human response, namely, obedience to God's instructions, are inseparable. Since humans, because of their sins, are absolutely incapable of a perfect observance of the torah, God through his mercy compensates for human inadequacy (15.13).

Psalms of Solomon 14 communicates the high esteem that the torah enjoyed in the groups that stand behind the Psalms of Solomon. It is nevertheless striking that we scarcely ever hear of the need to insist on the observance of specific *material* contents of the torah; nor is there any discussion or exposition of individual instructions or commandments. Instead, the torah functions as a differentiator between the righteous and the sinners, and the sinners include not only the gentiles, but also the lawless in Israel. This leads me to propose the thesis that *in the Psalms of Solomon, the delimitation vis-à-vis the lifestyle of the gentiles is the principle of exposition of the torah.*

1.5. Delimitation vis-à-vis the Gentiles as the Principle of Exposition of the Torah

Psalms of Solomon 2.13, speaking of the "daughters of Jerusalem," castigates the "disorder of mingling" in the context of unchastity or prostitution (2.11–12). This gives us our first sight of the problems associated with the mingling with the foreign culture that is dangerous but attractive, with its foreign gods and lifestyles. In 3.8, reconciliation for the transgressions committed in ignorance takes place through fasting and humbling oneself; humbling should be understood as the insight into one's own sinfulness and the conscious submission to God's will and commandments. Fasting as a means to attain the forgiveness of unconscious sins is implicitly here a competitor to the cultic animal sacrifices that are prescribed for this purpose by Lev 4–5: the torah is interpreted to mean that the cultic prescriptions have lost their significance, in view of the conviction that the immoral behavior of the priests has made the temple impure.[27] Fasting, confessing one's sins, and continuous prayer (praise) are the attitudes through which the righteous remain in the salvific relationship to God and that delimit them vis-à-vis the sinners (in Israel!). Psalms of Solomon

---

Seifrid, eds, *Justification and Variegated Nomism*, 2 vols., WUNT 140, 181 (Tübingen: Mohr Siebeck, 2001, 2004); Gerd Theissen and Petra von Gemünden, *Der Römerbrief: Rechenschaft eines Reformators* (Göttingen: Vandenhoeck & Ruprecht, 2016), 42–45.

27. See Atkinson, "Enduring the Lord's Discipline," 160.

15 and 16 demand attentiveness to the presence of God: Pss. Sol. 15.2–6 recommends the continuous praise of God, which keeps fellowship with God alive (as the antithesis of the "lawlessness" [ἀνομία] of the sinners in 15.8, 10), and Pss. Sol. 16.1–4 warns against allowing the soul to fall asleep, since this takes one far from God. It too encourages the praise of God and the continuous remembrance of God (16.5–6, 9).

The historical background to what the Psalms of Solomon see as the necessity to draw a boundary vis-à-vis the pagan lifestyle becomes clearly visible in Pss. Sol. 17. The "lawless one" (ἄνομος) in 17.11 comes from a foreign race, from the gentiles (17.7, 13), and has brought death and destruction to Israel. In terms of contemporary history, the author (and the readers) will have had in mind Pompey or the Roman military power in Israel, whose actions in Jerusalem are equated with those of the gentiles in their cities (17.14). Psalms of Solomon 17.15 is interesting, because it states that "the sons of the covenant" (Israel) surpassed even the gentiles in their wicked deeds (cf. 1.8; 8.13). This makes it clear that the sinners in Israel cultivated the same lifestyle as the gentiles, thereby turning their backs on the traditional way of life in Israel, which is represented by the torah.[28] In 17.18, the "lawless ones" (ἄνομοι) are identical with the peoples that have scattered Israel over the whole earth. The sinners in Israel are to be found in every class of society, from the ruler to the lowliest, as 17.20 underlines: they were in every kind of sin—"the king in transgression [παρανομία], and the judge in disobedience, and the people in sin." For the Psalms of Solomon, a question mark hovers over the traditional way of life, over the very existence of Israel!

Psalms of Solomon 17 then projects the delimitation vis-à-vis the pagan lifestyle into the messianic future. The messiah, as mediator and God's agent, will establish this boundary line perfectly. The messiah who

---

28. This raises the question of the group of "bearers" of the Psalms of Solomon. A few years ago, one could speak of a consensus that attributed these texts to the Pharisees, but today, in view of the plurality of currents in early Judaism, it is impossible to attribute them unambiguously to any one of the known groups. See Stefan Schreiber, *Gesalbter und König: Titel und Konzeptionen der königlichen Gesalbtenerwartung in frühjüdischen und urchristlichen Schriften*, BZNW 105 (Berlin: de Gruyter, 2000), 161–62; Atkinson, *I Cried to the Lord*, 6–8; Wright, *Psalms of Solomon*, 7–10. Trafton ("Bible," 434) thinks of "an anti-Hasmonean Jewish sentiment that had affinities with both Pharisaism and Essenism, but which cannot be identified with either." One should also bear in mind the influence of sapiential currents (see Schreiber, "Can Wisdom Be a Prayer?").

is awaited will destroy unjust rulers and "lawbreaking peoples" (ἔθνη παράνομα), and he will drive away the sinners from the inheritance, calling into question their membership of Israel (17.22–24).²⁹ Accordingly, the messiah will gather together a "holy people" (λαὸν ἅγιον) and "judge the tribes of the people" (κρινεῖ φυλὰς λαοῦ) that "is sanctified by the Lord his God" (17.26). The delimitation becomes even clearer in the promise that then there will be no more injustice among them and that there will not dwell among them anyone who knows evil. "Neither settler [πάροικος] nor alien [ἀλλογενής] shall live among them any more" (17.27–28). The settler is an inhabitant who lacks the rights of a citizen, and an alien comes from another people. All those who do not truly belong to Israel, and thus their dangerous, different culture, will no longer pose a threat to the people of God—the delimitation is perfect!

Once the messiah has reestablished the pure, original state of things in Jerusalem (17.30), an eschatological promise envisages a possible entry of the gentiles, but only on the premise that they are oriented to Israel: there will be "peoples of the gentiles" (λαοὺς ἐθνῶν) who serve the messiah under his yoke,³⁰ and there will be gentiles (ἔθνη) who come from the end of the earth to see his glory, "bringing as gifts her children who had fainted." Their function is the eschatological bringing back of the Jews from the diaspora to Jerusalem (17.30–31; cf. the motif in Isa 49:22 LXX). According to 17.34, he will be merciful to all the gentiles who fear him,³¹ and according to 17.43, he will rule "in the midst of sanctified peoples [λαῶν]." An eschatological opening of the λαός Israel is thus envisaged for those gentiles who submit to the rule of the messiah.³²

---

29. Influences from Ps 2 are discernible in the text. See John J. Collins, "The Royal Psalms and Eschatological Messianism," in *Aux origines des messianismes juifs*, ed. David Hamidović, VTSup 158 (Leiden: Brill, 2013), 85.

30. The "yoke" of the messiah has political connotations; see Joel Willitts, "Matthew and *Psalms of Solomon*'s Messianism: A Comparative Study in First-Century Messianology," *BBR* 22 (2012): 38. This concept, which is also used in 7.9, may indicate that the sovereignty of the messiah comes about in accordance with the torah, which the gentiles adopt.

31. The term Φόβος has positive connotations here (see Willitts, "Matthew and *Psalms of Solomon*'s Messianism," 47–48).

32. The concept of λαός does not have a univocal reference in the Psalms of Solomon. It is frequently employed for Israel as the people of God (and is then used in the singular): 9.8; 10.6; 17.20, 26, 35, 36, 43. In 5.11; 9.2; 17.29, 30, 33, it stands (in the

This opening onto the peoples of the world is, however, only conceivable in eschatological terms, in the saving rule of the messiah, when he makes this rule secure and guarantees it. The psalm closes, therefore, with a prayer that God may save Israel "from the uncleanness of unholy enemies" (17.45). In the present time, delimitation is commanded. This is the visibly lived belonging to the God of Israel in a life for which the torah provides the orientation. A life in accordance with the torah is evidence of this belonging.[33] The group behind the Psalms of Solomon formulates here a clear directive for Israel's conduct in the present time.

2. Paul's Letter to the Galatians and the Torah

2.1. The Demarcation Is Abolished

What remains an eschatological perspective in the Psalms of Solomon becomes in Paul a present-day conflict: the inclusion of the gentiles. As we have seen, the torah functions in general in the Psalms of Solomon to draw a boundary line between Israel and the gentiles, and more specifically to draw a boundary line within Israel between the pious Jews and those who adapt to the Gentile way of life. In Paul's dialogue situation, where, as a consequence of the eschatological Christ-event, persons from Judaism and from the gentiles together form the community of the end-time, it is precisely the delimitation between Jews and gentiles that he wants to overcome. In Paul's eyes, after the Christ-event, access to God stands open for persons from the gentiles too. These gentiles are integrated into the community of Christ without first becoming proselytes. The so-called Antioch incident, which is recalled in Gal 2:11–14,[34] shows that the resulting coexistence of Jewish and gentile Christians, which was actualized substantively in their common meal (Gal 2:12), aroused suspicion on the Jewish

---

plural) for the peoples of the earth. Pss. Sol. 12.2 uses it in general for "people." In 8.2, λαός πολύς refers to Roman troops.

33. This does not, however, mean that observance of the torah has a soteriological function. For a different view, see Mark A. Seifrid, *Justification by Faith: The Origin and Development of a Central Pauline Theme*, NovTSup 68 (Leiden: Brill, 1992), 130–33.

34. On the historical background: Dietrich-Alex Koch, *Geschichte des Urchristentums: Ein Lehrbuch*, 2nd ed. (Göttingen: Vandenhoeck & Ruprecht, 2014), 238–43; Udo Schnelle, *Die ersten 100 Jahre des Christentums 30–130 n.Chr. Die Entstehungsgeschichte einer Weltreligion*, UTB 4411 (Göttingen: Vandenhoeck & Ruprecht, 2015), 232–34.

side. Under the influence of a group of Jewish Christians from Jerusalem (whom Paul calls "James's people"), even Barnabas (who had accompanied Paul for many years on the mission to gentiles that did not demand circumcision) and Peter withdrew into the old pattern of delimitation, and *this* is what forms Paul's criticism of Peter in Gal 2:14: "If you, though a Jew, live like a Gentile and not like a Jew, how can you compel the Gentiles to live like Jews?" The delimitation of the Jews vis-à-vis the gentiles has lost its basis, since all who belong to Christ possess a common identity. This relativizes other, typically Jewish, patterns of identity.

The overcoming of the boundary between Jews and gentiles in the community of Christ—an overcoming that becomes visible in the coexistence of the two groups in the central spheres of life—is the problem that the Letter to the Galatians takes up. Paul's rivals demand that the gentile Christians[35] in Galatia also accept circumcision, which has been the sign of the covenant since the days of Abraham (Gen 17:11), as a decisive mark of Israel's identity (Gal 5:2–3, 6; 6:12–13, 15). As proselytes, these Christians would possess a clear identity, and they would be able to demonstrate clearly through the classic Jewish identity markers that they belonged to the people of Israel, in a visible delimitation vis-à-vis the pagan milieu. These rivals must have had a considerable influence, since some Galatians were clearly on the point of getting circumcised (1:6; 4:9, 17, 21; 5:4). In order to defend his new praxis, Paul must interpret the torah in such a way that the visible marks of delimitation, such as circumcision and commandments concerning diet and purity, are relativized. It seems natural to relate the central syntagma works of the law in Gal 2:16 to these identity markers of Judaism.

This identifies the goal of Paul's argumentation with regard to the concrete problem in Galatia. But in order to understand the affirmations of the Letter to the Galatians in their theological depth, we must go on to ask: when Jews become adherents of Christ, does nothing change in their understanding of the torah?

---

35. Gal 4:8 indicates that the addressees of the letter were primarily gentile Christians.

2.2. The Structure in Paul's Thinking: The Relationship to the God of Israel in Christ

This question leads us to the fundamental structure in Paul's thinking. At its center stands the relationship between God and the human person. Paul presupposes that, with Christ, the final age has dawned, and God turns toward Israel or to human beings in a new way in Christ, opening up the relationship to his own self. Paul affirms the eschatological significance of the Christ-event already in the prescript of the letter, at Gal 1:4: Jesus's gift of himself snatches us out of the present evil aeon, and this implies that we are freed in principle from the power of sin.[36] This leads to a new, eschatologically transformed existence in Christ: it is "Christ who lives in me; and the life I now live in the flesh I live in trust in the Son of God, who loved me and gave himself for me" (2:20). And in 6:15, he speaks of the human being who is in Christ as a "new creation," implying an eschatological change of status. Galatians 2:16 sums up this salutary turning of God to human beings by means of the motif of justifying. On God's part, this means that human beings are welcomed and saved and that their sins are forgiven.

"Justifying" (δικαιοῦσθαι) in Gal 2:16, or "righteousness" in 2:21, denotes an action on the part of God that puts the human being in the right relationship to God and gives fellowship with God. The human being himself cannot do this. This is something that God must do.[37]

The decisive point now is how Paul defines the part played by the human being. How does the human being behave in the new relationship to God? The Christ-event brings about here the central difference that Paul formulates as a sharp antithesis at 2:16: the basis (ἐκ) of justification is no longer the works of the law but the "solid relationship to Christ" (πίστις Ἰησοῦ Χριστοῦ).[38]

In classical linguistic usage, πίστις means confidence, fidelity, and reliability within a relationship and a conviction.[39] The genitive term πίστις

---

36. Cf. Gal 4:4–5: "But when the fullness of time had come, God sent forth his Son ... to redeem those who were under the law."

37. Cf., e.g., LXX Ps 142[143]:1–2; Mic 7:9; Dan 9:14–16. In the linguistic usage of the LXX, the righteousness of God means his salvific turning to his people, cf. Ps 40[41]:11; 70[71]:15; 97[98]:2; Isa 45:8; 46:13; 51:5; 56:1; 59:17; 4 Ezra 8:26.

38. On this antithesis, see also Gal 2:21; 3:2, 5, 10–14; 5:4–5.

39. See Schreiber, *Der erste Brief an die Thessalonicher*, 93–96; Thomas Schum-

Ἰησοῦ Χριστοῦ, which is the object of controversial discussion among scholars, is best translated as "solid relationship to Jesus Christ," where the *reciprocity* of the relationship is decisive.[40] Accordingly, 2:17 can employ the formulation "to be justified *in Christ*," that is to say, in the sphere of the relationship to him.

For Paul, justification passes, after the eschatological Christ-event, via the relationship to Christ. Accordingly, he has "put his trust in Christ Jesus" (2:16). The new fellowship with God in Christ creates a new perspective on the torah that is contrary to the traditional Jewish understanding, which Paul describes by means of the syntagma works of the law.

2.3. The Works of the Law

Paul continues to understand the torah as a Jew. At 2:15, he explicitly numbers himself among the Jews and adopts the customary Jewish delimitation that sees the gentiles in principle—in contradistinction to the Jews—as sinners.[41] But, as 2:16 underlines three times, Paul is convinced that, after the Christ-event, a human being "is not justified by works of the law [ἐξ ἔργων νόμου]." Here (as also in the Psalms of Solomon) the meaning is not that one merits God's righteousness through religious achievements. Rather, the question is how the relationship to God is lived. The works of the law are now useless as a response to justification.

The concept of ἔργα achieves a vital differentiation here. In linguistic terms, it makes it impossible to deny completely the significance of the torah. Works of the law does not in the least have the general meaning of behaving and living in accordance with the torah, with the intention of attaining righteousness before God. It means *actions that make visible one's belonging to God* (as the human side within the relationship between God and the human being). Those who perform the works of the law thereby

---

acher, *Zur Entstehung christlicher Sprache: Eine Untersuchung der paulinischen Idiomatik und der Verwendung des Begriffes* πίστις, BBB 168 (Göttingen: Vandenhoeck & Ruprecht, 2012).

40. This neutralizes the disputed question whether πίστις Ἰησοῦ Χριστοῦ is to be understood as an objective genitive ("faith in Christ," according to classic German scholarship) or as a subjective genitive ("the fidelity of Jesus in his death," as many English-language scholars prefer). See further Martinus C. de Boer, *Galatians: A Commentary*, NTL (Louisville: Westminster John Knox, 2011), 148–50.

41. Cf. Isa 14:5; 1 Macc 1:34; 2:48; Pss. Sol. 1.1–8.

show that they are living the torah in the classically Jewish manner, which also finds a representative in the Psalms of Solomon. The concept of ἔργα points to concrete prescriptions or modes of conduct that can be plainly seen to be a consequence of the law. In the dialogue situation of the Letter to the Galatians, we should think of these as pointedly Jewish identity markers that make the Jewish identity visible in demarcation vis-à-vis the pagan world—first and foremost, circumcision, the Sabbath commandment, and commandments about eating and purity.[42] For Paul, these are dangerous, not only because of their function of demarcation, but also because they signify an access to God that has become obsolete.

The reference of the syntagma ἐξ ἔργων νόμου is extremely disputed among exegetes.[43] Above all, there is no agreement about whether this refers to following the entire torah or only particular modes of conduct that mark the special character of Judaism (in the so-called new perspective, these are called identity or boundary markers). Martin Luther's general distinction between legalism (that is to say, every compliance with laws of the state and of religion) and divine grace has left a lasting mark on the discussion. This is connected with the theological question of whether works of the law are to be understood as human achievements that are meant to establish a claim on God. Paul would strictly reject such an idea, combating it by proclaiming the divine grace. Scholars also discuss a distinction between prescriptions and concrete actions.[44]

---

42. Cf. 4Q398 14 II, 2–7 (part of 4QMMT): "And also we have written to you some of the precepts of the Torah [ma'aseh ha-Torah] ... and it shall be reckoned to you as justice when you do what is good and upright before him." These words are preceded by some precepts that were understood as torah and that were important for the group behind this text. These are concerned above all with ritual purity and fulfill the function of marking boundaries between groups within Judaism. Josephus (A.J. 20.42, 43, 46) uses the expression "to do the work" (πράσσειν τὸν ἔργον) in the sense of "carrying out circumcision" in the context of conversion to Judaism. On this understanding, see James D. G. Dunn, *The New Perspective on Paul: Collected Essays*, rev. ed. (Grand Rapids: Eerdmans, 2008), esp. 1–88, 109; Dunn, *Theology of Paul*, 354–59.

43. On the state of the discussion, see Ivana Bendik, *Paulus in neuer Sicht? Eine kritische Einführung in die „New Perspective on Paul,"* Judentum und Christentum 18 (Stuttgart: Kohlhammer, 2010), esp. 165–74; Stefan Schreiber, "Paulus und die Tradition. Zur Hermeneutik der 'Rechtfertigung' in neuer Perspektive," *TRev* 105 (2009): 91–102; Michael Wolter, *Der Brief an die Römer*, vol. 1, EKKNT 6.1 (Neukirchen-Vluyn: Neukirchener, 2014), 1:233–37.

44. Michael Bachmann ("Keil oder Mikroskop? Zur jüngeren Diskussion um den Ausdruck 'Werke des Gesetzes,'" in *Lutherische und Neue Paulusperspektive: Beiträge*

The intention to make one's own belonging to the God of Israel visible in the ἔργα νόμου is, *per se*, positive. But for Paul, this has been rendered obsolete through the eschatological Christ-event, since God has now opened up in Christ a new possibility of belonging. The fulfilling of the torah changes both for the Jewish adherents of Christ and for those who come from the gentiles (ἔθνη).[45] For the Jewish Christians, the relationship to Christ means that the customary torah actions that express Israel's belonging to its God lose their relevance; in addition to the identity markers mentioned above, these also include cultic actions in the temple in Jerusalem, or the fasting that is recommended in Pss. Sol. 3.8 to atone for the sins committed in ignorance; the latter is irrelevant, since the sins have now been removed through Christ's gift of himself (Gal 1:4). And for the adherents from the gentiles, it is the relationship to Christ that makes possible in the first place their belonging to the God of Israel without accepting circumcision and commandments concerning matters such as food—in short, without becoming proselytes. Like the Jewish adherents, those from the gentiles find their orientation in the torah and its picture of God, but they understand this in a special manner, from the perspective of the Christ-event. It is precisely against the background of the Psalms of Solomon that we can grasp that when Paul's rivals in Galatia saw this opening for the ἔθνη, they could accuse him of interpreting the torah in such a way that it meant a cheap assimilation to the pagan culture.[46]

---

zu einem Schlüsselproblem der gegenwärtigen exegetischen Diskussion, ed. Michael Bachmann, WUNT 182 [Tübingen: Mohr Siebeck, 2005], 69–134) holds that only regulations of the law are meant. Against this, see James D. G. Dunn, "The Dialogue Progresses," in Bachmann, *Lutherische und Neue Pauluspersektive*, 400. Philo (*Praem.* 82–83, 126) and Josephus (*C. Ap.* 2.291–292) already note that it is only works that implement the laws.

45. From the perspective of the history of scholarship, the new theological evaluation of the regulations of the torah that make one's belonging to the God of Israel come alive is inseparable from the sociological consequence, that is to say, the admission of persons from the gentiles to the communities of Christ. The latter is strongly emphasized by the New Perspective (the function as boundary markers).

46. When Paul defends himself in Gal 1:10 against the charge that he wants to please human beings (ἀνθρώποις ἀρέσκειν), his rivals were probably making the same kind of accusations that the Psalms of Solomon too could raise against the "sinners" (Pss. Sol. 4.7, 19).

For Paul, the consequence of the new fellowship with God *in Christ* is a new interpretation of the torah. Let me conclude by at least indicating briefly in four points what has changed in Paul's understanding of the torah in comparison to that in the Psalms of Solomon.

2.4. The Interpretation of the Torah in Christ

First, Paul defines the significance of the figure of Abraham anew by means of an interpretation that is unusual in early Judaism. In the Psalms of Solomon, Abraham stands for the election of Israel, which distinguishes it from the gentiles (Pss. Sol. 9.9), and for the beginning of the covenant with God (10.4); an allusion to Gen 17:13, 19 can be heard here.[47] But Gal 3:6–18 begins at an earlier point in the story of Abraham, in order to show that God made it possible for Abraham to enter into a relationship with him through Abraham's trust in God's promise—even before circumcision. Gal 3:6 quotes from Gen 15:6 LXX: "Abraham believed God, and it was reckoned to him as righteousness." The gentiles (ἔθνη), too, are blessed in this attitude of trust (Gen 12:3 is quoted); according to Gal 3:7–9, οἱ ἐκ πίστεως ("those from the relationship of trust") are the children of Abraham; the gentiles are included here from the outset. Paul thus uses Abraham to demonstrate that God always favored the attitude of πίστις; the law, which came later, does not change this in any way (Gal 3:17).[48] In Gal 3:29, he states that all who belong to Christ are descendants of Abraham. The torah is given the function of bearing witness that the correct attitude of the human being in the relationship to God is πίστις: this applies both to Abraham (Gen 15:6) and to his descendants (Gen 12:3).

Second, the Psalms of Solomon do not speak of a *curse* of the law. Here, Paul elaborates an interpretation that is generated by the perspective of the Christ-event. According to Gal 3:10–13, all who live out of works

---

47. In early Judaism, Abraham was regarded as the founding father of Israel when he accepted circumcision. He already observed the torah before it was given on Sinai; cf. Gen^{LXX} 26:5; Sir^{LXX} 44:20–21; Jub. 24.11. Cf. Oda Wischmeyer, "Wie kommt Abraham in den Galaterbrief? Überlegungen zu Gal 3,6–29," in *Umstrittener Galaterbrief: Studien zur Situierung und Theologie des Paulus-Schreibens*, ed. Michael Bachmann and Bernd Kollmann, Biblisch-theologische Studien 106 (Neukirchen-Vluyn: Neukirchener, 2010), 119–63.

48. According to Gal 3:17, the law was given 430 years later. This figure is taken from Exod 12:40–41 LXX; cf. Josephus, *A.J.* 2.318.

of the law are under a curse. In support of this affirmation, Paul quotes Deut 27:26,[49] where the curse falls on everyone who "does not abide by all things written in the book of the law." The fundamental idea, already established in this quotation, is that no one is able to keep the torah perfectly. This means that all who rely on works of the law are in fact always under the curse.[50] The thesis that Paul's starting point is the inability of the (Jewish) human being to fulfill the entire torah has often been criticized by scholars who assert that early Judaism considered obedience to the law as practicable; it required no impossible perfection but made provision for atonement and repentance.[51] But as we have seen, the Psalms of Solomon already place the emphasis on God's mercy. In other words, they presuppose that even the righteous are always in need of this mercy, since no one can keep the torah perfectly ("sinful righteous"). And they no longer regarded the sacrificial cult as reliable, because the priests had incurred impurity. Unlike Paul, however, the Psalms of Solomon still envisage the strict observance of the torah as the path on which one can live in God's mercy. Paul interprets the inability of the human being to do the torah perfectly *in malam partem* through the idea of the curse in order to show that works of the law and the relationship to Christ are not equally valuable alternatives as a basis for fellowship with God.

The quotation from Lev 18:5 LXX places the accent on *doing* the torah. The Septuagint version of Lev 18:5 already underlines that this

---

49. Michael Bachmann ("Zur Argumentation von Gal 3.10–12," *NTS* 53 [2007]: 524–44) defines Gal 3:10–12 formally as two linked syllogisms. It seems to me more important that we have here an interpretation of scripture, probably a thematic pesher (cf., e.g., 4Q174 III; Acts 2:14–42).

50. Ottenheijm, "Which If a Man Do Them," 316: "In Paul's vision no person is able to keep the Law outside the realm of Christian faith." The dying "through the law" of which Gal 2:19 speaks (διά with the genitive denotes the law as mediator) is probably to be understood on the basis of this curse. The "dying to the law" in the same verse is a metaphor for the separation, the distance vis-à-vis the law (cf. Rom 6:2, 10–11; 7:6), that opens up a new standpoint in relation to the torah and a new interpretation. Gal 5:1, 3 speaks, with reference to circumcision, of the "yoke [ζυγός] of slavery," which apparently means that the entire torah must be kept.

51. Dunn, *Theology of Paul*, 361; cf. N. T. Wright, *The Climax of the Covenant: Christ and the Law in Pauline Theology* (repr. London: T&T Clark, 2004), 145. R. Barry Matlock discusses alternative drafts and convincingly defends the inability explanation in "Helping Paul's Argument Work? The Curse of Galatians 3.10–14," in *The Torah in the New Testament*, ed. Michael Tait and Peter Oakes (London: T&T Clark, 2009), 154–79.

means keeping the *entire* torah ("all my instructions and all my legal decisions")—something that Paul sees as impossible, so that, on this basis, the curse must necessarily fall.[52]

In Gal 3:11–12, there is a contrast between two scriptural quotations, Hab 2:4 ("The righteous will live out of trust [ἐκ πίστεως]") and Lev 18:5 (the one "who does [these commandments] shall live by them"). The motif of life links the two texts and places the accent on the opposition, already made pointedly at Gal 2:16, between trust and doing the torah; in both cases, the goal is life with God. Life has a comprehensive meaning here, including both the present day and the inalienable life with God.[53] Leviticus 18:5 focuses life on the delimited sphere of doing the torah, whereas the relationship of trust in God breaks open the boundary, leading to a new understanding of the torah.

For Paul, therefore, belonging to God can be realized and lived only in an inadequate manner on the basis of fulfilling the torah. But Christ ransomed humans from the curse of the law (not from the law as such!)[54] by taking upon himself the curse uttered in Deut 21:23 LXX ("Cursed [be] everyone who hangs on the wood"), shared it with all other human beings under the law, and—as Christ, as God's representative—liberated them from the curse with an eschatological effect (Gal 3:13).

Third, in Gal 3:19–4:7, Paul can assign certain *functions* of the torah to *the past*. The caesura is formed by the Christ-event, which divides the

---

52. On various interpretations of Paul's use of Lev 18:5, see Friedrich Avemarie, "Paul and the Claim of the Law according to the Scripture: Leviticus 18:5 in Galatians 3:12 and Romans 10:5," in *The Beginnings of Christianity*, ed. Jack Pastor and Menachem Mor (Jerusalem: Yad Ben-Zvi, 2005), 125–48. Cf. Nicole Chibici-Revneanu, "Leben im Gesetz: Die paulinische Interpretation von Lev 18:5 (Gal 3:12; Rom 10:5)," *NovT* 50 (2008): 105–19.

53. Gathercole, "Torah, Life, and Salvation" 143–45, sees Paul "in dialogue with a Judaism that thought in terms of obedience, final judgment, and eternal life" and argues against the view that "obedience to Torah is not the means of salvation but rather marks out covenant membership" (144)—a view maintained, e.g., by N. T. Wright (*Climax of the Covenant*, 149–50). In my opinion, the supposition of a *causal* relationship between observance of the torah and the reward of eternal life does not go far enough, since it omits from view the entire relationship to God that the torah seeks to shape; the theology of the antecedent covenant influences the soteriology of the Psalms of Solomon (esp. 9.8–11). The new interpretation of the torah by Paul after the Christ-event is the decisive point of conflict.

54. *Pace* de Boer, *Galatians*, 210: "the law itself is a curse."

whole of history into a period before Christ and a period after Christ. This dichotomy of the ages means that the time between Abraham and Christ loses its contours; Moses, David, and the prophets play no role. In this provisional, dark time, the law too has only a provisional function. According to Gal 3:19, the law was added "because of transgressions," in order to prevent the worst from happening, or in order to bring to light hidden, unconscious transgressions and make people conscious of them.[55] This function is temporary, until the coming of the "offspring" (Christ). According to 3:21–22, there never existed a righteousness "by the law," because everything, including the torah, was enclosed under sin and dominated by sin. Prior to the "relationship of trust [πίστις]," the law had the function of guarding (3:23) and of a "tutor" (παιδαγωγός, 3:24). This reflects an ambivalent view. Guarding can mean protection but also imprisonment,[56] and the "tutor"—a slave who took boys to school or the gymnasium and back and watched over them—could protect but also chastise. He was responsible for protection from dangers and bad influences, but he was also mocked, because the tutor was often a slave whose age or handicap meant that he could not be used for any other work. The function of the tutor recalls Pss. Sol. 7.9 and 10.1–4, but once again Paul sees it as temporary, until the coming of the relationship to Christ. Now that Christ has come, faithful are no longer under the tutor (Gal 3:25).

Psalms of Solomon 4.4–5 summarizes the significance of the coming of Christ: through the sending of his Son by God, the "fullness of time," the eschaton, has come. Since the Son himself was subject to the conditions of humans ("born of a woman"), and specifically Jewish existence ("born under the law"), he was able to redeem those who are "under the law," so that they receive "divine childhood"—that is, new life in the relationship, in immediate closeness to God in the end-time. The motif of education, whereby the torah played a central role as guideline, is central to the Psalms of Solomon, but this has become obsolete in Paul, thanks to God's salvific action in Christ. A new interpretation of the torah is both possible and necessary.

Fourth, the *commandment of love* from Lev 19:18 becomes the new *criterion of interpretation of the torah* in Gal 5:14: "For the whole law is fulfilled in one (single) word, 'You shall love your neighbor as yourself.'"

---

55. But not "to produce the transgressions" (thus de Boer, *Galatians*, 231).

56. Paul uses the verbs φρουρέω (transitive: to guard, to protect, but also of a garrison: to occupy) and συγκλείω (to enclose, to shelter, to encircle, to shut in).

Love for one's neighbor, welcoming and accepting the other person, getting involved on behalf of the other, means the fulfillment of the torah.[57] This is in accord with the new relationship to Christ, so that 5:6 speaks of "πίστις that becomes operative through ἀγάπη." Love of neighbor is a consequence of the relationship to Christ and is thus the key to the interpretation of the torah in Christ. It is here that Paul's specific hermeneutic of the torah becomes visible. Leviticus 19:18 itself comes from the torah, which means that Paul does not leave Judaism through his interpretation. In Gal 6:2, he speaks of "the law of Christ." This is not a new law, but the law that is qualified through Christ. He defines it by means of the exhortation: "Bear one another's burdens"—which is in keeping with the intention of Lev 19:18. Love of neighbor becomes the new identity marker of the community, which sets its stamp upon the community's ethos and demarcates it *ad extra*, while Jews and gentile Christians are united precisely in this love. Galatians 6:1 states that dealing with a "transgression" (παράπτωμα) is the task of the community, which consists of persons filled with the Spirit (πνευματικοί) and can bring the transgressor back onto the right path. The community takes on a task that is God's: in Pss. Sol. 13.10, it was God himself who removed the transgressions of the righteous through his education.

3. Conclusion

This comparison with the Psalms of Solomon shows that Paul's new interpretation touches a raw nerve of the Jewish understanding of the torah: Abraham as the beginning of the election of Israel, the torah as a good path of righteousness, the educational function of the torah. In these areas, Paul develops new paths and summarizes his understanding of the torah in the commandment of love, which is his hermeneutical key. The Psalms of Solomon and Paul share a central interest in God's turning to Israel, which is expressed in his "righteousness" and his "mercy" (Psalms of Solomon) or his "love" (Gal 2:20). In the Psalms of Solomon, doing the torah corresponds to the righteousness of God, and whoever lives in accordance with the torah can be called righteous and may hope for the forgiveness

---

57. Rom 13:8–10 also quotes Lev 19:18 as the summary of the torah. Such summaries were known in early Judaism. See Stefan Schreiber, "Law and Love in Romans 13.8–10," in *The Torah in the Ethics of Paul*, ed. Martin Meiser, LNTS 473 (London: T&T Clark, 2012), 100–19.

of his or her sins (one does not merit God's righteousness; one lives in it).[58] For Paul, on the other hand, the righteousness of God finds a new place in Christ, whereby also sins are forgiven. In Christ, God opens up for his people (and also for the gentiles) a new access to himself, a new relationship that makes one free for a new interpretation of the torah that relativizes the instructions that delimit the Jews vis-à-vis the gentiles and thus also gives the gentiles who belong to Christ the eschatological access to the people of God.

---

58. Atkinson ("Enduring the Lord's Discipline," 159) emphasizes the elements that are shared by the Psalms of Solomon and Paul: the fulfilling of the law does not make one righteous before God; all human beings sin; the pious know this, and they acknowledge the righteousness of God.

Coping with Dissonance: Theodicy, Genre, and Epistemology in the Psalms of Solomon

Shani Tzoref

1. Introduction

This discussion of theodicy and genre in the Psalms of Solomon builds upon Kenneth Atkinson's chapter, "Theodicy in the Psalms of Solomon," in Antti Laato and Johannes C. de Moor's comprehensive collection, *Theodicy in the World of the Bible*, and recent studies on the genre of the Psalms of Solomon.[1] I begin by reorganizing the presentation of some of

---

I am very grateful to Patrick Pouchelle for inviting me to join the Psalms of Solomon research group and to participate in the stimulating and fruitful conference at which a preliminary version of this paper was presented. Responses from fellow participants advanced my thinking and contributed to my formulations in this essay, which nevertheless remains a work-in-progress, as the Psalms of Solomon begins to receive the attention it deserves. My English translations of the Psalms of Solomon follow Kenneth Atkinson, "Psalms of Solomon," in *A New Translation of the Septuagint*, ed. Albert Pietersma and Benjamin G. Wright III (Oxford: Oxford University Press, 2007), 763–76, with some adaptation (throughout, I have substituted "mercy" for "pity"). References to the Greek text follow Robert B. Wright, *The Psalms of Solomon: A Critical Edition of the Greek Text*, Jewish and Christian Texts in Contexts and Related Studies 1 (London: T&T Clark, 2007).

1. Kenneth Atkinson, "Theodicy in the Psalms of Solomon," in *Theodicy in the World of the Bible*, ed. Antti Laato and Johannes C. de Moor (Leiden: Brill, 2003), 546–75; Brad Embry, "Some Thoughts on and Implications from Genre Categorization in the Psalms of Solomon," in *The Psalms of Solomon: Language, History, Theology*, ed. Eberhard Bons and Patrick Pouchelle, EJL 40 (Atlanta: SBL Press, 2015), 59–78; Rodney A. Werline, "The Experience of God's *Paideia* in the Psalms of Solomon," in *Linking Text and Experience*, vol. 2 of *Experientia*, ed. Colleen Shantz and Rodney A.

the key passages explored by Atkinson, which he addressed from a thematic perspective, and assigning them to categories of theodicy laid out by Laato and de Moor in their introduction.[2] I then describe a proposed correlation between these approaches to theodicy and genres of biblical and related literature. Finally, within this rubric, I discuss the genre hybridity of the Psalms of Solomon, especially with respect to its epistemological concerns.

I maintain that the Psalms of Solomon presumes and advocates a variation of a naïve theodicy that is typical of conventional wisdom—a more pious version of the view characterized by Klaus Koch as *Tun-Ergehen-Zusammenhang*.[3] In applying this rationalist worldview to historical and personal experience, the Psalms of Solomon adapts and develops certain generic features of biblical psalms, prophecy, and sapiential writings, while avoiding alternative skeptical and supernatural perspectives. Like its biblical precursors, the Psalms of Solomon addresses theodicy from a stance that relates explicitly to knowledge of God and God's ways. In this study, I treat the Psalms of Solomon as a unity, without endeavoring to incorporate redactional analysis. Despite its drawbacks, this approach avoids the flaw of circularity that typically arises in attempts to identify diachronic layers in the absence of sufficient external evidence.[4]

Werline, EJL 35 (Atlanta: Society of Biblical Literature, 2012), 17–44; Werline, "The Psalms of Solomon and the Ideology of Rule," in *Conflicted Boundaries in Wisdom and Apocalypticism*, ed. Lawrence M. Wills and Benjamin G. Wright III, SymS 35 (Atlanta: Society of Biblical Literature, 2005), 69–88.

2. Antti Laato and Johannes C. de Moor, "Introduction," in Laato and de Moor, *Theodicy*, vii–liv.

3. Klaus Koch, "Gibt es ein Vergeltungsdogma im Alten Testament?," in *Gesammelte Aufsätze*, vol. 1 of *Spuren des hebräischen Denkens: Beiträge zur alttestamentlichen Theologie* (Neukirchen-Vluyn: Neukirchener, 1991), 1–42.

4. Scholarly consensus views the Psalms of Solomon as a collection of works produced by multiple authors who worked within a common environment and historical era and a shared worldview. See Atkinson, "Theodicy," 553; George B. Gray, "The Psalms of Solomon," APOT 2:628; Robert B. Wright, "The Psalms of Solomon," OTP 2:641; Mikael Winninge, *Sinners and the Righteous: A Comparative Study of the Psalms of Solomon and Paul's Letters*, ConBNT 26 (Stockholm: Almqvist & Wiksell, 1995), 19–21. For diachronical analysis, see Kenneth Atkinson, *I Cried to the Lord: A Study of the Psalms of Solomon's Historical Background and Social Setting*, JSJSup 84 (Leiden: Brill, 2004); Werline, "Experience of God's *Paideia*," 20–21.

My heuristic starting point is the widely accepted conception of a trilemma at the heart of theodicy in monotheistic worldviews, as formulated for example by Ronald M. Green:[5]

> The "problem of theodicy" arises when the (1) experienced reality of *suffering* is juxtaposed with two sets of beliefs traditionally associated with ethical monotheism. One is (2) the belief that *God is absolutely good and compassionate*. The other is (3) the belief that he controls all events in history, that he is both *all-powerful* (*omnipotent*) and *all-knowing* (*omniscient*).

2. Approaches to Theodicy in the Hebrew Bible and in the Psalms of Solomon

As discussed at length by Laato and de Moor in the introduction to their volume, the term *theodicy* is sometimes used narrowly to denote a justification, or defense of God, arguing the truth of God's absolute goodness and absolute power.[6] The term can also be used more broadly, however, to describe the experience of grappling with the problem of badness in the world, both suffering and wrong-doing.[7] Suffering and

---

5. Ronald M. Green, "Theodicy," *EncRel* 14:430–441 (numbering and emphases have been added). The formulation as a trilemma is attributed to Epicurus in Lactantius, *De Ira Dei* 13, cited in Marcel Sarot, "Theodicy and Modernity," in Laato and de Moor, *Theodicy*, 1–26. The term *theodicy* was first used by Gottfried Wilhelm Leibniz, who presumed a monotheistic, specifically Christian, perspective (*Essais de théodicée: Sur la bonté de Dieu la liberté de l'homme et l'origine du mal* [Amsterdam: François Changuion, 1710]). The philosophical problem of human suffering is, of course, universal, and the religious dimension is not exclusive to monotheism. See below. Sarot ("Theodicy and Modernity") offers a detailed discussion of the variegated usage of the term theodicy in modern times.

6. Thus, Leibniz, *Essais de théodicée*. Green, "Theodicy," adopts this approach. See Laato and de Moor, "Introduction," x; Sarot, "Theodicy and Modernity," 3–4. Note the title of James L. Crenshaw's important contribution to the field, *Defending God: Biblical Responses to the Problem of Evil* (Oxford: Oxford University Press, 2005).

7. This broader usage is associated especially with Max Weber, *Gesammelte Aufsätze zur Religionssoziologie*, vol. 1. (Tübingen: Mohr Siebeck, 1920). See Laato and de Moor, "Introduction," x–xiii. The term *badness* is my rendering of Hebrew רע. By "grappling with the problem," I mean both the existential struggle with the reality of רע as well as the intellectual challenge posed by the existence of רע in a world that is believed to be created and governed by an all-good, all-powerful God.

sin are theologically problematic in a world that is believed to have been created by, and to be governed by, a beneficent supreme Divine Being.[8]

Laato and de Moor survey a variety of schemes for categorizing approaches to theodicy in the Hebrew Bible.[9] For the sake of maximal consistency in the discourse, I employ their taxonomy here:[10]

1. Retribution Theodicy
2. Educative Theodicy
3. Eschatological Theodicy
4. The Mystery of Theodicy[11]
5. Communion Theodicy
6. Human Determinism[12]

---

8. The premises of the trilemma, and perhaps the challenge itself, are fundamental to the canonical biblical tradition, in which God created the world to be good (טוב in Gen 1:4, 10, 12, 18, 21, 25) and even "very good," with טוב מאד associated particularly with the creation of human beings (Gen 1:31). The descriptor *omnipotent* is an overstatement, as Eberhard Bons pointed out in response to my oral presentation of this paper. The Hebrew Bible does not seem to attribute omnipotence to God, but rather a high degree of power. For some discussion of special aspects of the monotheistic context for considering the problem of theodicy, see Laato and de Moor, "Introduction," viii–xi, xx–xxiii. See also above.

9. Laato and de Moor include a brief survey of nonbiblical resolutions of the problem in which one or more of the premises of the trilemma is denied ("Introduction," xx–xxix). Green emphasizes that any theodicy—in the sense of a justification—will necessarily downplay or compromise at least one of the propositions. For example, some approaches open up the possibility that God may not be in absolute total control of the world, while others redefine suffering so that it is seen as a moral good rather than רע.

10. Laato and de Moor, "Introduction," xxx–liv, listed on xxx.

11. Laato and de Moor also use the label *Theodicy Deferred* for this category, to indicate that the process of theodicy is deferred, i.e., the struggle with the question or justification is put off, or deflected. This invites confusion with the eschatological theodicy in which the actual implementation of divine justice itself is viewed as deferred.

12. The determinist theodicy described by Laato and de Moor involves an acceptance of reality; it is fatalist in the philosophically submissive sense of the word. In the Hebrew Bible and in Second Temple writings, even the most deterministic works struggle with the problem of suffering and sin and tend to rely also on one of the other theodicies to confront the difficulty. For example, in Qohelet, determinism is not a coping mechanism for dealing with futility but a symptom and cause. The composition includes a variety of responses to the problem, including despair, relentless inquiry, and a shift to anthropodicy. Only the coda advocates acceptance, and it does

The first four of these six categories are relevant for evaluating the theodicy and genre of the Psalms of Solomon, and they frame the following discussion. Psalms of Solomon 2 serves as my exemplar for the retribution theodicy, which is foundational for the composition. The educative and eschatological theodicies are prominent in a number of psalms, as variants or supplements to the basic retribution theodicy. I do not detect the mystery theodicy in the Psalms of Solomon. Rather, I explore the possibility that the composition may constitute a reaction to the notion of the inscrutability of divine justice.

The premise of the retribution theodicy is that if suffering exists as a punishment for human wrong-doing, then human suffering is, in fact, good and not bad. The natural world order is just.[13] Suffering need not be viewed as a theological problem because it is a basic component of divine justice and is experienced as a deserved and fair consequence of sin. This view is fundamental to much of biblical and early postbiblical Jewish literature, and it is foundational to the Psalms of Solomon. The retribution theodicy is articulated especially throughout Pss. Sol. 2. Thus, Pss. Sol. 2.3–4 reads:

> 3. *Because* [ἀνθ' ὧν] the sons of Jerusalem had defiled the sanctuary of the Lord, had profaned the gifts of God with acts of lawlessness. 4. *Because of these things* [ἕνεκεν τούτων] he said: Cast them far from me.

Similarly, verse 7 states: "According to their sins [κατὰ τὰς ἁμαρτίας αὐτῶν] he dealt with them."[14] This latter expression hints at an especially

---

so in a way that is closer to the mystery theodicy. In apocalyptic literature, determinism is built into a belief in precise cosmic order and an affirmation that divine justice will prevail; it is a function of an eschatological theodicy. On free will in the Psalms of Solomon, see Eberhard Bons, "Philosophical Vocabulary in the Psalms of Solomon: The Case of Ps. Sol. 9:4," in Bons and Pouchelle, *Psalms of Solomon*, 49–58.

13. See Jonathan P. Burnside, "Rethinking Natural Law," section vii of ch. 3 in *God, Justice, and Society: Aspects of Law and Legality in the Bible* (Oxford: Oxford University Press, 2011), 92–101.

14. Cf. Pss. Sol. 2.25, "Do not delay, O God, to *repay* them [ἀποδοῦναι] on their heads, to declare in *dishonor* the *arrogance* of the dragon"; and 2.31, "It is he who raises me up to *glory* and puts the arrogant to sleep for everlasting destruction in *dishonor, because* they knew him not." Embry describes the cause-effect relationship in Pss. Sol. 2 in terms of covenantal relationship ("Genre Categorization," 70). Werline

strong form of the retribution theodicy, the principle of fitting the punishment to the crime. The belief in such divine poetic justice, which is related to the civic legal principle of *lex talionis*, later finds fuller expression in the rabbinic *measure for measure*.[15] The principle is possibly implied in verses 8–9, where the reason given for divine inattention to the people ("turned away his face") is "for they had done evil once again in not listening." It is evidenced in verse 13:

> And the daughters of Jerusalem were *profane* (or "polluted" [βέβηλοι]) according to [κατὰ] your judgment, because [ἀνθ' ὧν] they had *defiled themselves* with improper intercourse.

---

emphasizes the Deuteronomic ideology of sin-punishment in the covenantal political framework of the Psalms of Solomon ("Psalms of Solomon and the Ideology of Rule," 72–74).

15. Cf. t. Soṭah 3:1–4, 10, "By the same measure by which a man metes out, so too is meted out to him" (and similarly, Matt 7:1–2; Mark 4:24), and in later amoraic terminology, "measure for measure." Comprehensive discussion of the theological principle and its variegated applications and functions in ancient Jewish literature is found in Yehoshua Amir, "Measure for Measure in Talmudic Literature and in the Wisdom of Solomon," in *Justice and Righteousness: Biblical Themes and Their Influence*, ed. Henning Graf Reventlow and Yair Hoffman (Sheffield: JSOT Press, 1992), 29–46. See also, Ishay Rosen-Zvi, *The Mishnaic Sotah Ritual: Temple, Gender and Midrash*, JSJSup 160 (Leiden: Brill, 2012). In the Wisdom of Solomon, the description of the divine punishment of the Egyptians through the plagues, and of divine beneficence to Israel in the wilderness, is summarized as: "one is punished by the very things by which one sins" (11:16); "for through the very things by which their enemies were punished, they themselves received benefit" (11:5); and "for by the same means by which you punished our enemies you called us to yourself and and glorified us" (18:8). On the connection between the civil law of talion and conceptions of divine justice, see Chrysostome Larcher, *Le Livre de la Sagasse ou la Sagesse de Salomon* (Paris: Librairie Lecoffre, 1985), 656–59; Sandra Jacobs, "Natural Law, Poetic Justice and the Talionic Formulation," *Political Theology* 14 (2013): 691–99; John Barton, "Natural Law and Poetic Justice in the Old Testament," *JTS* 30 (1979): 1–14. For ancient Mesopotamian thought on this widespread premise, see Sandra Jacobs, "Talion: The Divine Prerogative," in Sandra Jacobs, *The Body as Property: Physical Disfigurement in Biblical Law*, LHBOTS 582 (London: Bloomsbury T&T Clark, 2014), 77–78; for Graeco-Roman sources, see Jan Rothkamm, *Talio esto: Recherches sur les origines de la formule 'œil pour œil, dent pour dent' dans les droits du Proche-Orient ancien, et sur son devenir dans le monde gréco-romain* (Berlin: de Gruyter, 2011).

The idea of matching the punishment to the transgression intersects with the trope of God as judge, particularly a righteous judge, as in verse 18, "God is a righteous judge, and is not impressed by appearances."[16] This in turn is associated with the metaphor of God as king, and king of kings in verses 30–32:

> 30. He is king over the heavens, also judging kings and authorities.... 32. And now see, the nobles of the earth, the judgment of the Lord, for he is a great and righteous king, judging what is under heaven.[17]

With the emphasis on justice, retribution is one side of the coin of belief in divine recompense, the other being reward, and specifically the reward of the righteous.[18] Dualistic presentations of reward and punishment are frequent in biblical and postbiblical literature, often with theological as well as literary stylistic valence.[19] Psalms of Solomon 2 generally adopts the most conventional form of the retribution theodicy, in which suffering is the lot of sinners and not the righteous, as stated explicitly in verse 16 above. This dualism is assumed also in the conclusion of the psalm:

---

16. For God as judge, see, e.g., Pss. Sol. 4.24; 8.23–26; 9.2 It is noteworthy that one of the key functions of the messianic ruler in Pss. Sol. 17 is to judge. Many of the attributes of this Davidic king (as compiled and discussed in Joseph L. Trafton, "What Would David Do? Messianic Expectations and Surprise in Ps. Sol. 17," in Bons and Pouchelle, *Psalms of Solomon*, 155–74), are pervasive in descriptions of God throughout the Psalms of Solomon.

17. For God as king, see also Pss. Sol. 5.18–19; 17.3, 46, and the previous footnote. For the connection between law and theology in conceptions of divine kingship and theodicy, see Reinhard Gregor Kratz, *Das Judentum im Zeitalter des Zweiten Tempels*, FAT 42 (Tübingen: Mohr Siebeck, 2004), 187–226.

18. On individual reward and punishment in ancient Jewish thought, see Jonathan Klawans, *Josephus and the Theologies of Ancient Judaism* (Oxford: Oxford University Press, 2012), esp. chapter 2 on divine providence.

19. See Matthew Goff, "Looking for Sapiential Dualism at Qumran," in *Dualism in Qumran*, ed. Géza G. Xeravits (London: T&T Clark, 2010), 20–38, and the sources cited there; Miryam Brand, *Evil within and Without: The Source of Sin and Its Nature as Portrayed in Second Temple Literature* (Göttingen: Vandenhoeck & Ruprecht, 2013); Winninge on the doctrine of retribution in *Sinners and the Righteous*, 179. Gray ("Psalms of Solomon," 2:628) comments on the dualistic division in the Psalms of Solomon and in many biblical psalms and lists terminology employed for sinners and the righteous.

> 34. to separate between righteous and sinner, to repay [ἀποδοῦναι] the sinners forever according to their works. 35. And to have mercy [ἐλεῆσαι] on the righteous from the humiliation of the sinner, and to repay [ἀποδοῦναι] the sinner for what he has done to the righteous. 36. For the Lord is kind [χρηστὸς] to all those who call on him with endurance, treating his devout according to his mercy, setting them continuously before him in strength.

Embedded in this affirmation of divine justice, however, is a recognition of one of the conventional challenges to the retribution theodicy: the empirical reality of the suffering of the righteous. By charging the sinner with victimization of the righteous, the psalmist acknowledges that the righteous experience affliction. He does not address the question of the (in)justice of this pain but only indirectly minimalizes the problem by emphasizing relief through divine salvation, and by introducing the quality of mercy. Earlier, in verse 14, the psalmist referred to his own personal anguish. There, the near-complaint is counter-balanced by his affirmation that the painful reality that he has witnessed is ultimately good because it is the implementation of divine justice. Belief in divine retribution is thus explicitly designated as the basis for the psalmist's theodicy, in the narrow sense of justification of God:

> 14. I am troubled in my heart/entrails and my inward parts over these things. 15. I will justify you, O God, in uprightness of heart, for in your judgments is your righteousness, O God. 16. For you have repaid the sinners according to [κατὰ] their works, and according to [κατὰ] their sins, which were very wicked.[20]

Psalms of Solomon 2 also addresses another challenge to the retribution theodicy: the ethical problem of punishing those who serve as instruments for divine punishment of Israel.[21] The psalmist resolves this

---

20. Werline ("Psalms of Solomon and the Ideology of Rule," 73) aptly identifies this verse as typifying a *Gerichtsdoxologie*, using the terminology of Gerhard von Rad (*Theologie des Alten Testaments*, vol. 1 [Munich: Kaiser, 1957], 354–55, following Friedrich Horst, "Die Doxologien im Amosbuch," *ZAW* 47 [1929]: 45–54). See also Rodney A. Werline, "The Formation of the Pious Person in the Psalms of Solomon," in Bons and Pouchelle, *Psalms of Solomon*, 139–47.

21. A *locus classicus* for this problem in modern scholarship is the hardening of Pharaoh's heart. See Cornelis Houtman, "Theodicy in the Pentateuch," in Laato and de

problem by pointing to the enemies' selfish motivations in verse 24: "For it was not out of zeal that they acted, but out of the desire of the soul, so as to pour out their wrath upon us in plunder." The culpability and instrumentality of the enemy are reflected also in the opening verses of the psalm: "When the sinner became proud, he struck down fortified walls … and you did not prevent him" (2.1), and "he abandoned them into the hands of those who prevail" (2.7). Throughout the psalm, the focus of the accusation is upon the enemy, with God refraining from preventing the enemy, though 2.22 does venture further in addressing God: "your hand has been heavy on Jerusalem in bringing the nations upon her."[22]

Most noteworthy in Pss. Sol. 2 is how both of these conventional challenges—empirical evidence of the suffering of the righteous and the punishments of the agents of retribution—are harnessed to *support* the retribution theodicy. The psalmist appeals to empirical evidence in his claim that Pompey's dramatically ignominious death was a direct (measure-for-measure) divine punishment for his insolent arrogance:

> 26. And I did not wait long until God showed me his insolence, pierced, on the mountains of Egypt, more than the least despised on land and sea. 27. His body, carried about on the waves in great insolence, and there was no one to bury, for he had rejected him in dishonor.

This is an unusual case in which observed reality is brought to support the retribution theodicy, rather than to challenge it. In his framing of this evidence, the psalmist makes a particularly strong case for the efficacy of supplicative prayer.[23] Psalms of Solomon 2 asserts experientially, not just theoretically, that the wicked king received recompense and that this followed from the psalmist's prayer. The efficacy of prayer is a common tenet in many texts that feature the retribution theodicy and an essential premise of penitential prayers.[24] Psalms of Solomon 2.22–25 records

---

Moor, *Theodicy*, 168–71. The question is contextualized within the larger problem of determinism and free will.

22. See Werline, "Experience of God's *Paideia*," 31–32.

23. See section 3.1 below, on the generally lamented mismatch between experience and doctrine.

24. See Rodney A. Werline, *Penitential Prayer in Second Temple Judaism: The Development of a Religious Institution*, EJL 13 (Atlanta: Scholars Press, 1998).

the psalmist's prayer for revenge upon the enemy nations headed by the arrogant dragon. God's prompt slaying of Pompey in 2.26–29 exemplifies both the reward of the righteous, by hearkening to their prayers, and the punishment of sinners in Pompey's humiliating demise.[25]

2.2. Educative Theodicy and Eschatological Theodicy

Like the retribution theodicy, the educative and eschatological theodicies adopt the theological stance that suffering results from sin. They address the observable and troubling fact that, in actual experience, suffering is not limited to sinners and some sinners do not suffer but rather prosper. Presuming a dualistic system of divine justice, the educative theodicy primarily attempts to respond to the question: how can an all-powerful good and just God cause *the righteous* to suffer? Above, I noted that Pss. Sol. 2 makes some allowance for this reality and copes with it by downplaying the degree to which the righteous suffer (Pss. Sol. 2.35) and emphasizing relief through divine intervention. Elsewhere in the Psalms of Solomon we find more direct engagement with the problem of the suffering of the righteous and attempted resolutions, especially the educative and eschatological theodicies.[26] The eschatological theodicy addresses the prosperity of the wicked as well as the suffering of the righteous.[27]

---

25. The theodicy of Pss. Sol. 8 shares many features with Pss. Sol. 2, and similarly focuses on the retribution theodicy, including empirical evidence of God's justice. It describes how the wicked nations wrought destruction upon Jerusalem, as punishment for the extreme sinfulness of the city's inhabitants, with allusive reference to specific current events (8.15–21). This psalm is generally dated after Pompey's invasion, but before his death, and its prayer contains supplication and affirmation of trust, but no thanksgiving. Pss. Sol. 8.5 is similar to 2.14, in describing the anguish of the (righteous) psalmist, followed by justification through consideration of God's just judgments in Pss. Sol. 8.7 as in Pss. Sol. 2, and again in vv. 23–26. Unlike Pss. Sol. 2, Pss. Sol. 8 explicitly describes the hiddenness of the sins prior to divine exposure (8.8–10).

26. Below, I address the approach based on hiddenness, which accounts for situations in which righteous people seem to suffer by maintaining that the sufferers are in fact wicked, having sinned in secret.

27. In much later eras, reconceptualizations of the educative theodicy came to be used also to address the prosperity of the wicked, to the extent that comfort and success came to be sources of anxiety. See, e.g., Gregory the Great's *Moralia on Job*, cited in Sarot, "Theodicy and Modernity," 17.

Educative Theodicy

The educative theodicy admits that the righteous do, in fact, suffer but maintains that this reality brings about atonement and repentance. If suffering is a form of *discipline* of the righteous, then it is, in fact, not bad but good. It is a means toward ensuring a greater more lasting goodness, and as such it may even be seen as yet another form of reward for the righteous—an expression of divine mercy as well as justice.

The most succinct and vivid formulation of the educative theodicy in the Psalms of Solomon is at 16.4: "He pricked me, like a goad for a horse, that I might awaken unto Him." Psalms of Solomon 10 offers another prominent example:

> 1. Happy is the man whom the Lord remembers with reproving, and who is *fenced from the evil road* by a whip, that he may be cleansed from sin, *that it may not increase*. 2. He who prepares his back for lashes will be cleansed, for the Lord is kind to those who endure discipline. 3 For he will *straighten the ways of the righteous*, and will not turn them aside by discipline.

This passage lends support to both of the two important explanations that recent scholarship has offered for the function of *paideia* in the Psalms of Solomon: atonement and behavior modification. Mikael Winninge describes the primary function of discipline in the Psalms of Solomon as cleansing, a process in which the righteous earn forgiveness through submission to the divine will.[28] Atkinson similarly emphasizes atonement and maintains further that divine discipline serves to keep the righteous within a covenantal relationship.[29] On the other hand, Rodney Werline and Patrick Pouchelle have effectively demonstrated the pragmatic role of *paideia* in the Psalms of Solomon.[30] The suffering of the righteous does not only

---

28. Winninge, *Sinners and the Righteous*, 136–40.
29. Atkinson, "Theodicy," 562–72.
30. Werline, "Experience of God's *Paideia*," esp. 27–31, 44; Patrick Pouchelle, "Prayers for Being Disciplined: Notes on παιδεύω and παιδεία in the Psalms of Solomon," in Bons and Pouchelle, *Psalms of Solomon*, 115–32. More generally, on *paideia* as a theological concept in biblical and classical writings, see now Patrick Pouchelle, *Dieu éducateur: Une nouvelle approche d'un concept de la théologie biblique entre Bible Hébraïque, Septante et littérature grecque classique* (Tübingen: Mohr Siebeck, 2015).

wipe clear heavenly ledgers, to use the metaphor that is implicit in Winninge's and Atkinson's views.[31] Rather, it serves as an alarm notification to enable them to alter their deeds. This is not a simple grace that counteracts or tempers justice with mercy but is an educative process that promotes justice, preventing further sin and ensuring that the righteous behave righteously and thereby earn their just reward.[32] The transformative educative purpose of *paideia* is highlighted in Pss. Sol. 3:

> 4. The righteous does not despise being disciplined [παιδευόμενος] by the Lord; his good will is always before the Lord. 5. The righteous stumbled and justified the Lord; he fell and watches what God will do for him; he eagerly watches whence his salvation will come. 6. The truth of the righteous is from their divine savior; in the house of the righteous sin upon sin does not lodge. 7. *The righteous always searches his house, to remove his injustice in transgression.* 8. He made atonement for sins of ignorance by fasting and humiliation (/afflicting) of his soul, and the Lord cleanses every devout man and his house.

Psalms of Solomon 3 is primarily a psalm in praise of the righteous, stating that it is the nature of the righteous person who sins to continue to look to God and to search his house in order to improve his ways.[33] From another angle, the passage offers an implicit defense of God, presuming the educative theodicy.[34] The punitive suffering of the righteous is justified because it serves as a means to get the righteous to investigate and improve their ways. The propensity to self-examination is both a testament to the merits of the righteous, for which he deserves divine reward, and a testament to

---

31. Gary A. Anderson, *Sin: A History* (New Haven: Yale University Press, 2009). Cf. Pss. Sol. 13.10, below.

32. See Pss. Sol. 16.11, "if I sin, you discipline me to return to you"; 18.4 "to turn back the obedient soul from ignorant stupidity"; 18.8, "to direct a man in works of righteousness in fear of God." Pouchelle ("Prayers for Being Disciplined," 132) notes similarities in Ben Sira (see esp. 23:2–3) and 2 Maccabees and cites the later formulation in the Talmud, b. Ber. 5a, "if a man sees suffering coming upon him, let him scrutinize his actions."

33. See Atkinson, "Theodicy," 556; cf. the expectations of the protagonist's friends in the book of Job.

34. The text presumes an educative theodicy, such that this praiseworthy soul-searching and rehabilitation is an actualization of the result intended by God.

the justice and mercy of God, through which God enables his faithful followers to attain righteous behavior, through which they will merit divine reward.

Psalms of Solomon 13.7 takes care to distinguish between the retribution meted out to sinners and the educative punishment of the righteous:

> 7. For not the same is the discipline of the righteous [παιδεία] [for sins done] in ignorance, and the destruction of the sinners. 8. The righteous is disciplined [παιδεύεται] with distinctness[35] so that the sinner may not rejoice over the righteous. 9. For he will admonish the righteous as a beloved son, and his discipline is as that of a firstborn. 10. For the Lord will spare his devout and will wipe away their transgressions with discipline. 11. For the life of the righteous is forever, but sinners shall be taken away into destruction, and their memorial shall never be found.

The element of secrecy and sins committed "in ignorance" in 13.7–8 is taken up below. With its references to eternity, the passage also invokes Laato and de Moor's third category, the eschatological theodicy. As noted by Pouchelle, in Pss. Sol. 17 and 18 one of the blessings of the messianic era is that the righteous will be "under the rod of discipline of the Lord's anointed."[36] Divine discipline is viewed so positively that it not only justifies current suffering but is retained as an ideal in the vision of the future righteous society.

Eschatological Theodicy

This approach again presumes the basic foundation of a retribution theodicy. A noteworthy feature of the eschatological theodicy is that it often addresses the problem of an *absence* of suffering. It responds to the empirical observation of the flourishing of sinners as well as the suffering of the righteous, by assuring a future rectification of the current injustice.[37]

---

35. See Pouchelle, "Prayers for Being Disciplined," 125–27, on the difficulty of the word περιστολῇ here.

36. Pouchelle, "Prayers for Being Disciplined," 130.

37. The most developed future-oriented theodicies in the Hebrew Bible and early postbiblical writings anticipate an end-time, but this is not always the case. Even texts that refer to ʿahryt hymym may not necessarily refer to the end of days.

Adapting Gershom Scholem's distinction between "restorative" and "utopian" messianism, we can discern two types of eschatological ideals in the Psalms of Solomon: a *historical* messianic theodicy found especially in Pss. Sol. 17, and an eternal *transhistorical* theodicy, which is prominent in Pss. Sol. 12–15, particularly in the conclusions of these psalms.[38]

Unlike most of the incipits in the Psalms of Solomon, the heading of Pss. Sol. 17 is representative of the content of the psalm and may even be original: "A Psalm. Pertaining to Solomon. With Song. Pertaining to the King." This psalm asserts that justice will prevail in the future at a national level, and 17.21–44 describes in detail how this will be achieved through the restoration of a Davidic messiah ruling from Jerusalem.[39] Elsewhere in the Psalms of Solomon a number of passages feature a *transhistorical* theodicy, declaring the everlasting destruction of sinners and eternal reward of the righteous, including eternal life. So, for example, Pss. Sol. 13.11 cited above and Pss. Sol. 14:

> 1. Faithful is the Lord to those who love him in truth, to those who endure his discipline, 2. to those who walk in the righteousness of his ordinances, in the law which he commanded us that we might live.[40] 3. The devout of the Lord shall live by it *forever*; the orchard of the Lord, the *trees of life*, are his devout. 4. Their plant-

---

On the question of whether *'ahryt hymym* ought to be interpreted as signifying last days or simply latter days, see Annette Steudel, "B'hryt hymym in the Texts from Qumran," *RevQ* 16 (1993): 225–46, and the sources cited there, as well as Laato and de Moor, "Introduction," xlliv.

38. See Gershom Scholem, *The Messianic Idea in Judaism* (New York: Schocken, 1971), 1–36. In Second Temple studies, Scholem's model has been adopted, inter alia, by Shemaryahu Talmon, "Types of Messianic Expectation at the Turn of the Era," in *King, Cult, and Ancient Israel* (Jerusalem: Magnes, 1987), 202–24; Talmon, "The Concepts of Masîaḥ and Messianism in Early Judaism," in *The Messiah: Developments in Earliest Judaism and Christianity*, ed. James H. Charlesworth (Minneapolis: Fortress, 1992), 79–115; and Lawrence H. Schiffman, "Messianic Figures and Ideas in the Qumran Scrolls," in Charlesworth, *Messiah*, 270–85. On a related, but not identical, distinction between historical and transcendent eschatology, see John J. Collins, *The Apocalyptic Imagination: An Introduction to Jewish Apocalyptic Literature*, 3rd ed. (Grand Rapids: Eerdmans, 2016), 14–15.

39. See also the conclusion of Pss. Sol. 7, "And you will direct us in the time of your help, showing mercy to the house of Jacob on the day you promised them" (v. 10).

40. Cf. Deut 4:1; 5:33; 8:1: (ן)למען תחיו; Jer 35:7: למען תחיו ימים רבים על האדמה. The psalmist takes "life" to indicate eternal life.

ing is rooted *forever*; they shall not be plucked up *all the days of heaven*.... 9. Therefore their ["the sinners and transgressors of the law"] inheritance is Hades and darkness and destruction, and they shall not be found in the day when the righteous obtain mercy. 10. But the devout of the Lord shall inherit life with joy.

Similarly, Pss. Sol. 15.10–13 reads:

10. And the inheritance of sinners is destruction and darkness, and their acts of lawlessness shall pursue them to Hades below. 11. Their inheritance shall not be found for their children, for sins shall lay waste the houses of sinners. 12. And sinners shall perish *forever* in the day of the Lord's judgment, when God visits the earth with His judgment. 13. But those who fear the Lord shall find mercy on it, and they shall live by the mercy of their God; but sinners shall perish *forever* and anon.[41]

A theme that may perhaps be related to eternal reward and punishment is the depiction of ignominious death as retribution for sin.[42] In addition to the death of Pompey in Pss. Sol. 2, this is attested in the prayer in Pss. Sol. 4, detailing the punishments that the psalmist asks God to inflict upon the hypocrites, including, "may the flesh of the men-pleasers be scattered by wild beasts, and may the bones of the transgressors lie before the sun in dishonor. May ravens pick out the eyes of hypocrites" (4.18–20).[43]

---

41. See also, Pss. Sol. 12.6 ("The salvation of the Lord is upon Israel his servant forever, and may the sinners perish altogether from the presence of the Lord, and may the devout of the Lord inherit the promises of the Lord"); Pss. Sol. 3.9–12. On the question of whether the Psalms of Solomon attests to a belief in resurrection, see Atkinson, "Theodicy," 572 n. 72. Note that references to eternal reward in Second Temple literature are often vague and general, and it is frequently unclear whether mention of eternal life in a given text refers to immortality of the soul or bodily resurrection. See Klawans, *Josephus*, 92–136.

42. Cf. Doron Mendels, "A Note on the Tradition of Antiochus IV's Death," *IEJ* 31 (1981): 53–56. For biblical roots of this trope, see, e.g., the talionic death of Absalom (2 Sam 14:25–26; cf. 2 Sam 18:9, m. Soṭah 1:8); the death of Jezebel (2 Kgs 9; cf. Jacobs, *Body as Property*, 71–72).

43. See also Pss. Sol. 13.3. The graphic curse in Pss. Sol. 4 calls to mind biblical and classical descriptions of crucifixion. Cf. Shani L. Berrin [Tzoref], *The Pesher Nahum Scroll from Qumran: An Exegetical Study of 4Q169*, STDJ 53 (Leiden: Brill,

Consistent with Scholem's rubric, the historical restorative vision in the Psalms of Solomon is concerned primarily with the well-being of the nation, while references to eternity focus more on personal reward. Both of these are combined in Pss. Sol. 18.7–8. From an even broader perspective, the most striking reflection of a temporal theodicy in the Psalms of Solomon is not its affirmation of future latter or last days but the insistence that present reality validates divine justice.

2.3. Mystery of Theodicy

The mystery-of-theodicy approach to the problem of suffering sees God as transcendent and unfathomable, so that human perception of injustice in the world is indicative of humans' incapability to comprehend divine justice. Even more than the educative and eschatological theodicies, this approach struggles with the dissonance between doctrinal assertions of divine retributive justice and observed reality. It is typical of works generally described as "skeptical" or even "anti-wisdom," such as Qohelet and Job. This is quite different from the stance we have seen in the Psalms of Solomon, which affirms the manifestation of God's justice rather than the unknowability of his ways. The Psalms of Solomon does, however, exhibit great interest in hidden transgressions, God's omniscience, and the limitations of human knowledge. The mystery approach to theodicy challenges conventional views about retribution and settles for a quasi-resolution by determining that comprehension of such hidden things must remain in the heavenly domain. The Psalms of Solomon utilizes the concept of hiddenness to *affirm* the retribution theodicy, and it represents human experience as visible evidence of the results of divine omniscience. What is notable about the Psalms of Solomon is that unlike many Second Temple compositions that are concerned with the imperfection of human knowledge and divine revelation, this composition maintains that knowledge

---

2004). As a stereotypical denigration, it is unlikely to offer a clue to the historical provenance of the Psalms of Solomon or to the identity of these opponents, particularly if the text is taken at face value as having been composed prior to the anticipated punishment. If taken as an *ex eventu* declaration, it could carry more historical valence. Pesher Nahum is generally understood to apply the reference to carrion in Nah 2:12 to Alexander Jannaeus's crucifixion of his Pharisaic opponents, which raises resonances with the "hypocrites" and "man-pleasers" who are the targets of the psalmist's anger in Pss. Sol. 4.

of good and evil, and reward and punishment, can be attained through empirical observation rather than being mediated through textual or scholarly instruction. As noted in the previous section, the faithful are portrayed as direct recipients of divine instruction, as they observe the suffering of the wicked through divine retribution and their own suffering as divine discipline toward righteousness.

Hiddenness: Concealed Sins and Inadvertent Sins

Psalms of Solomon 1 presents an unusual variation on the retribution and eschatological (or temporal) theodicies. Retribution theodicy is the unstated premise of this lament by personified Zion. She had presumed that her security was guaranteed by the righteousness of her inhabitants (1.2), but experience proved otherwise. The psalm resolves the problem by asserting that Zion's children did in fact deserve severe punishment, only this had not been widely recognized since they sinned in secret.[44] A similar theme is taken up in Pss. Sol. 4, in the harsh condemnation of the hypocrites, or "man-pleasers," who maintain an outward appearance of propriety while secretly transgressing. In Pss. Sol. 9.3, the psalmist affirms that God's omniscience ensures his just punishment of concealed sins: "For none that does injustice will be hidden from your knowledge" (cf. Pss. Sol. 14.8–9).

There is another set of references to hidden sins of a different sort—the unknown sins of the righteous, which are made known to them through God's discipline and through fear of God's discipline, as discussed above in the context of the educative theodicy.[45] In contrast to the sinful man-pleasers, the righteous worship God in truth (ἐν ἀληθείᾳ) (Pss. Sol. 3.6; 6.9; 10.3, 14.1, 15.2, 16.10). Their sins are committed in ignorance.

---

44. See Atkinson, "Theodicy," 556. The psalmist copes with the fact that reality does not seem to match the presuppositions of conventional retribution theodicy by reinterpreting reality in an attempt to preserve and reassert the theodicy: Zion's suffering is just recompense for its sins, hitherto undisclosed. The earlier prosperity of Zion's children had been mistakenly attributed to their presumed righteousness, and it was only upon their experiencing divine retribution that their hidden sinfulness became exposed.

45. See Atkinson, "Theodicy," 546, 556; ἀγνοίᾳ in Pss. Sol. 3.7–8; 13.7; 18.4. The fact that punishment stimulates the righteous to search their sins in Pss. Sol. 3 highlights the point that his sins are inadvertent and unknown, in need of being uncovered.

I suggest that we can gain insight into the psalmists' concern with concealed sins by considering these texts in relation to the mystery of theodicy, within the context of recent research by Aharon Shemesh, Cana Werman, and myself on *nistarot* and *niglot* in the Dead Sea Scrolls and related literature. This recent scholarship has expanded upon Lawrence Schiffman's initial observation that the terms *niglot* and *nistarot* in Qumran texts function to distinguish between generally known laws that are explicitly recorded in the Torah and esoteric sectarian laws that were made known only to the members of the community.[46] In fact, both the rabbinic and the Qumranic corpora, as well as other Second Temple writings use the term *nistarot* to designate (1) eschatologically and theologically significant esoterica, or mysteries, (2) laws that become known through progressive revelation, and (3) juridical categories of transgressions.[47] Legal and regulatory ("rules") texts tend to use the word *nistarot* to denote laws or to describe culpability and punishments for hidden sins, while apocalyptic texts employ the term *nistarot* to refer to knowledge of transcendent matters. I have argued that the book of Jubilees applies the concepts of *niglot* and *nistarot* broadly, legally, judicially, and epistemologically.[48]

In the Psalms of Solomon, the theme of hiddenness recurs in the context of theological concern about divine punishment. Unlike the theological function of *nistarot* at Qumran, however, this interest in hiddenness does not tend to pertain to the revelation of esoteric knowledge but rather is of a judicial sort. Secrecy is primarily associated with concealed sins, which are known to God and exposed through divine retribution, and secondarily with inadvertent sins which are made known to righteous sinners through disciplinary suffering. The composition does engage with

---

46. Lawrence H. Schiffman, *The Halakhah at Qumran*, SJLA 16 (Leiden: Brill, 1975), 22–32.

47. The technical use of the terms derives from Deut 29:29[28], "The *secret things* belong to the Lord our God, but the *revealed things* belong to us and to our children forever, to observe all the words of this law." See Aharon Shemesh and Cana Werman, "Hidden Things and Their Revelation," *RevQ* 18 (1998): 409–27; Shani Tzoref, "The 'Hidden' and the 'Revealed': Esotericism, Election, and Culpability in Qumran and Related Literature," in *The Dead Sea Scrolls at Sixty: The Scholarly Contributions of NYU Faculty and Alumni*, ed. Lawrence H. Schiffman and Shani Tzoref, STDJ 89 (Leiden: Brill, 2010), 299–324, a translation and revision of Tzoref, "The 'Hidden' and the 'Revealed': Progressive Revelation of Law and Esoterica" [Hebrew], *Meghillot* 7 (2009): 157–90.

48. Tzoref, " 'Hidden' and the 'Revealed.' "

hiddenness in the context of a concern about knowledge, but it is not interested in human acquisition of legal, eschatological, or cosmological data through verbal or textual transmission, as in Qumran, rabbinic, and apocalyptic texts. Rather, the Psalms of Solomon seeks to identify and affirm the revelation of divine justice in human experience, particularly historical events. God knows the concealed sins of those who maintain a false appearance of righteousness, and he knows the inadvertent sins of the genuinely righteous of which they themselves might be unaware. When God punishes people for those sins, divine knowledge and righteous judgment become manifest, as in Pss. Sol. 2.17 "you have exposed their sins that your judgment might be evident."[49]

In response to claims of a disparity between observed reality and divine justice, the Psalms of Solomon affirms that experience actually corroborates belief in divine justice. Its educative and eschatological theodicies are distinctly nonmystery oriented. Knowledge of God's ways is not an unfathomable heavenly secret but is revealed on earth before our eyes. This affirmation is in contrast not only with the view of skeptics who believe that such understanding is unattainable, but also with the various forms of apocalyptic traditions which look to special revelation of heavenly wisdom to the elect, through texts, cryptic omens visions, and mediated instruction: Enoch, Daniel, Qumran instruction and mysteries texts, the Hodayot, and pesharim. Recent scholarship has appropriately rejected earlier identifications of the Psalms of Solomon as apocalyptic.[50] It is significant that there is not just an absence of concern with access to heavenly

---

49. Cf. Pss. Sol. 4.7; 8.8, 27–29; 9.3; Atkinson, "Theodicy," 556. It has been suggested that another form of secrecy is mentioned in Pss. Sol. 13.8, where it is stated that God punishes the righteous ἐν περιστολῇ so as to spare them from humiliation (see above). Following his thorough philological discussion of this word, Pouchelle concludes that it is unlikely that the text refers to the secret punishment of the righteous, since the whole point of the discipline is to reveal their sins so as to modify behavior ("Prayers for Being Disciplined," 125–27). Through comparison with Sir 23:2–3, he argues that the avoidance of humiliation is achieved by the prevention of further sin. The text remains difficult. A discrete punishment could reveal the sin of a righteous person to him while concealing it from his antagonists. Against this position is the fact that this idea does not appear elsewhere in the Psalms of Solomon, in contrast to most of the themes we have investigated which recur frequently, both implicitly and explicitly.

50. See Werline, "Psalms of Solomon and the Ideology of Rule"; Embry, "Genre Categorization," 65–66; Collins, *Apocalyptic Imagination*, 176–77.

secrets but a pointed alternative. The psalmists do not need the teachings of Enoch, or the Teacher of Righteousness, or a Mebin or a Maskil; they just need to be patient and observe reality.[51]

Perhaps a hint of an alternative approach related to the mystery theodicy may be found in one passage in Pss. Sol. 6 that addresses the suffering of the righteous. The overt message in these verses is an affirmation of the staunch faithfulness of the righteous ones, but the evocative description may belie the assertion of confidence: "His soul will not be disturbed with the sight of evil dreams; when he crosses rivers and when the seas swell, he will not be terrified" (Pss. Sol. 6.3). I propose, tentatively, a psychological interpretation of a form of theodicy in these verses, such that the psalmist is aiming to suppress his doubts and bolster a form of denial: the reference to dreams simultaneously offers a vivid representation of the relentlessness of the suffering and an attempt to disassociate the experience from reality.[52] Similarly, the metaphor of rivers and seas is at once a powerful image of tempestuousness and a sort of distancing from one's personal experience. The following verse poses a contrast: "He arose from his sleep and blessed the name of the Lord. In firmness of heart he sang a hymn to the name of his God."

Possibly in Pss. Sol. 6.3, and more definitively in the references to hiddenness and most explicitly in the descriptions of the punishment of Zion in Pss. Sol. 1, 2, 8, and 9, as well as of God's general kindness in Pss. Sol. 5, the Psalms of Solomon demonstrates the psalmists' concerted efforts to see actual experience as the fulfillment of their expectations about God.

---

51. In this, I would disagree with Atkinson's statement, "the writers of the Psalms of Solomon present a unique explanation of a theodicy that seeks to defend God's justice in the face of evidence which suggests that God is actually indifferent to the suffering of the righteous" ("Theodicy," 547). This is true for Pss. Sol. 1, with its creative resolution in terms of concealed sin. The general thrust of the composition, however, is that the evidence shows that God is very interested in the suffering of the righteous. As Atkinson himself states, discipline is viewed as a sign of God's mercy ("Theodicy," 565). As noted above, the anticipation of the messianic era is not an anticipation of the replacement of injustice with justice, but rather an expectation of a merging of justice and mercy, with the eradication of sinners and effective discipline of the righteous.

52. For disturbed sleep as a form of suffering, see Job 4:13–14 and the punishment that the Psalms of Solomon seeks for the man-pleasing sinners in 4.15–16. On sleep in the Psalms of Solomon, see Sven Behnke, "Die Rede vom Schlaf in den Psalmen Salomos und ihr traditionsgeschichtlicher Hintergrund," in Bons and Pouchelle, *Psalms of Solomon*, 97–114.

Summary of section 2: Divine retribution is presumed throughout the Psalms of Solomon in a dualistic system in which wicked sinners are justly punished whereas the righteous are treated mercifully. The educative and eschatological theodicies are attested as well, in particularly rationalist empiricist forms. The educative theodicy is manifest in two forms, as the suffering of the righteous both atones for their sins and guides them toward future righteous behavior. As such, it is a form of instruction. The eschatological theodicy is also represented in two conventional forms, anticipating both a messianic restoration as well as some kind of everlasting reward for the righteous, along with the eternal erasure of the sinners. The psalmist's triumph over the death of Pompey in Pss. Sol. 2, and even the hopeful reactions to the crisis of the enemy invasion, desecration, plunder and exile may also be seen as a sort of eschatological theodicy, or temporal theodicy, in the sense that it affirms God's just intervention in history, in due time. The psalmists seek to know God and to be assured of divine reward, but they do not yearn for special divine revelation through omens, esoteric traditions, or inspired exegesis. They express their confidence that experience alone is God's method of revealing good and evil and appropriate recompense for these.

3. Genre and Theodicy

3.1. Genre and Theodicy in the Hebrew Bible

The foregoing observations about the rationalist empirical approach of the Psalms of Solomon and its theodicies can enrich current discourse about the genre of the work. One interesting feature of Laato and de Moor's *Theodicy in the World of the Bible* is that a significant portion of the volume is structured canonically according to the books of the Hebrew Bible.[53] Although the editors do not explain the rationale for their decision, a distinct advantage to the arrangement is that it highlights a correlation between genre and approach to theodicy.[54]

---

53. A potential drawback of this structure is that it could give a misimpression of homogeneity, or of a logical or chronological linear development in the composition of the corpus.

54. The connection between genre and approach to theodicy is brought out in their overview of the categories of theodicy (Laato and de Moor, "Introduction," xxix–liv). See also Lorenzo DiTommaso's summary in his review of the volume: review of

Laato and de Moor situate basic retribution theodicy of the Hebrew Bible within the framework of Covenant Theology, which is "deeply rooted in the ancient Near Eastern culture." They specify "ancient law documents," vassal treaties, and "the ancient oriental wisdom literature" as influential formal precursors.[55] The retribution theodicy thus underlies Pentateuchal legal texts and drives much of the national historical narrative in the Hebrew Bible, with some variation in emphasis, for example, on covenant (the Deuteronomistic History), divine grace (Ezra and Nehemiah), or divine reward (Chronicles).[56] In biblical sapiential tradition, the retribution theodicy is assumed as a framework for understanding and guiding personal experience and behavior. One can find roots for this conception of retribution as *Erfahrungswissen* ("knowledge from experience") in ancient Near Eastern sapiential writings, and it is the underlying theology of the Babylonian Theodicy.[57] All of these biblical genres and corresponding approaches to the retribution theodicy have left their mark on the Psalms of Solomon.

The correlation between genre and the educative theodicy in the Hebrew Bible is more complex. Laato and de Moor identify the chief expressions of the educative theodicy in the book of Job and some additional wisdom writings, in postexilic historical narrative, and in some strata of prophecy.[58] The understanding that the sinner is chastised for his

---

Antti Laato and Johannes C. de Moor, eds., *Theodicy in the World of the Bible: The Goodness of God and the Problem of Evil*, RBL (February 2007).

55. Laato and de Moor, "Introduction," xxx–xxxviii (the quoted text is on xxx).

56. See Antti Laato, "Theodicy in the Deuteronomic History," in Laato and de Moor, *Theodicy*, 183–235; Sara Japhet, "Theodicy in Ezra-Nehemiah and Chronicles," in Laato and de Moor, *Theodicy*, 429–69.

57. Karel van der Toorn, "Theodicy in Akkadian Literature," in Laato and de Moor, *Theodicy*, 57–89.

58. Laato and de Moor, "Introduction," xxxix–xli. Again, comparison with Babylonian precursors is illuminating. Cf. van der Toorn, "Theodicy in Akkadian Literature." The educative theodicy is particularly prominent in the book of Ben Sira (cf. Kratz, *Das Judentum*, 187–226). Exodus and Numbers contain notices to the educational function of suffering in these accounts, including the idea that Pharaoh's suffering was intended to educate Israel and other nations about the greatness of God. Jethro's statement, "Now I know that God is great, for by the matter in which they schemed against them" (Exod 18:11), is possibly the basis for the development of the measure for measure principle in these narratives, e.g., in the Wisdom of Solomon (see above). From this perspective, God's greatness was made known to all because of how the plagues fit the crimes. The verse was likely taken as elliptically stating that "by

own good in order to learn from the experience is well-suited to a wisdom orientation, with its emphasis on empirical knowledge and pedagogy.

The eschatological theodicy is naturally associated primarily with prophetic and apocalyptic writings, and it also appears in some sapiential psalms.[59]

The mystery theodicy is typical of late works that reacted to conventional sapiential affirmations of divine justice. With some adjustments, Klaus Koch's description of *Tun-Ergehen-Zusammenhang* as a fundamental principle of biblical sapiential texts has stood the test of time. The concept of deed-consequence connection, which underlies the retribution theodicy, posits a direct cause and effect between sinful action and suffering, and righteous—and wise—action and reward. This *Weltanschauung* supposes a world that is ordered and rational and therefore fair and good.[60] Justice is presumed as a positive reality. People must learn and adopt righteous behavior in order to benefit from divine justice. In many biblical psalms, however, as in Lamentations and the books of Job and Qohelet, the doctrine of retribution is "experienced as a problem" rather than functioning as an effective theodicy strategy.[61] This is due to the dissonance between the conventional belief and reality as lived and observed.

---

the very matter in which the Egyptians schemed [so did God punish them]." Measure for measure retribution is thus not only an effective legal and judicial principle, but also an effective instructional tool.

59. Laato and de Moor, "Introduction," xxxii–xxxiii, xlii–xlv.

60. In some texts, there is a conflation of natural consequences of righteous conduct and divine reward. Cf. Werline, "Experience of God's Paideia," 30. Japhet is careful to note that this is not the case in Chronicles: "Yet we should be careful not to mistake this aspect of retribution for an 'automatic' result of the deed itself. It is always the retributive act of God, not the inherent, mechanical reaction of the deed" (Japhet, "Theodicy in Ezra-Nehemiah and Chronicles," 459). A somewhat atypical perspective on theodicy is found in Pss. Sol. 2.9: "And the heaven was weighed down and the earth detested them." In the Hebrew Bible, the two main processes through which suffering is understood to result from sin are either divine intervention or direct, natural, consequence. Pss. Sol. 2.9 presents a more metaphysical variation of consequence, which is reminiscent of the common ancient Near Eastern formulae of curses and blessings that have been adopted in some of the covenantal language of Deuteronomy.

61. Fredrik Lindström, "Theodicy in the Psalms," in Laato and de Moor, *Theodicy*, 256–303. The summary quotation is from Laato and de Moor, "Introduction," xxxiii. This is true of corresponding genres in Akkadian literature as well. See van der Toorn, "Theodicy in Akkadian Literature," on Babylonian penitential psalms and their resolutions to the problem (62); on Man and His God (63–64); and on the Babylonian Theodicy (65–76).

In the classic sapiential tradition, knowledge, including knowledge about reward and punishment and about how to achieve proper conduct, is achieved through instruction and through empirical observation, *Erfahrungswissen*. Wisdom texts aim not only to instruct their pupils toward specific proper conduct but more generally to instruct toward acceptance of a traditional sapiential worldview itself. This pedagogical priority can be effective to the extent that the instruction is grounded in tradition—the teaching of the fathers. But since wisdom texts also give great weight to empirical observation, the concept of *Tun-Ergehen-Zusammenhang* can fail to satisfy, since it is falsifiable by actual observed reality.

Karel van der Toorn describes such an epistemological crisis, and a resolution, in Mesopotamian thought and literature. In the "traditional theology of the Mesopotamian scholars … the doctrine of retribution is a law of nature, so to speak, that does not require an act of disclosure on the part of the gods. It can be known from observation, extrapolation, and speculation on the principle of similarity." This tradition is reiterated in the skeptical Babylonian Theodicy 18, 21–22, even as this work also challenges the accepted premise that "when you look at humankind as a whole" this confirms that "he who looks to his gods has a protector, the humble man who fears his goddesses accumulates wealth."[62] Van der Toorn describes a "paradigm change" in first millennium Babylonian writings:

> The scepticism concerning the retribution doctrine voiced in the theodicy texts … forced the Babylonian scholars of the [first] millennium to reconsider the foundational foundations of their lore. The cuneiform tradition shows that the first millennium witnessed a development in which the corpus of codified knowledge was gradually brought under the banner of 'revelation.'

The traditional Babylonian sciences of divination, and then exorcism, were claimed to have "celestial origin[s]."

> In the course of the first millennium BCE the entire scholarly tradition as it was laid down in texts obtained the status of revealed knowledge. Texts of all genres had a colophon qualifying the contents of the tablets as secret…. Religious knowledge was also secret in the sense that it was,

---

62. Van der Toorn, "Theodicy in Akkadian Literature," 61.

by its very nature, hidden from human intelligence; it was a mystery that could only be known through revelation.[63]

Subsequently, the Neo-Assyrian theory of religious knowledge came to posit that "contemporary scholars were the heirs of scholars from antiquity, known as *apkalu*, who had received their knowledge out of the hands of the gods themselves." Van der Toorn summarizes: "If the theodicy question is an expression of scepticism, scepticism can be said to have bred the counter-dogma of revelation."[64]

The theologizing trajectory that van der Toorn observes in Mesopotamian theology is paralleled in biblical and postbiblical writings about theodicy. We can trace the same development in Israelite and early Jewish literature, from common sense beliefs in divine retribution, to anxiety and skepticism, to philosophies of mystery and apocalypticism.[65]

Thus, the conventional wisdom view is asserted explicitly, for example, in Prov 1:31–33:

> 31. Therefore they shall eat the fruit of their way and be sated with their own devices. 32. For waywardness kills the simple, and the complacency of fools destroys them; 33. but those who listen to me will be secure and will live at ease, without dread of disaster.

The mystery theodicy of skeptical wisdom literature, sometimes called "anti-wisdom" texts, was a product of serious struggle with the traditional dogma.[66] When Qohelet observes that one fate awaits all beings, or when Job rejects his friends' insistence that his suffering must be the result of sin—because he knows he has not sinned—these are not simply rejections

---

63. Van der Toorn, "Theodicy in Akkadian Literature," 88.
64. Van der Toorn, "Theodicy in Akkadian Literature," 89.
65. Van der Toorn, "Theodicy in Akkadian Literature," 86–89. My somewhat informal outline of the theologizing development in the Hebrew Bible has been anticipated by Hans Heinrich Schmid, *Eine Untersuchung zur altorientalischen und israelitischen Weisheitsliteratur*, BZAW 101 (Berlin: Töpelmann, 1966). I thank Reinhard Kratz for this reference.
66. See Antoon Schoors, "Theodicy in Qohelet," in Laato and de Moor, *Theodicy*, 375–409. Schoors states: "Qohelet does not accuse God, neither does he defend him" (407). See also Laato and de Moor, "Introduction," xlvi–xlvii; James L. Crenshaw, "Introduction: The Shift from Theodicy to Anthropodicy," in *Theodicy in the Old Testament*, ed. James L. Crenshaw (Philadelphia: Fortress, 1983), 1–16.

of conventional wisdom. These are self-reflective stances that indicate a high degree of what I term epistemological anxiety.[67] The characters and authors have embraced the wisdom hermeneutic of *Erfahrungswissen*, and they have embraced the wisdom belief in reward and punishment. When the knowledge that one acquires through experience does not match the belief in just consequences for one's actions, this creates a conflict between two major tenets of the wisdom tradition. If the value of knowledge-through-experience is irreconcilable with the belief in divine retribution, how can one know anything? The first-person speakers in these skeptical works are thus not only concerned with the seeming lack of order in the world, but also, self-consciously, with the futility of their own efforts to try to make sense of the world in light of the clash between conventional teachings and observed reality. If the doctrine of retribution is a problem, it is because the premise of divine justice is accepted as a philosophical and theological given. The difficulty arises in the application to real life, that is, in the gap.[68]

Experiencing their current existence as absurd,[69] some heirs to the wisdom tradition coped with the dissonance between their traditional beliefs and their empirical reality by envisioning a resolution in alternative dimensions of space and time. The mystery theodicy posited that knowledge about such heavenly matters as divine justice was unattainable to human beings. Apocalyptic tradition maintained that this knowledge was difficult to attain but accessible through divine revelation to elect individuals and communities. Qumran literature contains fusions of the apocalyptic notions of revelation with conventional wisdom concepts of instruction.[70]

---

67. Contrast the rejectionist skepticism of the sinners and rebels who question reward and punishment, e.g., in Jer 44:15–19: Isa 29:15–16 (as noted in James L. Crenshaw "Theodicy and Prophetic Literature," in Laato and de Moor, *Theodicy*, 254–55).

68. In some relevant Psalms in particular, the anxiety focuses especially on the flourishing of the wicked alongside the suffering of the righteous. This is evidenced quite strongly, for example, in Ps 37 (where, however, in its current form, a resolution is offered through the eschatological theodicy). What is particularly noteworthy in many of these texts is that what is considered bad (distressing, morally and theologically problematic) is an absence of bad (suffering): the psalmist is troubled by the fact that the wicked are *not* suffering for their sins. It is accepted that human suffering is actually good, not bad.

69. See Schoors, "Theodicy in Qohelet, " 375–76.

70. Armin Lange, "Die Weisheitstexte aus Qumran: Eine Einleitung," in *The Wisdom Texts from Qumran and the Development of Sapiential Thought*, ed. Charlotte

In the Psalms of Solomon, there are only brief references to the anxiety that underlies the mystery theodicy, and rapid resolution is offered in each case. I have argued above that the essence of the work is affirmation of confidence in God's justice as manifest in experience, utilizing and developing the conventional theodicies. I further propose that this theological stance offers a helpful lens for considering the genre affinities of the Psalms of Solomon.

3.2. Theodicy and the Genre of Psalms of Solomon

It is illuminating to map the correlations between biblical genre and theodicy in section 3.1 onto the question of the genre of the Psalms of Solomon in light of sections 1 and 2 of this study.[71] The generic features examined here are form, content, and worldview, which align with biblical influences from psalms, prophecy, and wisdom.[72] The most significant formal generic feature of the work is that it is a collection of poems, specifically prayers. The content may be summarized as reflections upon the manifestation of divine justice in the national sphere and in personal experience and expressions of hope for future reward for the righteous. The essence of the worldview is, as I have argued above, confidence in God's goodness and the belief that divine justice is made known to the righteous through divine recompense at the personal and national levels, in the present and future.

Form: Mixed Psalms

The poems of the Psalms of Solomon are primarily prayers, which adopt and adapt the typical forms that have been identified in the biblical psalms: individual and collective laments or complaints, and expressions

---

Hempel, Armin Lange, and Hermann Lichtenberger, BETL 159, (Leuven: Peeters, 2001), 3–30; Matthew Goff, *The Worldly and Heavenly Wisdom of 4QInstruction*, STDJ 50 (Leiden: Brill, 2003).

71. See the excellent summaries of suggested identifications of the genre of the Psalms of Solomon in Atkinson, "Theodicy," 550–51; Winninge, *Sinners and the Righteous*, 16–19; and Embry, "Genre Categorization." See also the additional sources cited in n. 1 above.

72. Cf. George J. Brooke, "Qumran Pesher: Towards the Redefinition of a Genre," *RevQ* 10 (1981): 483–503; Shani Berrin [Tzoref], "Qumran Pesharim," in *Biblical Interpretation at Qumran*, ed. Matthias Henze (Grand Rapids: Eerdmans, 2005), 110–33.

of appreciation in the form of thanksgiving psalms and hymns.[73] Many of the Psalms of Solomon have been aptly labelled "penitential prayers," and Werline's work has demonstrated the significance of the form for considering the *Sitz im Leben* of the work and its performative aspects.[74] Brad Embry has critiqued what he sees as an over-emphasis on form and biblical psalms in determining the genre of the Psalms of Solomon.[75] He argues convincingly for the need to give more weight to other factors. I suggest, nevertheless, that we should take care not to err in the opposite direction of discounting the significance of the psalmic features. The content and worldview of laments and hymns are inseparable from their forms. It is thus instructive to consider the ways in which the Psalms of Solomon is both similar to, and different from, MT Psalms with respect to theodicy.

It is not surprising that our first-century BCE collection exhibits freer variation and greater hybridity as compared to the more rigid conformity to *Gattungen* within the biblical Psalter.[76] Nevertheless, the pattern of the deviations offers cumulative evidence of a *Tendenz*. Most noteworthy for the current study is the near-absence of the positioning of the psalmists

---

73. See Claus Westermann, *Praise and Lament in the Psalms*, 5th ed. (Atlanta: Westminster John Knox, 1981); Svend Holm-Nielsen, "Die Psalmen Solomos," *JSHRZ* 4 (1977): 55–59. Pss. Sol. 1, 2, 7, 8, 9, 11, 17, 18 concern the nation, and Pss. Sol. 3, 4, 5, 6, 10, 12, 13, 14, 15, 16 concern the righteous.

74. Werline, "Experience of God's *Paideia*," 31–37; Werline, *Penitential Prayer in Second Temple Judaism*, 185–88; Werline, "Ideology of Rule," 83; Werline, "Formation of the Pious Person," 139–47.

75. Embry, "Genre Categorization," 61–67. He argues against giving very much weight to the influence of the biblical Psalter in determining the genre of the Psalms of Solomon. Note, however, that Eberhard Bons demonstrates that "the terminology of the Psalms of Solomon is largely borrowed from the Septuagint Psalter" (Bons, "Philosophical Vocabulary," 49). The obvious genre hybridity of the Psalms of Solomon supports a qualitative analysis of how different biblical genres were used, rather than an attempt to evaluate the relative degree of impact.

76. Some original features are, e.g., the fact that Pss. Sol. 3 begins as an apostrophe to the soul calling for praise of God (3.1–2). This turns the biblical convention of concern about God's sleep upon the psalmist himself. Pss. Sol. 4 addresses the wicked sinner. This is quite radical and possibly emphasizes the treachery of the man-pleasers—they had previously been perceived as insiders and leaders of the psalmist's community. The subsequent prayer/curse is a more conventional form, though its content is more graphic and original than standard biblical prayers for punishment of the wicked.

in the Psalms of Solomon as distressed victims. A conventional feature of complaints and thanksgiving songs is vivid emotional description of the psalmists' suffering and divine deliverance. With different degrees of emphasis and perspective, these psalmic forms include: (1) a report of a painful and distressing situation; (2) a crying out to God for relief; and (3) a description of God's positive response to the prayer, either as an expression of hope, as confidence for future salvation, or as gratitude for past and ongoing succor. In the Psalms of Solomon, the elements related to distress are downplayed and often depersonalized, while there is consistent emphasis on the affirmation of divine justice.

Expressions of Distress (focus on first-person discourse): In the Psalms of Solomon, the descriptions of suffering are generally detached, almost clinical, third person reports. The brief occurrences of emotional first-person expressions of anguish are quickly resolved (Pss. Sol. 2.14; 8.1–5; 13.5; 15.1). These resolutions are not brought about by a reversal of the distressing situation but by recognition and affirmation that the suffering of Jerusalem was just retribution (Pss. Sol. 2.15–21; 8.7: "I justified"). In Pss. Sol. 1, the first-person opening of the composition, with the classic "I cried to the Lord" formula, leads to a *negation* of the lament. Zion reveals that her perception of injustice had been a misapprehension. Psalms of Solomon 13 begins with an affirmation of confidence. It contains a confession of past fear during the terrible crisis that has passed, but the actual terrors of the destruction are described as having been the lot of the sinners. The suffering of the psalmist's community consisted in their having witnessed the terror and in their fear of being swept along in the punishment. They themselves are expressly excluded from the actual experiences of sword, famine, death, and bone-crushing wrought upon the guilty.[77] In Pss. Sol. 15, distress is mentioned only in the opening verse, "When I was in distress, I called upon the name of the Lord," in order to provide the setting for a psalm that is an affirmation of confidence. Psalms of Solomon 16 does contain a description of a particular situation from which the psalmist was saved. The situation, however, was a lapse in

---

77. Gray ("Psalms of Solomon," 2:628) noted that although both sinners and righteous suffered during the enemies' attack, the particular experience of exile is specifically associated with the wicked (Pss. Sol. 2.3–15; 8.21–22, 9.1, 3; 13.4). Those who were taken captive were thus subject to retribution and a form of excision, whereas the psalmists' own community were educated by the crisis.

his righteousness (16.1–3). The salvation for which he thanks God was effected not through a cessation of suffering, as in biblical psalms. Rather, in a dramatic inversion, it is divine affliction (16.4, 14–15) for which he expresses gratitude.

Supplication (focus on second-person address): A few of the supplications in the Psalms of Solomon are similar to conventional appeals for relief or revenge in MT Psalms. The most classic supplication style is found in Pss. Sol. 2.22–25, the plea to curtail the punishment of Jerusalem and wreak vengeance upon the enemy inflicting the attack. Even here, however, unlike the norm in biblical laments or complaints, the psalmist affirms the justice of the situation[78] and only asks that the suffering not become excessive. In Pss. Sol. 4.6–25, the psalmist pleads for divine justice. The harsh, graphic, one might even say sadistic, description of the wished-for retribution of sinners is presented primarily as a plea for justice, not revenge, and is quite impersonal. The requests on behalf of the righteous include the conventional plea for God to "save them from deceitful men and sinners," as well as from sin (4.23), and a general plea for mercy (4.25). But they also contain the less typical self-conscious concern with theodicy itself: "may the devout justify the judgment of their God" (4.8).[79] Psalms of Solomon 7 begins with a prayer for protection from potential (not actual) attack by sinners[80] and proceeds with a plea for divine instruction, and for moderation in punishment—acceptance of suffering as a form of mercy, rather than a request to be spared.

Psalms of Solomon 12 is a plea for deliverance: "deliver my soul from the man who is a transgressor of the law and wicked" (12.1; cf. 12.4). The description of the sins and plots of the transgressors are, however, impersonal. Contrast, for example, the development of this theme and form in the Qumran Hodayot, where a central concern is being targeted by sin-

---

78. This affirmation is typical of such Deuteronomistic prayers as Neh 9, Dan 9, Ps 89[88] and other historical psalms of the Psalter.

79. Explicit concern with theodicy is not absent from MT Psalms, but it is not prominent. When it does occur, the focus is upon the psalmists' anxiety. On the problem-poetry (Pss 37, 39, 49, 73), see Lindström, "Theodicy," 296–303. Such anxiety is also discernible in other psalms in a similar frame and register—e.g., Ps 3:3, which refers to a psycho-emotional component of the attacks by the psalmist's enemies: "many say of me, 'There is no deliverance for him through God.'"

80. Similarly, Pss. Sol. 9.8–11 asks for prevention of attack, rather than deliverance.

ners, and the desired divine response is protection. In Pss. Sol. 12, the focus is on divine judgment. As noted above, the psalmist's request in Pss. Sol. 16 is for righteousness, and for divine affliction to achieve that aim, rather than a cessation of affliction.

Thanksgiving, Praise, and Affirmation: Following from the above, the emotions and descriptions in the Psalms of Solomon are overwhelmingly positive or neutral, as in late biblical psalms of confidence.[81] What is distinctive is that every psalm affirms God's justice. Some notable examples: in the first half of Pss. Sol. 2, the second-person "justification" in verses 15–17 praises God not for salvation or for ending suffering but for having meted out proper justice through punishing Jerusalem. In Pss. Sol. 3, the formulaic "why do you sleep" is directed not against God, as in biblical psalms, but internally, as the psalmist rebukes his own soul for delay in praising God. The hymn proceeds to praise the righteous explicitly and, indirectly, God, for strengthening and rewarding the righteous and punishing sinners. Statements of confidence in the efficacy of the prayer of the righteous appear in Pss. Sol. 1.1–2; 2.22–26; 5.5, 8, 12; 6.1, 5–6; 7.7, 10. The strongest affirmation is the depiction of Pompey's death as an immediate response to the psalmist's supplicatory prayer in Pss. Sol. 2.[82] The psalmist sees real-life evidence of God's positive response to the prayers of the righteous.

In canonical psalms, the retribution theodicy is a problem that is experienced through national and personal crisis and generates epistemological crisis. In the Psalms of Solomon, retribution theodicy is the solution to the crises.

---

81. See Westermann, *Praise and Lament in the Psalms*, 55; C. Hassell Bullock, *Encountering the Book of Psalms: A Literary and Theological Introduction* (Grand Rapids: Baker, 2001), 166–76.

82. Atkinson describes the Psalms of Solomon as a community's "attempts to make sense of their present crisis" ("Theodicy," 546) and, similarly, to "seek to explain why God has apparently abandoned their righteous community and the city of Jerusalem in its time of need" (552). I agree to an extent, but this is an etic description. The sense in which the suffering in Jerusalem is depicted as their crisis is distinctive, and the psalms do not describe the community as having suffered abandonment. The psalmists consider themselves as witnesses to a crisis that warrants explanation, but as sufferers of a more limited discipline that is readily explicable. The stance of Pss. Sol. 2, at least, is a posttraumatic one, in which the psalmist feels that justice has been served, and he has achieved some degree of vindication.

Content: Prophecy

Embry's description of the "prophetic worldview" of the Psalms of Solomon captures the subject matter as well as the theological perspective of the work:

> By addressing the particular historical situation that he and his community faced—the invasion and dominance of Rome—through the "religious utilization of history," the author was able to produce a document that addressed this crisis with a certain, theohistorical sangfroid.[83]

Embry further describes the perspective as the belief that "restoration, through miraculous and interventive means, follows from God's punishment, which is a response to the sins and covenantal infidelities on the part of the community of God." He structures his analysis according to the salient features of prophecy identified by Gerhard von Rad: the "new eschatological word," the "old election tradition," and the "personal situation." In terms of the use of scripture, he notes that even Werline, after categorizing the Psalms of Solomon as "a collection of psalms," proceeded to refer almost exclusively to the prophetic corpus and Deuteronomy in describing the use of scripture in the Psalms of Solomon's presentation of its ideology. The elements of election, the personal situation, and eschatology, as well as the historicization described by Embry as prophetic features indeed align with the theodicies outlined above. The dualistic formulation of the retribution theodicy distinguishes between the sinners and the elect righteous, the educative theodicy addresses the personal situation of the righteous, and the eschatological theodicy incorporates historical and eschatological elements. The setting within current events moves the alignment of the Psalms of Solomon along a spectrum from prophecy toward pesher.[84]

Like the shifting of psalmic forms to accommodate an emphasis on affirmation of trust, so too, the adoption of subject matter associated with

---

83. Embry, "Genre Categorization," 59–60.

84. On the continuum of biblical prophecy and Qumran pesher, see Anselm Hagedorn and Shani Tzoref, "Attitudes to Gentiles in the Minor Prophets and in Corresponding Pesharim," *DSD* 20 (2013): 470–507; Reinhard Gregor Kratz, "Der Pescher Nahum und seine biblische Vorlage," in *Prophetenstudien: Kleine Schriften II* (Tübingen: Mohr Siebeck, 2011), 99–145.

prophecy is directed toward demonstrating the fulfillment of anticipated acts of divine intervention. In Qumran pesher, current events are viewed as fulfillment of prophetic texts. In the Psalms of Solomon, current events are viewed as fulfillment of prophetic and sapiential expectations. It might be even more appropriate to flip the perspective and consider that the authors of the Psalms of Solomon used the prophetic worldview as a hermeneutic for interpreting their experiences.[85] This is how I understand Embry's terminology of the "historicization of prophetic hope." In an earlier study, I compared the Psalms of Solomon and Pesher Nahum:

> Both texts employ allusive language in their presentation of this historical event, since they both "theologize" or, more specifically (if less grammatically) "theodicize" the text. That is to say, both *Psalms of Solomon* and *Pesher Nahum* are interested in the violence and disgrace of Jerusalem insofar as these historical events reflect divine reward and punishment. *Pesher Nahum* focuses upon the punishment of the Pharisees and, more briefly, upon the punishment of the Sadducees. Psalm 2 in its current form focuses upon the punishment of Pompey, but the guilt of the "sons of Jerusalem" is stressed as well, and global statements about reward and punishment pervade the psalm. Some dualistic elements may also be detected in both works.[86]

Embry observes that "one of the features often noted by von Rad in his treatment of Isaiah's prophecy is that not one of the prophet's utterances about Zion came true."[87] The Psalms of Solomon maintains that history shows that prophecies do come true. In this sense, a similarity could also be drawn to Chronicles, about which Sara Japhet remarked, "the stronger and more pervasive expression of theodicy in Chron. is the application of

---

85. Thus, Klaus Bringmann stated about Pss. Sol. 2 that "the pious inhabitants of the country interpreted the extraordinary happenings ... as God's punishment for the sins of the rulers and the people" (Klaus Bringmann, *Geschichte der Juden im Altertum: Vom babylonischen Exil bis zur arabischen Eroberung* [Stuttgart: Klett-Cotta, 2005], 166; cited in Benedikt Eckhardt, "The Psalms of Solomon as a Historical Source," in Bons and Pouchelle, *Psalms of Solomon*, 14).

86. Shani L. Berrin [Tzoref], "*Pesher Nahum, Psalms of Solomon* and Pompey," in *Reworking the Bible: Apocryphal and Related Texts at Qumran*, ed. Esther G. Chazon, Devorah Dimant, and Ruth A. Clements, STDJ 58 (Leiden: Brill, 2005), 65–84.

87. Embry, "Genre Categorization," 75. He cites Gerhard von Rad, *The Message of the Prophets* (London: SCM, 1968), 137.

God's justice to the historical course itself."[88] Japhet contrasts Chronicles with Ezra and Nehemiah, "where programmatic statements of faith, and especially penitential prayers—affirm God's justice as the theological basis for the prayer's historical view," but this belief is not applied in reports of the returnees' actual experiences.[89] The rhetorical passages in Ezra and Nehemiah describe God's justice as the "decisive factor in Israel's past" and God's mercy as the basis for Israel's appeals to God. In the explanations given for their personal contemporary experience, however, suffering is blamed on wicked human opponents, and reward is portrayed as resulting from God's benevolence.[90] In the Psalms of Solomon, the rhetoric is applied to actual experience. The composition contains general descriptions of divine involvement in history, and to a lesser extent in nature, like MT Psalms, and it also includes references to actual, historical current events, like prophecy and pesher.[91]

Worldview: Sapiential Writings

The dependence of the Psalms of Solomon on wisdom literature is evident in its focus on empirical observation and real-life experience, as well as its adaption of models of human instruction to apply to divine instruction of the righteous. The educative theodicy in the composition presumes divine

---

88. Japhet, "Theodicy in Ezra-Nehemiah and Chronicles," 449. Japhet also discusses the measure-for-measure principle in Chronicles (447–48). Cf. Kratz, *Das Judentum*, 187–226 on the theocratic writings of, e.g., Chronicles (in contrast to DtrH), Ben Sira, 1 and 2 Macc.

89. Japhet, "Theodicy in Ezra-Nehemiah and Chronicles," 435–37.

90. Japhet, "Theodicy in Ezra-Nehemiah and Chronicles," 430–49.

91. An additional similarity that has been noted between the Psalms of Solomon and pesher is the use of sobriquets, particularly in Pss. Sol. 2, 4, 8, and 17 (see the contribution of Werline in this volume). The most notable example is the reference to Pompey as the dragon in Pss. Sol. 2.25. See Atkinson, *I Cried*, 10–11 for a list of these epithets, which function as specific, but not explicit, historical references. See also Eckhardt, "Psalms of Solomon as a Historical Source," 13, 17–18. The reason for the use of sobriquets in Psalms of Solomon is not obvious to me. It may have roots in biblical prophecy, where colorful descriptors are a common feature of prophetic *Kunstprosa*. The use of epithets accommodates typological reinterpretation and facilitates reuse of the texts in subsequent liturgical settings. In pesher, I believe that the use of sobriquets is related to the esoteric nature of the revealed, but still veiled, interpretations. See Atkinson, *I Cried*, 10–11 for additional proposed explanations for the use of sobriquets in pesher.

justice as a positive reality, and even as a type of divine mercy. As noted in section 3.1 above, most biblical texts assume divine retribution. In some texts, the disparity between this belief and empirical experience is cause for lament or questioning or supplication. Sapiential texts, including sapiential psalms, incorporate an extensive amount of explicit self-conscious engagement with the question of theodicy as an epistemic challenge. They are concerned with knowledge of the ways of God, or deficiencies of such knowledge, and with the whys and wherefores of human suffering. In the sapiential Deuteronomic tradition of the Psalms of Solomon, the doctrine of retribution is actively asserted through purported empirical evidence. This is quite unusual in extant Second Temple writings. By the mid-second century BCE, the dissonance that had previously been cause for anxiety had given rise to worldviews that maintained that current existence does not conform to expected beliefs.

The Psalms of Solomon seems to present a counter-counter-dogma. Whether as a corrective to skepticism and apocalypticism, a polemic, or a parallel line of thought, the Psalms of Solomon insists upon a pre-apocalyptic worldview.[92] It presents the fulfillment of divine covenantal promise as unfolding in reality. That which comes into being is not a mystery like the *raz nihyeh* of the Qumran corpus, whose meaning needs to be sought in esoteric textual exegesis or the interpretations of charismatic mediators of the divine word.[93] Rather, God instructs his righteous followers by punishing and rewarding individuals and nations. One need only pay attention and learn the lessons (educative theodicy) in order to be confident of divine justice and faithfulness (retribution theodicy). This justice is already manifest in the present—even the horrifying present; it will be further corroborated imminently with the arrival of the messianic king; and also eternally (eschatological theodicy). The eschatological theodicy is not a discontinuity that will resolve a current absurdity. It is rather a continuity of current justice, only more perfect, and without evildoers or evil. The search for divine justice is not a cause for epistemological anxiety to be resolved in some celestial revelation of a mystery or corrective historical upheaval. In order to understand God's justice and earn divine reward, the

---

92. See the distinction drawn by Kratz between theocratic and apocalyptic worldviews in *Das Judentum*, 187–226.

93. On the translation of the term *raz nihyeh*, see Matthew Goff, *Discerning Wisdom: The Sapiential Literature of the Dead Sea Scrolls*, VTSup 116 (Leiden: Brill, 2007), 51–79.

righteous are wakeful and watchful, and they pragmatically monitor their actions. Revelation takes place here-and-now as divine exposure undoes the hiddenness of sins and sinfulness (Pss. Sol. 2.17; 4.7; 8.8–10).

A question that is worthy of further consideration is whether the return to the naïve retribution theodicy in the Psalms of Solomon is best understood as a rejection, perhaps even a polemic, against skepticism and apocalypticism, or whether it reflects a parallel track continuing conventional thought. Are the psalmists like Job's friends, who criticized his refusal to acknowledge the teachings of his fathers and to recognize that his suffering must be retributive or educative?[94] Do they go even further in opposing the mystery theodicy, rejecting the skeptics' denial of human beings' capacity to understand and appreciate God's justice in this world? What about the descriptions of sin being revealed and exposed and made known through historical and personal experience of divine retribution? Is such rationalist reassertion of the conventional retribution and educative theodicies a simple alternative to revelatory strands of Jewish thought or an expression of opposition them?

The Absence of Mythological Elements

One biblical genre in which the retribution theodicy is key is conspicuously absent from the Psalms of Solomon, namely, myth.[95] Cornelis Houtman has remarked: "The entire primeval, history (Gen 1–11) may be interpreted as a justification of God. Human sin and rebellion are the causes of evils that beset men—death, pain, murder, violence etc."[96] The immanence of the divine and the inclusion of supernatural elements and heavenly beings are key features of these opening narratives of the Pentateuch. Their cryptic allusions have been viewed by some as taming and polemicizing against myths that are known from ancient Near Eastern

---

94. See, e.g., Pss. Sol. 3.9: "the sinner stumbled, and he curses his life, the day of his birth and his mother's birth pangs." This may be seen as a repudiation of Job, in Job 3:1–3 "After this Job opened his mouth and cursed the day of his birth. And Job said: 'Let the day perish on which I was born, and the night that said, "A man is conceived."'"

95. The dragon in Pss. Sol. 2.25 functions only as a sobriquet, without any mythic texture.

96. Houtman, "Theodicy in the Pentateuch," 152 n. 4. Cf. Laato and de Moor, "Introduction," xxxii: "The Yahwistic account of creation in Gen 2–3 presents this classic understanding of the retribution theodicy."

writings. In particular, it has been argued that the Hebrew Bible polemicizes against Babylonian depictions of the human-like caprice of the gods, insisting that Yahweh/Elohim is just, that he is to be propitiated through proper conduct rather than an appeal to sensory or aesthetic pleasures and that he rewards goodness rather than behaving toward humans on the basis of arbitrary whims.[97] The mythical elements that are subdued in Genesis and elsewhere in scripture are highlighted and developed in the apocalyptic literature of the Second Temple era, such as Enoch and Jubilees.[98] Such elements are absent from the Psalms of Solomon. The biblical myths and later apocalyptic writings are particularly interested in the question of the origin of sin, which is a topic that is not given very much attention elsewhere in the Pentateuch, and none at all in the Psalms of Solomon.

4. Conclusion

The Psalms of Solomon copes with suffering and sin by combining a variety of biblical concepts and genres to affirm the validity of the doctrine of divine justice in lived experience. The composition adopts and adapts psalmodic poetic forms to express a theological interpretation of current events and personal experience in historicized modes that are derived from biblical prophecy. The hermeneutical lens used to interpret lived reality is fashioned out of sapiential ideas concerning instruction, consequences, and empirical observation, with a theological overlay. The Psalms of Solomon shares some features with historical apocalypses, especially insofar as it anticipates a future era in which the righteous of Israel flourish, in righteousness, under messianic rule. It differs from apocalyptic texts in that it pointedly lacks the key apocalyptic generic factor of mediated revelation of heavenly secrets to an elect human individual. Turning away from the epistemological anxiety of skepticism and apocalypticism, the foundational claim of the Psalms of Solomon is confidence that divine justice is

---

97. See Yehezkel Kaufmann, *The Religion of Israel from Its Beginnings to the Babylonian Exile* (Chicago: Chicago University Press, 1960), 292–95, 322–23; Nahum M. Sarna, *Understanding Genesis* (New York: Schocken), 1972.

98. On mythological aspects of apocalypticism, see Collins, *Apocalyptic Imagination*, 17–26. On the connection between mythological elements and the origin of evil in the Hebrew Bible, see Jon D. Levenson, *Creation and the Persistence of Evil* (San Francisco: Harper, 1985).

manifest in the reality of national and personal experience, already in the present and assuredly in the future.

The Imaginative Experiencing of Psalms of Solomon 8

Angela Kim Harkins

This paper presents a discussion of Pss. Sol. 8 with special attention to the ways in which scriptural allusions to foundational events can contribute to an experience of the text in which God's presence is made perceptible in his absence.

The association that the Psalms of Solomon have with the biblical king Solomon is long and widely attested. The eighteen Psalms of Solomon comprise a discrete collection that was transmitted in antiquity both independently as a separate collection and also alongside other Solomonic corpora such as the Wisdom of Solomon and the book of Sirach.[1] The Psalms of

---

1. Ancient sources like the fifth-century Codex Alexandrinus attest to the independent circulation of the Psalms of Solomon. Six of the eleven Greek manuscripts of the Psalms of Solomon present this collection together with the Wisdom of Solomon and Sirach. Robert R. Hann, *The Manuscript History of the Psalms of Solomon*, SCS 13 (Atlanta: Scholars, 1982), 113. One can infer that the association of this collection with the biblical figure of Solomon was very ancient and undisputed. For studies on the Psalms of Solomon, see Herbert E. Ryle and Montague R. James, *Psalms of the Pharisees Commonly Called the Psalms of Solomon* (Cambridge: Cambridge University Press, 1891); Joseph Viteau, *Les Psaumes de Salomon: Introduction, texte grec et traduction, avec les principales variantes de la version syriaque par François Martin*, Documents pour l'étude de la Bible (Paris: Letouzey et Ané, 1911); Gerhard Maier, *Mensch und freier Wille nach den jüdischen Religionsparteien zwischen Ben Sira und Paulus*, WUNT 12 (Tübingen: Mohr Siebeck, 1971), 264–301; Svend Holm-Nielsen, "Die Psalmen Salomos," *JSHRZ* 4 (1977): 51–112; Joachim Schüpphaus, *Die Psalmen Salomos: Ein Zeugnis Jerusalemer Theologie und Frömmigkeit in der Mitte des vorchristlichen Jahrhunderts*, ALGHJ 7 (Leiden: Brill, 1977); Hann, *Manuscript History*; Robert B. Wright, "The Psalms of Solomon," *OTP* 1 (1983): 639–70; Joseph L. Trafton, *The Syriac Version of the Psalms of Solomon: A Critical Evaluation*, SCS 11 (Atlanta: Scholars Press, 1985); Mark A. Seifrid, *Justification by Faith: The Origin and Development of a Central Pauline Theme*, NovTSup 68 (Leiden: Brill, 1992), 109–35; Mikael Winninge,

Solomon were also circulated with the forty-two Odes of Solomon to form a nonbiblical corpus of Solomonic pseudepigrapha of sixty compositions.[2]

One question that this complex textual history of the Psalms of Solomon raises is how an ancient reader or hearer would have experienced this text? While a codex apparatus would allow for the possible experiencing of these compositions through random access, a scroll apparatus would not allow for such freedom of access, thus highlighting the importance of the order and arrangement of compositions and the consideration of how emotions can build up over the course of the collection. Related to this question is also that of the effect of reading and hearing these texts and certain limitations to how modern scholars imagine this process.

1. A General Orientation to the Methodological Perspective

Thirty years ago, Paul N. Franklyn's study of the Psalms of Solomon helpfully highlighted how the Psalms of Solomon are liturgical, not simply lit-

---

Sinners and the Righteous: A Comparative Study of the Psalms of Solomon and Paul's Letters, ConBNT 26 (Stockholm: Almqvist & Wiksell, 1995); Joseph L. Trafton, "The Psalms of Solomon in Recent Research," *JSP* 12 (1994): 3–19.

2. The Psalms of Solomon have long been associated with the collection known as the Odes of Solomon. Early evidence exists for the sequence of Psalms of Solomon + Odes of Solomon in the copy of the Pistis Sophia preserved in Codex Askew, a Coptic manuscript which dates to the fourth-fifth century CE. Michael Lattke, *Die Oden Salomos in ihrer Bedeutung für Neues Testament und Gnosis*, 4 vols., OBO 25.1–4 (Gottingen: Vandenhoek & Ruprecht, 1979–1998), 1:24–31. There, the ode that is labeled as the nineteenth one is not identical with what is known as the nineteenth Ode of Solomon to us today, and so is thought by scholars to be the long-lost first Ode of Solomon. Lattke, *Die Oden Salomos* 1:216–17; Lattke, "The Gnostic Interpretation of the Odes of Solomon in the Pistis Sophia," *Bulletin de la Société d'Archéologie Copte* 24 (1982): 75. According to Lattke's commentary, there is medieval evidence for the sequencing of the Psalms of Solomon after the Odes of Solomon. The fragmentary manuscripts known as Codex Nitriensis (N) from the ninth-tenth century CE and the later medieval manuscript known as Codex Harris (H) both sequence the Psalms of Solomon collection after the Odes of Solomon, effectively renumbering the Psalms of Solomon as numbers 43–60 in the combined collection of Odes + Psalms. Codex N shows that Pss. Sol. 1 is copied after the last ode numbered 42. While the manuscript is fragmentary, it is possible to see that the Psalms of Solomon follow the Odes. So too, Codex H is not a completely intact manuscript, but it is possible to see that the end of Ode 42.20 is followed immediately by the first Psalms of Solomon, which is numbered Ode 43 in the heading to that text. For further details on Codex N and H, see Michael Lattke, *Odes of Solomon: A Commentary*, Hermeneia 86 (Minneapolis: Fortress, 2009), 4.

erary texts, by noting the deliberate way the collection has been arranged.³ Franklyn noted with some confidence that the reading of the entire Psalms of Solomon collection would have taken approximately one hour: "It requires at most 55 minutes to read the collection aloud from start to finish in Greek, and even less in Hebrew; though the entire collection may not have been read at once in a worship situation."⁴ His flat-footed assessment does not express any part of the degree or intensity of the performative act of ritualized reading within religious groups. Michael Swartz does well to note that process of reading is far more complex from an integrative perspective than most text-based scholars may be willing to keep in mind: "Indeed, the force of recitation needs to be taken quite seriously as a potent form of ritual behavior and as an example of the actualization of sacred space in time. Memorization, recitation and performance, we must remember, are physical acts, requiring intensive preparation, stamina, and physical prowess."⁵ The performative reading of the Psalms of Solomon involves the integration of the body and the mind. Included is also a level of cognitive engagement that literary theorist Anežka Kuzmičová calls "enactive reading," a process by which the mind's perception of sensorimotor experiences are at work during the imaginative reading of a text.⁶ In line with Swartz's and Kuzmičová's perspectives, which attend to the embodied aspects of reading, this paper seeks to add a degree of complexity to how scholars imagine the experience of reading a collection like the Psalms of Solomon by examining the experiential effect of emotionally re-experiencing the events described in Pss. Sol. 8. This paper uses integrative approaches, especially those that attend to the body's experiences of emotion, in order to texture and complicate how modern scholars imagine the effect that the reading of these Psalms of Solomon may have had on their readers and hearers.

---

3. Paul N. Franklyn, "The Cultic and Pious Climax of Eschatology in the Psalms of Solomon," *JSJ* 18 (1987): 1-17.

4. Franklyn, "Cultic and Pious Climax," 5.

5. Michael D. Swartz, "Ritual about Myth about Ritual: Towards an Understanding of the Avodah in the Rabbinic Period," *The Journal of Jewish Thought and Philosophy* 6 (1997): 153. See too, Ophir Münz-Manor, "Narrating Salvation: Verbal Sacrifices in Late Antique Liturgical Poetry," in *Jews, Christians, and the Roman Empire: The Poetics of Power in Late Antiquity*, ed. Natalie B. Dohrmann and Annette Yoshiko Reed (Philadelphia: University of Pennsylvania Press, 2013), 154-66.

6. Anežka Kuzmičová, "Literary Narrative and Mental Imagery: A View from Embodied Cognition," *Style* 48 (2014): 275-93.

The push to recover the complexities of the on-the-ground experience of ancient texts within their readers and hearers reflects a shift that took place in the 1980s in the social sciences to move away from over-determined models of social structures that presumably exerted influence on people through institutionalized practices and discourses (e.g., political systems, kinship structures, cultural histories, symbolic meanings). Scholars have done well to consider how embodied experiences and materiality might offer insights into the lived experience of religion.[7] While the recovery of individual experiences has long been recognized as difficult, *not* considering subjective experiences as data for understanding the past can lead to over-determined monochromatic images of the other that inevitably reserve high-definition texturing such as complexity, contingencies, and ambivalence to the world of the observer alone.[8] One way of recovering textured experiences of the past is to look to interdisciplinary explanatory theories of religion from anthropology and cognitive science of religion that seek to describe the range of bodily experiences that are involved in the processing of emotions and memory and the formation of subjectivity.[9] The interdisciplinary studies used here offer heuristic theories about human emotion and memory and draw upon ethnographic studies of contemporary societies that examine how highly imaginative embodied meditative practices and emotion contribute to the experience of simultaneity between the time of the ancient reader and hearer and the foundational scriptural event that is being evoked.[10]

---

7. Robert Desjarlais and C. Jason Throop, "Phenomenological Approaches in Anthropology," *Annual Review of Anthropology* 40 (2011): 96. An important texturing of the communities of D appears in Maxine L. Grossman, *Reading for History in the Damascus Document: A Methodological Study*, STDJ 45 (Leiden: Brill, 2002), 184–209. It is worth mentioning the important contributions of feminist studies to these understandings of embodiment, subjectivity, and intersubjectivity, a point that was well made by Elliot R. Wolfson, "The Body in the Text: A Kabbalistic Theory of Embodiment," *JQR* 95 (2005): 479.

8. Desjarlais and Throop, "Phenomenological Approaches in Anthropology," 95–96; Stephen S. Bush, "Are Religious Experiences Too Private to Study?," *JR* (2012): 199–223.

9. Amira Mittermaier, *Dreams that Matter: Egyptian Landscapes of the Imagination* (Berkeley: University of California Press, 2011); Mittermaier, "Dreams from Elsewhere: Muslim Subjectivities beyond the Trope of Self-Cultivation," *Journal of the Royal Anthropological Institute* 18 (2012): 247–65.

10. Pascal Boyer, *The Naturalness of Religious Ideas* (Berkeley: University of Cali-

This paper, as an exploratory inquiry into how integrative research into cognitive and emotion processes, can shed light on new ways of understanding how these texts may have been experienced by the ancient readers and hearers by taking a look at the specific composition known as Pss. Sol. 8. This question should also be examined from the perspective of the cumulative effect of such experiences from reading and rereading—one that is not typically taken up on the scholarship on the Psalms of Solomon, but which is a worthwhile consideration nonetheless. The reexperiencing of the emotions according to the theological pattern of covenant breaking and terrifying chastisement in the form of dispersion can be understood as constructing a malleable framework of vivid experiences within which each reader, even those who have not openly violated any law, could have imagined him- or herself.[11]

2. Who Are the Implied Readers and Hearers of the Psalms of Solomon?

Various references throughout the collection known as the Psalms of Solomon suggest that the implied speaker understands himself as a righteous person; even so, it becomes apparent that this righteous individual is wres-

---

fornia Press, 1994); Boyer, *Religion Explained: The Evolutionary Origins of Religious Thought* (New York: Basic Books, 2001); Robert N. McCauley and Emma Cohen, "Cognitive Science and the Naturalness of Religion," *Philosophy Compass* 5 (2010): 779–92. Michael D. Swartz speaks about the experiential dimension of ritual simultaneity in "Judaism and the Idea of Ancient Ritual Theory," in *Jewish Studies at the Crossroads of Anthropology and History: Authority, Diaspora, Tradition*, ed. Raʿanan S. Boustan, Oren Kosansky, and Marina Rustow (Philadelphia: University of Pennsylvania Press, 2011), 315–16. Other useful anthropological discussions of compelling (phenomenological) experiences of performativity include Thomas Csordas, "Embodiment as a Paradigm for Anthropology," *Ethos* 18 (1990): 5–47; Csordas, "Imaginal Performance and Memory in Ritual Healing," in *The Performance of Healing*, ed. Carol Laderman and Marina Roseman (London: Routledge, 1996), 91–114; Tanya M. Luhrmann, *Persuasions of the Witches' Craft: Ritual Magic in Contemporary England* (Oxford: Blackwell, 1989); Luhrmann, *When God Talks Back: Understanding the American Evangelical Relationship with God* (New York: Knopf, 2012); Saba Mahmood, *Politics of Piety: The Islamic Revival and the Feminist Subject* (Princeton: Princeton University Press, 2005).

11. It is in this way that the present study shares the concern of Angela Kim Harkins, "The Emotional Re-experiencing of the Hortatory Narratives Found in the Admonition of the Damascus Document," *DSD* 22 (2015): 285–307.

tling with the problem of lived suffering. As Kenneth Atkinson has well-noted, the question of soteriology is a central concern for these texts.[12]

The righteousness of the authors of the Psalms of Solomon is made clear in the opening to the collection in which the speaker states: "He will hear me because I am righteous; I reminded myself that I am indeed righteous; hadn't I prospered and given birth to many children?" (1.2–3). Such a statement epitomizes the classic wisdom ideal of the worldly manifestations of the person who is reckoned as righteous by God. The Psalms of Solomon go on to describe what it means to be considered righteous by contrasting the righteous readers and hearers of the collection with those who are not righteous. In Pss. Sol. 3, the speaker states that even though both groups may experience the same stumbling, the righteous respond with an even more scrupulous examination of their deeds, while the wicked are led to sin even graver sins as a result (Pss. Sol. 3.3). In other words, according to the Psalms of Solomon, to be counted among the righteous does not mean that one lives without suffering or without blame. The righteous are also said to be disciplined (quietly) for mistakes done out of ignorance (Pss. Sol. 13.7–8, 10). The implied readers and hearers of the Psalms of Solomon collection are described in highly esteemed terms as "a firstborn son" (Pss. Sol. 18.4), one who is chastised. Of this group, we read that God "brings back the one who heeds well from stupidity and ignorant" (18.4). In addition to having the qualities of righteousness, the readers and hearers are also called "the pious ones of God" (οἱ ὅσιοι τοῦ θεοῦ; 8.23, 34).

Several recent studies have explored well the topic of language and identity, especially during the late Second Temple period.[13] These studies are relevant given the passages that suggest the speaker's self-understanding as a righteous diaspora Jew who strongly identifies with Jerusalem. Various textual markers and appeals to what can be known about the larger historical context of first-century BCE Jerusalem support the widely

---

12. Kenneth Atkinson, "Enduring the Lord's Discipline: Soteriology in the Psalms of Solomon," in *This World and the World to Come: Soteriology in Early Judaism*, ed. Daniel M. Gurtner (London: T&T Clark, 2011), 145–63.

13. Catherine Hezser, *Jewish Literacy in Roman Palestine* (Tübingen: Mohr Siebeck, 2001); Chris Keith, *Jesus' Literacy: Scribal Culture and the Teacher from Galilee* (New York: T&T Clark, 2011); Michael O. Wise, *Language and Literacy in Roman Judaea: A Study of the Bar Kokhba Documents* (New Haven: Yale University Press, 2015).

recognized dating and locale for the Psalms of Solomon.[14] The first century shows evidence of a sustained interest in the Hebrew language as the preferred language for religious writings, a phenomenon that is borne out by the Dead Sea Scrolls. Even so, significant Jewish interest in Greek language texts can be observed during the time that the Psalms of Solomon are thought to be produced. Examples of this include the Minor Prophets Scroll from Naḥal Ḥever, which revises the LXX of this collection in light of the MT, along with the various additions to the LXX which begin to emerge during this time.[15] First-century Jerusalem was a diverse urban context in which Jewish groups took serious interest in the LXX and in the production of Greek texts.

The beginning of Pss. Sol. 9 also makes clear that the speaker is in exile. Scholars have made the observation that the Greek of the Psalms of Solomon shows a preference for LXX phrases and wording, giving witness to a larger interest in the Greek. Even so, the content of the compositions themselves are Jerusalem focused, with strong concerns for the temple and a desire for the ingathering of the exiled righteous and Jerusalem's restoration (17.30–31). These observations offer important insights into a more complex understanding of the speaker or putative author of these texts by challenging long-standing assumptions about language, locale, and identity that restrict and oversimplify cultural identity and regional markers.

3. How a Text May Generate Experience

Embodied reading that vividly enacts the experiences that are described (also called "enactive reading")[16] allows for the formation of egocentric

---

14. Kenneth Atkinson, "Psalms and Odes of Solomon: Psalms of Solomon," in *Deutero-Canonical Scriptures*, vol. 2 of *Textual History of the Bible*, ed. Matthias Henze and Frank Feder (Leiden: Brill, 2019), 332–50, esp. 336–39. The discussion of the Greek of the Psalms of Solomon indicates that the translation of these texts into Greek must have been very early in the transmission history.

15. See, for example, Adrian Schenker, "What Were the Aims of the Palestinian Recensions, and What Did They Achieve? With Some Biographical Notes on Dominique Barthélemy," in *The Legacy of Barthélemy: Fifty Years after Les Devanciers d'Aquila*, ed. Anneli Aejmelaeus and Tuukka Kauhanen (Göttingen: Vandenhoeck & Ruprecht, 2017), 14–22.

16. During enactive reading, compelling reference to an object can stimulate sensory and motor areas in the brain that govern the appropriate visualizing and phenomenal handling of that object. It can also arouse other bodily states, including

episodic memories that are crucial for the mind's ability to anticipate future events such as the divine punishments that result unfailingly from treachery. One of the aims of the vivid imagery found in the Psalms of Solomon, I propose, is to encourage those readers who are already counted among the righteous to an even more intense scrupulosity by generating a vivid palpable presence of a deity whose presence in history is either punitive or providential. The bodily imagery that appears in this psalm can assist readers in enactive reading, a cognitive process that engages the regions of the brain that govern motor and sensory processing. In this sense, emotion and the public strategic arousal of emotion can generate first-hand experiences of the events that are described, including the perceptible presence of a deity who is otherwise invisible.

Sensations of presence are conveyed by suggestive words of physicality that reference the deity's embodiment: his fiery manifestation causes the earth (and the speaker) to tremble (Pss. Sol. 8.1–4), God's mixing and giving a drink in a cup, and whose deeds of righteous judgment can be viewed or beheld by the speaker (Pss. Sol. 8.25). The vivid sense of presence of an otherwise invisible deity can assist in the cultivation of a religious subjectivity that is predisposed to obey the law (without predetermining obedience) because the invisible God knows all things that are done in hidden places, even those under the earth (Pss. Sol. 8.8–9). For the spiritually elite readers and hearers of Pss. Sol. 8, the text may be able to generate an ever more intense scrupulosity and conscientiousness to follow the law. The image of the mighty foreign leader being led securely to Jerusalem (8.19) in order to deliver God's righteous punishment to its inhabitant alludes to the providential way that God provided for the Israelites to be led during their wanderings in the wilderness. Again, God's presence, either providential or punitive, is made perceptible to the readers and hearers of this text.

4. An Appeal to the Deuteronomistic View of History

The Psalms of Solomon were used and read long after the presumed composition date. In this paper, rather than mining the Psalms of Solomon for historical references that date to the time of the putative author, I wish to

---

appropriate emotional responses. See Anežka Kuzmičová, "Presence in the Reading of Literary Narrative: A Case for Motor Enactment," *Semiotica* 189 (2012): 23–48, esp. 25–26.

explore how the imagery and intertextual references in this psalm might assist the later readers and hearers of this text to cultivate the subjectivity of the implied speaker—biblical Israel. One way in which this is done is through the use of common theological traditions such as the Deuteronomistic view of history, which emphasizes the righteousness and mercy of God and the sinfulness of the people. Such allusions could be considered as aids to help readers experientially recover access to foundational events in Israel's history or to God's primeval deeds, but especially important here are the foundational experiences of covenant breaking and remaking. Such an inquiry into how the past would have been experienced in the time of the reader is guided by the text itself which appeals to God's judgments since the beginning of time (Pss. Sol. 8.7).

Scholars have long observed the strong Deuteronomistic understanding of history in these texts, which, in the case of Pss. Sol. 8 is epitomized by passages like verse 29: "We stiffened our neck, and you are the one who disciplines us." In Pss. Sol. 8, such statements are accompanied by repeated references to God's righteousness judgments, which are heavily concentrated in the latter part of Pss. Sol. 8 (8.7, 8, 23, 25, 26, 32, 34) and which are intended to give a vivid and lasting impression of the otherwise invisible God's role, both punitive and providential, in history. A Deuteronomistic view understands the experiences of chosenness and chastisement together as driving the recurring pattern of covenant making, political disaster, and the expectation of covenant remaking throughout Israel's history. The events recounted in the center portion of the Pss. Sol. 8 of the mighty foreign ruler can be understood as the fulfillment of the Deuteronomic curse that Israel will become conquered and besieged for not obeying the covenant law. This ruler who is said to have peaceably entered Jerusalem (8.15–18) has long been identified as Pompey, whose entry into Jerusalem marked the end of the Hasmonean dynasty in 63 BCE.[17] There are as many as five underlying Semitic allusions here to the root form of

---

17. Pompey captured the walled city (8.19), killed its leaders (8.20), and slaughtered the inhabitants of the city (8.20). The psalmist speaks from a state of dispersion when he petitions God: "Gather together the dispersion of Israel with mercy and goodness, for your faithfulness is with us" (8.28). These general events can be situated within a Deuteronomistic understanding of history in which the experience of dispersion in the present is understood as a fulfilment of the curses for disobeying the law as stated in Deut 28:25—"And you shall be in dispersion in all of the kingdoms of the earth."

Solomon's name (שׁ'ל'ם), both in the name of Jerusalem and also in the references to "peace" in Pss. Sol. 8.15-19.

4.1. "My Ear Heard Distress and the Sound of War": Pss. Sol. 8.1-6

Psalms of Solomon 8 uses vivid imagery of the body to describe events that are situated in Jerusalem and the temple. Rather than examining the historical allusions found in this composition, a concern that has been well executed by many already, it is worthwhile to consider how language is rhetorically expressed to arouse certain emotional states within the reader and hearer of this text. In particular, I wish to examine how the images in the opening of Pss. Sol. 8 might assist the speaker and reader in cultivating the subjectivity of Israel. It is important that the Pss. Sol. 8 concludes with a verse in which the pious ones stand in synonymous parallel to Israel.

Psalms of Solomon 8 begins with battle imagery that is viscerally mediated to the reader through the experiences that take place in the speaker's body: the *sounds* of warfare are made manifest in the *physical tremors* in the speaker's loins, knees, heart palpitations, and rattling bones. Terror is especially expressed in the weakening of the speaker's loins, which are otherwise the seat of courage and manly strength. These opening lines of the Pss. Sol. also allow for the reinvigoration of the experiences that are associated with the covenant making and covenant breaking experience in Exod 32 // Deut 9. The mention of a "sound of war" (Φωνὴ πολέμου) referenced here at the very opening of Pss. Sol. 8.1 is the very expression used in the LXX account of Joshua's report to Moses, just prior to the realization that Israel has engaged in the making of a false calf cult (Exod 32:17-18). The shaking that is called to mind by the speaker's report of his own bodily tremors anticipate both the dramatic events that unfold on the mountain, but more importantly, introduce stereotypical language for theophanic experiences and call to mind the encounter with the terrifying warrior deity who causes Israel and all of creation to tremble at Sinai (Exod 19:16, 18). This phenomenon can be compared to other biblical references that speak of the effects of trembling during the moment of encounter (cf. Judg 5:4-5; Joel 2:10; Isa 13:13).[18]

---

18. Samuel E. Loewenstamm, "The Trembling of Nature during the Theophany," in *Comparative Studies in Biblical and Ancient Oriental Literatures*, AOAT 204 (Neukirchen-Vluyn: Neukirchener Verlag, 1984), 173-89. According to Loewenstamm, the image likely comes from ancient Akkadian literature (e.g., "The Prayer to Ishtar").

The internalization and vivid imaginative reenactment of the perceptible effects of a theophanic encounter are expressed in Pss. Sol. 8.4–5:

(4) I heard a sound in Ierousalem, city of a holy precinct.
(5) My lower back was crushed from the report,
My knees weakened;
My heart was afraid;
My bones were shaken like flax

Just as the earth trembles at the approach of the great warrior deity, the psalmist describes his/her own body's physical and psychological (heart) response to the encounter. The speaker's emotional experiences mirror the commonly known response of the created world and also script an emotional response within the reader who could take on these experiences through the first-person "I."[19]

Allusions to Sinai, the site where Israel encountered the invisible deity, reinvigorate foundational memories of covenant-making and also the grave cultic apostasy that took place there. The psalmist speaks of "the roaring firestorm sweeping down through the wilderness" (ὡς καταιγὶς πυρὸς πολλοῦ φερομένου δι' ἐρήμου, Pss. Sol. 8.2), thereby simultaneously evoking the wilderness of Sinai (τὴν ἔρημον τοῦ Σινα, Exod 19:1) and the foundational event where "God descended upon Mt. Sinai in fire" (τὸ δὲ ὄρος τὸ Σινα ἐκαπνίζετο ὅλον διὰ τὸ καταβεβηκέναι ἐπ' αὐτὸ τὸν θεὸν ἐν πυρί, καὶ ἀνέβαινεν ὁ καπνὸς ὡς καπνὸς καμίνου, καὶ ἐξέστη πᾶς ὁ λαὸς σφόδρα, Exod 19:18).

Language and imagery can work together to arouse similar emotions that were had by the Israelites at the foundational covenant moment at Sinai. Because emotions are refelt in the body with the same intensity whether they are first-hand or second-hand experiences, the imaginative reexperiencing of events as they might have been at Sinai can assist the otherwise spiritually righteous and pious speaker and readers of Pss. Sol. 8 to imaginatively cultivate the subjectivity of what it would have been like to stand trembling at Sinai, a cultural and religious event where every

---

19. On the effects of the psalmist's first-person voice as a performative scripting of emotional experiences, see Suzanne Gillmayr-Bucher, "Body Images in the Psalms," *JSOT* 28 (2004): 301–26; Angela Kim Harkins, *Reading with an "I" to the Heavens: Looking at the Qumran Hodayot through the Lens of Visionary Traditions*, Ekstasis 3 (Berlin: de Gruyter, 2012), 69–113.

Israelite stood guilty before God.[20] The golden calf was a scandalous event of cultic apostasy, closely identified with Aaron, the progenitor of what would later become Israel's priesthood. Psalms of Solomon 8.1–5 allude to the foundational event of theophany and covenant-making and also point proleptically to the foundational event of cultic violation by the priest Aaron, the eponymous ancestor of the priestly class of Israel. These elements also fit well the concern to highlight the cultic pollution of the Jerusalem temple, a special concern of Pss. Sol. 8.12.

Physical tremors move through the speaker's loins, knees, heart, and bones. While various parts of the speaker's extended body are enumerated, interestingly, there is no report of visual perception here; the speaker does not refer to what he *sees*, only to what he *hears*. On the one hand, the absence of visual references could suggest some distance between the speaker and the events that are being described, possibly indicating that the speaker and the readers themselves presumably are not close enough to the events on Mount Sinai to see what is transpiring. On the other hand, the bodily range of perceptions that are reported themselves suggest a very close proximity to the events themselves. Such a strategic location could allow a reader or hearer to imagine himself as one of the Israelites at Mount Sinai whose position at the bottom of the holy Mount would have prevented them from fully viewing the events that transpired at the top of the mountain. In other words, the bodily experiences can help to imaginatively cultivate the subjectivity of what it would have been like to have been physically present at the golden calf apostasy, where a position at the base of the mountain was the closest that one could come to the terrifying theophany that was taking place at the top of the mountain. If we think too about the reception of Pss. Sol. 8 by later communities in the fourth–fifth centuries, other theophanic mountaintop events such as the transfiguration (Matt 17:1–9; Mark 9:2–10; Luke 9:28–36) also presuppose that the witnesses (Peter and the sons of Zebedee) took on the posture of falling face-down on the mountainside (Matt 17:6), also preventing the complete visual apprehension of events.

Even so, the absence of visual detail here in the opening scene suggests some removal from events and possibly expresses the psalmist's experience of exile from Jerusalem; an inference that is also corroborated by Pss.

---

20. Of course, only Moses and Joshua were absent from the cultic apostasy at Sinai. For a similar study of the emotional reexperiencing of Sinai, see Harkins, "Emotional Re-experiencing of the Hortatory Narratives," 299–307.

Sol. 8.28, which assumes that the speaker is among the scattered of Israel ("Gather together the dispersion of Israel with pity and kindness, for your faithfulness is with us," Pss. Sol. 8.28). Notably, it is only at the end of this psalm, after the multitude of references to the decisive acts of the warrior deity, when the speaker reports that his visual apprehension of the mighty God through his magnificent righteous deeds; it is only at this point that Pss. Sol. 8.25 states, "Behold, now, O God, you have shown us your judgment in your righteousness; *Our eyes have seen* your judgments, O God."

The Sinai event is one of Israel's foundational experiences. It can be understood as a malleable frame through which the contemporary experiences of the psalmist during the first century BCE can be understood and one which the later readers and hearers of this text could imaginatively access. The set of emotional experiences that fit into this Deuteronomistic understanding of history effectively constructs a malleable framework of experiences within which each reader and hearer, regardless of his or her spiritual standing, could imagine him/herself.[21] In this way, foundational narratives can be updated to accommodate changing circumstances while retaining the powerful emotional contours of the foundational event.[22] Embodied reading, which vividly enacts the experiences that are described (enactive reading), can allow for the formation of egocentric episodic memories that are crucial for the mind's ability to anticipate future events such as the divine punishments that result unfailingly from treachery.[23] These egocentric imagined scenarios of God's punitive judgment can thus function effectively as a constraint on behavior and contribute to the moral decision-making processes of the readers and hearers of this psalm. Because ritually aroused emotions are reexperienced in the body, even community members who had never committed open treason against the group could have imagined the decisive consequences of disobedience with the vividness of first-hand events. Rebecca Sachs Norris

---

21. Lawrence W. Barsalou et al., "Embodiment in Religious Knowledge," *Journal of Cognition and Culture* 5 (2005): 23.

22. Pascal Boyer, "What Are Memories For? Functions of Recall in Cognition and Culture," in *Memory in Mind and Culture*, ed. Pascal Boyer and James V. Wertsch (Cambridge: Cambridge University Press, 2009), 3–28.

23. Kuzmičová, "Presence in the Reading of Literary Narrative," 25–26. This kind of ego-centric foresight is often referred to as mental time-travel in the literature and recognized as exerting an important force in moral decision-making. Boyer, "What Are Memories For?," 13–14.

writes: "That emotion can be refelt in the present when it is recalled enables religious feelings to be layered and developed, because each time a ritual gesture is repeated the emotion is recalled and new emotional memories laid down in association with the old ones to be recalled the next time."[24] The emotional reexperiencing of the events in Pss. Sol. 8 could thus effectively shape future decision-making processes by predisposing pious community members to obey the laws of the covenant (without predetermining that they would do so), perhaps resulting in an even more meticulous scrupulosity among the righteous readers and hearers of these psalms.

4.2. Age-Old Crimes against the Covenant: "I Considered the Judgments of God since the Creation of Heaven and Earth" (Pss. Sol. 8.7–14)

The next unit of the psalm about the wicked in 8.7–14 shifts from the psalmist speaking about his own experiences to describing primordial crimes against the covenant—offenses that have the capacity to defile the sanctuary. This unit begins by mentioning various sexual and moral sins that are hidden but which have become exposed to the light of day. These sexual sins have the capacity to compromise the holiness of the land.[25] The specific view that the sanctuary of the Lord was polluted by these sexual sins was shared by the Psalms of Solomon and other Second Temple texts known as the Testament of Levi and the Damascus Document.[26]

The orientation to a primordial time resembles the admonitory narratives in the Damascus Document.[27] Scholars have previously observed the striking similarities between the Psalms of Solomon and the Damascus Document, especially in the way they conceptualize sin (CD IV, 13–18; cf. Pss. Sol. 1.7–8; 4.5). These associations with the Essene communities described in the ancient sources are interesting, especially in light of the speaker's own account of being at some remove from the city of Jerusalem,

---

24. Rebecca Sachs Norris ("Examining the Structure and Role of Emotion: Contributions of Neurobiology to the Study of Embodied Religious Experience," *Zygon* 40 [2005]: 192–93). Instead of emotions *recalling* memories, it is better to think of emotions as *reinvigorating* or *reconstituting* them.

25. Jonathan Klawans, *Impurity and Sin in Ancient Judaism* (Oxford: Oxford University Press, 2000), 43–60.

26. Klawans, *Impurity and Sin in Ancient Judaism*, 56–60 (e.g., T. Levi 9.9; 14.5–15.1).

27. Harkins, "Emotional Re-experiencing of the Hortatory Narratives," 287–95.

although as scholars have noted before, these connections are inconclusive.[28] Psalms of Solomon 8.7–14 identifies three types of sins that resemble those in the Damascus Document as the "Three Snares of Belial": fornication, wealth, and defiling the sanctuary (CD IV, 13–18). The speaker of Pss. Sol. 8 speaks of incestuous relations (8.9–10) and other forms of sexual pollution (8.12) done in secret.[29] Jonathan Klawans observes that sexual sins become more prominently associated with the defilement of the sanctuary in Second Temple times (in contrast to having only an effect on the land).[30] The specific sin of improper sexual relations, expressed by the language of "mingling" (συνεφύροντο) in Pss. Sol. 8.9, is the same one that appears in a passage detailing the sexual transgressions of Israel in Hos 4:14, a passage that can be understood as a further layering of the foundational cultic apostasy: the golden calf.[31] The bovine references in the book of Hosea, especially at 4:12–19,[32] alludes to the calf cult at Sinai and also strongly indicts various northern shrines of Gilgal and Beth-aven (also known as Bethel) and reinvigorate images of Jeroboam's calf cults of at Bethel and Dan (Hos 4:15–19). These apostate cults were understood to be the cause of the division of the United Kingdom according to the Deuteronomistic Historian (2 Kgs 17:16, 21–23).[33]

---

28. Kenneth Atkinson, *I Cried to the Lord: A Study of the Psalms of Solomon's Historical Background and Social Setting*, JSJSup 84 (Leiden: Brill, 2004), 220–22.

29. The speaker states "with menstrual blood they defiled the sacrifices as though they were common flesh" (8.12).

30. Klawans, *Impurity and Sin in Ancient Judaism*, 59.

31. Pss. Sol. 8.9: ἐν καταγαίοις κρυφίοις αἱ παρανομίαι αὐτῶν ἐν παροργισμῷ· υἱὸς μετὰ μητρὸς καὶ πατὴρ μετὰ θυγατρὸς συνεφύροντο. Hos 4:14: καὶ οὐ μὴ ἐπισκέψωμαι ἐπὶ τὰς θυγατέρας ὑμῶν, ὅταν πορνεύωσιν, καὶ ἐπὶ τὰς νύμφας ὑμῶν, ὅταν μοιχεύωσιν, διότι καὶ αὐτοὶ μετὰ τῶν πορνῶν συνεφύροντο καὶ μετὰ τῶν τετελεσμένων ἔθυον, καὶ ὁ λαὸς ὁ συνίων συνεπλέκετο μετὰ πόρνης.

32. It is possible that this passage from Hos 4 is the scriptural allusion that stands behind CD I, 12–II, 1; see the analysis by Maxine L. Grossman, "Cultivating Identity: Textual Virtuosity and 'Insider' Status," in *Defining Identities: We, You, and the Other in the Dead Sea Scrolls*, ed. Florentino García Martínez and Mladen Popović, STDJ 70 (Leiden: Brill, 2008), 6–10.

33. This intertextual connection between Exod 32 and 1 Kgs 12 (see Exod 32:4, 8 and 1 Kgs 12:28) was well noted by Moses Aberbach and Leivy Smolar, "Aaron, Jeroboam, and the Golden Calves," *JBL* 86 (1967): 129–40; and has since been discussed by Nicolas Wyatt, "Of Calves and Kings: The Canaanite Dimension in the Religion of Israel," *SJOT* 6 (1992): 68–91; Gary N. Knoppers, "Aaron's Calf and Jeroboam's Calves," in *Fortunate the Eyes That See: Essays in Honor of David Noel Freedman in*

Notably the catalogue of sins that are done "in secret" (Pss. Sol. 8.7–14) are also the transgressions that the invisible God has full knowledge. These sins are also not incompatible with the crimes done at the foundation event of covenant breaking of the golden calf event at which moment the newly created covenant was polluted. The suggestion of sexual impropriety can also be seen in the golden calf event in which the people sat down to eat and drink and then arose "to play" (וישב העם לאכל ושתו ויקמו לצחק) (καὶ ἐκάθισεν ὁ λαὸς φαγεῖν καὶ πιεῖν καὶ ἀνέστησαν παίζειν) in Exod 32:6. The verb that appears here has a sexual connotation in Gen 26:8: "And after Isaac had been there for a long time, Abimelech, king of the Philistines, looked out of a window and he saw that behold! Isaac was playing with Rebecca his wife" (pun in Hebrew on the name of the patriarch, יצחק and the verb for "playing" מצחק).[34] This is often taken to refer to some kind of sexual playing or fondling, as it is at this moment when King Abimelech realizes that Isaac and Rebecca are husband and wife. These allusions to the sexual crimes and cultic pollution during the foundational event of the golden calf apostasy are not incompatible with the general crimes that are highlighted in these lines of Pss. Sol. 8.

The specific language that is used in this part of Pss. Sol. 8 is notable as it reinvigorates memories of the dramatic Sinai event in multiple ways. Verses 7–14 succeed in constructing a perception of the deity's presence through active language; God is the one who "exposed their sins before the sun" (8.8), "mixed for them a spirit of confusion" (8.14), and "gave them a cup of undiluted wine to drink" (8.14). God's active role in the exposition and judgment of these secret sins thus creates the perception of his presence in in his absence (invisibility). In this way, the text contributes to the cultivation of virtue in the reader and hearer, predisposing him or her to do the law, even if no appears to be watching, since the invisible God sees all sexual transgressions done in secret—and distributes justice accordingly, even though he himself cannot be seen. In this way, the text can assist in the construction of an ethical constraint on decision-making for an individual who vividly imagines the things described in the psalm.[35]

Celebration of His Seventieth Birthday, ed. Astrid B. Beck (Grand Rapids: Eerdmans, 1995), 92–104.

34. ἐγένετο δὲ πολυχρόνιος ἐκεῖ· παρακύψας δὲ Αβιμελεχ ὁ βασιλεὺς Γεραρων διὰ τῆς θυρίδος εἶδεν τὸν Ισαακ παίζοντα μετὰ Ρεβεκκας τῆς γυναικὸς αὐτοῦ (Gen 26:8).

35. Boyer, "What Are Memories For?," 13–14.

4.3. Honor (τιμή) and Faithfulness (πίστις)

The final section of Pss. Sol. 8 returns to the imagery of God as a military warrior. In Pss. Sol. 8.26–28, the image of God as the military warrior returns the reader back to the opening of the psalm. The speaker states that "we have justified your name which is honored forever" (ἐδικαιώσαμεν τὸ ὄνομά σου τὸ ἔντιμον εἰς αἰῶνας, 8.26) and pleads for "God's mercy and compassion towards us, in gathering the scattered of Israel with mercy and kindness, because your faithfulness] is with us" (ὅτι ἡ πίστις σου μεθ᾽ ἡμῶν, 8.28). The word *faithfulness* (ἡ πίστις) has a wide-ranging meaning, but among its many connotations is one connected to the context of military leaders in the classical literature.[36] The effect is to express confidence in God's military success. It also contrasts the reign of God to that of a tyrant in whom the people do not have faith. In so doing, the text draws readers and hearers to respond to the described event and participate in thoughts of the covenant relationship.

In Pss. Sol. 8, there are two places where the Greek mentions "God's pious ones" (οἱ ὅσιοι τοῦ θεοῦ), and, notably, both instances are associated with the praise of God. The first appears in the Pss. Sol. 8.23 in which the speaker says that "God's **pious ones** are like innocent lambs (οἱ ὅσιοι τοῦ θεοῦ ὡς ἀρνία ἐν ἀκακίᾳ ἐν μέσῳ αὐτῶν) in their midst." The text goes on to say that the Lord is worthy of praise (αἰνετὸς κύριος). Later on in Pss. Sol. 8, the pious ones are again associated with the activity of praising God. In the Pss. Sol. 8.34 it is said that "the Lord is worthy to be praised [αἰνετὸς κύριος] for his judgments by the mouths of the pious ones [ἐν στόματι ὁσίων]." The association of the pious ones and the praise of God can perhaps indicate that the very act is itself worthy of emulation as the right response to divine chastisement.[37]

---

36. Teresa Morgan, "Is Pistis/Fides Experienced as an Emotion in the Late Roman Republic, Early Principate, and Early Church?," in *Emotions in Greece and Rome: Texts, Images, Material Culture*, vol. 2 of *Unveiling Emotions*, ed. Angelos Chaniotis and Pierre Ducrey; Heidelberger Althistorische Beitrage und Epigraphische Studien 55 (Stuttgart: Franz Steiner, 2013), 199–200.

37. The reference "pious ones" (οἱ ὅσιοι), interestingly, is the same term used to refer to the Essenes in a quote attributed to Philo, preserved in Eusebius, *Praep. ev.* 8.11 (see also Pss. Sol. 8.34: ἐν στόματι ὁσίων).

5. Conclusion

How were the Psalms of Solomon experienced in the ancient world? While we cannot answer this question with absolute certainty, it is worthwhile revisiting the ways in which we imagine the reading process to have taken place in individual readers and hearers of the past. For a collection like the Psalms of Solomon, the predominance of scriptural language and the dramatic and vivid style of the text suggest that the text aimed to have a desired effect upon the reader and hearer that goes beyond the simple expression of content or the rote recitation of the psalms and moves toward an integrative experience of the text that imagines how embodied cognition work together in the cultivation of an experience.

This paper has examined how language about foundational events can rhetorically construct experiences about the body that have the vividness of first-hand experiences. Language and imagery along with a Deuteronomistic theology could have aroused emotional states that are not incompatible with the foundational experience at Sinai: the covenant making, apostasy of the golden calf, and covenant remaking. The effect of active imaginative engagement of Sinai could help to make present an otherwise invisible deity through the reinvigoration of tales of his providential and punitive presence in Israel's history. This emotional reexperiencing of the otherwise invisible God can participate in guiding an already pious reader or hearer to an even more intense scrupulosity since even those who have never openly committed the sins against the covenant that are detailed in Pss. Sol. 8.7–14 or of apostasy could know with a first-hand intensity what it was like to be guilty at Sinai and to receive a righteous punishment from the hand of God.

Social Memory Features in the Psalms of Solomon

Rodney A. Werline

1. Introduction

While in popular thought memory may be imagined as nostalgic rumination or recollection of facts, modern investigation into memory has shown that the process of memory is quite complicated and is socially constructed in the individual.[1] Maurice Halbwachs was the first to put forward this understanding of memory, doing so having been influenced by Emile Durkheim. Halbwachs asserted the following about memory:

> But individual memory is nevertheless a part or an aspect of group memory, since each impression and each fact, even if it apparently concerns a particular person exclusively, leave a lasting memory only to the extent that one has thought it over—to the extent that it is connected with the thoughts that come to us from the social milieu.[2]

This basic premise introduced by Halbwachs has remained a foundational component in social memory theory. Like the founder of the theory, Barry Schwartz claims that memory and social memory theory can be summed up quite simply:

> Memory is a fundamental property of the mind, an indispensable component of culture, and an essential aspect of tradition. Although individuals alone possess the capacity to remember the past, they never

---

1. Alan Kirk, "Social and Cultural Memory," in *Memory, Tradition and Text: Uses of the Past in Early Christianity*, ed. Alan Kirk and Tom Thatcher, SemeiaSt 52 (Atlanta: Society of Biblical Literature, 2005), 2.

2. Maurice Halbwachs, *On Collective Memory*, ed. and trans. Lewis A. Coser (Chicago: University of Chicago Press, 1992), 53.

do so singly; they do so with and against others situated in different groups and through the knowledge and symbols that predecessors and contemporaries transmit to them.³

Both quotes bear the unmistakable markings of Durkheim's elevation of the collective consciousness of the community over the individual members of the group.⁴

Some theorists, especially some in the field of cognitive science, have pushed back against cultural anthropological approaches to memory, in which they see Durkheimian cultural determinism as erasing individual autonomy and psychology. Pascal Boyer lays out the basic contours of this debate in his essay "What Are Memories For? Functions of Recall in Cognition and Culture."⁵ Boyer hails from the cognitive study of religion approach and gives significant privilege to these methods, and he has less sympathy for anthropological approaches to memory. While he can appreciate Halbwachs's contribution of social memory theory, Boyer complains that Durkheim and the tradition that flowed out of his work ignored social psychology for cultural interpretation.⁶ He thinks that social memory wrongly over-emphasizes that the individual is determined by the dominant cultural construction of memory and leaves little room for individual reaction to culture. Boyer wants to know "why humans remember?," and by this he wonders how memory served some evolutionary purpose. Boyer must admit that memory, though it seems to be about the past, is actually not about the past, for, as he states, "memory has a biological function to the extent that it serves to organize current behavior."⁷ Drawing on the theories of Thomas Suddendorf and Michael C. Corballis, Boyer suggests that humans, in part, developed memory because "recall evolved as a precious way of providing relevant information to organisms faced with complex choices," "a way to provide organisms with a range of complex examples against which to com-

---

3. Barry Schwartz, "Where There's Smoke, There's Fire: Memory and History," in *Memory and Identity in Ancient Judaism and Early Christianity: A Conversation with Barry Schwartz*, ed. Tom Thatcher, SemeiaSt 78 (Atlanta: SBL Press, 2014), 9.

4. For a brief discussion of collective consciousness within the context of social memory theory, see Schwartz, "Where There's Smoke, There's Fire," 19.

5. Pascal Boyer, "What Are Memories For? Functions in Recall of Cognition and Culture," in *Memory in Mind and Culture*, ed. Pascal Boyer and James V. Wertsch (Cambridge: Cambridge University Press, 2009), 3–28.

6. Boyer, "What Are Memories For?," 11.

7. Boyer, "What Are Memories For?," 3.

pare present situations and select the most beneficial course of action."[8] Further, in order to maintain social stability, he says, "it would make great sense to store episodes of social interaction in great detail as a means to form impressions about the reliability of other agents."[9] Finally, for the interests of this essay, Boyer also recognizes that episodic recollection provides a person with an affective experience—"the possibility of experience (at least part of) the emotional impact as well as the details of the revisited scene."[10]

So, social memory theorists and cognitive scientists at least agree that memory's primary focus lies not on the past but on the present moment. Further, Boyer must give some nod to the fact that cultures do share a common memory and that memories are in part culturally formed. Further, one might ask Boyer how frequently a need to organize current behavior is the result of a culturally generated demand upon an individual.

If the past is invoked in light of the needs of the present, then memory is no longer history but a construction for the present moment. This does not reduce memory to mere fantasy but emphasizes that memory is a reconstructed history from the perspective of present needs.[11] This observation would, in part, explain the difficulty in reconstructing history from texts such as the Psalms of Solomon, as well as biblical and Second Temple Jewish texts in general. Loren Stuckenbruck has expressed this issue very well in his analysis of the attempted reconstructions of the Teacher of Righteousness in the Qumran pesharim. He encourages interpreters to focus more attention on what can be learned about the authors of the pesharim "by studying what they have to say about their community's formative past" and, thus, less on historical reconstructions of the Teacher of Righteousness.[12] As a result, the most important past that the text makes

---

8. Boyer, "What Are Memories For?," 14.
9. Boyer, "What Are Memories For?," 15.
10. Boyer, "What Are Memories For?," 15.
11. For this problem, see Holly Hearon, "The Construction of Social Memory in Biblical Interpretation," *Enc* 67 (2006): 349; Schwartz, "Where There's Smoke, There's Fire," 17–26. Schwartz adopts a somewhat optimistic stance on the limitations on the way in which a society or historian can distort a memory in relation to the historical event: "No one can doubt that every story of every historical event of figure is modified by the way it is told from one generation to the next, but it is equally certain that such a story loses plausibility if it fails to acknowledge minimal claims of accepted knowledge" (23).
12. Loren T. Stuckenbruck, "The Legacy of the Teacher of Righteousness in the Dead Sea Scrolls," in *New Perspectives on Old Texts, Proceedings of the Tenth*

available resides in the moment the text was generated, rather than the authors own past they claim to depict.

This essay primarily assumes a cultural anthropological approach to memory in the Psalms of Solomon, although it occasionally draws on insights from cognitive science as well as some features of trauma theory. The essay is only an initial foray into the usefulness of social memory theory for analyzing aspects of the Psalms of Solomon. It assumes that much more detailed and extensive analysis should be conducted.

A number of basic features of the Psalms of Solomon makes the collection ideal for using social memory theory in order to better understand the first-century BCE group that valued the collection. First, several psalms (1, 2, perhaps 7, 8, 17, 18) are a response to the early decades of Roman occupation in Palestine after Pompey marches into Judea in 63 BCE and enters the Jerusalem temple.[13] While it is unclear how much time passes between that event and the production of at least those particular psalms, those texts are looking back and structuring the memory of that event for those who hear the psalms in a later era. The authors speak about this turning-point in their history with language traditionally used to describe their more remote past; that is, they draw on sacred traditions. Second, if the psalms do go through an additional redaction sometime during or after Herod's reign, the timing of that update might be significant. In this case, we find another reapplication of collective memory to a changing situation. Further, even the hope for a messianic figure in Pss. Sol. 17 draws on language from the sacred past with the present in mind. In this instance, future hope is also shaped by the past, but in the process, the author is especially commenting on the contemporary setting in Judea. Third, even in what George E. Nickelsburg labelled as the psalms of the individual (Pss. Sol. 3, 4, 5, 6, 9–16), collective memory weighs heavily. Most fascinating are the psalms in which the poet reflects on a moment in his own past. Even texts that address the present in a seemingly individualistic manner still do so with a sense of memory shaped by culture; that is, the past, or cultural language from the past, impinges on the present conversation.

International Symposium of the Orion Center for the Study of the Dead Sea Scrolls and Associated Literature, 9–11 January, 2005, ed. Esther G. Chazon and Betsy Halpern-Amaru, STJD 88 (Leiden: Brill, 2010), 49.

13. For the designation "Psalms of the Nation," see George W. E. Nickelsburg, *Jewish Literature between the Bible and the Mishnah*, 2nd ed. (Minneapolis: Fortress, 2005), 238–44. Nickelsburg also includes psalm 11 in this group.

Finally, in retelling the past in both the psalms of the nation and the individual, memory enjoys a special relationship with commemoration, even though the precise setting in which such commemorations took place remains unclear. For social memory theory, this recitation of memory is also important. As Jan Assmann explains, cultural memory is about "the handing down of meaning," and in this process "rituals are part of cultural memory because they are the form through which cultural meaning is both handed down and brought to present life."[14] Alan Kirk introduces the importance of commemoration in the following manner:

> Communication is essential for the formation of memory. Memory emerges in coherent, durable form to the extent remembrances find articulation and reinforcement in communicative interaction within a group, and conversely, a person's remembrances fade to the extent they are not taken up in the groups with which he or she is affiliated.[15]

On this point, Kirk certainly follows Halbwachs and Assmann's positions. Generally, one might think of commemoration as specifically reserved for large ceremonies of grand historical events, for example, July 4, Bastille Day, or Passover. However, commemoration and recitation can happen in much more daily, mundane, or quotidian ways—even in liturgical practice. As far as can be determined, the psalms do not seem to be connected to any specific Jewish festivals. The psalms, however, seem to have been performed in the gatherings of the pious (cf. 10.7; 17.16, 43). Whether the gatherings should be understood as worship in a synagogue remains difficult to determine and historically problematic.[16] While the evidence limits our understanding of how these psalms were used within the community, in form and in content they at least imagine a communal, not private, setting. However, even if the psalms were only involved in private use, their content reflects culturally constructed memories and indicates that the social has invaded the private.

---

14. Jan Assmann, *Cultural Memory and Early Civilization: Writing, Remembrance and Political Imagination* (Cambridge: Cambridge University Press, 2011), 7.
15. Kirk, "Social and Cultural Memory," 3.
16. Nadav Sharon in a conversation about this passage in the Psalms of Solomon urged caution in assuming that "gatherings" refers to worship in a synagogue as one would find in a later period.

2. Reflections on Remembering: Pss. Sol. 3, 6, 16

The Psalms of Solomon speak about the process of remembering. Three excellent examples appear in Pss. Sol. 3, 6, and 16. The uses of a form of the word "to remember" and the context in which they appear allow confidence in a conclusion that the authors are actually consciously reflecting on the memory process.[17]

> Why do you sleep, soul, and do not praise the Lord?
>   Sing a new song to God, who is worthy to be praised
> Sing and be aware of how he is aware of you.
>   for a good psalm to God is from a glad heart
> The righteous remember the Lord all the time,
> δίκαιοι μνημονεύουσιν διὰ παντὸς τοῦ κυρίου
>   by acknowledging and proving the Lord's judgments right
>   ἐν ἐξομολογήσει καὶ δικαιώσει τὰ κρίματα κυρίου (Pss. Sol. 3.2)

> Happy is the man whose heart is ready to call on the name of the Lord;
>   when he remembers the name of the Lord, he will be saved.
> μακάριος ἀνήρ οὗ ἡ καρδία αὐτοῦ ἑτοίμη ἐπικαλέσασθαι τὸ ὄνομα κυρίου
> ἐν τῷ μνημονεύειν αὐτὸν τὸ ὄνομα κυρίου σωθήσεται.
> His ways are directed by the Lord,
>   and the works of his hands are protected by the Lord his God (Pss. Sol. 6.1–2)

> I will give thanks to you, O God, who came to my aide for my salvation
>   and who did not count me with the sinners for my destruction.
> Do not take your mercy away from me, O God,
>   nor your memory from my heart until death.
> ἐξομολογήσομαί σοι ὁ θεός ὅτι ἀντελάβου μου εἰς σωτηρίαν
>   καὶ οὐκ ἐλογίσω με μετὰ τῶν ἁμαρτωλῶν εἰς ἀπώλειαν
> μὴ ἀποστήσῃς τὸ ἔλεός σου ἀπ' ἐμοῦ ὁ θεός
>   μηδὲ τὴν μνήμην σου ἀπὸ καρδίας μου ἕως θανάτου (Pss. Sol. 16.5–6)

---

17. All English translations come from Robert B. Wright, "Psalms of Solomon," *OTP* 2:639–70. For the Greek text, see Alfred Rahlfs, ed. *Septuaginta* (Stuttgart: Deutsche Bibelgesellschaft, 1935/1979) as it appears in Bible Works 9. Translations of the Bible are from the NSRV.

First, in all three passages cited above a cognate of "to remember" lies either in parallelism to or in close proximity to an act of speaking: Pss. Sol. 3: μνημονεύουσιν / ἐξομολογήσει καὶ δικαιώσει; Pss. Sol. 6: ἐπικαλέσασθαι / ἐν τῷ μνημονεύειν; Pss. Sol. 16: ἐξομολογήσομαί / τὴν μνήμην. While remembering includes an inward moment, the text also emphasizes the outward action of the process—the recital or a confession or perhaps acclamation. Within each psalm as a whole, the recital is said to take the shape of a prayer, or perhaps it is the psalm itself as it is performed before the community. William Horbury assesses the situation as follows,

> In the Psalms of Solomon ... the remembrance of God has become a prominent theme, especially in the three psalms concerned with the topic of prayer (3, 6, 16). This remembrance is now clearly cherished in the heart as well as uttered; it implies reflection as well as recital, and belongs to a system of piety in which liturgical practices are interpreted with regard to morality and the soul's health. The two poles of remembrance of God are recital and moral internalization.[18]

However, as his exposition continues, Horbury eventually gives more weight to the internal aspect of memory: "When the verb *zakhar* is used in passages on remembrance of the deity, recital can still be important, but the mental activity of remembering comes more plainly into view."[19] This assertion that interiorizes key aspects of remembering may reflect the western tradition's separation of mind and body or a theological preference that moves away from practice to internalization—the inward experience of grace over the outward expression of works. Thus, this interpretive move may also reflect the lingering effects of Protestant theology.

By contrast, there is something important about the embodiment of the memory in these texts—the memory is embedded, sustained, and made alive in practice, which sometimes includes recitation before a community. This is sometimes the case in the Hebrew Bible in regards to memory. To remember YHWH includes something more than merely thinking about God but doing something—keeping the commandments, singing a hymn, offering a prayer, or offering a sacrifice. Likewise, when

---

18. William Horbury, "The Remembrance of God in the Psalms of Solomon," in *Memory in the Bible and Antiquity: The Fifth Durham-Tübingen Research Symposium (Durham, September 2004)*, ed. Stephen C. Barton, Loren T. Stuckenbruck, and Benjamin G. Wold, WUNT 212 (Tübingen: Mohr Siebeck, 2007), 112.

19. Horbury, "Remembrance of God in the Psalms of Solomon," 114.

God remembers the people, there is an action—God does not just think about the people. While much more detailed examination could be done on the connection between memory and action in the Hebrew Bible, these texts provide some examples of the close relationship between the two:

> But God remembered Noah and all the wild animals and all the domestic animals that were with him in the ark. And God made a wind blow over the earth, and the waters subsided. (Gen 8:1)

> Moses said to the people, "Remember this day on which you came out of Egypt, out of the house of slavery, because the LORD brought you out from there by strength of hand; no leavened bread shall be eaten." (Exod 13:3)

> Remember the sabbath day, and keep it holy. (Exod 20:8)

> You have the fringe so that, when you see it, you will remember all the commandments of the LORD and do them. (Num 15:39)

> So you shall remember and do all my commandments, and you shall be holy to your God. (Num 15:40)

Similarly, in the New Testament, taking the Lord's Supper is an act of remembering:

> And when he had given thanks, he broke it and said, "This is my body that is for you. Do this in remembrance of me." In the same way he took the cup also, after supper, saying, "This cup is the new covenant in my blood. Do this, as often as you drink it, in remembrance of me." (1 Cor 11:24–25)

Thus, remembering is not simply internal reflection; it is something that one enacts and embodies. Memory's connection to action also generally leads to a particular kind of moral life, as the person who remembers also honors the relationship that the person has with another person or with God.

Recitation in the Psalms of Solomon undoubtedly had pedagogical purposes. The psalms provided a model of and for ideal moral behavior in the community.[20] Halbwachs recognized this feature of social memory in the early days of the history of the methodology: "Memory retains only those events that are of a pedagogic character."[21] Further, recitation in a communal setting, before witnesses or with a congregation, as ritualized action establishes obligation upon the speaker or community as a whole. Assmann asserts this role for cultural memory as follows:

> "Memory culture" is concerned with social obligation and is firmly linked to the group. The question here is: "What must we not forget?" This question is generally a more or less explicit and relatively central element of any group.... In other words, memory culture is linked to the 'memory that forms a community.'"[22]

Roy Rappaport also recognized this feature of ritual action. For him, ritual's primary office was to establish obligation:

> To *perform* a liturgical order, which is by definition a more or less *invariant* sequence of formal acts and utterances *encoded by someone other than the performer* himself, is *necessarily to conform to it*.[23]

In each of the psalms quoted above, the act of remembering God is also closely aligned with God's deliverance of the individual. In Pss. Sol. 3, the righteous person acknowledges God's just disciple, that is, correction, of his sins. The righteous person receives God's punishment and understands that this averts piling sin upon sin:

> The confidence of the righteous (comes) from God their savior;
> sin after sin does not visit the house of the righteous

---

20. This, of course, plays on Clifford Geertz famous use of this phrase and the double function of a blueprint. See Clifford Geertz, *The Interpretation of Cultures* (New York: Basic, 1973), 93. Barry Schwartz (*Abraham Lincoln and the Forge of Memory* [Chicago: University of Chicago Press, 2000], 18) also applies Geertz words in this context.
21. Halbwachs, *On Collective Memory*, 23.
22. Assmann, *Cultural Memory and Early Civilization*, 16. At least some of Assmann's quotations seem to come from a work by Pierre Nora, though the documentation seems unclear and no page number is cited.
23. Roy A. Rappaport, *Ritual and Religion in the Making of Humanity*, Cambridge Studies in Social and Cultural Anthropology 110 (Cambridge: Cambridge University Press, 1999), 118, emphasis original.

> The righteous constantly searches his house
> to remove his unintentional sin. (Pss. Sol. 3.6–7)

The wicked do not engage in this cycle and replace thankfulness for discipline with curses:

> The sinner stumbles and curses his life,
> the day of his birth, and his mother's pains.
> He adds sin upon sin in his life;
> he falls—his fall is serious—and he will not get up. (Pss. Sol. 3.9–10)

In a wordplay, the wicked will experience a disastrous ironic twist when they are swept away from God's memory:

> The destruction of the sinner is forever,
> and he will not be remembered when (God) looks after the righteous. (Pss. Sol. 3.11)

This verse also uses the language of salvation in relation to remembrance.

In Pss. Sol. 6, the poet once again connects remembering the name of God and deliverance. In this instance, the psalmist explains that calling on the name (6.1), blessing the name (6.4), singing in honor of the name (6.4), and praying to the Lord (6.5) enact a life of confidence. Thus, remembering again appears within the context of several pious actions that involve performance and perhaps some kind of recitation.

Somewhat similar to the theme of psalm 3, Pss. Sol. 16 depicts the psalmist in a dangerous moment. The author recalls a moment when his "soul was drawn away from the Lord God of Israel" (16.3). According to the psalmist, he was even "near the gates of Hades with the sinner" (16.2). The turning point for the psalmist occurs much like psalm 2 explains—God visits the wandering righteous person with discipline: "He jabbed me as a horse is goaded to keep awake; my savior and protector of all times saved me" (16.4). This evokes a response of thanks and the request that God never remove God's memory from the psalmist's heart (16.5–6). At this juncture, the psalm pivots to requests help in living a moral life. The struggle to remain righteous is cast in the vocabulary of tradition, as the text echoes with language from Psalms and Proverbs and is placed within a report, not just for himself, but for his community (16.7–11). When the reader shared the memory with a gathered group, the community also experienced the past memory as something for their present situation, and they are being shaped by this past.

While these texts seem to focus on the individual, the practice is socially constructed and the act of remembering is modeled by many passages found in the Hebrew Bible. By taking up the language of the culture for the recital, the speaker situates the experience within the cultural history of the people. In the language of Pierre Bourdieu, the authors of the Psalms of Solomon draw from their own *habitus* and quickly and artfully adapt their language and action to their current needs. Worth noting in this process is that some of what constitutes *habitus* has been constructed through the process of social memory. The present sounds like the past, or, perhaps, the past sounds forth again in the present. For example, Pss. Sol. 3 draws its language about a "new song" from language manifested in Pss 33:3; 40:3; 96:1; 98:1; 144:9; 149:1; and Isa 42:10, poetic texts which often propose song as a response to God's saving deeds. As Kenneth Atkinson suggests, the question "Why do you sleep?" may be an adaptation of the lament in Ps 44:2, as the psalmist turns the inquiry upon himself instead of God.[24] Again, this is reminiscent of the ideas of Halbwachs, who, in his social memory theory, noted that sacred texts become ritualized in the practice of religion and that they take on a material form: "Rites consist of a body of gestures, words, and liturgical objects established in a material form. From this point of view, sacred texts have a ritual character."[25] Kirk affirms this with his quote from Yosef Yerushalmi: "Memory flowed through two channels, ritual and recital."[26]

3. Memory of Pompey and Herod the Great in Pss. Sol. 1, 2, 8, 17

As explained, social memory theory distinguishes between events as they really were and the development of a narrative which a culture employs to organize the selected the events. As mentioned above, Pss. Sol. 1, 2, 8, and 17 contain a cultural reconstruction of the events of 63 BCE and perhaps

---

24. Kenneth Atkinson, *An Intertextual Study of the Psalms of Solomon* (Lewiston, NY: Mellen, 2001), 56.
25. Halbwachs, *On Collective Memory*, 116.
26. Kirk, "Social and Cultural Memory," 9. His quote is from Yosef Yerushalmi, *Zakhor: Jewish History and Jewish Memory* (Seattle: University of Washington Press, 1982), 11.

may have been updated after Herod came to power in Judea. The authors are not interested in presenting a linear retelling of the events leading up to Roman occupation. Instead, the events are told in such a way to say something about the present situation of the people and the future for which they hope. In this process, societies also reveal how they view themselves, as Assmann explains: "I investigate *how* societies remember, and how they visualize themselves in the course of their remembering."[27] This certainly bears out in these psalms.

As many interpreters have noted, and Atkinson argued, these chapters in the Psalms of Solomon teem with language from Israel's traditions. Thus, the author is primarily interested in retelling this more recent past through language, images, and theology found in the people's ancient memories. How the people remember Israel's much longer story also undergoes change in their current presentation. In social memory theory, talking about one event and telling it through language that is often related to other events, or one particular event, is called "keying."[28] This frequently occurs in religious texts because there is often a sacred tradition through which the present is being read. However, political speeches often employ this same technique.

3.1. Pss. Sol. 1–2

The authors of the psalms about the nation attribute everything that happened in Roman invasion and subsequent rule as the result of the people's sins. Psalms of Solomon 1 and 2, as the text of the Psalms of Solomon now exists, seem to go together, especially emphasize this. Psalms of Solomon 1 establishes the voice of the two psalms as Mother Zion. She expresses her surprise at the arrival of foreign armies (1.1–3), until she discovers that the people had sinned in secret (1.7). Psalms of Solomon 2 explains the extent of the people's sins, though the text still lacks enough detail to determine the precise arguments that the group had with other Jews at that time. Further, the depiction of the people's sins falls into traditional polemical language, making a specific analysis of the authors' disagreement with other groups almost impossible to reconstruct in detail (2.9–13). Such language

---

27. Assmann, *Cultural Memory and Early Civilization*, 4.
28. Schwartz, "Where There's Smoke, There's Fire," 16.

is connotative, and it probably does not literally describe the opponents but simply casts them as the opponents.[29]

The language that especially keys the memory to the Deuteronomic tradition, to use social memory terminology, is found in 2.15–18:[30]

> I shall prove you right, O God, in uprightness of heart;
>   for your judgments are right, O God.
> For you have rewarded the sinners according to their actions,
>   and according to their extremely wicked sins.
> You have exposed their sins, that your judgment might be evident;
>   you have obliterated their memory from the earth.
> God is a righteous judge and he will not be impressed by appearances.
> (Pss. Sol. 2.15–18)

The declaration of God's righteous (*Gerichtsdoxologie*) became a standard feature of penitential prayers that sprang from Deuteronomic tradition, and it holds a crucial position in the Psalms of Solomon.[31] Through these acclamations, the community ritually acknowledged God's discipline in their own time. Thus, the psalms diagnosed current struggles as like those of Israel's past—even problems displayed continuity with the past. My earlier analysis of *paideia* in the Psalms of Solomon led to a conclusion that collection played a crucial role in the formation of the pious members of the community.[32] Acclamations by the community of God's righteousness in all God's actions contributed to that formation. As I have argued elsewhere, "the *Psalms of Solomon* reveals a community that understood how practice shapes the dispositions of individuals and communities."[33] This current analysis shows that part of that formation included providing the framework and language to form the pious' social memory, and by

---

29. Luke T. Johnson, "The New Testament's Anti-Jewish Slander and the Conventions of Ancient Polemic," *JBL* 108 (1989): 419–44.

30. Rodney A. Werline, *Penitential Prayer in Second Temple Judaism: The Development of a Religious Institution*; EJL 13 (Atlanta: Scholars Press, 1998), 185–88.

31. Rodney A. Werline, "The Formation of the Pious Person in the Psalms of Solomon," in *The Psalms of Solomon: Language, History, Theology*, ed. Eberhard Bons and Patrick Pouchelle, EJL 40 (Atlanta: SBL Press, 2015), 139–47.

32. Rodney A. Werline, "The Experience of God's *Paideia* in the Psalms of Solomon," in *Linking Text and Experience*, vol. 2 of *Experientia*, ed. Colleen Shantz and Rodney A. Werline;, EJL 35 (Atlanta: Society of Biblical Literature, 2012), 17–44.

33. Werline, "Formation of the Pious Person in the Psalms of Solomon," 154.

forming their memory the psalms formed their moral life and vision. Brad Embry has also recently emphasized the presence of prophetic language, especially from Ezekiel, in psalm 2.[34]

3.2. Pss. Sol. 8

Upon hearing the sounds of war at Jerusalem, the anonymous speaker in Pss. Sol. 8 remembers his own reaction:

> My ear heard distress and the sound of war,
>   the blast of the trumpet sounding slaughter and destruction.
> The sound of many people as of a violent storm,
>   as a raging fire storm sweeping through the wilderness.
> And I said to my heart, Where, then, will God judge it?
> I heard a sound in Jerusalem, the holy city.
> My stomach was crushed at what I heard;
>   my knees were weak, my heart was afraid,
>   my bones shook like reeds. (Pss. Sol. 8.1–5)

The speaker in the psalm presents himself as a witness to the events surrounding the Romans arrival at Jerusalem and their assault on the city, though the report focuses on hearing the gathering armies and the attack instead of seeing the assault. Like Mother Zion in psalm 1, the author expresses surprise that God would bring judgment against the city: "I said, they directed their ways in righteousness" (Pss. Sol. 8.6; cf. Pss. Sol. 1.3–4). However, the psalmist somehow realizes that their sins were in secret, in places "underground," which God now lays open to the world (Pss. Sol. 8.8–10).

Rome's capture of the Jerusalem was catastrophic. The siege lasted three months, and it came to end with great bloodshed. Josephus reports that when the Romans breached the temple area, they slaughtered the priests as they were offering sacrifices (Josephus, *A.J.* 14.63–67). Josephus numbers the Jewish dead at "some twelve thousand" (*A.J.* 14.71). Aristobulus II, his family members, and other Jewish leaders were taken to Rome as prisoners. Undoubtedly, such an experience was traumatic for

---

34. Brad Embry, "Some Thoughts on and Implications from Genre Categorization in the Psalms of Solomon," in *The Psalms of Solomon: Language, History, Theology*, ed. Eberhard Bons and Patrick Pouchelle, EJL 40 (Atlanta: SBL Press, 2015), 68–72.

the victims, which would include all the people who watched the events transpire and suddenly found themselves under another brutal imperial rule. As a result, trauma theory might complement social memory theory at this point by providing tools for examining the way the Psalms of Solomon speak about his horrific experience.

As Judith Herman has explained, humans respond to such traumatic events with a "complex, integrated system of reactions, encompassing both body and mind."[35] The bodily sensations mentioned in the psalm would fit with Herman's observation that a "threat initially arouses the sympathetic nervous system, causing the person in danger to feel an adrenalin rush and go into a state of alert."[36] At the sound of the attack, the psalmist declares: "My stomach was crushed.... My knees were weak, my heart was afraid, my bones shook like reeds" (Pss. Sol. 8.5). Clearly the psalmist has an embodied emotional response to the sound of the battle. Other members of the community undoubtedly shared with the psalmist a similar reaction.

With this expression of terror as a response to the catastrophe, the psalmist may provide a valuable service to the community. Herman explains, "Traumatic memories lack verbal narrative and context; rather, they are encoded in the form of vivid sensations and images."[37] Further, trauma fragments the victim's "complex system of self-protection that normally functions in an integrative fashion."[38] Thus, the psalmist, and perhaps all the psalms related to the fate of the people in the collection, supplies the language to organize and express the traumatic experience. If so, the authors of the psalms may also be following a model that they found in their sacred traditions. David Carr has recently examined the production of the Hebrew Bible in light of trauma theory. He observes the crucial role that Israel's fall to Assyria, Jerusalem's fall to Babylon, and the Babylonian exile have played in the collection of texts. These were integrated

---

35. Judith Herman, *Trauma and Recovery: The Aftermath of Violence from Domestic Abuse to Political Terror* (New York: Basic Books, 1992), 34. Herman's investigations reveal that victims of traumatic events may even enter an altered state of consciousness, sometimes even experiencing themselves as out of their own body. She proposes that these altered states "might be regarded as one of nature's small mercies, a protection against unbearable pain" (43)

36. Herman, *Trauma and Recovery*, 34.

37. Herman, *Trauma and Recovery*, 38.

38. Herman, *Trauma and Recovery*, 35.

into a "master narrative" that gave shape to the group's identity, which had been shredded by the trauma.[39] By the choice of language, the authors of the Psalms of Solomon affirm a similar master narrative, or perhaps incorporate their experience into the master narrative that occurs in many Hebrew Bible texts, and adapt it for themselves and their own community.

The author's memory in psalm 8 about the event also bears some resemblance to what cognitive scientists call "flashbulb memories." Robert N. McCauley and E. Thomas Lawson identify flashbulb memories as those that "concern our recall for the circumstances in which we learned of some significant event that, usually, was unexpected."[40] The flashbulb metaphor highlights the "brevity, surprise, and indiscriminate illumination (of the circumstances at learning)" about the event.[41] Drawing on the work of Roger Brown and James Kulik, McCauley and Lawson suggest that "a special neural mechanism may automatically register all available information connected with the context when learning suddenly of a 'significant novelty' that is emotionally arousing."[42]

3.3. Pss. Sol. 17

The future hope found in psalm 17 offers another fascinating place to explore social memory within these psalms. This psalm, as is well-known, anticipates the appearance of a messianic figure who will deliver the people from oppressive rule and will establish a just society. As in Pss. Sol. 1, 2, and 8, Pss. Sol. 17 draws on Deuteronomic ideology and identifies sin as the cause for the catastrophes that have come upon the people: "But (because of) our sins, sinners rose up against us, they set upon us and drove us out" (Pss. Sol. 17.5). The author goes on to describe a society that is collapsed, as just has disappeared, especially as it relates to the com-

---

39. David Carr, *Holy Resilience: The Bible's Traumatic Origin* (New Haven: Yale University Press, 2014), 8.

40. Robert N. McCauley and E. Thomas Lawson, *Bringing Ritual to Mind: Psychological Foundations of Cultural Forms* (Cambridge: Cambridge University Press, 2002), 56. After an overview of the phenomenon of flashbulb memories, McCauley and Lawson review various studies about the accuracy of these memories after some time passes since the actual event. In general, they examine how humans remember rituals and their meaning in order to pass them to the next generation.

41. McCauley and Lawson, *Bringing Ritual to Mind*, 57.

42. McCauley and Lawson, *Bringing Ritual to Mind*, 57.

munity who produced the text.[43] Drawing especially on language from Pss 2:9; 104:7, and Isa 11:2–4, the author envisions the arrival of a messiah who will smash the wicked and will restore justice in the land. Following this, in accordance with prophetic images, the gentiles will come to Jerusalem. However, the future does not simply look like past prophecies, for the author's presentation of the messiah casts him according to the interests and ideology of the scribes responsible for the Psalms of Solomon.[44] Assmann perfectly summarizes this process as follows:

> Thus collective memory operates simultaneously in two directions: backward and forward. It not only reconstructs the past but it also organizes the experience of the present and the future. It would therefore be absurd to draw a contrast between the "principle of memory" and the "principle of hope," because each conditions the other and each is unthinkable without the other."[45]

Features of Pss. Sol. 17 suggest that the text was probably updated following Herod's rise to power.[46] The text seems to depict the last days of Hasmonean rule, when Herod essentially hunted down members of the Hasmonean line (Pss. Sol. 17.9b). The description of the oppressive ruler as acting like the gentiles better fits Herod's actions (17.14), since Pompey did not remain in Jerusalem. Further, the reference to a famine at the time of the siege of the city (17.18b–19a) also occurred at the time of Herod's approach and not during Pompey's assault.[47]

---

43. See Rodney A. Werline, "The Psalms of Solomon and Ideology of Rule," in *Conflicted Boundaries in Wisdom and Apocalypticism*, ed. Benjamin G. Wright III and Lawrence M. Wills, SymS 35 (Atlanta: Society of Biblical Literature, 2005), 77–82.

44. See Werline, "Psalms of Solomon and Ideology of Rule," 77–85.

45. Assmann, *Cultural Memory and Early Civilization*, 28.

46. Werline, "Psalms of Solomon and the Ideology of Rule," 70–71; Kenneth Atkinson, "On the Herodian Origin of Militant Davidic Messianism at Qumran: New Light from *Psalms of Solomon 17*," *JBL* 118 (1999): 435–60. Cf. Marinus de Jonge, "The Expectation of the Future in the Psalms of Solomon," in *Jewish Eschatology, Early Christian Christology, and the Testaments of the Twelve Patriarchs*, ed. Marinus de Jonge, NovTSup 63 (Leiden: Brill, 1991), 14.

47. See Atkinson, "On the Herodian Origin of Militant Davidic Messianism at Qumran," 443 n. 21. Cf. Josephus, *B.J.* 1.17–18; *A.J.* 14.16. For a fuller treatment on these features of the text, see Werline, "Psalms of Solomon and the Ideology of Rule," 70–71.

These new events would have naturally invited textual updates. First, the community needed an explanation for this historic shift in how Rome administered its rule in Judea. Further, the new developments may have tested the community's hope that the situation could improve. Herod's rise to power, a person of partial Idumean descent appointed as a client king over the people, turned history in an unexpected direction. Finally, the rise of Herod and the redaction of the text come about thirty years after the initial arrival of the Romans. Assmann has argued that the forty-year mark is important for social memory, as the narrative needs to be firmed up and in place as a new generation begins to emerge. However, I would also argue that any community crisis could prompt the solidification or updating or, better, a reapplication of the memory. Could these two factors converge in some way as to move the community toward the hope for a Davidic king? Was a bolder hope and statement needed, drawn up from the tradition, in order to stabilize community cohesion and to maintain membership numbers? These questions are probably impossible to answer, but they invite interesting conversation and thought.

4. Sobriquets

The Psalms of Solomon refuses to include the names of contemporary figures and instead refers to them with sobriquets.[48] The use of the sobriquets in the text would not necessarily be to hide the identity of the historical persons. Rather, these often appear in poetic and mythic kinds of texts. Real names of real historical persons seem to be used when they become idealized figures. The Psalms of Solomon names David (Pss. Sol. 17.4, 6, 21) and Abraham (Pss. Sol. 9.9; 18.3) because they are idealized and already possess connotative power. The reference to Abraham arises in order to evoke the covenant that God has with the people (Pss. Sol. 9.9–10) and God's continuing love for faithfulness to the people (Pss. Sol. 18.3). As already mentioned, references to David arise in the depiction of a coming messiah in Pss. Sol. 17. But, no psalm mentions Hycranus II, Aristobulus II, Pompey, or Herod by name. Apparently, the "the dragon" in Pss. Sol. 2.25 is Pompey. One might also include

---

48. See also Kenneth Atkinson, *I Cried to the Lord: A Study of the Psalms of Solomon's Historical Background and Social Setting*, JSJSup 84 (Leiden: Brill, 2004), 10–11.

cryptic phrases attributed to an anonymous character. The phrase "for there rose up against them a man alien to our race" (Pss. Sol. 17.7) may have originally alluded to Pompey, but if there was an updating of the Psalms of Solomon during the time of Herod, the designation may have been reapplied to Herod. The same is true for the phrase "the lawless one laid waste to the land" (Pss. Sol. 17.11). "The lawless one" may have first referred to Pompey and later to Herod. The Hasmoneans, apparently, are the "sinners who rose up against us" (Pss. Sol. 17.5), who set up "a monarchy because of their arrogance" so that they "despoiled the throne of David" (Pss. Sol. 17.6). The text characterizes the Hasmoneans or the Jerusalem leadership in general as "pagans" who "exalt themselves to the stars" (Pss. Sol. 1.5). The words may echo Isaiah's taunt of Babylon: "You said in your heart, 'I will ascend to heaven; I will raise my throne above the stars of God'" (Isa 14:13). Pompey, apparently, makes a similar vaunted claim in Pss. Sol. 8: "He did not consider that he was a man, for the latter do not consider (this). He said, 'I shall be lord of land and sea' and he did not understand that it is God who is great, powerful in his great strength. He is king over the heavens" (Pss. Sol. 2.28–30a).

By not using names, the authors can discredit these figures and tune the narrative so that it has a mythic quality. This fits quite well in a repetitive, commemorative setting in which the psalms might be recited across many eras. Assmann charts this move toward the mythic in social memory. First, as he explains, "Cultural memory ... focuses on fixed points in the past, but again it is unable to preserve the past as it was. This tends to be condensed into symbolic figures to which memory attaches itself—for example, tales of the patriarchs, the Exodus."[49] Second, the focus on these founding figures and events "show that cultural memory is imbued with an element of the sacred. The figures are endowed with religious significance, and commemoration often takes the form of a festival."[50] Given this characteristic of social memory, it only makes sense that more recent enemies of the community should not achieve named status within community's memory but be called by names that connote that they are the enemy. Thus, designations like "dragon" or a generic title like "lawless one" or "profaner" (Pss. Sol. 4.1) preserve the mythic quality of the cultural memory.

---

49. Assmann, *Cultural Memory and Early Civilization*, 38.
50. Assmann, *Cultural Memory and Early Civilization*, 38.

5. Memory and the Challenge to Power

As I have argued in other places, the authors of the Psalms of Solomon seem to be marginalized. If they indeed come from a scribal class, their fates were tied to the fates of their patrons. In a change like the one in Jerusalem at the beginning of Roman occupation, the fortunes of many groups shifted. The community of the Psalms of Solomon may have found itself on the margins and struggling. For marginalized people, memory is often contested, because there are competing memories. Something new, must be able to pass as tradition. As Kirk explains, the rulers are also constructing a memory of the past for the present moment. For those oppressed, that hegemonic memory falsifies and fabricates the past: "Anti-hegemonic memory exposes this mendacity, and it utters a 'true' past."[51] Assmann similarly shows that memory can also become "a weapon against oppression."[52] Quoting Herbert Marcuse, Assmann asserts memory's power:

> Remembrance of the past may give rise to dangerous insights, and the established society seems to be apprehensive of the subservice contents of memory. Remembrance is a mode of dissociation from the given facts, a mode of 'mediation' that breaks for short moments the omniscient power of the given facts. Memory recalls the terror and the hope that passed.[53]

Further, the events that led to Pompey's death in 48 BCE after the battle of Pharsalus are not reported as history but within the context of God's continuing activity of punishing arrogant rulers who oppress God's people and defile the sanctuary (Pss. Sol. 2.26–27). The frequent references to God as "savior" (Pss. Sol. 2.32; 8.33; 17.1, 3, 34, 46), while finding its roots in the Hebrew Bible, challenges Roman propaganda. Greco-Roman rulers could call themselves "savior." Thus, the invocation of this title for God demonstrates a way in which the present can be keyed by a past memory in order to discredit or subvert a constructed countermemory.[54]

---

51. Kirk, "Social and Cultural Memory," 14–15.
52. Assmann, *Cultural Memory and Early Civilization*, 69.
53. Assmann, *Cultural Memory and Early Civilization*, 69. His quotation is from Herbert Marcuse, *The One-Dimensional Man* (Boston: Beacon Press, 1964), 64.
54. For a full treatment of this challenge to rule, see Werline, "Psalms of Solomon and the Ideology of Rule," 75–77.

6. Conclusion

In the language of social memory theory, the Psalms of Solomon contains commemorations that seek to fix meaning and purpose in an enduring form for a community at a crucial time. These commemorations prevent the rupture between the community and the past. Ritual achieves this even at the individual level. In the participation of a ritual act that is tied to social memory, the individual envisions his or her own unique situation as part of a larger story, as perhaps even the focal point of that story. In so doing, the act of remembering can fit a range of present needs. Memory, once constituted, becomes a semantic frame that has the power to give shape to the experience of the present, which then also has the power to frame hope.

A "Song with a Happy Heart": A Response

Rodney A. Werline

Introduction

This fine collection of essays, largely emerging from conference papers delivered at the meeting in Paris in 2015, ends with this response. Like most concluding responses, it will consider the thesis of each paper and focus on facets that remind us of the critical issues that scholars should consider as their research on the Psalms of Solomon continues. As the reader has seen, some of the early theories about the origins of the Psalms of Solomon, for example, that they were the product of the Pharisees, no longer have credence, while some of the most fundamental issues related to the interpretation of the Psalms of Solomon resist resolutions. Obviously, we will never achieve certainty on many of these unsolved matters. Still, on-going analysis of the available evidence might help us sharpen the picture that we have about these texts and the groups that produced, protected, and transmitted them. Further, analysis of these texts, and texts exhibiting similar interpretive problems, should invite comparisons that could produce new insights, as some of the essays in this volume have demonstrated.

Analysis and Response

Patrick Pouchelle and G. Anthony Keddie open the volume with an essay that rehearses the beginning of the more modern era of the study of the Psalms of Solomon. That rediscovery of the text commenced in a period fraught with religious conflict. Tensions between Catholics and Protestants ran hot through the era—the late sixteenth through the seventeenth centuries—as the early work on the Psalms of Solomon began in the years leading up to and during the Thirty Years War, a war which would at various points involve nearly all of western Europe. However, the story the two authors tell contains moments in which scholarship rose above the bitterness. First, they recognize and honor, as they write, the work of Jesuit scholars on the Psalms of Solomon, who carried out their scholarship with what one might now call an ecumenical spirit. Pouchelle and Keddie's account is fascinating on several levels. The rediscovery and rekindled interest in the Psalms of Solomon sits within the flurry of general interest in ancient manuscripts—both classical and religious—during that era. At the beginning of the sixteenth century, Erasmus had published his Greek text. Further, during that same period, Codex Alexandrinus, containing a list of texts that included the Psalms of Solomon, made its way west from Constantinople to England. Unfortunately, the eighteen psalms were missing from the manuscript.[1] Second, the essay serves as a reminder of how humanistic passion could rise above confessional contentions. The humanist Erasmus, who could not resist sharp, witty criticism of the Catholic Church and Martin Luther, found it difficult to float above the conflicts of religious parties. The Enlightenment scholars of the Psalms of Solomon, by contrast, reached across religious and national boundaries—quite a difficult feat in a polarized and growing nationalistic era. As Pouchelle and Keddie state, the study of the Psalms of Solomon in this era stands as "a tribute to the Jesuits' willingness to collaborate with others and to advance humanistic inquiry through the preservation and discussion of little-known texts during times of interreligious strife."

Whatever the limitations, sins, and problems of the Enlightenment era and its philosophies—several of which still linger with us—there were moments of great achievement within humanistic intellectual endeavors of the time. All of us who work in this area hope that dedication to the pursuit of knowledge also helps us to correct prejudices and presuppositions. Further, in our own era of the diminution of funding for humanities in general society and in institutions of higher education, which obviously includes faculty staffing and promotion of liberal arts education, the significance of the story affirms the social value of joint pursuits of knowledge and shared projects. Modern scholars in the humanities need to recognize the cross-disciplinary feature of this story, which takes place before schol-

---

1. Robert B. Wright, "Psalms of Solomon," *OTP* 2:639 believes that the space for the missing leaves at the end of the manuscript probably contained the Psalms of Solomon. He believed the same is possible for missing pages in Codex Sinaiticus.

ars constructed and then retreated into their specialty silos. The Jesuits participated in a larger movement in the era, and they obviously benefited from its energy and the knowledge it was generating.

As in the previous volume of collected essays, Eberhard Bons continues to challenge the position that the Psalms of Solomon were translated from an original Hebrew text. Bons's analysis in this volume also alerts the interpreter to the complex and complicated nature of determining the original language of the Psalms of Solomon. He focuses on the use of ἄλογος with θυμός and ὀργή in Pss. Sol. 16.10. While θυμός and ὀργή appear frequently in Psalms and Proverbs, ἄλογος is a rarity in the Septuagint. Somewhat in line with his essay in the previous volume, he argues for the influence of Greek philosophical moral tradition on the texts of the Psalms of Solomon. The influence would not necessarily need to be direct but simply that the author of Pss. Sol. 16 had some knowledge of the philosophical tradition.

The determination of the original language of the Psalms of Solomon shapes all proposals about the social setting of the authors, early editors, and community, a matter often overlooked in interpretation. If the original composer of Pss. Sol. 16 did write in Greek and did have some knowledge of the philosophical concepts attached to the term ἄλογος in verse 10, then we have to assume that he had access to some formal training or circles in Jerusalem that had a bit more formal familiarity with Greek thought. This would mean either that the authors of various psalms had traveled outside Jerusalem or that they had some access in Judea to conversations or even instruction that had some kind of connections to Greek philosophical traditions. If the author was working with a Septuagint tradition, then one would have to surmise that the authors were connected to a group of scribes or scholars in Jerusalem for whom the production of Greek texts was important. Finally, since this is a collection of psalms and, thus, had some connection to worship, there would seem to be a community in Jerusalem in which Greek was prominent enough that the language could be used in worship. I refer to Jerusalem as the setting for the production of many of the psalms because at least psalms 1, 2, 8, and 17 focus on the city. For me, these complicated issues related to proposing that the original language of the psalms was Greek and that these authors had philosophical knowledge seem to weigh against the position. However, I must concede that so much of the textual history of these psalms remains shrouded in mystery, and we cannot rule out the possibility that those who received these traditions made alterations.

While not wholly unrelated to the issues of setting raised by Bons, the essays by Atkinson, Keddie, Harkins, and myself more directly address matters about the social settings. Kenneth Atkinson's work in this volume differs, however, from Keddie and myself in that he pursues more traditional historical and literary methodologies. He has taken up a comparison of the Psalms of Solomon to the Dead Sea Scrolls. In general, comparisons of the scrolls and the Psalms of Solomon are rare, even though the two sets of text seem to invite the exercise. As Atkinson shows in striking fashion, the Dead Sea Scrolls include a large number of prayer and liturgical texts. Further, several texts, such the 1QS and 1QM, include prayers and other liturgical material. He has done his readers a genuine service by cataloging many of the different features of the prayer and liturgical texts. Atkinson's work is a welcome advance over the old cursory and largely uncritical comparisons of the two collections of texts.

Instead of focusing on similar wording, phrases and syntactical constructions between the Psalms of Solomon and Qumran texts, Atkinson analyzes larger themes and issues in both collections and then compares them. In the process, he puts forth a key principle: "What has been overlooked in much Qumran scholarship is the possibility that nonsectarian texts took on new meanings there, especially when read alongside sectarian texts." I think that this would include traditional vocabulary, phrases, and themes within texts. Religious language generally reveals itself as quite pliable to the unique and idiosyncratic interpretations and understandings of almost any group. Members of movements can easily pump their own definitions into the metaphorical language of their texts. In this way, groups hear even more widely accepted texts in a different register than other groups. In a kind of circular process, the group then hears its own ideas confirmed in these more widely used texts.

Any comparisons between the Psalms of Solomon and the scrolls, Atkinson demonstrates, must avoid generalities and be specific about the texts under consideration. The similarities between the scrolls and the Psalms of Solomon that he notices, however, cast a broad light on what are perhaps some of the broader characteristics of prayer in the era. He includes the following: (1) the prayers are not "excessively long"; (2) both stress "the practice of regular prayer"; a variety of genres are used, but evidence from the era contain many examples of these same genres; (3) diverse types of prayers can occur in a single scroll; (4) "ample use of intertextuality"; (5) both "have undergone a considerable process of alteration, whose extent of is unknown"; and (6) some prayers are incorporated with other liturgical texts, which indicates their ongoing use by worshippers. Atkinson concludes that the evidence does not support the notion that the Qumran scrolls and the Psalms of Solomon are in some way directly connected. Rather, both corpora display some of the hallmarks of liturgy and prayers caught up in the disappointments, sufferings, frustrations, and hopes of several Second Temple Jewish groups.

Keddie seeks to bring more clarity to the understanding of suffering and poverty in the Psalms of Solomon by looking briefly at the historical setting of the text and possible historical allusions within it. As he says in the opening of his essay, scholars generally accept that the Psalms of Solomon arises from a suffering community. The tone of psalms 1, 2, 8, and 17, especially, shapes that perception. However, added to these palms about the suffering of the nation is, for example, psalm 4, which speaks of the suffering of the individual and which Keddie carefully examines. Besides these, the psalms often speak of those seemingly connected to these texts as "the poor." In some regards, Keddie does not actually abandon the position that the Psalms of Solomon arise out of suffering. I might add here that I have not been especially confident about identifying the historical figures behind the ciphers in the text as Keddie suggests. Nevertheless, from his assessment of the data, Keddie argues for the following: "The psalms do not reflect real material conditions but refract them with a political lens. In this way, the text was a resource used by its producers in an attempt to obtain power by delegitimizing opponents and objectifying socioeconomic structures as exploitative." Part of this observation—that suffering as depicted in ancient texts might be on a continuum—is not new. Counter to those who argued several generations ago that what they labelled "apocalyptic" originated during intense suffering and persecution, some scholars suggested that the suffering only needed to be perceived. However, Keddie's observation differs from these earlier positions in its nuanced analysis, which he achieves through his reliance on modern theorists such as Pierre Bourdieu. The authors of the psalms certainly experienced marginalization and the pain of Roman domination, but they respond, he seems to explain, with a well-crafted counter argument and counter-narrative (as I borrow language and ideas from the work of Anathea Portier-Young[2]) that intends to delegitimize those in power positions.

---

2. Anathea Portier-Young, *Apocalypse against Empire: Theologies of Resistance in Early Judaism* (Grand Rapids: Eerdmans, 2011).

In looking at how the composers of the psalms accomplish this, Keddie explores how they manage language about suffering and poverty in comparison to apocalyptic and sapiential traditions. His assessment leads to this conclusion "that the Psalms of Solomon mediate sapiential and apocalyptic discourses on inequality, generating a class subjectivity that awkwardly construes poverty positively as self-sufficiency, yet attributes the cause of poverty to unjust sociopolitical authorities and allows for prayer as the only form of agency through which humans can ameliorate it." In some ways, Keddie seems to say that the authors want the best of both the apocalyptic and sapiential rhetorical-ideological worlds.

While Keddie basically maintains the old categories of apocalyptic and sapiential, I think that his conclusions contribute to the current argument that these two categories simply cannot hold together as previous generations assumed.[3] That the authors of the Psalms of Solomon drew from both traditions suggests that the boundaries between the categories are not as neat as assumed; an author is not of one camp and not the other. Rather, the genres and the uses of them are much more fluid than modern scholarly categories allowed for. In other words, Keddie's conclusion contributes to the deconstruction of rigid modern approaches to these categories.

Further, his discoveries about the mediated constructed response tell us something more about the character of the scribe. The scribe acquired knowledge about many traditions, learned how to draw on them and combine them, and then could also construct them into liturgical pieces. To return to the language of Bourdieu, the scribe's *habitus* could include a variety of traditions, which the scribe could craft together into liturgical forms. The scribe did not acquire this ability simply through discursive instruction alone, but also through embodied practice. Scholarship has undervalued, if not minimalized, this aspect of scribal life—the practice of faith among scribes—and this despite the many examples of the place of prayer in the production of texts and scribes. The basic features of this practice cut across all the traditional categories that we have mentioned—apocalyptic and sapiential. Ben Sira, the Dead Sea Scrolls, Daniel, the Enochic traditions, and the Psalms of Solomon all testify to scribes who

---

3. The early exploration into the collapsing of the categories appears in Rodney A. Werline, "The Psalms of Solomon and the Ideology of Rule," in *Conflicted Boundaries in Wisdom and Apocalypticism*, ed. Lawrence M. Wills and Benjamin G. Wright III, SymS 35 (Atlanta, GA: Society of Biblical Literature 2005), 69–87.

understood the function of prayer and other rituals, and they all knew how to incorporate them into their work. While these texts all have varied and multiple functions, on some occasions the scribes intend for the liturgical practices to shape their audience. In some instances, the rituals in the text, when performed, drew in the audience or even included the audience in the world of the text. Thus, Keddie's analysis contributes to the conclusion that among their many skills, many scribes had specialized liturgical and ritual skills and knowledge.

If we wonder how a text might shape the experience of a person who encountered it, or draw an audience into the world of the text, Angela Kim Harkins considers this phenomenon. Her approach builds on her recent work on emotions, especially as presented in her monograph on the Hodayot.[4] However, Harkins's focus in this essay widens beyond the community that first valued the Psalms of Solomon to those who received them through the years: "Rather than mining the Psalms of Solomon for historical references that date to the time of the putative author, I wish to explore how the imagery and intertextual references in this psalm might assist the later readers and hearers of this text to cultivate the subjectivity of the implied speaker—biblical Israel." While many of the psalms come into view in her contribution, she is especially interested in the emotions found in Pss. Sol. 8 and the way in which a reader and audience might embody those emotions through the performance of the text. While her methodology is quite detailed and nuanced, we could summarize her interests with her following statement: "Embodied reading that vividly enacts the experiences that are described (also called 'enactive reading') allows for the formation of egocentric episodic memories that are crucial for the mind's ability to anticipate future events such as the divine punishments that result unfailingly from treachery." She contends that the Deuteronomistic ideology that permeates most psalms, especially Pss. Sol. 2 and 8, becomes the filter through which authors present scenes of temple defilement. In the process, they also allude to disastrous moments of moral failure in Israel's story. As a result, readers, who assume they are among the righteous, feel the tug "to an even more intense scrupulosity by generating a vivid palpable presence of a deity whose presence in history is either punitive or providential." In an era in which we focus so

---

4. Angela Kim Harkins, *Reading with an "I" to the Heavens: Looking at the Qumran Hodayot through the Lens of Visionary Traditions*, Ekstasis 3 (Berlin: de Gruyter, 2012).

much on reconstructing origins, histories, and communities, it is quite helpful to consider how authors sought to connect with audiences and future readers and their audiences. Discovering these rhetorical strategies or hooks is beginning to take root in scholarship, and more work should follow. While I am not ready to discard questions related to histories and communities, Harkins has perhaps reminded us about the real reason for writing a psalm in the first place—to convince and shape an audience in some way.

My own essay, I believe, lands somewhere between the approaches of Keddie and Harkins and perhaps Tzoref. On the one hand, the essay examines how the community constructs social memory. This includes the adaptation of the larger framework of an understanding of Israel's history. Within this framework, the authors drew on specific traditions and rhetoric to address their current situation. On the other hand, I recognize the trauma and accompanying emotions that generated the text, as well as those that the text might trigger. One result of this process is that the experience of the present, or very recent past, is mediated and constructed by social memory. Further, even future hopes are shaped by an understanding of the past. Given the nature of the texts from the Second Temple period, this approach could find extensive use, and it could help bring to life crucial aspects of the texts' meanings. The method also explores the way in which ritual functions within a community. Since the Psalms of Solomon are psalms[5] and at least imagine a performance if they were not actually performed, they exemplify the role of ritual in the process of shaping and preserving memory. In doing so, they are not simply the production of a community, but they shape the community and the individuals within it. In ritual performance, the community embodies the past as well as proclaims it.

As one begins the essay by Pouchelle that compares the Psalms of Solomon to the Assumption of Moses, one wonders what the two could possibly have in common. On some levels, indeed, they have little in common. However, Pouchelle reveals how the two texts have presented scholars with similar types of issues as they try to recover the earliest versions of the texts and the original historical events and persons depicted in the texts. The upshot of Pouchelle's analysis is the difficulty of identifying the original historical settings referred to in the Assumption of Moses and Psalms of

---

5. As explored in the essay by Shani Tzoref in this volume.

Solomon. Especially his list of assaults on Jerusalem from Antiochus to the fall of the temple in 70 CE is a reminder of the difficulties and sufferings of the era. Drawing on the conclusions of Atkinson, Pouchelle observes that the recurring assaults on the people and the city may reveal the authors' thoughts that the Deuteronomic cycle continued to churn along. Pouchelle and Atkinson describe the situation in this manner: "Accordingly, this succession of sieges of Jerusalem may explain why some communities may read these events as cycles[6] with the same typological analysis based in the Antiochian crisis." His final line in section three is mostly likely accurate, though perhaps difficult for modern scholars to digest: "It is probably an illusion to think that we could reach the original versions of these texts, to identify them with precise historical events, and to reconstruct all of their developments." The problems that have arisen in the interpretation of the Dead Sea Scrolls, the largest collection of texts from Judea, have unfortunately alerted scholars to the difficulty of interpretation even when in possession of multiple texts belonging to a community (we presume).

In some ways, Stefan Schreiber's essay parallels Pouchelle's quest, for he also compares two texts from different historical and social contexts. While Pouchelle noticed that both texts—the Psalms and Solomon and the Assumption of Moses—are reacting to the cycle of violence in Judea and that both texts seem to undergo revisions as editors appropriate the text for a new context, Schreiber's analysis appears to be mostly controlled by Paul's special problem—can the torah save? I'm not sure that we would ask this question of the Psalms of Solomon without the influence of Paul's theology. In handling the issues, Schreiber eventually turns to E. P. Sanders's construct of "covenantal nomism." When he lays out the Psalms of Solomon's historical-social setting, Schreiber especially focuses on Pss. Sol. 2, 3, 4, 8, 9, and 14. Because he cannot find specific halakic arguments against the community's opponents, Schreiber believes that the problem resides in the lawbreakers adopting Hellenistic culture: "The association with the sinful conduct of the peoples is interesting because this may be a further indication of the intention with which the lawbreakers interpret the torah: in the eyes of Psalms of Solomon, they are conforming to the lifestyle of the Hellenistic world." This position resonates with the old theories held by interpreters like Martin Hengel. However, I am more inclined toward

---

6. Kenneth Atkinson, "On the Herodian Origins of Militant Davidic Messianism at Qumran: New Light from Psalms of Solomon 17," *JBL* 118 (1999): 148–49.

Atkinson's position that the authors of the Psalms of Solomon disputed with priests in Jerusalem over proper interpretations of the torah.[7] The list of the leaders' secret sins (Pss. Sol. 8.8–10) seems to be a typical polemical tirade that emerges in arguments about torah, for similar accusations appear in CD V, 7–12.[8] However, polemical language sometimes has a connotative function instead of denotative; that is, the language intends to identify a group as opponents rather than precisely enumerate their actual misdeeds.[9] This different interpretation, then, would also mean that the vision of a new era in Pss. Sol. 17 would be slightly different from the way in which Schreiber has characterized it. These matters aside, both Pouchelle and Schreiber signal the value of comparing the Psalms of Solomon to other texts to see what new insights might emerge.

Johanna Erzberger also compares two texts to one another: Pss. Sol. 11 and Bar 4:5–5:9. The texts relate to one another because both discuss the return of the Jewish diaspora to Jerusalem. As Erzberger notes, that upbeat tone of the text is somewhat rare in the Psalms of Solomon. According to her interpretation of Pss. Sol. 11, the psalm is not interested in establishing any discernable historical event or personages. This makes the psalm unlike most other psalms in the collection that speak of Jerusalem. Further, while there are several similarities between Pss Sol. 11 and Baruch, Baruch is also much more conscious of historical setting and draws on the Babylonian exile to code events actually belonging to a later era. These characteristics alter the psalm's understanding of history, as she concludes: "Pss. Sol. 11 forgoes all historical references and places God's act of final salvation in the eschatological future."

As I considered Shani Tzoref's essay, it struck me how rarely—unfortunately—we engage in this kind of interpretation. So often we search for origins, settings, and sources but never actually get around to considering the purpose and teaching of a text from the era. Treating the collection of

---

7. Kenneth Atkinson, *I Cried to the Lord: A Study of the Psalms of Solomon's Historical Background and Social Setting*, JSJSup 84 (Leiden: Brill, 2004). See especially his conclusion (211–22); Atkinson, "Herod the Great, Sosius, and the Siege of Jerusalem (37 B.C.E.) in Psalm of Solomon 17," *NovT* 38 (1996): 435–60. However, I do not follow Atkinson's position that the Psalms of Solomon authors had cut themselves off completely from the Jerusalem temple, as his essay in this volume again states.

8. Cf. Werline, "Psalms of Solomon and the Ideology of Rule," 73.

9. Cf. Luke T. Johnson, "The New Testament's Anti-Jewish Slander and the Conventions of Ancient Polemic," *JBL* 108 (1989): 419–41.

psalms as a whole, she draws us into an intellectual world that is solidly grounded in the social and historical realities of the era—the very real struggles of the period. She considers these in the way that the Psalms of Solomon considers these: why does such evil and suffering exist? As she writes, she has in mind the results of the comprehensive treatment, *Theodicy in the World of the Bible*, edited by Antti Laato and Johannes C. de Moor.[10] She arrives at the following conclusion about the issue of suffering in the Psalms of Solomon: "The essence of the work is affirmation of confidence in God's justice as manifest in experience, utilizing and developing the conventional theodicies. I further propose that this theological stance offers a helpful lens for considering the genre affinities of the Psalms of Solomon." On one level, the Psalms of Solomon see suffering as "retribution." As Tzoref states, "The premise of the retribution theodicy is that if suffering exists as a punishment for human wrong-doing, then human suffering is, in fact, good and not bad. The natural world order is just." In line with some biblical and postbiblical Jewish texts, suffering does not present itself as a "theological problem" because "it is a basic component of divine justice and is experienced as a deserved and fair consequence of sin." On a second level, suffering in the Psalms of Solomon has a pedagogical function: "The educative theodicy admits that the righteous do, in fact, suffer but maintains that this reality brings about atonement and repentance. If suffering is a form of *discipline* of the righteous, then it is, in fact, not bad but good."

Finally, Tzoref also explores the relationship between the genre of the Psalms of Solomon and its message. She maintains, as I and many do, that this is at its most basic level a collection of psalms or prayers. However, the Psalms of Solomon differs from the MT Psalms in the following manner:

> In canonical Psalms, the retribution theodicy is a problem that is experienced through national and personal crisis and generates epistemological crisis. In the Psalms of Solomon, retribution theodicy is the solution to the crises.

Thus, psalmic forms are adjusted to "accommodate an emphasis on affirmation of trust." The authors do this through appropriation of sapiential, Deuteronomic, and prophetic material. In doing so, Tzoref shows that the

---

10. Antti Laato and Johannes C. de Moor, eds., *Theodicy in the World of the Bible* (Leiden: Brill, 2003).

Psalms of Solomon greatly differs from approaches to suffering in a variety of texts such as Qohelet, Jubilees, 1 Enoch, and several Dead Sea Scrolls.

Tzoref's explorations not only provide real benefits for understanding the Psalms of Solomon but also the broader field of Second Temple Judaism. First, she is able to bring together the ideas of several authors, including Atkinson, Pouchelle, and myself, in a systematic manner. She can then place these within the larger intellectual movements found in the Hebrew Bible and in Second Temple literature scholarship. Second, she provides a way to ask more theological and interpretive questions without having the presuppositions of such questions distort the meaning of the text. What I have already noticed in these essays appears here again: the value of comparing texts while allowing them to speak for themselves is manifest.

Considering the Future

As I mentioned in the introduction, some of the foundational work in the process of interpretation remains problematic when reading the Psalms of Solomon. As discussed, Bons's work on the text again highlights how complicated the determination of the original language has become. Like Atkinson, I continue to think that the Psalms of Solomon originally appeared in Hebrew. However, as Atkinson has argued, the extant texts of the psalms are from a much later era than the time of their original production. We cannot rule out the likelihood that they have undergone substantial redacting and editing. Further, as is now apparent in the analysis of writings that eventually land in the Masoretic Text, these ancient texts were not stable, and we have no way of knowing the transmission history of the Psalms of Solomon, if they were written in Hebrew before they were translated into Greek.

The issue of the original language clearly trickles into many of the other problems related to interpreting these psalms. The original language directly relates to social setting in which the Psalms of Solomon were produced. As I mentioned earlier, as best as we can determine, the texts seem to have been written in Jerusalem, since several psalms focus on the city. In addition, it is difficult not to think that their composition began at the time in which Rome gained control over Judea. However, if they were first composed in Greek, then was there a community of scribes in Jerusalem who composed psalms in Greek? Further, would we not need to assume that, since they are *psalms*, they were composed for worship or with worship in mind? Was there a collection of people who worshiped using Greek psalms or included Greek psalms within a worship that primarily took place in Hebrew? Answering these basic questions impacts the way in which we think of the community that produced the psalms, its relationship to contemporaneous groups, its relationship to leaders, and the sort of training these scribes underwent and where they acquired it. Decisions on this not only change how we see this text but could also force us to reconsider other texts from their era, their authors, their communities, and their transmissions. Thus, the consideration of the original language has a much larger impact than we might first imagine. In a chain reaction, these decisions affect the work of Keddie and myself in this volume and to some degree the conclusions of Atkinson and Harkins, among others.

Finally, I return briefly to the work of Tzoref in this volume. Her work reminded me, again, how much our discipline is focused on historical origins of texts and the communities related to them, sometimes to the point of diminishing any interest in what the text might actually be saying or what it might mean. Of course, historical origins have a direct bearing on what texts mean, but the work is not completed with determinations of historical origins. After all, the text is written to communicate something to an audience. Further, this message sits within the context of issues from the same basic era. Additionally, the text sits within the ongoing discussions that humans have about the meaning of being human and the problems associated with our existence.

Bibliography

Abegg, Martin G., Jr. "4QMMT, Paul and 'Works of the Law.'" Pages 203–16 in *The Bible at Qumran: Texts, Shape, and Interpretation*. Edited by Peter W. Flint and James C. VanderKam. Grand Rapids: Eerdmans, 2001.

———. "Concordance of Proper Nouns in the Non-biblical Texts from Qumran." Pages 229–84 in *The Texts from the Judaean Desert Indices and an Introduction to the Discoveries in the Judaean Desert Series*. Edited by Emanuel Tov. DJD 39. Oxford: Clarendon, 2002.

———. "The Time of Righteousness (4Q251a): A Time of War or a Time of Peace?" Pages 1–12 in *Prayer and Poetry in the Dead Sea Scrolls and Related Literature: Essays in Honor of Eileen Schuller on the Occasion of Her Sixty-Fifth Birthday*. Edited by Jeremy Penner, Ken M. Penner, and Cecilia Wassen. STDJ 98. Leiden: Brill, 2012.

Abegg, Martin G., Jr., with James E. Bowley and Edward M. Cook. *The Non-biblical Texts from Qumran*. Vol. 1.2 of *The Dead Sea Scrolls Concordance*. Leiden: Brill, 2003.

Ábel, František. *The Psalms of Solomon and the Messianic Ethics of Paul*. WUNT 2/416. Tübingen: Mohr Siebeck, 2016.

Aberbach, Moses. "The Historical Allusions of Chapters IV, XI, and XIII of the Psalms of Solomon." *JQR* 41 (1950): 379–96.

Aberbach, Moses, and Leivy Smolar. "Aaron, Jeroboam, and the Golden Calves." *JBL* 86 (1967): 129–40.

Adams, Samuel L. *Social and Economic Life in Second Temple Judea*. Louisville: Westminster John Knox, 2014.

Adams, Sean A. *Baruch and the Epistle of Jeremiah: A Commentary Based on the Texts in Codex Vaticanus*. Septuagint Commentary Series. Leiden: Brill, 2014.

Albrecht, Felix. *Psalmi Salomonis*. SVTG 12.3. Göttingen: Vandenhoeck & Ruprecht, 2018.

———. "Zur Notwendigkeit einer Neuedition der Psalmen Salomos." Pages 110–23 in *Die Septuaginta—Text, Wirkung, Rezeption*. Edited by Wolfgang Kraus and Siegfried Kreuzer. WUNT 325. Tübingen: Mohr Siebeck, 2014.

Amir, Yehoshua. "Measure for Measure in Talmudic Literature and in the Wisdom of Solomon." Pages 29–46 in *Justice and Righteousness: Biblical Themes and Their Influence*. Edited by Henning Graf Reventlow and Yair Hoffman. Sheffield: JSOT Press, 1992.

Amphoux, Christian-Bernard, and Arnaud Serandour. "La date de la forme courte de Jérémie." Pages 25–35 in *Eukarpa: Études sur la Bible et ses exégètes*. Edited by Mireille Loubet and Didier Pralon. Paris: Cerf, 2011.

Anderson, Gary A. *Charity: The Place of the Poor in the Biblical Tradition*. New Haven: Yale University Press, 2013.

———. "The Praise of God as a Cultic Event." Pages 15–33 in *Priesthood and Cult in Ancient Israel*. Edited by Gary A. Anderson and Saul M. Olyan. JSOTSup 125. Sheffield: JSOT Press, 1991.

Andreau, Jean. "Twenty Years after Moses I. Finley's *The Ancient Economy*." Pages 33–52 in *The Ancient Economy*. Edited by Walter Scheidel and Sitta von Reden. Edinburgh: Edinburgh University Press, 2002.

Ashbrook Harvey, Susan. "The Holy and the Poor: Models from Early Syriac Christianity." Pages 43–66 in *Through the Eye of a Needle: Judeo-Christian Roots of Social Welfare*. Edited by Emily Albu Hanawalt and Carter Lindberg. Kirksville: Thomas Jefferson University Press, 1994.

Assmann, Jan. *Cultural Memory and Early Civilization: Writing, Remembrance and Political Imagination*. Cambridge: Cambridge: University Press, 2011.

Atkinson, Kenneth. "Biblical 'Land' Texts in the Dead Sea Scrolls: The Wilderness Experience Revived at Qumran." Paper Presented at the Society of Biblical Literature Annual Meeting, Atlanta, GA, 21 November 2015.

———. "Enduring the Lord's Discipline: Soteriology in the *Psalms of Solomon*." Pages 145–66 in *This World and the World to Come: Soteriology in Early Judaism*. Edited by Daniel M. Gurtner. London: T&T Clark, 2011.

———. "Herod the Great as *Antiochus Redevivus*: Reading the Testament of Moses as an Anti-Herodian Composition." Pages 134–49 in vol. 1 of *Of Scribes and Sages: Ancient Versions and Traditions*. Edited by Craig A. Evans. 2 vol. Edinburgh: T&T Clark, 2004.

———. "Herod the Great, Sosius, and the Siege of Jerusalem (37 B.C.E.) in Psalm of Solomon 17." *NovT* 38 (1996): 313–22.

———. *I Cried to the Lord: A Study of the Psalms of Solomon's Historical Background and Social Setting.* JSJSup 84. Leiden: Brill, 2004.

———. "The Identification of the 'Wicked Priest' Reconsidered: The Case for Hyrcanus II." Pages 93–109 in *Sibyls, Scriptures, and Scrolls: John Collins at Seventy.* Edited by Joel Baden, Hindy Najman, and Eibert Tigchelaar. Leiden: Brill, 2017.

———. *An Intertextual Study of the Psalms of Solomon.* Lewiston, NY: Mellen, 2000.

———. "Psalms of Solomon." Pages 763–76 in *A New Translation of the Septuagint.* Edited by Albert Pietersma and Benjamin G. Wright. Oxford: Oxford University Press, 2007.

———. "On the Herodian Origin of Militant Davidic Messianism at Qumran: New Light from Psalm of Solomon 17." *JBL* 118 (1999): 435–60.

———. "Perceptions of the Temple Priests in the Psalms of Solomon." Pages 79–86 in *The Psalms of Solomon: Language,* in *The Psalms of Solomon: Language, History, Theology.* Edited by Eberhard Bons and Patrick Pouchelle. EJL 40. Atlanta: SBL Press, 2015.

———. "Psalms of Solomon: Greek." Pages 332–41 in *Deutero-Canonical Scriptures.* Vol. 2 of *The Textual History of the Bible.* Edited by Matthias Henze and Frank Leder. Leiden: Brill, 2019.

———. "Psalms of Solomon: Syriac." Pages 341–50 in *Deutero-Canonical Scriptures.* Vol. 2 of *The Textual History of the Bible.* Edited by Matthias Henze and Frank Leder. Leiden: Brill, 2019.

———. "Representations of History in 4Q331 (4QpapHistorical Text C), 4Q332 (4QHistorical Text D), 4Q333 (4QHistorical Text E), and 4Q468e (4QHistorical Text F): An Annalistic Calendar Documenting Portentous Events?" *DSD* 14 (2007): 125–51.

———. "Response." Pages 175–91 in *The Psalms of Solomon: Language, History, Theology.* Edited by Eberhard Bons and Patrick Pouchelle. EJL 40. Atlanta, GA: SBL Press, 2015.

———. "Taxo's Martyrdom and the Role of the *Nuntius* in the '*Testament of Moses*': Implications for Understanding the Role of Other Intermediary Figures." *JBL* 125 (2006): 453–76.

———. "Theodicy in the Psalms of Solomon." Pages 546–75 in *Theodicy in the World of the Bible.* Edited by Antti Laato and Johannes C. de Moor. Leiden: Brill, 2003.

———. "Toward a Redating of the *Psalms of Solomon*: Implications for Understanding the *Sitz im Leben* of an Unknown Jewish Sect." *JSP* 17 (1998): 85–112.

Atkinson, Kenneth, and Jodi Magness. "Josephus's Essenes and the Qumran Community." *JBL* 129 (2010): 317–42.

Avemarie, Friedrich. "Paul and the Claim of the Law according to the Scripture: Leviticus 18:5 in Galatians 3:12 and Romans 10:5." Pages 125–48 in *The Beginnings of Christianity*. Edited by Jack Pastor and Menachem Mor. Jerusalem: Yad Ben-Zvi, 2005.

Babota, Vasile. *The Institution of the Hasmonean High Priesthood*. JSJSup 165. Leiden: Brill, 2014.

Bachmann, Michael. "Keil oder Mikroskop? Zur jüngeren Diskussion um den Ausdruck 'Werke des Gesetzes.'" Pages 69–134 in *Lutherische und Neue Paulusperspektive: Beiträge zu einem Schlüsselproblem der gegenwärtigen exegetischen Diskussion*. Edited by Michael Bachmann. WUNT 182. Tübingen: Mohr Siebeck, 2005.

———. "Zur Argumentation von Galater 3.10–12." *NTS* 53 (2007): 524–44.

Ball, Warwick. *Rome in the East: The Transformation of an Empire*. London: Routledge, 2000.

Balogh, Amy. "Negotiating Moses's Divine-Human Identity in LXX Exodus." *JSCS* 52 (2019): 91–101.

Barsalou, Lawrence W., Aron K. Barbey, W. Kyle Simmons, and Ava Santos. "Embodiment in Religious Knowledge." *Journal of Cognition and Culture* 5 (2005): 14–57.

Bartels, Jens, and Werner Eck. "Sosius." *BNP* 13 (2008):660–62.

Barton, John. "Natural Law and Poetic Justice in the Old Testament." *JTS* 30 (1979): 1–14.

Bazzana, Giovanni. "Galilean Village Scribes as the Authors of the Sayings Gospel Q." Pages 133–48 in *Q in Context II*. Edited by Markus Tiwald. BBB 173. Göttingen: Vandenhoeck & Ruprecht, 2015.

———. *Kingdom of Bureaucracy: The Political Theology of Village Scribes in the Sayings Gospel Q*. BETL 274. Leuven: Peeters, 2015.

Behnke, Sven. "Die Rede vom Schlaf in den Psalmen Salomos und ihr traditionsgeschichtlicher Hintergrund." Pages 97–114 in *The Psalms of Solomon: Language, History, Theology*. Edited by Eberhard Bons and Patrick Pouchelle. EJL 40. Atlanta: SBL Press, 2015.

Bendik, Ivana. *Paulus in neuer Sicht? Eine kritische Einführung in die „New Perspective on Paul."* Judentum und Christentum 18. Stuttgart: Kohlhammer, 2010.

Berlin, Andrea M. "Herod the Tastemaker." *NEA* 77 (2014): 108–19.
Bévenot, Maurice. "An 'Old Latin' Quotation (II Tim. 3.2), and Its Adventures in the MSS. of St. Cyprian's *De unitate ecclesiae* Chap. 16." Pages 249–52 in *Papers Presented to the Second International Conference on Patristic Studies Held at Christ Church, Oxford, 1955*. Edited by K. Aland and Frank L. Cross. TUGAL 63. StPatr 1.1. Berlin: Akademie, 1957.
Bianchini, Giuseppe. *Vindiciae Canonicarum Scriptarum Vulgatae Latinae Editionis*. Rome: S. Michaelis, 1740.
Black, Matthew. *The Book of Enoch, or, I Enoch: A New English Edition with Commentary and Textual Notes*. SVTP 7. Leiden: Brill, 1985
Boer, Martinus C. de. *Galatians: A Commentary*. NTL. Louisville: Westminster John Knox, 2011.
Bons, Eberhard. "Philosophical Vocabulary in the Psalms of Solomon: The Case of Ps. Sol. 9:4." Pages 49–78 in *The Psalms of Solomon: Language, History, Theology*. Edited by Eberhard Bons and Patrick Pouchelle. EJL 40. Atlanta: SBL Press, 2015.
Bons, Eberhard, and Patrick Pouchelle. Introduction to *The Psalms of Solomon: Language, History, Theology*. Edited by Eberhard Bons and Patrick Pouchelle. EJL 40. Atlanta, GA: SBL, 2015.
Bourdieu, Pierre. *Distinction: A Social Critique of the Judgement of Taste*. Translated by R. Nice. Cambridge: Harvard University Press, 1984.
Boyer, Pascal. *The Naturalness of Religious Ideas*. Berkeley: University of California Press, 1994.
———. *Religion Explained: The Evolutionary Origins of Religious Thought*. New York: Basic Books, 2001.
———. "What Are Memories For? Functions in Recall of Cognition and Culture." Pages 3–28 in *Memory in Mind and Culture*. Edited by Pascal Boyer and James V. Wertsch. Cambridge: Cambridge University Press, 2009.
Brand, Miryam. *Evil within and Without: The Source of Sin and Its Nature as Portrayed in Second Temple Literature*. Göttingen: Vandenhoeck & Ruprecht, 2013.
Bringmann, Klaus. *Geschichte der Juden im Altertum: Vom babylonischen Exil bis zur arabischen Eroberung*. Stuttgart: Klett-Cotta, 2005.
Brooke, George J. "Aspects of the Theological Significance of Prayer and Worship in the Qumran Scrolls." Pages 35–54 in *Prayer and Poetry in the Dead Sea Scrolls and Related Literature: Essays in Honor of Eileen Schuller on the Occasion of Her Sixty-Fifth Birthday*. Edited by Jeremy

Penner, Ken M. Penner, and Cecilia Wassen. STDJ 98. Leiden; Brill, 2012.

———. "Between Scroll and Codex: Reconsidering the Qumran Opisthographs." Pages 123–38 in *On Stone and Scroll: Essays in Honour of Grahm Ivor Davies*. Edited by J. K. Aitken, Katharine J. Dell, and Brian A. Mastin. BZAW 420. Berlin: de Gruyter, 2011.

———. "Body Parts in Barkhi Nafshi and the Qualifications for Membership of the Worshipping Community." Pages 79–94 in *Sapiential, Liturgical and Poetical Texts from Qumran: Proceedings of the Third Meeting of the International Organization for Qumran Studies, Published in Memory of Maurice Baillet*. Edited by Daniel K. Falk, Florentino García Martínez, and Eileen Schuller. STDJ 35. Leiden: Brill, 2000.

———. "Qumran Pesher: Towards the Redefinition of a Genre." *RevQ* 10 (1981): 483–503.

Broshi, Magen, and Esther Eshel. "The Greek King Is Antiochus IV (4QHistorical Text=4Q248)." *JJS* 48 (1997): 120–29.

Bullock, C. Hassell. *Encountering the Book of Psalms: A Literary and Theological Introduction*. Grand Rapids: Baker, 2001.

Burkes, Shannon. "Wisdom and Law: Choosing Life in Ben Sira and Baruch." *JSJ* 30 (1999): 253–76.

Burnside, Jonathan P. *God, Justice, and Society Aspects of Law and Legality in the Bible*. Oxford: University Press, 2011.

Bush, Stephen S. "Are Religious Experiences Too Private to Study?" *JR* (2012): 199–223.

Butcher, Kevin. *Roman Syria and the Near East*. London: British Museum Press, 2003.

Canfora, Luciano. *Convertire Casaubon*. Milan: Adelphi, 2002.

Caquot, André. "Les Hasmonéens, les Romains et Hérode: Observations sur Ps. Sal. 17." Pages 213–18 in *Hellenica et Judaïca, Hommage à Nikiprowetzky*. Edited by André Caquot, Mireille Hadas-Lebel, and Jean Riaud. Collection de la Revue des Études Juives 3. Leuven: Peeters, 1986.

Cardellini, Innocenzo. *Numeri 1,1–10,10: Nuova versione, introduzione e commento*. I libri biblici 4. Milan: Paoline, 2013.

Carson, Donald A., Peter T. O'Brien, and Mark A. Seifrid, eds. *Justification and Variegated Nomism*. 2 vols. WUNT 140, 181. Tübingen: Mohr Siebeck, 2001, 2004.

Carr, David. *Holy Resilience: The Bible's Traumatic Origin*. New Haven: Yale University Press, 2014.

Casali, Sergio. "Agudezas virgilane nel commento all'Eneide di Juan Luis de la Cerda." Pages 33–61 in *Esegesi dimenticate di autori classici*. Edited by Carlo Santini and Fabio Stok. Testi e studi di cultura classica 41. Pisa: Edizioni ETS, 2008.

Cavallera, Ferdinand. "Un chef-d'œuvre de la littérature apocryphe: Les Psaumes de Salomon; Bulletin de patrologie." *Études* 118 (1909): 789–805.

Cerda, Juan Luis de la. *Adversaria Sacra*. Lyon: Louis Prost, 1626.

Ceriani, Antonius M. *Monumenta Sacra et profana ex codicibus praesertim Bibliothecae Ambrosianae*. 5 vols. Milan: Biblioteca Ambrosiana, 1861–1868.

Chae, Young S. *Jesus as the Eschatological Davidic Shepherd*. WUNT 2/216. Tübingen: Mohr Siebeck, 2006.

Charles, R. H. *The Assumption of Moses Translated From the Latin Sixth Century MS., the Unemended Text of Which Is Published Herewith, Together With the in Its Restored and Critically Emended Form*. London: Adam & Charles Black, 1897.

Charlesworth, James H. *The Pesharim and Qumran History: Chaos or Consensus?* Grand Rapids: Eerdmans, 2002.

Charlesworth, James H., and Dennis T. Olson. "Prayers for Festivals (1Q34–1Q34[bis]; 4Q507–509)." Pages 107–53 in *The Dead Sea Scrolls: Hebrew, Aramaic, and Greek Texts with English Translations; Pseudepigraphic and Non-Masoretic Psalms and Prayers*. Edited by James H. Charlesworth and Henry W. L. Rietz. PTSDSSP 4A. Louisville: Westminster John Knox, 1997.

Chatelain, Jean-Marc. "Les receuils d'adversaria aux XVIe et XVIIe siècles: Des pratiques de la lecture savante au style de l'érudition." Pages 169–86 in *Le livre et l'historien: Études offertes en l'honneur du professeur Henri-Jean Martin*. Edited by Frédéric Barbier, Annie Parent-Charon, Francois Dupuigrenet Desroussilles, Claude Jolly, and Dominique Varry. Histoire et civilisation du livre 24. Paris: Droz, 1997.

Chazon, Esther G. "The Function of the Qumran Prayer Texts: An Analysis of the Daily Prayers (4Q503)." Pages 217–25 in *The Dead Sea Scrolls Fifty Years after Their Discovery: Proceedings of the Jerusalem Congress, July 20–25, 1997*. Edited by Lawrence H. Schiffman, Emanuel Tov, and James C. Vanderkam. Jerusalem: Israel Exploration Society, 2000.

———. "Is *Diveri ha-me'orot* a Sectarian Prayer." Pages 3–17 in *The Dead Sea Scrolls: Forty Years of Research*. Edited by Devorah Dimant and Urial Rappaport. STDJ 10. Leiden: Brill, 1992.

———. "Psalms, Hymns, and Prayers." *EDSS* 2:710–15.

———. "The Words of the Luminaries and Penitential Prayer in Second Temple Times." Pages 177–86 in *The Development and Impact of Penitential Prayer in Second Temple Judaism*. Vol. 2 of *Seeking the Favor of God*. Edited by Mark J. Boda, Daniel K. Falk, and Rodney A. Werline. EJL 22. Atlanta: Society of Biblical Literature, 2007.

Chibici-Revneanu, Nicole. "Leben im Gesetz: Die paulinische Interpretation von Lev 18:5 (Gal 3:12; Rom 10:5)." *NovT* 50 (2008): 105–19.

Clemen, Carl. *Die Himmelfahrt des Mose*. KlT 10. Bonn: Marcus & Weber, 1904.

Collins, John J. *The Apocalyptic Imagination: An Introduction to Jewish Apocalyptic Literature*. 3rd ed. Grand Rapids: Eerdmans, 2016.

———. *Beyond the Qumran Community*. Grand Rapids: Eerdmans, 2010.

———. "The Date and Provenance of the Testament of Moses." Pages 15–32 in *Studies on the Testament of Moses*. Edited by George W. E. Nickelsburg. SCS 4. Cambridge: Society of Biblical Literature, 1973.

———. Review of *Studies on the Hasmonean Period*, by Joshua Efron. *CBQ* 52 (1990): 372.

———. "The Royal Psalms and Eschatological Messianism." Pages 73–89 in *Aux origines des messianismes juifs*. Edited by David Hamidović. VTSup 158. Leiden: Brill, 2013.

———. "Some Remaining Traditio-Historical Problems in the Testament of Moses." Pages 38–43 in *Studies on the Testament of Moses*. Edited by George W. E. Nickelsburg. SCS 4. Cambridge: Society of Biblical Literature, 1973.

Cook, Johann. *The Septuagint of Proverbs—Jewish and/or Hellenistic Proverbs? Concerning the Hellenistic Colouring of LXX Proverbs*. VTSup 69. Leiden: Brill, 1997.

Cosme, Pierre. "Les *Res gestae divi Augusti*: Une autobiographie d'Auguste?" Pages 33–46 in *Autobiographies souveraines*. Edited by Pierre Monnet and Jean-Claude Schmitt. Histoires anciennes et médiévales 112. Paris: Sorbonne, 2012.

Crenshaw, James L. *Defending God: Biblical Responses to the Problem of Evil*. Oxford: University Press, 2005.

———. "Introduction: The Shift from Theodicy to Anthropodicy." Pages 1–16 in *Theodicy in the Old Testament*. Edited by James L. Crenshaw. Philadelphia: Fortress, 1983.

———. "Theodicy and Prophetic Literature." Pages 236–55 in *Theodicy in the World of the Bible*. Edited by Antti Laato and Johannes C. de Moor. Leiden: Brill, 2003.

Csordas, Thomas. "Embodiment as a Paradigm for Anthropology." *Ethos* 18 (1990): 5–47.

———. "Imaginal Performance and Memory in Ritual Healing." Pages 91–114 in *The Performance of Healing*. Edited by Carol Laderman and Marina Roseman. London: Routledge, 1996.

Davila, James R. "(How) Can We Tell If a Greek Apocryphon or Pseudepigraphon Has Been Translated from Hebrew or Aramaic?" *JSP* 15 (2005): 3–61.

———. *The Provenance of the Pseudepigrapha: Jewish, Christian, or Other?* JSJSup 105. Leiden: Brill, 2005.

Denis, Albert-Marie. *Introduction à la littérature religieuse judéo-hellénistique*. 2 vols. Turnhout: Brepols, 2000.

Desjarlais, Robert, and C. Jason Throop. "Phenomenological Approaches in Anthropology." *Annual Review of Anthropology* 40 (2011): 87–102.

Dibelius, Martin, and Hans Conzelmann. *The Pastoral Epistles*. Edited by Helmut Koester. Translated by Philip Buttolph and Adela Yarbro. Hermeneia. Philadelphia: Fortress, 1973.

Dider, Hugues. "La vie et la pensée de Juan Eusebio Nieremberg." PhD diss., Université Lille, 1974.

DiTommaso, Lorenzo. "The Development of Apocalyptic Historiography in Light of the Dead Sea Scrolls." Pages 497–522 in *Celebrating the Dead Sea Scrolls: A Canadian Collection*. Edited by Peter W. Flint, Jean Duhaime, and Kyung S. Baek. EJL 30. Atlanta: Society of Biblical Literature, 2011.

———. Review of *Theodicy in the World of the Bible: The Goodness of God and the Problem of Evil*, ed. Antti Laato and Johannes C. de Moor, *RBL* (February 2007).

———. "Penitential Prayer and Apocalyptic Eschatology in Second Temple Judaism." Pages 115–33 in *Prayer and Poetry in the Dead Sea Scrolls and Related Literature: Essays in Honor of Eileen Schuller on the Occasion of Her Sixty-Fifth Birthday*. Edited by Jeremy Penner, Ken M. Penner, and Cecilia Wassen. STDJ 98. Leiden: Brill, 2012.

Donceel, Robert. *Khirbet Qumrân (Palestine): Le Locus 101 et ses vestiges d'activité artisanale*, QC 17. Cracow: Enigma, 2005.

Dorival, Gilles. *Les Nombres: Traduction du texte grec de la Septante, Introduction et notes*. BA 4. Paris: Cerf, 1994.

Dunn, James D. G. "The Dialogue Progresses." Pages 389–430 in *Lutherische und Neue Pauluserspektive. Beiträge zu einem Schlüsselproblem der gegenwärtigen exegetischen Diskussion*. Edited by Michael Bachmann. WUNT 182. Tübingen: Mohr Siebeck, 2005.

———. *The New Perspective on Paul: Collected Essays*. Rev. ed. Grand Rapids: Eerdmans, 2008.

———. *The Theology of Paul the Apostle*. Grand Rapids: Eerdmans, 1998.

Eckhardt, Benedikt. "'An Idumean, That Is, a Half-Jew': Hasmoneans and Herodians between Ancestry and Merit." Pages 91–115 in *Jewish Identity and Politics between the Maccabees and Bar Kokhba: Groups, Normativity, and Rituals*. Edited by Benedikt Eckhardt. JSJSup 155. Leiden: Brill, 2012.

———. "The Psalms of Solomon as a Historical Source." Pages 7–29 in *The Psalms of Solomon: Language, History, Theology*. EJL 40. Edited by Eberhard Bons and Patrick Pouchelle. Atlanta: SBL Press, 2015.

———. "PsSal 17, die Hasmonäer und der Herodompeius." *JSJ* 40 (2009): 465–92.

Eckstein, Arthur M. *Moral Vision in The Histories of Polybius*. Berkeley: University of California Press, 1995.

Eder, Klaus. *The New Politics of Class: Social Movements and Cultural Dynamics in Advanced Societies*. London: Sage, 1993.

Efron, Joshua. "The Psalms of Solomon, the Hasmonean Decline and Christianity." Pages 219–86 in *Studies on the Hasmonean Period*. SJLA 39. Leiden: Brill, 1987.

Eissfeldt, Otto. *The Old Testament: An Introduction*. Translated by P. R. Ackroyd. New York: Harper & Row, 1965.

Elßner, Thomas R. "Das Wagnis der Hoffnung—Ein Bund auch für uns geschlossen (PsSal 9,10)." Pages 123–37 in *Weisheit als Lebensgrundlage, Texte imprimé: Festschrift für Friedrich V. Reiterer zum 65. Geburtstag*. Edited by Renate Egger-Wenzel, Karin Schöpflin, and Johannes Friedrich Diehl. DCLS 15. Berlin: de Gruyter, 2013.

Embry, Brad. "The *Psalms of Solomon* and the New Testament: Intertextuality and the Need for a Re-evaluation." *JSP* 13 (2002): 99–136.

———. "The Name 'Solomon' as a Prophetic Hallmark in Jewish and Christian Texts." *Hen* 28 (2006): 47–62.

———. "Some Thoughts on and Implications from Genre Categorization in the Psalms of Solomon." Pages 59–78 in *The Psalms of Solomon: Language, History, Theology*. Edited by Eberhard Bons and Patrick Pouchelle. EJL 40. Atlanta, GA: SBL Press, 2015.

Erzberger, Johanna. "One Author's Polyphony: Zion and God Parallelized (Bar 4:5–5:9)." Pages 79–96 in *Studies on Baruch: Composition, Literary Relations, and Reception*. Edited by Sean A. Adams. Berlin: de Gruyter, 2016.

Eshel, Hanan. "4Q386: An Allusion to the Death of Pompey in 48 BCE?" [Hebrew]. *Shnaton* 14 (2004): 195–203.

———. "The Fate of the Scrolls and Fragments: A Survey from 1946 to the Present." Pages 33–49 in *Gleanings from the Caves*. Edited by Torleif Elgvin. London: Bloomsbury T&T Clark, 2016.

———. "Publius Quinctilius Varus in Jewish Sources." *JJS* 59 (2008): 112–19.

Fabricius, Johannes Albertus. *Codex Pseudepigraphus Veteris Testamenti collectus, castigatus, testimoniisque, censuris et animadversionibus illustratus*. 2 vols. Hamburg: Felginer: 1722–1723.

Fahey, Michael A. *Cyprian and the Bible: A Study in Third-Century Exegesis*. BGBH 9. Tübingen: Mohr Siebeck, 1971.

Falk, Daniel K. *Daily, Sabbath, and Festival Prayers in the Dead Sea Scrolls*. STDJ 27. Leiden: Brill, 1998.

———. "Material Aspects of Prayer Manuscripts at Qumran." Pages 33–87 in *Literature or Liturgy? Early Christian Hymns and Prayers in Their Literary and Liturgical Context in Antiquity*. Edited by Clemens Leonhard and Hermut Löhr. WUNT 363. Tübingen: Mohr Siebeck, 2014.

———. "Petition and Ideology in the Dead Sea Scrolls." Pages 135–59 in *Prayer and Poetry in the Dead Sea Scrolls and Related Literature: Essays in Honor of Eileen Schuller on the Occasion of Her Sixty-Fifth Birthday*. Edited by Jeremy Penner, Ken M. Penner, and Cecilia Wassen. STDJ 98. Leiden: Brill, 2012.

———. "Psalms and Prayers." Pages 7–56 in *The Complexities of Second Temple Judaism*. Vol. 1 of *Justification and Variegated Nomism*. Edited by Donald A. Carson, Peter T. O'Brien, and Mark A. Seifrid. WUNT 140. Tübingen: Mohr Siebeck, 2001.

Feingold, Mordechai. Preface to *Jesuit Science and the Republic of Letters*. Edited by Mordechai Feingold. Cambridge: MIT Press, 2003.

Finley, Moses I. *The Ancient Economy*. Berkeley: University of California Press, 1973.

Fischer, Irmtraud. *Women Who Wrestled with God: Biblical Stories of Israel's Beginnings*. Collegeville, Minnesota: Liturgical Press, 2005.

Fouilloux, Etienne, and Bernard Hours, eds. *Les jésuites à Lyon: XVIe–XXe siècle*. Lyon: ENS éditions, 2005.

Fox, Michael V. *Proverbs: An Electic Edition with Introduction and Textual Commentary.* HBCE. Atlanta: SBL Press, 2015.

Franklyn, Paul N. "The Cultic and Pious Climax of Eschatology in the Psalms of Solomon." *JSJ* 18 (1987): 1–17.

Frede, Hermann Josef. *Epistulae ad Thessalonicenses Timotheum, Titum, Philemonem, Hebraeos.* VL 25.1. Freiburg: Herder, 1975–1982.

Friesen, Steven J. "Injustice or God's Will? Early Christian Explanations of Poverty." Pages 17–36 in *Wealth and Poverty in Early Church and Society.* Edited by Susan R. Holman. Grand Rapids: Baker, 2008.

———. "Poverty in Pauline Studies: Beyond the So-Called New Consensus." *JSNT* 26 (2004): 323–61.

García Martínez, Florentino. "Reconsidering the Cave 1 Texts Sixty Years after Their Discovery: An Overview." Pages 1–13 in *Qumran Cave 1 Revisited.* Edited by Daniel K. Falk et al. Leiden: Brill, 2010.

Gardner, Gregg. *The Origins of Organized Charity in Rabbinic Judaism.* Cambridge: University Press, 2015.

Garnsey, Peter. *Famine and Food Supply in the Graeco-Roman World: Responses to Risk and Crisis.* Cambridge: University Press, 1988.

Gathercole, Simon J. "Torah, Life, and Salvation: Leviticus 18:5 in Early Judaism and the New Testament." Pages 126–45 in *From Prophecy to Testament: The Function of the Old Testament in the New.* Edited by Craig A. Evans. Peabody: Hendrickson, 2004.

Gebhardt, Oscar von. *Die Psalmen Salomo's zum ersten Male mit Benutzung der Athoshandschriften und des Codex Casanatensis.* TUGAL 13.2. Leipzig: Hinrichs, 1895.

Geiger, P. Eduard Ephraem. *Der Psalter Salomo's, Herausgegeben und Erklärt.* Augsburg: Wolff, 1871.

Geertz, Clifford. *The Interpretation of Cultures.* New York: Basic, 1973.

Gillmayr-Bucher, Suzanne. "Body Images in the Psalms." *JSOT* 28 (2004): 301–26.

Goff, Matthew. *Discerning Wisdom: The Sapiential Literature of the Dead Sea Scrolls.* VTSup 116. Leiden: Brill, 2007.

———. "Looking for Sapiential Dualism at Qumran." Pages 20–38 in *Dualism in Qumran.* Edited by Géza G. Xeravits. London: T&T Clark, 2010.

———. *The Worldly and Heavenly Wisdom of 4QInstruction.* STDJ 50. Leiden: Brill, 2003.

Goldstein, Jonathan A. "The Apocryphal Book of I Baruch." *PAAJR* 47 (1980): 179–99.

Goodblatt, David M. *The Monarchic Principle: Studies in Jewish Self-Government in Antiquity.* TSAJ 38. Tübingen: Mohr Siebeck, 1994.

Goodman, Martin. *The Ruling Class of Judaea: The Origins of the Jewish Revolt against Rome A.D. 66–70.* Cambridge: University Press, 1987.

Gordley, Matthew E. "Creating Meaning in the Present by Reviewing the Past: Communal Memory in the Psalms of Solomon." *JAJ* 5 (2014): 368–92.

―――. "Psalms of Solomon as Solomonic Discourse: The Nature and Function of Attribution to Solomon." *JSP* 25 (2015): 52–88.

Gray, George Buchanan. "The Psalms of Solomon." *APOT* 2:625–52.

Green, Ronald M. "Theodicy." *EncRel* 14:430–41.

Greenblatt, Stephen. *The Swerve: How the World Became Modern.* New York: Norton, 2011.

Grierson, Fiona. "The Testament of Moses." *JSP* 17 (2008): 266–74.

Grossman, Maxine L. "Cultivating Identity: Textual Virtuosity and 'Insider' Status." Pages 1–11 in *Defining Identities: We, You, and the Other in the Dead Sea Scrolls.* Edited by Florentino García Martínez and Mladen Popović. STDJ 70. Leiden: Brill, 2008.

―――. *Reading for History in the Damascus Document: A Methodological Study.* STDJ 45. Leiden: Brill, 2002.

Gryson, Roger. *Esaias.* 2 vols. VL 12. Freiburg: Herder, 1987–1997.

Hadas-Lebel, Mireille. *Jerusalem against Rome.* Interdisciplinary Studies in Ancient Culture and Religion 7. Leuven: Peeters, 2006.

Hagedorn, Anselm, and Shani Tzoref. "Attitudes to Gentiles in the Minor Prophets and in Corresponding Pesharim." *DSD* 20 (2013): 470–507.

Halbwachs, Maurice. *On Collective Memory.* Edited and translated by Lewis A. Coser. Chicago: University of Chicago Press, 1992.

Hamel, Gildas. *Poverty and Charity in Roman Palestine, First Three Centuries.* Berkeley: University of California Press, 1990.

Hamidović, David. *L'écrit de Damas, le manifeste essénien.* Collection de la revue des études juives. Leuven: Peeters, 2011.

d'Hamonville, David-Marc. *Les Proverbes: Traduction du texte grec de la Septante, Introduction et notes.* La Bible d'Alexandrie 17. Paris: Cerf, 2000.

Hann, Robert R. "The Community of the Pious: The Social Setting of the Psalms of Solomon." *SR* 17 (1988): 169–89.

―――. *The Manuscript History of the Psalms of Solomon.* SCS 13. Atlanta: Scholars Press, 1982.

Harkins, Angela Kim. "The Emotional Re-experiencing of the Hortatory Narratives Found in the Admonition of the Damascus Document." *DSD* 22 (2015): 285–307.

———. *Reading with an "I" to the Heavens: Looking at the Qumran Hodayot through the Lens of Visionary Traditions*. Ekstasis 3. Berlin: de Gruyter, 2012.

Harris, William V. "The Late Republic." Pages 511–42 in *The Cambridge Economic History of the Greco-Roman World*. Edited by Walter Scheidel, Ian Morris, and Richard P. Saller. Cambridge: Cambridge University Press, 2013.

———. "On the Applicability of the Concept of Class in Roman History." Pages 598–610 in *Forms of Control and Subordination in Antiquity*. Edited by Tōru Yuge and Masaoki Doi. Leiden: Brill, 1988.

———. *Restraining Rage: The Ideology of Anger Control in Classical Antiquity*. Cambridge: Harvard University Press, 2001.

———. *Rome's Imperial Economy: Twelve Essays*. Oxford: University Press, 2011.

Hartman, Dorota. *Emozioni nella Bibbia: Lessico e passaggi semantici fra Bibbia ebraica e LXX*. Archivio di Studi ebraici 9. Naples: Centro di Studi ebraici, 2017.

Hearon, Holly. "The Construction of Social Memory in Biblical Interpretation." *Enc* 67 (2006): 343–59.

Hellholm, David. "The Problem of Apocalyptic Genre and the Apocalypse of John." *Semeia* 36 (1986): 13–64.

Hempel, Charlotte. *The Laws of the Damascus Document: Sources, Tradition and Redaction*. STDJ 29. Leiden: Brill, 1998.

Henderson, Ruth. *Second Temple Songs of Zion: A Literary and Generic Analysis of the Apostrophe to Zion (11QPs^a XXII 1–15), Tobit 13:9–18 and 1 Baruch 4:30–5:9*. DCLS 17. Berlin: de Gruyter, 2014.

———. "Structure and Allusion in the *Apostrophe Zion* (11QPs^a 22:1–15)." *DSD* 20 (2013): 51–70.

Hendrickson, Scott. *Jesuit Polymath of Madrid: The Literary Enterprise of Juan Eusebio Nieremberg (1595–1658)*. Leiden: Brill, 2015.

Henten, Jan Willem van. "Moses about Herod, Herod about Moses? *Assumptio Mosis* and Josephus' *Antiquities* 15.136." Pretoria. 27 August 2012. Thessaloniki. 25 April, 2013.

Herman, Judith. *Trauma and Recovery: The Aftermath of Violence from Domestic Abuse to Political Terror*. New York: Basic Books, 1992.

Hezser, Catherine. *Jewish Literacy in Roman Palestine*. TSAJ 81. Tübingen: Mohr Siebeck, 2001.

Hilgenfeld, Adolf. "Die Psalmen Salomo's und die Himmelfahrt des Moses, griechisch hergestellt und erklärt." *ZWT* 11 (1868): 273–309.

———. *Messias Judaeorum, Libris eorum Paulo ante et Paulo Post Christum natum conscriptis illustratus*. Leipzig: Fues, 1869.

———. "Mosis Assumptionis, quae supersunt nunc primum edita et illustrata." Pages 93–116 in *Novum Testamentum extra canonem receptum*. Leipzig: Weigel, 1866.

———. "Nachträge zu den Psalmen Salomo's und der Himmelfahrt des Moses." *ZWT* 11 (1868): 353.

Hofmann, Norbert Johannes. *Die Assumptio Mosis: Studien zur Rezeption massgültiger Überlieferung*. JSJSup 67. Leiden: Brill, 2000.

Hölscher, Gustav. "Über die Entstehungszeit der 'Himmelfahrt Moses.'" *ZNW* 17 (1916): 108–27, 149–58.

Hollenbach, Paul W. "Defining Rich and Poor Using the Social Sciences." Pages 30–63 in *Society of Biblical Literature 1987 Seminar Papers*. SBLSP 26. Atlanta, GA: Scholars, 1987.

Holm-Nielsen, Svend. "Die Psalmen Solomos." *JSHRZ* 4 (1977): 51–112.

———. "The Importance of Late Jewish Psalmody for the Understanding of the Old Testament Psalmodic Tradition." *ST* 14 (1960): 1–54.

Hopkins, Keith. "Rome, Taxes, Rents and Trade." Pages 190–232 in *The Ancient Economy*. Edited by Walter Scheidel and Sitta von Reden. Edinburgh: Edinburgh University Press, 2002.

Horbury, William. "'Gospel' in Herodian Judaea." Pages 80–103 in *Herodian Judaism and New Testament Study*. WUNT 193. Tübingen: Mohr Siebeck: 2006.

———. "Moses and the Covenant in the Assumption of Moses and the Pentateuch." Pages 191–208 in *Covenant as Context: Essays in Honour of E. W. Nicholson*. Edited by Andrew D. H. Mayes and Robert B. Salter. Oxford: Oxford University Press, 2003.

———. "The Remembrance of God in the Psalms of Solomon." Pages 111–28 in *Memory in the Bible and Antiquity: The Fifth Durham-Tübingen Research Symposium (Durham, September 2004)*. Edited by Steven C. Barton, Loren T. Stuckenbruck, and Benjamin G. Wold. WUNT 212. Tübingen: Mohr Siebeck, 2007.

Horgan, Maurya P. "Psalm Pesher 1 (4Q171=4QpPs^a =4QpPs37 and 45)." Pages 6–23 in *The Dead Sea Scrolls: Hebrew, Aramaic, and Greek Texts with English Translation; Pesharim, Other Commentaries, and Related*

Documents. Edited by James H. Charlesworth. PTSDSSP 6B. Louisville: Westminster John Knox, 1997.

Horn, Christoph, and Christof Rapp, eds. *Wörterbuch der antiken Philosophie*. Munich: Beck, 2002.

Horsley, Richard A. *Revolt of the Scribes: Resistance and Apocalyptic Origins*. Minneapolis: Fortress, 2010.

———. "Social Relations and Social Conflict in the Epistle of Enoch." Pages 100–15 in *For a Later Generation: The Transformation of Tradition in Israel, Early Judaism, and Early Christianity*. Edited by R. A. Argall, Beverly Bow, and Rodney A. Werline. Harrisburg: Trinity, 2000.

Horst, Friedrich. "Die Doxologien im Amosbuch." *ZAW* 47 (1929): 45–54.

Horst, Pieter Willem van der. *The Sentences of Pseudo-Phocylides: With Introduction and Commentary*. SVTP 4. Leiden: Brill, 1978.

Houtman, Cornelis. "Theodicy in the Pentateuch." Pages 151–82 in *Theodicy in the World of the Bible*. Edited by Antti Laato and Johannes C. de Moor. Leiden: Brill, 2003.

Humbert, Jean-Baptiste. "L'espace sacré a Qumrân. Propositions pour l'archéologie." *RB* 191 (1994): 161–214.

Hunt, Alice. *Missing Priests: The Zadokites in Tradition and History*. LHBOTS 452. London: T&T Clark, 2006.

Israeli, Edna. "'Taxo' and the Origin of the 'Assumption of Moses.'" *JBL* 128 (2009): 735–57.

Jacobs, Sandra. *The Body as Property: Physical Disfigurement in Biblical Law*. LHBOTS 582. London: T&T Clark, 2014.

———. "Natural Law, Poetic Justice and the Talionic Formulation." *Political Theology* 14 (2013): 691–99.

Janenskius, Georg. *Dissertationem historico criticam de Psalterio Salomonis*. Wittenberg: Christian Fincelius, 1687.

Japhet, Sara. "Theodicy in Ezra-Nehemiah and Chronicles." Pages 429–69 in *Theodicy in the World of the Bible*. Edited by Antti Laato and Johannes C. de Moor. Leiden: Brill, 2003.

Johnson, Luke T. *The First and Second Letters to Timothy*. AB 35A. New York: Doubleday, 2001.

———. "The New Testament's Anti-Jewish Slander and the Conventions of Ancient Polemic." *JBL* 108 (1989): 419–41.

Johnson, Nathan C. "Rendering David a Servant in *Psalm of Solomon* 17.21." *JSP* 26 (2017): 235–50.

Jokiranta, Jutta. *Social Identity and Sectarianism in the Qumran Movement*. STDJ 105. Leiden: Brill, 2013.

Jonge, Marinus de. "The Expectation of the Future in the *Psalms of Solomon*." Pages 3–27 in *Jewish Eschatology, Early Christian Christology and the Testaments of the Twelve Patriarchs*. Edited by Marinus de Jonge. NovTSup 63. Leiden: Brill, 1991.

Jüngling, Hans-Winfried, Hermann von Lips, and Ruth Scoralick. "Paroimiai/Proverbia/Sprichwörter/Sprüche Salomos." Pages 1950–2001 in *Psalmen bis Daniel*. Vol. 2 of *Septuaginta Deutsch: Erläuterungen und Kommentare zum griechischen Alten Testament*. Edited by Martin Karrer and Wolfgang Kraus. Stuttgart: Deutsche Bibelgesellschaft, 2011.

Kabasele Mukenge, André. *L'unité littéraire du livre de Baruch*. Études bibliques: Nouvelle Série 38. Paris: Gabalda, 1998.

Kaiser, Otto. *Die poetischen und weisheitlichen Werke*. Vol 3 of *Grundriß der Einleitung in die kanonischen und deuterokanonischen Schriften des Alten Testaments*. Gütersloh: Gütersloher Verlagshaus, 1994.

———. *Gott, Mensch und Geschichte: Studien zum Verstandnis des Menschen und seiner Geschichte*. Berlin: de Gruyter, 2010.

Kalimtzis, Kostas. *Taming Anger: The Hellenic Approach to the Limitations of Reason*. London: Bloomsbury, 2014.

Kallendorf, Craig. "Epic and Tragedy—Virgil, La Cerda, Milton." Pages 579–95 in *Syntagmatia: Essays on Neo-Latin Literature in Honour of Monique Mund-Dopchie and Gilbert Tournoy*. Edited by Dirk Sacré and Jan Papy. Leuven: Leuven University Press, 2009.

Karrer, Martin. *Der Gesalbte, die Grundlagen des Christustitels*. FRLANT 151. Göttingen: Vandenhoeck & Ruprecht, 1991.

Kassel, Rudolf, and Colin Austin, eds. *Menander: Testimonia et Fragmenta apud scriptores servata*. Vol. 6.2 of *Poetae comici graeci*. Berlin: de Gruyter, 1998.

Kaufmann, Yehezkel. *The Religion of Israel from Its Beginnings to the Babylonian Exile*. Chicago: Chicago University Press, 1960.

Keddie, G. Anthony. *Class and Power in Roman Palestine: The Socioeconomic Setting of Judaism and Christian Origins*. Cambridge: Cambridge University Press, 2019.

———. "Judaean Apocalypticism and the Unmasking of Ideology: Foreign and National Rulers in the *Testament of Moses*." *JSJ* 44 (2013): 301–38.

———. *Revelations of Ideology: Apocalyptic Class Politics in Early Roman Palestine*. JSJSup 189. Leiden: Brill, 2018.

Keith, Chris. *Jesus against the Scribal Elite: The Origins of the Conflict*. Grand Rapids: Baker, 2014.

Kim, Heerak Christian. *Zadokite Propaganda in the Late Second Temple Period: A Turning Point in Jewish History.* Lanham, MD: University Press of America, 2014.

Kirk, Alan. "Social and Cultural Memory." Pages 1–24 in *Memory, Tradition and Text: Uses of the Past in Early Christianity.* Edited by Alan Kirk and Tom Thatcher. SemeiaSt 52. Atlanta: Society of Biblical Literature, 2005.

Klawans, Jonathan. *Impurity and Sin in Ancient Judaism.* Oxford: Oxford University Press, 2000.

———. *Josephus and the Theologies of Ancient Judaism.* Oxford: Oxford University Press, 2012.

Kneucker, Johann Jakob. *Das Buch Baruch: Geschichte und Kritik, Übersetzung und Erklärung auf Grund des wiederhergestellten hebräischen Urtextes mit einem Anhang über den pseudepigraphischen Baruch.* Leipzig: Brockhaus, 1879.

Knoppers, Gary N. "Aaron's Calf and Jeroboam's Calves." Pages 92–104 in *Fortunate the Eyes That See: Essays in Honor of David Noel Freedman in Celebration of His Seventieth Birthday.* Edited by Astrid B. Beck. Grand Rapids: Eerdmans, 1995.

Koch, Dietrich-Alex. *Geschichte des Urchristentums: Ein Lehrbuch.* 2nd ed. Göttingen: Vandenhoeck & Ruprecht, 2014.

Koch, Klaus. "Gibt es ein Vergeltungsdogma im Alten Testament?" Pages 65–103 in *Gesammelte Aufsätze.* Vol. 1 of *Spuren des hebräischen Denkens: Beiträge zur alttestamentlichen Theologie.* Neukirchen-Vluyn: Neukirchener, 1991.

Kratz, Reinhard Gregor. *Das Judentum im Zeitalter des Zweiten Tempels.* FAT 42. Tübingen: Mohr Siebeck, 2004.

———. "Der Pescher Nahum und seine biblische Vorlage." Pages 99–145 in *Prophetenstudien: Kleine Schriften II.* Edited by R. G. Kratz. Tübingen: Mohr Siebeck, 2011.

Kraus, Wolfgang, and Martin Karrer, eds. *Septuaginta Deutsch: Das griechische Alte Testament in deutscher Übersetzung.* Stuttgart: Deutsche Bibelgesellschaft, 2009.

Kugel, James L. "Topics in the History of the Spirituality of the Psalms." Pages 125–87 in *Jewish Spirituality: From the Bible through the Middle Ages.* Edited by Arthur Green. New York: Crossroad, 1986.

Kuzmičová, Anežka. "Literary Narrative and Mental Imagery: A View from Embodied Cognition." *Style* 48 (2014): 275–93.

———. "Presence in the Reading of Literary Narrative: A Case for Motor Enactment." *Semiotica* 189 (2012): 23–48.

Laato, Antti. "Theodicy in the Deuteronomic History." Pages 183–235 in *Theodicy in the World of the Bible*. Edited by Antti Laato and Johannes C. de Moor. Leiden: Brill, 2003.

Laato, Antti, and Johannes C. de Moor. "Introduction." Pages vii–liv in *Theodicy in the World of the Bible*. Edited by Antti Laato and Johannes C. de Moor. Leiden: Brill, 2003.

———, eds. *Theodicy in the World of the Bible*. Leiden: Brill, 2003.

Laird, Andrew. "Juan Luis de la Cerda and the Predicament of Commentary." Pages 171–203 in *The Classical Commentary: Histories, Practices, Theory*. Edited by Roy K. Gibson and Christina Shuttleworth Kraus. Mnemosyne: Bibliotheca Classica Batava. Leiden: Brill, 2002.

Lange, Armin. "Die Weisheitstexte aus Qumran: Eine Einleitung." Pages 3–30 in *The Wisdom Texts from Qumran and the Development of Sapiential Thought*. Edited by Charlotte Hempel, Armin Lange, and Hermann Lichtenberger. BETL 159. Leuven: Peeters, 2001.

———. *Weisheit und Prädestination: Weisheitliche Urordnung und Prädestination in den Textfunden von Qumran*. STDJ 18. Leiden: Brill, 1995.

Lange, Armin, and Ulrike Mittmann-Richert. "Annotated List of the Texts from the Judaean Desert Classified." Pages 115–64 in *The Texts from the Judaean Desert: Indices and an Introduction to the Discoveries in the Judaean Desert Series*. Edited by Emanuel Tov. DJD 39. Oxford: Clarendon, 2002.

Laperrousaz, Ernest-Marie. "Le milieu d'origine du 17e des psaumes (apocryphes) de Salomon." *REJ* 150 (1991): 557–64.

———. *Le Testament de Moïse (généralement appelé 'Assomption de Moïse'). Traduction avec introduction et notes*. Semitica 10. Paris: Adrien-Maisonneuve, 1970.

Lapin, Hayim. "Temple, Cult, and Consumption in Second Temple Jerusalem." Pages 241–53 in *Expressions of Cult in the Southern Levant in the Greco-Roman Period: Manifestations in Text and Material Culture*. Edited by Oren Tal and Zeev Weiss. Contextualizing the Sacred 6. Turnhout: Brepols, 2017.

Larcher, Chrysostome. *Le Livre de la Sagesse ou la Sagesse de Salomon*. Paris: Librairie Lecoffre, 1985.

Lattke, Michael. *Die Oden Salomos in ihrer Bedeutung für Neues Testament und Gnosis*. 4 vols. OBO 25.1–4. Göttingen: Vandenhoeck & Ruprecht, 1979–1998.

———. "Die Psalmen Salomos: Orte und Intentionen." Pages 78–95 in *Die Septuaginta—Orte und Intentionen: 5. Internationale Fachtagung veranstaltet von Septuaginta Deutsch (LXX.D), Wuppertal 24.–27. Juli 2014*. Edited by Siegfried Kreuzer, Martin Meiser, and Marcus Sigismund. WUNT 361. Tübingen: Mohr Siebeck, 2016.

———. "The Gnostic Interpretation of the Odes of Solomon in the Pistis Sophia." *Bulletin de la Société d'Archéologie Copte* 24 (1982): 69–84.

———. *Odes of Solomon: A Commentary*. Hermeneia 86. Minneapolis: Fortress, 2009.

Le Déaut, Roger. "La Septante, un Targum?" Pages 147–95 in *Études sur le judaïsme hellénistique: Congrès de Strasbourg (1983)*. Edited by R. Kuntzmann and J. Schlosser. LD 119. Paris: Cerf, 1984.

Leibniz, Gottfried Wilhelm. *Essais de théodicée: Sur la bonté de Dieu la liberté de l'homme et l'origine du mal*. Amsterdam: François Changuion, 1710.

Levenson, Jon D. *Creation and the Persistence of Evil*. San Francisco: Harper, 1985.

Lévi, Israël. "Les Dix-huit bénédictions et les Psaumes de Salomon." *REJ* 32 (1896): 161–78.

———. "La mort de Titus." *REJ* 15 (1887): 62–69.

Licht, Jacob. "Taxo and the Apocalyptic Doctrine of Vengeance." *JJS* 12 (1961): 95–103.

Lindemann, Andreas. "Paulus—Pharisäer und Apostel." Pages 311–51 in *Paulus und Johannes. Exegetische Studien zur paulinischen und johanneischen Theologie und Literatur*. Edited by Dieter Sänger and Ulrich Mell. WUNT 198. Tübingen: Mohr Siebeck, 2006.

Lindström, Fredrik. "Theodicy in the Psalms." Pages 256–303 in *Theodicy in the World of the Bible*. Edited by Antti Laato and Johannes C. de Moor. Leiden: Brill, 2003.

Ling, Timothy J. M. *The Judaean Poor and the Fourth Gospel*. SNTSMS 136. Cambridge: University Press, 2006.

Loader, William. "Herod or Alexander Janneus? A New Approach to the *Testament of Moses*." *JSJ* 46 (2015): 28–43.

Loewenstamm, Samuel E. "The Trembling of Nature during the Theophany." Pages 173–89 in *Comparative Studies in Biblical and Ancient Oriental Literatures*. AOAT 204. Neukirchen-Vluyn: Neukirchener Verlag, 1984.

Looijer, Gwynned de. *The Qumran Paradigm: A Critical Evaluation of Some Foundational Hypotheses in the Construction of the Qumran Sect*. EJL 43. Atlanta, GA: SBL Press, 2015.

Luhrmann, Tanya M. *Persuasions of the Witches' Craft: Ritual Magic in Contemporary England*. Oxford: Blackwell, 1989.

———. *When God Talks Back: Understanding the American Evangelical Relationship with God*. New York: Knopf, 2012.

Machiela, Daniel A. "The Aramaic Dead Sea Scrolls: Coherence and Context in the Library of Qumran." Pages 244–58 in *The Dead Sea Scrolls at Qumran and the Concept of a Library*. Edited by Sidnie White Crawford and Cecilia Wassen. STDJ 116. Leiden: Brill, 2016.

———. "Prayer in the Aramaic Dead Sea Scrolls: Catalogue and Overview." Pages 285–305 in *Prayer and Poetry in the Dead Sea Scrolls and Related Literature: Essays in Honor of Eileen Schuller on the Occasion of Her Sixty-Fifth Birthday*. Edited by Jeremy Penner, Ken M. Penner, and Cecilia Wassen. STDJ 98. Leiden: Brill, 2012.

Maes, Léon. "Lettres inédites d'André Schott." *Muséon* 9 (1908): 368–411.

Magness, Jodi. "Were Sacrifices Offered at Qumran? The Animal Bone Deposits Reconsidered." *JAJ* 7 (2016): 5–34.

Mahmood, Saba. *Politics of Piety: The Islamic Revival and the Feminist Subject*. Princeton: Princeton University Press, 2005.

Maier, Gerhard. *Mensch und freier Wille nach den jüdischen Religionsparteien zwischen Ben Sira und Paulus*. WUNT 12. Tübingen: Mohr Siebeck, 1971.

Malina, Bruce J. "Wealth and Poverty in the New Testament and Its World." *Int* 41 (1987): 354–67.

Manning, J. G. *Land and Power in Ptolemaic Egypt: The Structure of Land Tenure*. Cambridge: University Press, 2003.

Marcuse, Herbert. *The One-Dimensional Man*. Boston: Beacon Press, 1964.

Martin, Henri-Jean. *Livre, Pouvoir et Sociétés à Paris au XVIIe siècle (1598–1701)*. 2 vols. Genève: Droz, 1969.

Martínez, Bernabé Bartolomé. "Educación y humanidades clásicas en el Colegio Imperial de Madrid durante el siglo XVII." *Bulletin hispanique* 97 (1995): 109–55.

Mathews, Mark D. *Riches, Poverty, and the Faithful: Perspectives on Wealth in the Second Temple Period and the Apocalypse of John*. SNTSMS 154. Cambridge: University Press, 2013.

Matlock, R. Barry. "Helping Paul's Argument Work? The Curse of Galatians 3.10–14." Pages 154–79 in *The Torah in the New Testament*. Edited by Michael Tait and Peter Oakes. London: T&T Clark, 2009.

Mayer, Ernst Emanuel. *The Ancient Middle Classes: Urban Life and Aesthetics in the Roman Empire 100 BCE–250 CE*. Cambridge: Harvard University Press, 2012.

Mazzochi, Giuseppe. "Los comentarios virgilianos del Padre Juan Luis de La Cerda." *AISO: Acàtas II* (1990): 663–75.

McCarter, P. Kyle, Jr. *I Samuel: A New Translation with Introduction, Notes and Commentary*. AB 8. Garden City, NY: Doubleday, 1980.

McCauley, Robert N., and Emma Cohen. "Cognitive Science and the Naturalness of Religion." *Philosophy Compass* 5 (2010): 779–92.

McCauley, Robert N., and E. Thomas Lawson. *Bringing Ritual to Mind: Psychological Foundations of Cultural Forms*. Cambridge: Cambridge University Press, 2002.

McCloud, Sean. *Divine Hierarchies: Class in American Religion and Religious Studies*. Chapel Hill: University of North Carolina Press, 2007.

McCloud, Sean, and William A. Mirola, eds. *Religion and Class in America: Culture, History, and Politics*. International Studies in Religion and Society 7. Leiden: Brill, 2009.

McDonald, Lee Martin. "The Odes of Solomon in Ancient Christianity: Reflections on Scripture and Canon." Pages 108–36 in *Sacra Scriptura: How "Non-canonical" Texts Functioned in Early Judaism and Early Christianity*. Edited by James H. Charlesworth and Lee Martin McDonald, with Blake A. Jurgens. Jewish and Christian Texts in Contexts and Related Studies 20. London: T&T Clark, 2014.

McGlynn, Moyna. "Authority and Sacred Space: Concepts of the Jerusalem Temple in Aristeas, Wisdom, and Josephus." *BN* 161 (2014): 115–40.

Meggitt, Justin J. *Paul, Poverty and Survival*. SNTW. Edinburgh: T&T Clark, 1998.

Meinhold, Arndt. *Sprüche Kapitel 16–31*. Vol. 2 of *Die Sprüche*. Zürcher Bibelkommentare. Zürich: Theologischer Verlag Zürich.

Mendels, Doron. "A Note on the Tradition of Antiochus IV's Death." *IEJ* 31 (1981): 53–56.

Meursius, Johannes. *Opera*. Florence: Tartinius & Franchius 1763.

Milgrom, Jacob. *Leviticus 1–16*. AB 3A. Yale: Yale University Press, 1998.

Mittermaier, Amira. "Dreams from Elsewhere: Muslim Subjectivities beyond the Trope of Self-Cultivation." *Journal of the Royal Anthropological Institute* 18 (2012): 247–65.

———. *Dreams that Matter: Egyptian Landscapes of the Imagination.* Berkeley: University of California Press, 2011.
Monson, Andrew. *From the Ptolemies to the Romans: Political and Economic Change in Egypt.* Cambridge: University Press, 2012.
Moore, Carey A. *Daniel, Esther, and Jeremiah: The Additions: A New Translation with Introduction and Commentary.* AB 44. New York: Doubleday, 1977.
Morgan, Teresa. "Is Pistis/Fides Experienced as an Emotion in the Late Roman Republic, Early Principate, and Early Church?" Pages 199–200 in *Emotions in Greece and Rome: Texts, Images, Material Culture.* Vol. 2 of *Unveiling Emotions.* Edited by Angelos Chaniotis and Pierre Ducrey. Heidelberger Althistorische Beitrage und Epigraphische Studien 55. Stuttgart: Franz Steiner, 2013.
Morley, Neville. *Theories, Models, and Concepts in Ancient History.* London: Routledge, 2004.
Movers, Franz Karl. "Apokryphen-Literatur." *Kirchen-Lexikon oder Encyclopädie der Katholischen Theologie und ihrer Hilfswissenschaften* 1 (1847): 339–41.
Münz-Manor, Ophir. "Narrating Salvation: Verbal Sacrifices in Late Antique Liturgical Poetry." Pages 154–66 in *Jews, Christians, and the Roman Empire: The Poetics of Power in Late Antiquity.* Edited by Annette Y. Reed and N. Dohrmann. Philadelphia: University of Pennsylvania Press, 2013.
Muraoka, Takamitsu. "Pairs of Synonyms in the Septuagint Psalter." Pages 36–43 in *The Old Greek Psalter: Studies in Honour of Albert Pietersma.* Edited by Robert J. V. Hiebert, Claude E. Cox, and Peter J. Gentry. JSOTSup 332. Sheffield: Sheffield Academic, 2001.
Murphy, Catherine M. *Wealth in the Dead Sea Scrolls and in the Qumran Community.* STDJ 40. Leiden: Brill, 2002.
Najman, Hindy. *Seconding Sinai: The Development of Mosaic Discourse in Second Temple Judaism.* JSJSup 77. Leiden: Brill, 2003.
Nakládalová, Iveta, ed. Facsimile of Francesco Sacchini, *De ratione libros cum profectu legendi libellus.* Bibliotheca Sphaerica 5. Barcelona: Seminario de Poética Europea del Renacimiento, Instituto Séneca, 2009.
Navarro, Víctor. "Tradition and Scientific Change in Early Modern Spain: The Role of the Jesuits." Pages 331–87 in *Jesuit Science and the Republic of Letters.* Edited by Mordechai Feingold. Cambridge: MIT, 2003.
Newsom, Carol A. "'Sectually Explicit' Literature from Qumran." Pages 167–87 in *The Hebrew Bible and Its Interpreters.* Edited by William

H. Propp, Baruch Halpern, and David Noel Freedman. Winona Lake: Eisenbrauns, 1990.

———. *The Self as Symbolic Space: Constructing Identity and Community at Qumran*. STDJ 52. Leiden: Brill, 2004.

Neyrey, Jerome H. *Give God the Glory: Ancient Prayer and Worship in Cultural Perspective*. Grand Rapids: Eerdmans, 2007.

Nickelsburg, George W. E. "An Antiochian Date for the Testament of Moses." Pages 15–32 in *Studies on the Testament of Moses*. Edited by George W. E. Nickelsburg. SCS 4. Cambridge: Society of Biblical Literature, 1973.

———. *Jewish Literature between the Bible and the Mishnah*. 2nd ed. Minneapolis: Fortress, 2005.

———. "Revisiting the Rich and Poor in 1 Enoch 92–105 and the Gospel according to Luke." *NTS* 25 (1978–1979): 324–44.

———. "Social Aspects of Palestinian Jewish Apocalypticism." Pages 641–54 in *Apocalypticism in the Mediterranean World and the Near East: Proceedings of the International Colloquium on Apocalypticism, Uppsala, August 12–17, 1979*. Edited by David Hellholm. Tübingen: Mohr Siebeck, 1983.

———. "Torah and the Deuteronomic Scheme in the Apocrypha and Pseudepigrapha: Variations on a Theme and Some Noteworthy Examples of Its Absence." Pages 222–35 in *Das Gesetz im frühen Judentum und im Neuen Testament: Festschrift C. Burchard*. Edited by Dieter Sänger and Matthias Konradt. NTOA 57. Göttingen: Vandenhoeck & Ruprecht, 2006.

Nickelsburg George W. E., and James C. VanderKam. *1 Enoch: A New Translation*. 2 vols. Hermeneia. Minneapolis: Fortress, 2004, 2012.

Nitzan, Bilhah. *Qumran Prayer and Religious Poetry*. Translated by Jonathan Chipman. STDJ 12. Leiden: Brill, 1994.

Norris, Rebecca Sachs. "Examining the Structure and Role of Emotion: Contributions of Neurobiology to the Study of Embodied Religious Experience." *Zygon* 40 (2005): 181–99.

Notley, R. Steven. "The Kingdom of Heaven Forcefully Advances." Pages 279–311 in *The Interpretation of Scripture in Early Judaism and Christianity*. Edited by Craig A. Evans. Sheffield: Sheffield Academic, 2000.

Ottenheijm, Eric. "'Which If a Man Do Them He Shall Live by Them': Jewish and Christian Discourse on Lev 18:5." Pages 303–16 in *The Scriptures of Israel in Jewish and Christian Tradition: Essays in Honour of Maarten J. J. Menken*. Edited by Bart J. Koet, Steve Moyise and Joseph Verheyden. NovTSup 148. Leiden: Brill, 2013.

Pajunen, Mika S. "From Poetic Structure to Historical Setting: Exploring the Background of the Barkhi Nafshi Hymns." Pages 355–76 in *Prayer and Poetry in the Dead Sea Scrolls and Related Literature: Essays in Honor of Eileen Schuller on the Occasion of Her Sixth-Fifth Birthday*. Edited by Jeremy Penner, Ken M. Penner, and Cecilia Wassen. STDJ 98. Leiden: Brill, 2012.

Passow, Franz. *Handwörterbuch der Griechischen Sprache*. 4 vols. 5th ed. Repr. Darmstadt: Wissenschaftliche Buchgesellschaft, 2008.

Pastor, Jack. *Land and Economy in Ancient Palestine*. London: Routledge, 1997.

Penner, Jeremy. "Mapping Fixed Prayers from the Dead Sea Scrolls onto Second Temple Period Judaism." *DSD* 21 (2014): 39–63.

———. *Patterns of Daily Prayer in Second Temple Judaism*. STDJ 104. Leiden: Brill, 2014.

Pernigotti, Carlo. *Menandri Sententiae*. Studi e testi per il Corpus dei papiri filosofici greci e latini 15. Florence: Olschki, 2008.

Pesch, Wilhelm. "Die Abhangigkeit des 11. Salomonische Psalms vom letzten Kapitel des Buches Baruch." *ZAW* 67 (1955): 251–63.

Pevarello, Daniele. "Psalms of Solomon." Pages 425–37 in *The T&T Clark Companion to the Septuagint*. Edited by James K. Aitken. London: T&T Clark, 2015.

Pfann, Stephen J. "List of the Texts from the Judaean Desert." Pages 27–114 in *The Texts from the Judaean Desert: Indices and an Introduction to the Discoveries in the Judaean Desert Series*. Edited by Emanuel Tov. DJD 39. Oxford: Clarendon, 2002.

Piñero Sáenz, Antonio. "Salmos de Salomón." Pages 239–69 in *Libros poéticos y sapienciales*. Vol. 3 of *La Biblia griega Septuaginta*. Edited by Natalio Fernández Marcos and María Victoria Spottorno Díaz-Caro. Salamanca: Ediciones Sígueme, 2013.

Piovanelli, Pierluigi. "'A Testimony of the Kings and the Mighty Who Possess the Earth': The Thirst for Justice and Peace in the Parables of Enoch." Pages 363–79 in *Enoch and the Messiah Son of Man: Revisiting the Book of Parables*. Edited by Gabrielle Boccaccini. Grand Rapids.: Eerdmans, 2007.

Pomykala, Kenneth E. *The Davidic Dynasty Tradition in Early Judaism, Its History and Significance for Messianism*. EJL 7. Atlanta: Scholars Press, 1995.

Portier-Young, Anathea. *Apocalypse against Empire: Theologies of Resistance in Early Judaism*. Grand Rapids: Eerdmans, 2011.

———. "Jewish Apocalyptic Literature as Resistance Literature." Pages 145–62 in *The Oxford Handbook of Apocalyptic Literature*. Edited by John J. Collins. Oxford: Oxford University Press, 2014.

———. "Theologies of Resistance in Daniel, The Apocalypse of Weeks, the Book of Dreams, and the Testament of Moses." PhD diss. Duke University, 2004.

Pouchelle, Patrick. *Dieu éducateur: Une nouvelle approche d'un concept de la théologie biblique entre Bible Hébraïque, Septante et littérature grecque classique*. FAT 77. Tübingen: Mohr Siebeck, 2015.

———. "Flatterers, Whisperers, and Other Hypocrites: New Denominations for Sinners in the Writings of the Second Temple Period." Pages 234–50 in *New Vistas on Early Judaism and Christianity*. Edited by Lorenzo DiTommaso and Gerbern Oegema. Jewish and Christian Texts in Contexts and Related Studies 22. London: T&T Clark, 2016.

———. "Prayers for Being Disciplined: Notes on παιδεύω and παιδεία in the Psalms of Solomon." Pages 115–32 in *The Psalms of Solomon: Language, History, Theology*. Edited by Eberhard Bons and Patrick Pouchelle. EJL 40. Atlanta: SBL Press, 2015.

———. "The Simple Bare Necessities: Is *Pss. Sol.* 5 a Wisdom Prayer?" Pages 138–54 in *Tracing Sapiential Traditions in Ancient Judaism*. Edited by Hindy Najman, Jean-Sébastien Rey, and Eibert J. C. Tigchelaar. JSJSup 174. Leiden: Brill, 2016.

Priest, John. "Testament of Moses." *OTP* 1 (1983): 919–34.

Prigent, Pierre. "Psaumes de Salomon." Pages 945–92 in *La Bible: Écrits Intertestamentaires*. Edited by André Dupont-Sommer, Marc Philonenko, and Daniel A. Bertrand. Bibliothèque de la Pléiade. Paris: Gallimard, 1987.

Rad, Gerhard von. *The Message of the Prophets*. London: SCM, 1968.

———. *Theologie des Alten Testaments*. Vol. 1. Munich: Kaiser, 1957.

Rahlfs, Alfred. *Psalmi cum Odis*. Septuaginta Societatis Scientiarum Gottingensis auctoritate 10. Göttingen: Vandenhoeck & Ruprecht, 1931.

Rahlfs, Alfred, and Robert Hanhart, eds. *Septuaginta*. Stuttgart: Deutsche Bibelgesellschaft, 2006.

Rappaport, Roy A. *Ritual and Religion in the Making of Humanity*. Cambridge Studies in Social and Cultural Anthropology 110. Cambridge: Cambridge University Press, 1999.

Reed, Annette Yoshiko. "The Modern Invention of 'Old Testament Pseudepigrapha.'" *JTS* 60 (2009): 403–36.
Reymond, Eric D. *New Idioms within Old: Poetry and Parallelism in the Non-Masoretic Poems of 11Q5 (=11QPsª)*. EJL 31. Atlanta: Society of Biblical Literature, 2011.
Rocca, Samuel. *Herod's Judaea: A Mediterranean State in the Classical World*. TSAJ 122. Tübingen: Mohr Siebeck, 2008.
———. "Josephus and the Psalms of Solomon on Herod's Messianic Aspirations: An Interpretation." Pages 313–33 in *Making History: Josephus and Historical Method*. Edited by Zuleika Rodgers. JSJSup 110. Leiden: Brill, 2007.
Rooke, Deborah W. *Zadok's Heirs: The Role and Development of the High Priesthood in Ancient Israel*. Oxford Theological Monographs. Oxford: Oxford University Press, 2000.
Rosen-Zvi, Ishay. *The Mishnaic Sotah Ritual: Temple, Gender and Midrash*. JSJSup 160. Leiden: Brill, 2012.
Rothkamm, Jan. *Talio esto: Recherches sur les origines de la formule 'œil pour œil, dent pour dent' dans les droits du Proche-Orient ancien, et sur son devenir dans le monde gréco-romain*. Berlin: de Gruyter, 2011.
Ryle, Herbert Edward, and Montague Rhodes James. *Psalms of the Pharisees Commonly Called the Psalms of Solomon*. Cambridge: Cambridge University Press, 1891.
Sacchini, Francesco. *De ratione libros cum profectu legendi libellus*. Ingolstadt: Elisabeth Angermaria, 1614.
Sæbø, Magne. *Sprüche*. Das Alte Testament Deutsch. Göttingen: Vandenhoeck & Ruprecht, 2012.
Saller, Richard P. "Framing the Debate over Growth in the Ancient Economy." Pages 251–69 in *The Ancient Economy: Evidence and Models*. Edited by J. G. Manning and Ian Morris. Stanford: Stanford University Press, 2005.
Sanders, E. P. "The Genre of Palestinian Jewish Apocalypses." Pages 447–59 in *Apocalypticism in the Mediterranean World and the Near East: Proceedings of the International Colloquium on Apocalypticism, Uppsala, August 12–17, 1979*. Edited by David Hellholm. Tübingen: Mohr Siebeck, 1983.
———. *Judaism: Practice and Belief, 63 B.C.E.–66 C.E.* London: SCM, 1992.
———. *Paul and Palestinian Judaism: A Comparison of Patterns of Religion*. Philadelphia: Fortress, 1977.

Sanders, James A. "Psalm 154 Revisited." Pages 296–306 in *Biblische Theologie und gesellschaftlicher Wandel: Für Norbert Lohfink*. Edited by Georg Braulik, Walter Gross, and Sean McEvenue. Frieburg: Herder, 1993.

———. *The Psalms Scroll of Qumran Cave 11 (11QPsᵃ)*. DJD 4. Oxford: Clarendon, 1965.

Sarna, Nahum M. *Understanding Genesis*. New York: Schocken, 1972.

Sarot, Marcel. "Theodicy and Modernity." Pages 1–26 in *Theodicy in the World of the Bible*. Edited by Antti Laato and Johannes C. de Moor. Leiden: Brill, 2003.

Sartre, Maurice. *The Middle East under Rome*. Translated by Catherine Porter and Elizabeth Rawlings. Cambridge: Harvard University Press, 2005.

Savage, Mike. *Class Analysis and Social Transformation*. Philadelphia: Open University Press, 2000.

Scheidel, Walter, and Steven J. Friesen. "The Size of the Economy and the Distribution of Income in the Roman Empire." *JRS* 99 (2009): 69–91.

Scheidel, Walter, Ian Morris, and Richard P. Saller, eds. *The Cambridge Economic History of the Greco-Roman World*. Cambridge: University Press, 2007.

Schenker, Adrian. "What Were the Aims of the Palestinian Recensions, and What Did They Achieve? With Some Biographical Notes on Dominique Barthélemy." Pages 14–22 in *The Legacy of Barthélemy: Fifty Years after Les Devanciers d'Aquila*. Edited by Anneli Aejmelaeus and Tuukka Kauhanen. Göttingen: Vandenhoeck & Ruprecht, 2017.

Schiffman, Lawrence H. "The Dead Sea Scrolls and the Early History of Jewish Liturgy." Pages 33–48 in *The Synagogue in Late Antiquity*. Edited by Lee I. Levine. Pittsburgh: American Schools of Oriental Research, 1987.

———. *The Halakhah at Qumran*. SJLA 16. Leiden: Brill, 1975.

———. "Messianic Figures and Ideas in the Qumran Scrolls." Pages 270–85 in *The Messiah: Developments in Earliest Judaism and Christianity*. Edited by James H. Charlesworth. Minneapolis: Fortress, 1992.

———. "Sacrifice in the Dead Sea Scrolls." Pages 89–106 in *The Actuality of Sacrifice: Past and Present*. Edited by Alberdina Houtman et al. Jewish and Christian Perspectives Series 28. Leiden: Brill, 2014.

Schmid, Hans Heinrich. *Eine Untersuchung zur altorientalischen und israelitischen Weisheitsliteratur*. BZAW 10. Berlin: Töpelmann, 1966.

Schmidt, Moriz, and Adalbert Merx. "Die Assumptio Mosis mit Einleitung und erklärenden Anmerkungen." *Archiv für wissenschaftliche Erforschung des Alten Testaments* 1 (1869): 111–52.

Schnelle, Udo. *Die ersten 100 Jahre des Christentums 30–130 n.Chr. Die Entstehungsgeschichte einer Weltreligion*. UTB 4411. Göttingen: Vandenhoeck & Ruprecht, 2015.

———. "Gerechtigkeit in den Psalmen Salomos und bei Paulus." Pages 365–75 in *Jüdische Schriften in ihrem antik-jüdischen und urchristlichen Kontext*. Edited by Hermann Lichtenberger and Gerbern S. Oegema. JSHRZ Studien 1. Gütersloh: Gütersloher, 2002.

Scholem, Gershom. *The Messianic Idea in Judaism*. New York: Schocken, 1971.

Schoors, Antoon. "Theodicy in Qohelet." Pages 375–409 in *Theodicy in the World of the Bible*. Edited by Antti Laato and Johannes C. de Moor. Leiden: Brill, 2003.

Schreiber, Stefan. "Can Wisdom Be Prayer? Form and Function of the Psalms of Solomon." Pages 89–106 in *Literature or Liturgy? Early Christian Hymns and Prayers in Their Literary and Liturgical Context in Antiquity*. Edited by Clemens Leonhard and Hermut Löhr. WUNT 363. Tübingen: Mohr Siebeck, 2014.

———. *Der erste Brief an die Thessalonicher*. ÖTK 13.1. Gütersloh: Gütersloher, 2014.

———. *Gesalbter und König: Titel und Konzeptionen der königlichen Gesalbtenerwartung in frühjüdischen und urchristlichen Schriften*. BZNW 105. Berlin: de Gruyter, 2000.

———. "Law and Love in Romans 13.8–10." Pages 100–119 in *The Torah in the Ethics of Paul*. Edited by Martin Meiser. LNTS 473. London: T&T Clark, 2012.

———. "Paulus und die Tradition: Zur Hermeneutik der 'Rechtfertigung' in neuer Perspektive." *TRev* 105 (2009): 91–102.

Schröter, Jens. "Gerechtigkeit und Barmherzigkeit: Das Gottesbild der Psalmen Salomos in seinem Verhältnis zu Qumran und Paulus." *NTS* 44 (1998): 557–77.

Schuller, Eileen M. "Prayers and Psalms from the Pre-Maccabean Period." *DSD* 13 (2006): 306–18.

———. "Recent Scholarship on the Hodayot 1993–2010." *CurBR* 19 (2011): 119–62.

Schuller, Eileen M., and Lorenzo DiTommaso. "A Bibliography of the Hodayot, 1948–1996." *DSD* 4 (1997): 55–101.

Schumacher, Thomas. *Zur Entstehung christlicher Sprache: Eine Untersuchung der paulinischen Idiomatik und der Verwendung des Begriffes* πίστις. BBB 168. Göttingen: Vandenhoeck & Ruprecht, 2012.

Schüpphaus, Joachim. *Die Psalmen Salomos: Ein Zeugnis Jerusalemer Theologie und Frömmigkeit in der Mitte des vorchristlichen Jahrhunderts.* ALGHJ 7. Leiden: Brill, 1977.

Schwartz, Barry. *Abraham Lincoln and the Forge of Memory.* Chicago: University of Chicago Press, 2000.

———. "Where There's Smoke, There's Fire: Memory and History." Pages 7–37 in *Memory and Identity in Ancient Judaism and Early Christianity: A Conversation with Barry Schwartz.* Edited by Tom Thatcher. SemeiaSt 78. Atlanta: SBL Press, 2014.

Schwartz, Joshua. Review of *Jewish Law and Identity: Academic Essays*, by Heerak Christian Kim. *RBL* 10 (2006).

Schwarzfuchs, Lyse. *L'hébreu dans le livre lyonnais au XVIe siècle: Inventaire chronologique.* Lyon: ENS éditions, 2008.

Scott, James M. *BACCHIUS IUDAEUS: A Denarius Commemorating Pompey's Victory over Judea.* SUNT 104. Göttingen: Vandenhoeck & Ruprecht, 2015.

Seifrid, Mark A. *Justification by Faith: The Origin and Development of a Central Pauline Theme.* NovTSup 68. Leiden: Brill, 1992.

Sewell, William H. *Logics of History: Social Theory and Social Transformation.* Chicago: University of Chicago Press, 2005.

Sharon, Nadav. "Between Opposition to the Hasmoneans and Resistance to Rome: The *Psalms of Solomon* and the Dead Sea Scrolls." Pages 41–54 in *Reactions to Empire: Sacred Texts in Their Socio-political Contexts.* Edited by John A. Dunne and Dan Batovici. WUNT 372. Tübingen: Mohr Siebeck, 2014.

———. *Judea under Roman Domination: The First Generation of Statelessness and Its Legacy.* EJL 46. Atlanta: SBL Press, 2017.

———. "Setting the Stage: The Effects of the Roman Conquest and the Loss of Sovereignty." Pages 415–46 in *Was 70 CE a Watershed in Jewish History? On Jews and Judaism before and after the Destruction of the Second Temple.* Edited by Daniel R. Schwartz and Zeev Weiss, with Ruth A. Clements. AJEC 78. Leiden: Brill, 2012.

Shemesh, Aharon, and Cana Werman. "Hidden Things and Their Revelation." *RevQ* 18 (1998): 409–27.

Skeggs, Beverly. *Class, Self, Culture.* London: Routledge, 2004.

Steck, Odil Hannes. *Das apokryphe Baruchbuch: Studien zu Rezeption und Konzentration 'kanonischer' Überlieferung*. FRLANT 160. Göttingen: Vandenhoeck & Ruprecht, 1993.
Steins, Georg. "Die Psalmen Salomos—Ein Oratorium über die Barmherzigkeit Gottes und die Rettung Jerusalems." Pages 121–41 in *Laetare Jerusalem*. Edited by Nikodemus C. Schnabel. Jerusalemer theologisches Forum 10. Münster: Aschendorff, 2006.
Stenhouse, William. "Greek Antiquities and Greek Histories in the Late Renaissance" Pages 177–197 in *Et Amicorum: Essays on Renaissance Humanism and Philosophy in Honour of Jill Kraye*. Edited by Anthony Ossa-Richardson and Margaret Meserve. Brill's Studies in Intellectual History 273. Leiden: Brill, 2018.
Steudel, Annette. "B'hryt hymym in the Texts from Qumran." *RevQ* 16 (1993): 225–46.
Stone, Michael. *Ancient Judaism: New Visions and Views*. Grand Rapids: Eerdmans, 2011.
Stuckenbruck, Loren T. *1 Enoch 91–108*. CEJL. Berlin: de Gruyter, 2007.
———. "The Legacy of the Teacher of Righteousness in the Dead Sea Scrolls." Pages 23–49 in *New Perspectives on Old Texts, Proceedings of the Tenth International Symposium of the Orion Center for the Study of the Dead Sea Scrolls and Associated Literature, 9–11 January, 2005*. Edited by Esther G. Chazon and Betsy Halpern-Amaru. STJD 88. Leiden: Brill, 2010.
———. "Temporal Shifts from Text to Interpretation: Concerning the Use of the Perfect and Imperfect in the *Habakkuk Pesher* (1QpHab)." Pages 124–49 in *Qumran Studies: New Approaches, New Questions*. Edited by Michael Thomas Davis and Brent A. Strawn. Grand Rapids: Eerdmans, 2007.
Sollamo, Raija. "Messianism and the 'Branch of David' Isaiah 11,1–5 and Genesis 49,8-12." Pages 357–70 in *The Septuagint and Messianism*. Edited by Michael A. Knibb. BETL 195. Leuven: Peeters, 2006.
Striker, Gisela. "Emotions in Context." Pages 286–302 in *Essays on Aristotle's Rhetoric*. Edited by Amélie Oksenberg Rorty. Berkeley: University of California Press, 1996.
Swartz, Michael D. "Judaism and the Idea of Ancient Ritual Theory." Pages 294–317 in *Jewish Studies at the Crossroads of Anthropology and History: Authority, Diaspora, Tradition*. Edited by R. S. Boustan, Oren Kosansky, and Marina Rustow. Philadelphia: University of Pennsylvania Press, 2011.

———. "Ritual about Myth about Ritual: Towards an Understanding of the Avodah in the Rabbinic Period." *The Journal of Jewish Thought and Philosophy* 6 (1997): 135–55.

Talmon, Shemaryahu. "The Concepts of Masîah and Messianism in Early Judaism." Pages 79–115 in *The Messiah: Developments in Earliest Judaism and Christianity*. Edited James H. Charlesworth. Minneapolis: Fortress, 1992.

———. "Types of Messianic Expectation at the Turn of the Era." Pages 202–24 in *King, Cult, and Ancient Israel*. Jerusalem: Magnes, 1987.

———. *The World of Qumran from Within: Collected Studies*. Jerusalem: Magnes, 1989.

Tauberschmidt, Gerhard. *Secondary Parallelism: A Study of Translation Technique in LXX Proverbs*. AcBib15. Atlanta: Society of Biblical Literature, 2004.

Theissen, Gerd, and Petra von Gemünden. *Der Römerbrief: Rechenschaft eines Reformators*. Göttingen: Vandenhoeck & Ruprecht, 2016.

Tigchelaar, Eibert. *To Increase Learning for the Understanding Ones*. STDJ 44. Leiden: Brill, 2001.

Toomer, G. J. *Eastern Wisdom and Learning: The Study of Arabic in Seventeenth-Century England*. Oxford: Clarendon, 1996.

Toorn, Karel van der. *Scribal Culture and the Making of the Hebrew Bible*. Cambridge: Harvard University Press, 2007.

———. "Theodicy in Akkadian Literature." Pages 57–89 in *Theodicy in the World of the Bible*. Edited by Antti Laato and Johannes C. de Moor. Leiden: Brill, 2003.

Torijano, Pablo A. *Solomon the Esoteric King: From King to Magus, Development of a Tradition*. JSJSup 72. Leiden: Brill, 2002.

Tov, Emanuel. Foreword to *The Meaning of the Dead Sea Scrolls: Their Significance for Understanding the Bible, Judaism, Jesus, and Christianity*. Edited by James C. VanderKam and Peter W. Flint. San Francisco: HarperSanFrancisco, 2002.

———. "The Impact of the LXX Translation of the Pentateuch on the Translation of the Other Books." Pages 183–94 in *The Greek and Hebrew Bible: Collected Essays on the Septuagint*. Edited by Emanuel Tov. VTSup 77. Leiden: Brill, 1999.

———. "Lists of Specific Groups of Texts from the Judaean Desert." Pages 203–28 in *The Texts from the Judaean Desert: Indices and an Introduction to the Discoveries in the Judaean Desert Series*. Edited by Emanuel Tov. DJD 39. Oxford: Clarendon, 2002.

———, ed. *The Texts from the Judaean Desert: Indices and an Introduction to the Discoveries in the Judaean Desert Series*. DJD 39. Oxford: Clarendon, 2002.

———. *Textual Criticism of the Hebrew Bible, Qumran, Septuagint: Collected Essays*. VTSup 3. Leiden: Brill, 2015.

———. "The Writing of Early Scrolls and the Literary Analysis of Hebrew Scripture." *DSD* 13 (2003): 339–47.

Trafton, Joseph L. "The Bible, the *Psalms of Solomon*, and Qumran." Pages 427–46 in *The Dead Sea Scrolls and the Qumran Community*. Vol. 2 of *The Bible and the Dead Sea Scrolls*. Edited by James H. Charlesworth. Waco, TX: Baylor University Press, 2006.

———. "The Psalms of Solomon in Recent Research." *JSP* 12 (1994): 3–19.

———. *The Syriac Version of the Psalms of Solomon: A Critical Evaluation*. SCS 11. Atlanta: Scholars Press, 1985.

———. "What Would David Do? Messianic Expectations and Surprise in Ps. Sol. 17." Pages 155–74 in *The Psalms of Solomon: Language, History, Theology*. Edited by Eberhard Bons and Patrick Pouchelle. EJL 40. Atlanta: SBL Press, 2015.

Tromp, Johannes. *The Assumption of Moses: A Critical Edition with Commentary*. SVTP 10. Leiden: Brill, 1993.

———. "The Sinners and the Lawless in Psalm of Solomon 17." *NovT* 35 (1993): 344–61.

———. "Taxo, the Messenger of the Lord." *JSJ* 21 (1990): 200–209.

Tsouna, Voula. *Philodemus, On Property Management*. WGRW 33. Atlanta: Society of Biblical Literature, 2012.

Tzoref, Shani L. [Berrin]. "The 'Hidden' and the 'Revealed': Esotericism, Election, and Culpability in Qumran and Related Literature." Pages 299–324 in *The Dead Sea Scrolls at Sixty: The Scholarly Contributions of NYU Faculty and Alumni*. Edited by Lawrence H. Schiffman and Shani Tzoref. STDJ 89. Leiden: Brill, 2010.

———. "The 'Hidden' and the 'Revealed': Progressive Revelation of Law and Esoterica" [Hebrew]. *Meghillot* 7 (2009): 157–90.

———. "*Pesher Nahum, Psalms of Solomon* and Pompey." Pages 65–84 in *Reworking the Bible: Apocryphal and Related Texts at Qumran*. Edited by Esther G. Chazon, Devorah Dimant, and Ruth A. Clements. STDJ 58. Leiden: Brill, 2005.

———. *The Pesher Nahum Scroll from Qumran: An Exegetical Study of 4Q169*. STDJ 53. Leiden: Brill, 2004.

———. "Qumran Pesharim." Pages 110–33 in *Biblical Interpretation at Qumran*. Edited by Matthias Henze. Grand Rapids: Eerdmans, 2005.

Udoh, Fabian E. *To Caesar What Is Caesar's: Tribute, Taxes, and Imperial Administration in Early Roman Palestine, 63 B.C.E.–70 C.E.* BJS 343. Providence: Brown Judaic Studies, 2005.

Viteau, Joseph. *Les Psaumes de Salomon: Introduction, texte grec et traduction, avec les principales variantes de la version syriaque par François Martin*. Documents pour l'étude de la Bible. Paris: Letouzé et Ané, 1911.

Volkmar, Gustav. *Mose Prophetie und Himmelfahrt: Eine Quelle für das Neue Testament zum ersten Male deutsch herausgegeben, im zusammenhang der Apokrypha und der Christologie überhaupt*. Handbuch der Apocryphen 3. Leipzig: Fues Verlag, 1867.

Wälchli, Stefan H. *Gottes Zorn in den Psalmen: Eine Studie zur Rede vom Zorn Gottes in den Psalmen im Kontext des Alten Testaments und des Alten Orients*. OBO 244. Vandenhoeck & Ruprecht: Göttingen, 2012.

———. "Zorn (AT)." *Wibilex*. https://www.bibelwissenschaft.de/stichwort/35502/.

Wallace, David H. "The Semitic Origin of the Assumption of Moses." *ThZ* 5 (1955): 321–28.

Weber, Max. *Gesammelte Aufsätze zur Religionssoziologie*. Vol. 1. Tübingen: Mohr Siebeck, 1920.

Webster, Brian. "Chronological Index of the Texts from the Judaean Desert." Pages 351–446 in *The Texts from the Judaean Desert: Indices and an Introduction to the Discoveries in the Judaean Desert Series*. Edited by Emanuel Tov. DJD 39. Oxford: Clarendon, 2002.

Wees, Hans van, and Nick Fisher. "The Trouble with 'Aristocracy.'" Pages 1–58 in *"Aristocracy" in Antiquity: Redefining Greek and Roman Elites*. Edited by Nick Fisher and Hans van Wees. Swansea: Classical Press of Wales, 2015.

Wellhausen, Julius. *Die Pharisäer und die Sadduzäer: Eine Untersuchung zur innerin jüdischen Geschichte*. Griefswald: Bamberg, 1874.

Werline, Rodney A. "Defining Penitential Prayer." Pages xiii–xvii in *The Origins of Penitential Prayer in Second Temple Judaism*. Vol. 1 of *Seeking the Favor of God*. Edited by Mark J. Boda, Daniel K. Falk, and Rodney A. Werline. EJL 21. Atlanta: Society of Biblical Literature, 2006.

———. "The Experience of God's *Paideia* in the *Psalms of Solomon*." Pages 17–44 in *Linking Text and Experience*. Vol. 2 of *Experientia*. Edited by

Colleen Shantz and Rodney A. Werline. EJL 35. Atlanta: Society of Biblical Literature, 2012.

———. "The Formation of the Pious Person in the Psalms of Solomon." Pages 133–54 in *The Psalms of Solomon: Language, History, Theology.* Edited by Eberhard Bons and Patrick Pouchelle. EJL 40. Atlanta: SBL Press, 2015.

———. *Penitential Prayer in Second Temple Judaism: The Development of a Religious Institution.* EJL 13. Atlanta: Scholars Press, 1998.

———. "The *Psalms of Solomon* and the Ideology of Rule." Pages 69–88 in *Conflicted Boundaries in Wisdom and Apocalypticism.* Edited by Lawrence M. Wills and Benjamin G. Wright III. SymS 35. Atlanta: Society of Biblical Literature, 2005.

Westermann, Claus. *Lob und Klage in den Psalmen.* Göttingen: Vandenhoeck & Ruprecht, 1977.

———, ed. *Praise and Lament in the Psalms.* 5th ed. Atlanta: Westminster John Knox, 1981.

Whitters, Mark F. "Taxo and His Seven Sons in the Cave (Assumption of Moses 9–10)." *CBQ* 72 (2010): 718–31.

Willitts, Joel. "Matthew and *Psalms of Solomon*'s Messianism: A Comparative Study in First-Century Messianology." *BBR* 22 (2012): 27–50.

Winninge, Mikael. *Sinners and the Righteous: A Comparative Study of the Psalms of Solomon and Paul's Letters.* ConBNT 26. Stockholm: Almqvist & Wiksell, 1995.

Wischmeyer, Oda. "Wie kommt Abraham in den Galaterbrief? Überlegungen zu Gal 3,6–29." Pages 119–63 in *Umstrittener Galaterbrief: Studien zur Situierung und Theologie des Paulus-Schreibens.* Edited by Michael Bachmann and Bernd Kollmann. Biblisch-theologische Studien 106. Neukirchen-Vluyn: Neukirchener, 2010.

Wise, Michael O. *Language and Literacy in Roman Judaea: A Study of the Bar Kokhba Documents.* New Haven: Yale University Press, 2015.

———. *Thunder in Gemini: And Other Essays on the History, Language and Literature of Second Temple Palestine.* JSPSup 15. Sheffield: JSOT Press, 1994.

Wold, Benjamin G. "Metaphorical Poverty in *Musar leMevin*." *JJS* 58 (2007): 140–53.

Wolfson, Elliot R. "The Body in the Text: A Kabbalistic Theory of Embodiment." *JQR* 95 (2005): 479–500.

Wolter, Michael. *Der Brief an die Römer.* Vol. 1. EKKNT 6.1. Neukirchen-Vluyn: Neukirchener, 2014.

Wright, Benjamin G. "The Categories of Rich and Poor in the Qumran Sapiential Literature." Pages 101–23 in *Sapiential Perspectives: Wisdom Literature in Light of the Dead Sea Scrolls*. Edited by John J. Collins, Gregory E. Sterling, and Ruth A. Clements. STDJ 51. Leiden: Brill, 2001.

Wright, Benjamin G., and Claudia V. Camp. "Who Has Been Tested by Gold and Found Perfect? Ben Sira's Discourse of Riches and Poverty." *Henoch* 23 (2001): 153–74.

Wright, N. T. *The Climax of the Covenant: Christ and the Law in Pauline Theology*. Repr. London: T&T Clark, 2004.

Wright, Robert B. "The Psalms of Solomon." *OTP* 2:639–70.

———. *The Psalms of Solomon: A Critical Edition of the Greek Text*. Jewish and Christian Texts in Contexts and Related Studies 1. London: T&T Clark, 2007.

———. "The Psalms of Solomon: The Pharisees and the Essenes." Pages 136–54 in *1972 Proceedings of the International Organization for Septuagint and Cognate Studies and the Society of Biblical Literature Pseudepigrapha Seminar*. Edited by Robert A. Kraft. SCS 2. Missoula: Society of Biblical Literature, 1972.

Wyatt, Nicolas. "Of Calves and Kings: The Canaanite Dimension in the Religion of Israel." *SJOT* 6 (1992): 68–91.

Yerushalmi, Yosef. *Zakhor: Jewish History and Jewish Memory*. Seattle: University of Washington Press, 1982.

Zacharias, H. Daniel. "The Son of David in Psalms of Solomon 17." Pages 73–87 in *"Non-canonical" Religious Texts in Early Judaism and Early Christianity*. Edited by Lee Martin McDonald and James H. Charlesworth. Jewish and Christian Texts in Contexts and Related Studies 14. London: T&T Clark, 2012.

Contributors

Kenneth Atkinson is a Professor of History at the University of Northern Iowa, USA. He is a specialist in Second Temple Jewish history and literature as well as the author of *I Cried to the Lord: A Study of the Psalms of Solomon's Historical Background and Social Setting* (Brill), *The Hasmoneans and Their Neighbors: New Historical Reconstructions from the Dead Sea Scrolls and Classical Sources* (Bloomsbury T&T Clark), *A History of the Hasmonean State: Josephus and Beyond* (Bloomsbury T&T Clark), *Queen Salome: Jerusalem's Warrior Monarch of the First Century B.C.E.* (McFarland), and *Empress Galla Placidia and the Fall of the Roman Empire* (McFarland).

Eberhard Bons has studied theology, philosophy and Romance languages at the universities of Mainz, Tübingen, Rome (Gregorian University), and Frankfurt (Faculty of Sankt Georgen). In 1988 he obtained a PhD degree from the University of Mainz. In 1993, he also earned a doctoral degree in theology (biblical exegesis) from the Philosophisch-Theologische Hochschule St. Georgen, Francfort. He received his habilitation in 2000 from the University of Strasbourg (France), where he teaches as a Professor of Old Testament Exegesis. Bons is a member of the editorial board of *Septuaginta Deutsch* (Stuttgart: Deutsche Bibelgesellschaft, 2009–2011) and editor of the *Historical and Theological Lexicon of the Septuagint* (Mohr Siebeck). Moreover, he has edited several books on Septuagint studies, Old Testament prophetism, and biblical monotheism, including *Textkritik und Textgeschichte: Studien zur Septuaginta und zum hebräischen Alten Testament* (Mohr Siebeck). Since 2015, he has been a member of the Accademia Ambrosiana (Milan), "Classe di Studi sul Vicino Oriente," sezione ebraica.

Johanna Erzberger is the Laurentius Klein Chair for Ecumenical and Biblical Theology and Dean of the Theologische Studienjahr Jerusalem/ Jerusalem School of Theology, Dormition Abbey, Jerusalem, Israel. She is also a research associate of the Department of Old Testament Studies at the University of Pretoria, South Africa. Her research interests include the book of Jeremiah, the book of Baruch, and Septuagint studies.

Angela Kim Harkins is an Associate Professor at Boston College, Boston, Massachusetts (USA). Her work on the lived experience of religion covers a range of Jewish and Christian writings from the Second Temple period. She is the author of *Reading with an "I" to the Heavens: Looking at the Qumran Hodayot through the Lens of Visionary Traditions* (2012) and more than three dozen articles and essays. She is also an editor of several volumes, the most recent of which is *Selected Studies on Deuterocanonical Prayers* (Peeters). Harkins was the recipient of a Marie Curie International Incoming Fellowship at the University of Birmingham, England in 2014–2015, and received a Fulbright fellowship for study at Hebrew University in 1997–1998. She has recently completed a book manuscript that applies cognitive literary theory to the early Christian work known as the Shepherd of Hermas. Harkins is the 2021 President of the New England/Eastern Canada region of the Society of Biblical Literature.

G. Anthony (Tony) Keddie is Assistant Professor of Early Christian History and Literature at the University of British Columbia in Vancouver, Canada. His research focuses on the social history of Jewish and Christian communities in antiquity, theory and methods for socioeconomic analysis of religious texts, and the reception of biblical texts in contemporary politics. He is the author of *Class and Power in Roman Palestine: The Socioeconomic Setting of Judaism and Christian Origins* (Cambridge University Press), *Revelations of Ideology: Apocalyptic Class Politics in Early Roman Palestine* (Brill), and *Jewish Fictional Letters from Hellenistic Egypt: The Epistle of Aristeas and Related Literature* (SBL Press, coauthored with L. Michael White).

Patrick Pouchelle is Assistant Professor of Old Testament at the Centre Sèvres, Jesuit faculties of Paris (France). His research focuses on Septuagint, Old Testament Pseudepigrapha and Second Temple Judaism. He is the author of *Dieu éducateur: Une nouvelle approche d'un concept de la théologie biblique entre Bible hébraïque, Septante et littérature grecque classique* (Tübingen: Mohr Siebeck), and he is preparing a new French translation of the Psalms of Solomon.

Stefan Schreiber has been professor of New Testament at the University of Augsburg (Germany) since 2010. From 2003 to 2010, he was professor of New Testament at the University of Münster (Germany). His research focuses on Paul and early Judaism, the New Testament writings in their political world, the history of early Christianity, the Johannine Letters, and New Testament hermeneutics and methodology.

Shani Tzoref is currently pursuing an M.A. in Digital Humanities at the CUNY Graduate Center, New York, and is an instructor of English in high schools in Rishon leZion, Israel. In her previous position of Professor of Hebrew Bible and Biblical Exegesis, she was a vigorous advocate for academic reforms in such spheres as diversity, open access, collaborative research, and ethical use of archaeological artefacts. Her primary areas of research are early biblical interpretation, especially Qumran studies, and the use of Hebrew Bible in contemporary sociopolitical discourse.

Rodney A. Werline is the Leman and Marie Barnhill Endowed Chair in Religious Studies and Professor of Religious Studies and the Director of the Center for Religious Studies at Barton College. Most recently, he co-edited the second edition of *Early Judaism and Its Modern Interpreters* (SBL Press). He continues to research in the area of prayer and ritual in early Judaism, the Hebrew Bible, and the New Testament.

Ancient Sources Index*

Ancient Near Eastern Works		49:26	47–48
		50:24	116
Babylonian Theodicy	186–87		
18	188	Exodus	
21–22	188	6:12	30
		6:15	117
The Prayer to Ishtar	212	12:40–41	159
		13:3	228
Hebrew Bible/Old Testament		16:35	117
(including LXX, Revisions, and Vulgate)		18:11	186
		19:1	213
Genesis		19:4	133
1–11	200	19:16	212
1:4	168	19:18	212–13
1:10	168	20:8	228
1:12	168	20:24–25	78
1:18	168	20:25	134
1:21	168	32	212, 217
1:25	168	32:4	217
1:31	168	32:6	218
2–3	200	32:8	217
2:21	72	32:17–18	212
8:1	228	34:6	27
12:3	159		
15:6	159	Leviticus	
17:11	154	4–5	150
17:13	146, 159	16:19	134
17:19	146, 159	18:4–5	148
26:5	159	18:5	148–49, 160–61
26:8	218	19:18	162–63
27	26	25:8–12	115
27:43–44	26	25:9–10	136

---

* The editors thank Thomas Ellison (BA Honours 2021, University of British Columbia) for his meticulous work helping to prepare the indices.

Leviticus (cont.)
26:12 — 143

Numbers
6:12 — 30
15:39 — 228
15:40 — 228
21:32 — 27

Deuteronomy
4:1 — 178
5:33 — 178
8:1 — 178
8:17 — 92, 101, 103
8:17–18 — 90
9 — 212
12:2 — 47
15:7–11 — 90, 92
21:23 — 161
26:12–16 — 90
27:26 — 160
28–32 — 144
28:25 — 211
29:29[28] — 182
32:10 — 104

Joshua
5:12 — 117
6:20 — 124

Judges
5:4–5 — 212

1 Samuel (1 Kingdoms)
20 — 26
20:9–10 — 26
20:13 — 26

2 Samuel (2 Kingdoms)
14:25–26 — 179
18:9 — 179

1 Kings (3 Kingdoms)
12 — 217
12:28 — 217

13:1–10 — 134

2 Kings (4 Kingdoms)
9 — 179
17:16 — 217
17:21–23 — 217
23:16 — 134

Nehemiah
9 — 194

Job
3:1–3 — 200
4:13–14 — 184
15:7 — 47
38:32 — 132
40:30 — 117

Psalms
2 — 152
2:9 — 237
3:3 — 194
18[17]:7 — 23
28[27]:1 — 23
33[32]:3 — 231
35[34]:22 — 23
37[36] — 74–75, 96, 190, 194
37[36]:14 — 96
39[38] — 194
39[38]:13 — 23
40[39]:3 — 231
40[39]:17 — 96
41[40]:11 — 155
44[43]:2 — 231
49[48] — 194
53[52] — 99, 117, 119
53[52]:6 — 119
65[64]:8 — 28
70[69]:5 — 96
71[70]:15 — 155
72[71] — 94
72[71]:4 — 96
72[71]:10 — 53
72[71]:12 — 96
73[72] — 194

74[73]:21	96	14:13	132–33, 239
78[77]:38	29	29:15–16	190
85[84]:4	29	40	47
86[85]:1	96	40:4	45–48
89[88]:10	28	40:4–5a	45, 47–48
96[95]:1	231	40:5	48
98[97]:1	231	41:19–20	47
98[97]:2	155	42:10	231
104[103]:7	237	45:8	155
107–109[106–108]	68	46:13	155
109[108]:1	23	49:1	53
109[108]:16	96	49:22	53, 152
109[108]:22	96	51:5	155
113[112]:7	96	52:1	50
114[113]:3–4	46	52:2	43
140[139]:12	96	52:7	115, 136
143[142]:1–2	155	56:1	155
144[143]:9	231	59:17	155
149:1	231	60:9	53
		60:19	53
Proverbs		61:10	50
1:31–33	189	61:17	43
2:16	29	63:9	133
5:8	29	66:10–11	67
6:1–5	94		
11:15	94	Jeremiah	
16:32	26–27	2:20	147
17:18	94	5:5	147
19:18	119	11:4	143
20:16	94	35:7	178
22:26–27	94	38:10	53
29:8	28	44:15–19	190
29:11	28	50[27]:39	53
30:8	29, 103	51[28]:9	132
Ecclesiastes (Qoheleth)		Lamentations	
6:9	120	2:21	126
7:9	28		
		Ezekiel	
Isaiah		9:6	126
1:11	134		
3:16	133	Daniel	
11:2–4	237	8:10	132
13:13	212	9	194
14:5	156	9:14–16	155

Hosea		11:17	91
4	217	11:21	91
4:12–19	217	11:22	91
4:14	217	13:24	91
4:15–19	217	14:14–17	91
6:6	134	17:22	92
		23:2–3	176, 183
Joel		29:12	92
2:1	53	29:14–20	92
2:10	212	29:21–22	91
		31:1–11	92
Amos		40:17	92
2:8	135	40:24	92
3:14	135	40:25–26	91
5:21	134	41:1–3	91
		44:6–7	91
Micah		44:10–15	91
7:9	155	44:20–21	159
		47:16	53
Nahum		51:26	147
2:12	180		
		Baruch	
Habakkuk		4:5	39, 44
2:4	161	4:5–29	39
		4:5–5:8	37
Zechariah		4:5–5:9	20, 36, 39–42, 50–51, 252
12:3	135	4:7	47
		4:9b–16	39
Malachi		4:11	43
1:7–10	134	4:17–29	39
		4:19	49
Apocrypha/Deuterocanonical Works		4:20	49–50
		4:23	43
Wisdom of Solomon		4:24	50
7:25	134	4:27	44
11:5	170	4:29	43
11:15	30	4:30–5:4	40
11:16	170	4:30–5:9	39
18:8	170	4:36	43–44, 51–52
		4:36–37	40, 42–44, 51
Sirach		4:36–5:9	67
3:30	92	4:37	42–44, 50, 52–53
5:1	92, 104	5	52–53
6:30	147	5:1	37–38, 49–50
8:13	92	5:1–2	49–50

5:1–9	41, 50	5	122–23
5:2	50	5.4	21, 133, 135
5:4	39–40, 46, 50–52	6	122–23
5:5	37, 40, 42–44, 47, 51	6.1	124, 126
5:5–6	38, 40, 42	6.2–7	126
5:5–8	36–37, 40–41, 47–48, 50, 54–55	6.6	121
5:5–9	39–41, 44, 52–53	6.8	122
5:6	40, 44, 50	6.8–9	126
5:7–8	37–38, 40, 45–48, 51	7	114, 122, 130
5:7	45–51	7–9	126
5:8	45, 47, 51	7.4	117
5:9	40, 43, 50	8	126
		8–9	122
1 Maccabees		8.5	133
1:30–32	128	9	126
1:34	156	9.3–7	112
1:54	133	10	113
1:59	135	10.1–10	126
2:48	156	10.2	115, 136
3:45	135	10.8–9	133
3:51	135	10.9	132
4:45	135	11.16	117
4:60	135		
6:16–17	128	2 Baruch	
		41.3	147
2 Maccabees			
3:9	128	1 Enoch	
8:2	135	7.3	93
9:5–6	128	37–71	93
		53.1	93
3 Maccabees		53.2	93
1:8–11	128	92–105	92–93, 101
5:40	30	94.8	93
		96.5	92
4 Maccabees		103.11	93
2:16–20	29		
14:14	30	2 Enoch	
14:18	30	34.1	147
		48.9	147
Pseudepigrapha			
		4 Ezra	
Assumption (Testament) of Moses		8:26	155
1.3	117		
1.8	116	Five Apocryphal Syriac Psalms	
2.4	117	151A	68

Five Apocryphal Syriac Psalms (cont.)
 154   68
 155   68

Jubilees
 24.11   159

Odes of Solomon
 1   204
 19   204
 42   204
 42.20   204
 43   204

Psalms of Solomon (numbering based on Oscar von Gebhardt's 1895 edition)
 1   10, 52, 55, 66–67, 145, 181, 184, 192–93, 204, 224, 231–32, 234, 236, 245, 247
 1.1   23
 1.1–2   195
 1.1–3   232
 1.1–6   145
 1.1–8   156
 1.2   181
 1.2–3   208
 1.3   65
 1.3–4   234
 1.4   96
 1.5   132, 239
 1.6   97
 1.7   232
 1.7–8   144, 216
 1.8   77, 145, 151
 2   36, 52, 55–56, 66, 72, 144, 169, 171–74, 179, 184–85, 192, 195, 197–98, 224, 230–32, 234, 236, 245, 247, 249, 251
 2–16   55
 2.1   10, 173
 2.1–2   145
 2.1–3   128
 2.1–5   142
 2.2   18, 134–35
 2.3–4   77, 169
 2.3–15   193
 2.4   4
 2.5   50
 2.7   169, 173
 2.8–9   170
 2.9   187
 2.9–13   232
 2.10   68
 2.11–12   150
 2.11–13   144
 2.11–14   142
 2.13   150, 170
 2.14   172, 174, 193
 2.14–16   172
 2.15   65, 147
 2.15–17   195
 2.15–18   68, 233
 2.15–21   193
 2.16   171
 2.17   183, 200
 2.19   50
 2.20   50, 135
 2.20–21   49–50
 2.21   50
 2.22   173
 2.22–25   173, 194
 2.22–26   195
 2.23   72
 2.24   173
 2.25   18, 169, 198, 200, 238
 2.25–29   128
 2.26   139
 2.26–27   173, 240
 2.26–29   174
 2.28–30a   239
 2.30–32   171
 2.31   50, 169
 2.32   240
 2.32–35   68
 2.34–36   172
 2.35   96, 174
 3   72, 176, 181, 192, 195, 208, 224, 226–27, 229–31, 251
 3–6   55
 3–7   144

3.1–2	192	4.23	142, 145, 194
3.2	65, 226	4.24	147, 171
3.3	68, 72, 77, 208	4.25	142, 147, 194
3.3–12	145	5	72, 102–6, 184, 192, 224
3.4	75	5.1	72, 77
3.4–8	176	5.1–4	68
3.6	181	5.2	23, 64, 96
3.6–7	230	5.4	64–65, 102
3.6–8	101, 146	5.5	103, 195
3.7	146	5.5–9	56
3.7–8	77, 181	5.8	62, 195
3.8	96, 146, 150, 158	5.10–14	103
3.9	200	5.11	64, 96, 152
3.9–10	230	5.12	96, 195
3.9–12	179	5.14	96
3.11	230	5.16	4, 23, 72, 97, 103–4
3.12	64	5.16–17	103
4	66, 72, 97, 99–102, 104–7, 140, 179–81, 192, 198, 224, 247, 251	5.17	149
		5.18	97
4.1	65, 98, 140, 145, 239	5.18–19	171
4.2–3	140	5.18–20 (Syriac)	104
4.2–5	147	6	72, 184, 192, 224, 226–27, 230
4.3	23, 101	6.1	65, 195, 230
4.4	101	6.1–2	72, 77, 226
4.4–5	140, 162	6.2	141
4.5	101, 140–41, 216	6.3	184
4.6	96, 140	6.4	65, 230
4.6–25	194	6.5	101, 230
4.7	141, 158, 183, 200	6.5–6	195
4.8	68, 73, 141, 194	6.9	181
4.9	67, 101, 141	7	72, 178, 192, 194, 224
4.10	102, 141	7–10	55
4.10–20	97–98	7.2	106
4.11	101	7.3	75
4.11–12	141	7.3–10	144
4.12	72–73, 101, 130	7.6–7	72, 77
4.15	96	7.7	195
4.15–16	101, 184	7.8	62, 144
4.16	141	7.9	75, 146, 152, 162
4.17	101	7.10	101, 178, 195
4.18–20	179	8	22, 36, 52–55, 66, 72, 106, 140, 174, 184, 192, 198, 203, 205, 207, 210–14, 216–19, 224, 231, 234, 236, 239, 245, 247, 249, 251
4.19	4, 65, 117, 120, 141–42, 158		
4.20	101–2, 140–41		
4.21	4, 101		
4.22	72, 140	8.1	53, 65, 212

Psalms of Solomon (cont.)

8.1–4	210	8.27	53, 62
8.1–5	193, 214, 234	8.27–29	183
8.2	153, 213	8.28	53, 62, 211, 215, 219
8.3	65, 145	8.29	75, 146, 211
8.4–5	213	8.30	62
8.5	65, 174, 235	8.32	68, 211
8.6	234	8.33	240
8.7	174, 193, 211	8.34	208, 211, 219
8.7–8	68	8.43	54
8.7–14	216–18, 220	9	54, 72, 117, 184, 192, 209, 251
8.8	183, 211, 218	9–16	224
8.8–9	210	9.1	73, 193
8.8–10	174, 200, 234, 252	9.2	143, 152, 171
8.9	142, 217	9.3	148, 181, 183, 193
8.9–10	217	9.4	23, 73, 142
8.9–12	142	9.4–5	148
8.9–14	144	9.4–7	104
8.10–12	77, 105	9.5	65, 68, 101
8.11	73, 106	9.6	148
8.11–13	77	9.6–7	143, 146
8.12	21, 133, 135, 214, 217	9.7	147
8.13	142, 151	9.8	62, 73, 143, 147, 152
8.14	218	9.8–11	143, 161, 194
8.14–22	142	9.9	143, 146, 159, 238
8.15	53	9.9–10	238
8.15–18	211	9.9–11	144
8.15–19	212	9.10	143
8.15–21	174	9.11	54, 101, 144, 147
8.16–18	128	10	72, 175, 192
8.17	52	10.1–2	146
8.17–19	127	10.1–3	145, 175
8.18	101	10.1–4	75, 148, 162
8.19	73, 210–211	10.3	146, 181
8.20	73, 211	10.3–4	147
8.21–22	193	10.4	146–47, 159
8.22	144–45	10.5	68
8.23	208, 211, 219	10.5–7	147
8.23–25	68	10.6	64, 96, 152
8.23–26	171, 174	10.6–7	147
8.24–26	147	10.7	108, 225
8.25	210–11, 215	10.8	54, 62, 101
8.25–34	144	10.14	139
8.26	75, 146, 211, 219	11	20, 35–37, 39–41, 44, 46, 49–50, 52–56, 62, 66–68, 72, 131, 192, 224, 252
8.26–28	219		

11.1	37–38, 49, 53–55, 66, 115, 136, 147	14.2–3	148
		14.3	148
11.1–9	147	14.3–5	144, 149
11.2	38, 42–44, 51–53	14.6–9	149
11.2–3	38, 40, 42–44, 53	14.8	65
11.2–6	50, 52–54	14.8–9	181
11.2–7	20, 36–38, 52–54	14.9–10	178–79
11.3	42, 44, 52–53, 56	14.10	149
11.4	45–48, 52	15	72, 151, 192–93
11.4–5	40, 45, 47–48	15.1	23, 64, 72, 77, 96, 193
11.4–6	38, 47	15.2	181
11.5	47	15.2–6	151
11.6	38, 48–50, 55, 73, 147	15.3	65
11.7	37–39, 49–50, 54, 144	15.5	73
11.7–9	37, 53–54	15.6	65
11.8	37–39, 50, 54, 80	15.8	68, 73, 145, 151
11.8–9	38	15.10	145, 151
11.9	37, 54, 147	15.10–13	179
12	54, 72, 101, 140, 143, 192, 194–95	15.11	65, 101
12–15	178	15.12	68
12–16	55, 145	15.13	147, 150
12.1	143, 194	16	24, 32–33, 72, 106–7, 151, 192–93, 195, 226–27, 230, 245
12.2	153		
12.3	65, 101	16.1	72
12.3–4	143	16.1–3	194
12.4	194	16.1–4	151
12.5	101, 143	16.2	230
12.6	54, 73, 179	16.3	147, 230
13	72, 192–193	16.4	75, 175, 194, 230
13.3	179	16.5–6	151, 226, 230
13.4	65, 193	16.6	147
13.5	143, 193	16.7–11	230
13.6–11	146	16.9	142, 151
13.7	75, 146, 177, 181	16.10	19, 24–25, 29–30, 32, 181, 245
13.7–8	177, 208	16.11	176
13.7–11	177	16.11–15	75
13.8	183	16.12–15	106
13.9	146	16.13	96
13.10	75, 146, 163, 176	16.14–15	96, 194
13.11	178	16.15	147
13.12	147	16.17–18	140
14	72, 150, 178, 192, 251	17	18, 22, 36, 52, 55–56, 66, 68, 72, 107, 112–13, 115, 123, 125–27, 131–32, 151, 171, 177–78, 192, 198, 224, 231, 236–38, 245, 247, 252
14.1	148, 181		
14.1–4	178–79		
14.2	139, 147–48		

Psalms of Solomon (cont.)

17.1	240	17.32	10, 54, 112
17.3	68, 147, 171, 240	17.33	107, 152
17.4	144, 238	17.34	147, 152, 240
17.4–6	17	17.35	67, 152
17.4–7	143	17.36	152
17.5	146, 236, 239	17.42	101
17.5–6	36, 126	17.43	54, 152, 225
17.5–8	144	17.45	147, 153
17.6	123, 238–239	17.46	171, 240
17.6–14	125	18	10, 55, 72, 177, 192, 224
17.7	36, 124, 151, 239	18.1	96
17.7–8	126	18.2	62, 64, 96
17.7–9	36	18.3	68, 143, 147, 238
17.8	141	18.4	23, 146, 176, 181, 208
17.9	125, 237	18.5	72–73, 112, 147
17.10	68	18.7	67, 112
17.11	36, 73, 125–27, 151, 239	18.7–8	180
17.11–14	126	18.8	142, 176
17.11–18	142	18.9	147
17.12	53	18.10	113
17.13	65, 151	18.10–12	68, 70, 77
17.14	128, 151, 237		
17.14–15	145	Testament of Benjamin	
17.15	151	4.5	119
17.15–20	126		
17.16	108, 127, 225	Testament of Levi	
17.16–17	126	9.9	216
17.18	102, 151	14.5–15.1	216
17.18–19	12, 237		
17.19–20	144	Dead Sea Scrolls and Related Texts	
17.20	151–52	Aramaic Levi Document	61
17.21	14, 238		
17.21–44	178	Book of Giants	61
17.21–46	126		
17.22–24	152	CD (Cairo Damascus Document)	95, 105, 107–8, 216–17
17.23	67	I, 12–II, 1	217
17.25	65	IV, 12–19	105
17.26	152	IV, 13–18	216–17
17.27	54	IV, 15–18	77
17.27–28	152	IV, 17	105
17.28	36, 107	V, 7–12	252
17.29	67, 152	VI, 14–17	105
17.30	152	XI, 17–21	135
17.30–31	152, 209		

Ancient Sources Index

Minor Prophets Scroll from Naḥal Ḥever (8QḤevXII gr)	209	1QS (Rule of the Community) 95, 107, 246	60, 64,
1Q20 (Genesis Apocryphon)	61	I, 11	65
		III, 8	65
1Q28b	60	III, 13–IV, 26	64–65
		V, 13–14	65
1Q34+34bis	60–61	IX, 26b–XI, 22	61
1–3	63	3Q6	60
1–3 I, 2	64		
3–5 II, 9	64	4Q87	60
1Q36	60	4Q88 (4QPs^f)	67–68
		VII, 14–VIII, 15	67
1Q39	60		
		4Q166 (4QpHos^a)	74
1QH^a (Hodayot^a) 20, 58, 60, 68, 70, 75, 77, 79, 95, 183, 194, 249		4Q169 (Pesher Nahum) 76, 99, 180, 197	
VI, 3–4	75		
IX, 36	75	4Q171 (Psalms Pesher)	20, 74–76
X, 14–16	99	II, 2, 15	75
X, 27–28	132	II, 2b–5a	75
X, 29	132	II, 9–12	75
X, 31–35	75	II, 9–14	75
XI, 25–29	76	IV, 8	74
XII, 7–14	99	IV, 9–10	75
XIII, 16	75		
XIII, 18	75	4Q174 (4QFlorilegium)	
XIII, 21	75	III	160
XIII, 22	75		
		4Q177 (4QCatena A)	66–67
1QH^{a-b}	60	3 4–6	67
1Q/4QInstruction	94–95, 101, 108	4Q179 (4QApocryphal Lamentations A) 60, 66	
1QM (War Scroll)	60, 64, 71, 79, 246		
X, 8–XII, 18	61	4Q180 (4QAges of Creation A)	66–67
XVIII, 5–XIX, 8	61	1 2	67
		2–4 II, 10	67
1QpHab (Pesher Habakkuk)			
VIII, 3–IX, 7	105	4Q215a	60
IX, 4–7	106		
XI	74–75	4Q242 (Prayer of Nabonidus)	61
XI, 6–8	74		
		4Q255–257	60

4Q262	60	4Q435–4Q437	65
4Q275	60	4Q437	
4Q280	60	2 I, 12	65
4Q284	60	4Q438	
4Q286–290	60	3 2	65
4Q291–293	60	4Q440a	60
4Q334	60	4Q441–443	60
4Q380–381	60	4Q444	60
4Q380 (4QNoncanonical Psalms A)	66	4Q446	60
4Q386	128	4Q448 (4QApocryphal Psalm and Prayer) 60, 66–67	
4Q392+393	60	4Q449–451	60
4Q398		4Q455	60
14 II, 2–7	157	4Q456	60
4Q400–407 (Songs of the Sabbath Sacrifice[a])	60–61, 76	4Q457b	60
4Q409	60	4Q471b	60
4Q411	60	4Q471c	60
4Q414	60	4Q475 (4QRenewed Earth)	67
4Q433	60	4Q496	65
4Q434		4Q499–501	60
1 I, 1	65	4Q502	60
1 I, 2	65		
1 I, 2–3	65	4Q503 (Daily Prayers)	60, 61, 63
4Q434–440	60	4Q504 (4QWords of the Luminaries[a]) 20, 60–64, 67, 70, 76	
4Q434–483	65	1–2 V-VI	62
		1–2 VI, 6–7	75

Ancient Sources Index 309

1–2 VI, 11	75	8Q5	60
1–2 VI, 11–14	62		
		11Q5 (11QPs^a)	20, 67–68, 70, 72, 79
4Q505	60–63	XXII, 1–10	67
4Q506	60–61, 65	11Q6	67–68
4Q507	60, 63	11Q11	60
4Q507–4Q509	61, 63	11Q13	136
		II, 4–23	115
4Q507–508	60		
		11Q15–16	60
4Q508	60, 63		
2 3	75	11Q17	60–61
2 4	64		
		11QPs^a	
4Q509	63, 65	XXVII, 2–11	68
16 3	75		
131–132	65	**Other Ancient Jewish Works**	
212 1	64		
		Josephus, *Antiquitates judaicae*	
4Q509+505	60	2.318	159
		13.257	125
4Q510–511	60	13.405–409	100
		13.416–447	98
4Q512	60	14.16	237
		14.41–45	127
4Q528	60	14.53–57	128
		14.58–63	142
4Q560	60	14.63–67	234
		14.71	234
4QH^{a–f}	60	14.74	88
		14.91	88
4QMMT (Miqṣat Ma'aśê ha-Torah)	157	14.200–206	89
		14.203	100
4QS^{d,e}	64	14.429–430	127
		14.475	102
5Q11	60	15.11–21	100
		17.73	127
5Q14	60	17.190	121
		17.286–291	127
6Q16	60	17.292	127
		17.294	128
6Q18	60	17.295	127

Josephus, Antiquitates judaicae (cont.)
17.297	127
17.301	127
17.304–314	127
18.3	105
20.42	157
20.43	157
20.46	157

Josephus, *Bellum judaicum*
1.17–18	237
1.107–112	100
1.131–132	142
1.142–143	128
1.142–147	142
1.169	128
1.170	88
1.253–255	128
2.14	105
2.66–71	127
2.72	127
2.72–75	128
2.74	128
2.75	127
2.77–78	127
2.84–93	127
2.163	105

Josephus, *Contra Apionem*
2.291–292	158

Philo, *De cherubim*
74	118

Philo, *De fuga et inventione*
81	118

Philo, *De Iosepho*
143	118

Philo, *De mutatione nominum*
221	118

Philo, *De posteritate Caini*
21	118

Philo, *De praemiis et poenis*
82–83	158
126	158

Philo, *De sacrificiis Abelis et Caini*
3	118
32	118
52	118

Philo, *De somniis*
2.219	118

Philo, *De specialibus legibus*
1.344	118

Philo, *Hypothetica*
11.14	118

Philo, *Legum allegoriae*
1.49	118
3.115	31
3.116	33
3.147	29
3.231	118

Philo, *Quod deterius potiori insidari soleat*
32	118
68	118
78	118

Philo, *Quod Deus sit immutabilis*
71	29

New Testament

Matthew
7:1–2	170
11:28–30	147
17:1–9	214
17:6	214

Mark
4:24	170
9:2–10	214

Luke
    9:28–36   214

Acts
    2:14–42   160
    15:10   147

Romans
    1:4   117
    6:2   160
    6:10–11   160
    7:6   160
    13:8–10   163

1 Corinthians
    11:24–25   228

2 Corinthians
    6:14   147

Galatians
    1:4   155, 158
    1:6   154
    1:10   158
    2:11–14   153
    2:12   153
    2:14   154
    2:15   156
    2:16   154–56, 161
    2:17   156
    2:19   160
    2:20   155, 163
    2:21   155
    3:2   155
    3:5   155
    3:6   159
    3:6–18   159
    3:7–9   159
    3:10–12   160
    3:10–13   159
    3:10–14   155
    3:11–12   161
    3:13   161
    3:17   159
    3:19   162
    3:19–4:7   161
    3:21–22   162
    3:23   162
    3:24   162
    3:25   162
    3:29   159
    4:4–5   155
    4:8   154
    4:9   154
    4:17   154
    4:21   154
    5:1   147, 160
    5:2–3   154
    5:3   160
    5:4   154
    5:4–5   155
    5:6   154, 163
    5:14   162
    6:1   163
    6:2   163
    6:12–13   154
    6:15   154–55

Ephesians
    6:6   119

Colossians
    3:22   119

2 Timothy
    3:2   118–19

Other Ancient Christian Works

Augustine, *De civitate Dei*
    14.13   119

Augustine, *Enarrationes in Psalmos*
    106.14   119

2 Clement
    13.1   120

Cyprian, *De catholicae ecclesiae unitate*
    16(14)   118

Cyprian, *Epistulae*
   3.3 — 119
   11.1 — 119

Eusebius, *Praeparatio evangelica*
   8.11 — 219

Gregory the Great, *Moralia*
   174

Hymns of Severus — 74

Ignatius, *Epistulae*
   11.9 (*recensio longior*) — 120

Patriarch Nicephorus, *Stichometria* — 74

Pistis Sophia — 204

Pseudo-Athanasius, *Synopsis Scripturae Sacrae* — 74

Tertullian, *De Pallio* — 8

Greco-Roman Literature

Appian, *Bella civilia*
   5.4 — 89
   5.75 — 89

Aristotle, *Rhetorica*
   1368b33–35 — 31
   1369a1–2 — 31
   1369a4 — 31
   1370a19 — 31

Cicero, *De provinciis consularibus*
   5.10 — 88

Cicero, *In Pisonem*
   41 — 88
   48 — 88

Cicero, *Pro Flacco*
   28.69 — 88

Cicero, *Pro Sestio*
   43.63 — 88

Dio Cassius, *Historiae romanae*
   39.56 — 88
   39.59 — 88

Herodotus, *Historiae*
   5.72 — 27

Menander, *Minor Fragments*
   742 [574K] — 32

Menander, *Sententiae*
   22 — 28

Petronius, *Satyricon* — 85

Plato, *Protagoras*
   321b — 30

Polybius, *Historiae*
   3.81.9 — 31
   6.56.11 — 31

Pseudo-Phocylides, *Sententiae*
   57 — 29

Thucydides, *Historiae*
   3.72 — 27

Rabbinic Works

b. Berakhot
   5a — 176

m. 'Abot
   3:5 — 147
   3:16 — 105

m. Soṭah
   1:8 — 179

m. Yoma
   8:1 — 18

t. Soṭah
- 3:1–4   170
- 3:10   170

Modern Authors Index

Abegg, Martin G., Jr. 66–67, 149
Ábel, František 16–17, 24
Aberbach, Moses 36, 217
Adams, Samuel L. 82, 88, 91–92, 94–95
Adams, Sean A. 39–40
Albrecht, Felix 4, 12, 19, 24, 29, 41, 112, 117, 140–41
Amir, Yehoshua 170
Amphoux, Christian-Bernard 51
Anderson, Gary A. 78, 90, 176
Andreau, Jean 83
Ashbrook Harvey, Susan 104
Assmann, Jan 225, 229, 232, 237–40
Atkinson, Kenneth 11–12, 15–16, 18, 20, 24, 36, 57–58, 61–62, 64–66, 72–77, 79, 82, 87, 95–100, 102, 106, 108, 112, 115, 122–25, 127, 129, 132, 139, 142, 144, 147, 149–51, 164–66, 175–76, 179, 181, 183–84, 191, 195, 198, 208–9, 217, 231–32, 237–38, 246–47, 251–52, 254–55
Austin, Colin 32
Avemarie, Friedrich 161
Babota, Vasile 124
Bachmann, Michael 157, 160
Ball, Warwick 89
Balogh, Amy 30
Barbey, Aron K. 215
Barsalou, Lawrence W. 215
Bartels, Jens 129
Bartolomé Martínez, Bernabé 7
Barton, John 170
Bazzana, Giovanni 108
Behnke, Sven 101, 184
Bendik, Ivana 157
Berlin, Andrea M. 85
Bévenot, Maurice 118
Bianchini, Giuseppe 119
Black, Matthew 94
Boer, Martinus C. de 156, 161–62
Bons, Eberhard 11–12, 19, 23–24, 73, 99, 104, 117, 168–69, 192, 245–46, 254
Bourdieu, Pierre 85, 87, 231, 247–248
Bowley, James E. 66
Boyer, Pascal 206–7, 215, 218, 222–23
Brand, Miryam 171
Bringmann, Klaus 197
Brooke, George J. 65–66, 71, 79, 191
Broshi, Magen 123
Bullock, C. Hassell 195
Burkes, Shannon 67
Burnside, Jonathan P. 169
Bush, Stephen S. 206
Butcher, Kevin 89
Camp, Claudia V. 91–92
Canfora, Luciano 2
Caquot, André 125
Cardellini, Innocenzo 30
Carson, Donald A. 149
Carr, David 235–36
Casali, Sergio 7
Cavallera, Ferdinand 10
Cerda, Juan Luis de la 1, 3–8, 11, 113
Ceriani, Antonio M. 111–12
Chae, Young S. 113
Charles, R. H. 114, 116, 121–22, 130–31
Charlesworth, James H. 63–65, 76, 78, 130
Chatelain, Jean-Marc 7–8
Chazon, Esther G. 59, 62–63, 78

Chibici-Revneanu, Nicole 161
Clemen, Carl 111
Cohen, Emma 207
Collins, John J. 66, 97, 120, 122–23, 152, 178, 183, 201
Conzelmann, Hans 118–19
Cook, Edward M. 66
Cook, Johann 27
Cosme, Pierre 4
Crenshaw, James L. 167, 189–90
Csordas, Thomas 207
Davila, James R. 12, 121
Denis, Albert-Marie 24, 113
Desjarlais, Robert 206
Dibelius, Martin 119
Dider, Hugues 9
DiTommaso, Lorenzo 58, 69, 185
Donceel, Robert 78–79
Dorival, Gilles 30
Dunn, James D. G. 149, 157–58, 160
Eck, Werner 129
Eckhardt, Benedikt 36, 100, 121, 124–25, 127, 197–98
Eckstein, Arthur M. 31–32
Eder, Klaus 85
Efron, Joshua 120
Eissfeldt, Otto 35
Elßner, Thomas R. 13
Embry, Brad 13–14, 82, 127, 165, 169, 183, 191–92, 196–97, 234
Erzberger, Johanna 19–20, 43, 252
Eshel, Esther 123
Eshel, Hanan 59, 122, 128
Fabricius, Johann Albert 10, 111
Fahey, Michael A. 119
Falk, Daniel K. 15, 60, 63, 67, 71
Feingold, Mordechai 2
Finley, Moses I. 83, 85
Fischer, Irmtraud 26
Fisher, Nick 83
Fouilloux, Etienne 9
Fox, Michael V. 27–28
Franklyn, Paul N. 35–36, 55, 204–5
Frede, Hermann Josef 118
Friesen, Steven J. 84, 91

García Martínez, Florentino 58
Gardner, Gregg 90–91
Garnsey, Peter 85
Gathercole, Simon J. 148, 161
Gebhardt, Oscar von 3–5, 112, 140
Geiger, P. Eduard Ephraem 40
Geertz, Clifford 229
Gemünden, Petra von 150
Gillmayr-Bucher, Suzanne 213
Goff, Matthew 95, 171, 191, 199
Goldstein, Jonathan A. 41, 47
Goodblatt, David M. 98
Goodman, Martin 89
Gordley, Matthew E. 13–14, 70
Gray, George Buchanan 64, 103, 166, 171, 193
Green, Ronald M. 167–68
Greenblatt, Stephen 6
Grierson, Fiona 111, 117, 121
Grossman, Maxine L. 206, 217
Gryson, Roger 136
Hadas-Lebel, Mireille 128
Hagedorn, Anselm 196
Halbwachs, Maurice 221–22, 225, 229, 231
Hamel, Gildas 96
Hamidović, David 135
d'Hamonville, David-Marc 28
Hanhart, Robert 140
Hann, Robert R. 87, 203
Harkins, Angela Kim 22, 109, 207, 213–14, 216, 246, 249–50, 255
Harris, William V. 30, 83–84
Hartman, Dorota 29
Hearon, Holly 223
Hellholm, David 81
Hempel, Charlotte 135
Henderson, Ruth 39–41, 44, 46–47, 49–50, 55, 67
Hendrickson, Scott 9
Henten, Jan Willem van 121
Herman, Judith 235
Hezser, Catherine 116, 208
Hilgenfeld, Adolf 113, 116–17, 120, 129, 131

Hofmann, Norbert Johannes 115, 134	Koch, Dietrich-Alex 153
Hölscher, Gustav 122	Koch, Klaus 166, 187
Hollenbach, Paul W. 85	Kratz, Reinhard Gregor 171, 186, 189,
Holm-Nielsen, Svend 24, 35–36, 114,	196, 198–99
139, 142, 192, 203	Kraus, Wolfgang 141
Hopkins, Keith 84	Kugel, James L. 78
Horbury, William 70, 101, 115, 136,	Kuzmičová, Anežka 205, 210, 215
227	Laato, Antti 165–68, 177–78, 185–87,
Horgan, Maurya P. 74	189, 200, 253
Horn, Christoph 31	Laird, Andrew 6–8
Horsley, Richard A. 81, 93, 100, 106	Lange, Armin 60–61, 64, 190
Horst, Friedrich 172	Laperrousaz, Ernest-Marie 114, 116,
Horst, Pieter Willem van der 29	121, 125, 130, 134
Hours, Bernard 9	Lapin, Hayim 84
Houtman, Cornelis 172, 200	Larcher, Chrysostome 170
Humbert, Jean-Baptiste 78	Lattke, Michael 15, 204
Hunt, Alice 16	Lawson, E. Thomas 236
Israeli, Edna 120	Le Déaut, Roger 30
Jacobs, Sandra 170, 179	Leibniz, Gottfried Wilhelm 167
James, Montague R. 3–4, 98–99, 102–3,	Levenson, Jon D. 201
105, 114, 116, 124, 203	Lévi, Israël 127–28
Janenskius, Georg 10	Licht, Jacob 122
Japhet, Sara 186–87, 197–98	Lindemann, Andreas 149
Johnson, Luke T. 119, 233, 252	Lindström, Fredrik 187, 194
Johnson, Nathan C. 14	Ling, Timothy J. M. 96
Jokiranta, Jutta 76	Lips, Hermann von 28
Jonge, Marinus de 35, 56, 237	Loader, William 121
Jüngling, Hans-Winfried 28	Loewenstamm, Samuel E. 212
Kabasele Mukenge, André 35–36, 38–	Looijer, Gwynned de 58
41, 43–47, 49–50, 52–53, 55	Luhrmann, Tanya M. 207
Kaiser, Otto 24, 55	Machiela, Daniel A. 69–70
Kalimtzis, Kostas 30	Maes, Léon 2
Kallendorf, Craig 7	Magness, Jodi 58, 78
Karrer, Martin 113, 141	Mahmood, Saba 109, 207
Kassel, Rudolf 32	Maier, Gerhard 203
Kaufmann, Yehezkel 201	Malina, Bruce J. 85
Keddie, G. Anthony 20–21, 64, 81, 88,	Manning, J. G. 88
117, 121, 243–44, 246–50, 255	Marcuse, Herbert 240
Keith, Chris 109, 208	Martin, Henri-Jean 9
Kim, Heerak Christian 16	Mathews, Mark D. 82, 86, 90, 92–95
Kirk, Alan 221, 225, 231, 240	Matlock, R. Barry 160
Klawans, Jonathan 105, 171, 179,	Mayer, Ernst Emanuel 83
216–17	Mazzochi, Giuseppe 7
Kneucker, Johann Jakob 41	McCarter, P. Kyle, Jr. 26
Knoppers, Gary N. 217	McCauley, Robert N 207, 236

McCloud, Sean 86
McDonald, Lee Martin 15
McGlynn, Moyna 142
Meggitt, Justin J. 84
Meinhold, Arndt 26–27
Mendels, Doron 179
Merx, Adalbert 113, 130
Meursius, Johannes 2–3, 6
Milgrom, Jacob 134
Mirola, William A. 86
Mittermaier, Amira 206
Mittmann-Richert, Ulrike 60–61
Monson, Andrew 88
Moor, Johannes C. de 166–68, 178, 185–87, 189, 200, 253
Moore, Carey A. 39, 41, 46
Morgan, Teresa 219
Morley, Neville 83
Morris, Ian 88
Movers, Franz Karl 123
Münz-Manor, Ophir 205
Muraoka, Takamitsu 29
Murphy, Catherine M. 75, 86, 94–95, 105
Najman, Hindy 13, 72
Nakládalová, Iveta 7
Navarro, Víctor 9
Newsom, Carol A. 63, 72
Neyrey, Jerome H. 109
Nickelsburg, George W. E. 35, 69, 92–94, 123, 128, 144, 224
Nitzan, Bilhah 58, 78
Norris, Rebecca Sachs 215–16
Notley, R. Steven 115, 136
O'Brien, Peter T. 149
Olson, Dennis T. 63–65, 78
Ottenheijm, Eric 148, 160
Pajunen, Mika S. 66
Passow, Franz 145
Pastor, Jack 88–89
Penner, Jeremy 59, 61, 63, 70
Pernigotti, Carlo 28
Pesch, Wilhelm 41, 48, 53–54
Pevarello, Daniele 12
Pfann, Stephen J. 65

Piñero Sáenz, Antonio 24
Piovanelli, Pierluigi 93
Pomykala, Kenneth E. 113
Portier-Young, Anathea 81, 121, 247
Pouchelle, Patrick 1, 11, 14–16, 21, 81, 99–100, 103–4, 112, 165, 175–77, 183, 243–44, 250–52, 254
Priest, John 131
Prigent, Pierre 64, 86, 130
Rad, Gerhard von 172, 196–97
Rahlfs, Alfred 119, 140, 226
Rapp, Christof 31
Rappaport, Roy A. 229
Reed, Annette Yoshiko 10
Reymond, Eric D. 67
Rocca, Samuel 36, 88–89, 100
Rooke, Deborah W. 16
Rosen-Zvi, Ishay 170
Rothkamm, Jan 170
Ryle, Herbert E. 3–4, 98–99, 102–3, 105, 114, 116, 124, 203
Sacchini, Francesco 7
Sæbø, Magne 27–28
Saller, Richard P. 83, 88
Sanders, E. P. 81, 88, 106, 149, 251
Sanders, James A. 68
Santos, Ava 215
Sarna, Nahum M. 201
Sarot, Marcel 167, 174
Sartre, Maurice 89
Savage, Mike 85
Scheidel, Walter 84, 88
Schenker, Adrian 209
Schiffman, Lawrence H. 78, 178, 182
Schmid, Hans Heinrich 189
Schmidt, Moriz 113, 130
Schnelle, Udo 145–46, 149, 153
Scholem, Gershom 178, 180
Schoors, Antoon 189–90
Schreiber, Stefan 14, 21, 141, 144, 151, 155, 157, 163, 251–52
Schröter, Jens 145, 147
Schuller, Eileen M. 58, 76
Schumacher, Thomas 155–56
Schüpphaus, Joachim 114, 203

Schwartz, Barry	221–23, 229, 232	Weber, Max	167
Schwartz, Joshua	16	Webster, Brian	62–63, 65, 67
Schwarzfuchs, Lyse	9	Wees, Hans van	83
Scoralick, Ruth	28	Wellhausen, Julius	98, 130
Scott, James M.	18–19	Werline, Rodney A.	15, 22, 61, 70, 82, 100–102, 109, 165–66, 169, 172–73, 175, 183, 187, 192, 196, 198, 233, 237, 240, 248, 252
Seifrid, Mark A.	149–50, 153, 203		
Serandour, Arnaud	51		
Sewell, William H.	87		
Sharon, Nadav	17–18, 82, 88, 98, 106, 143, 225	Werman, Cana	182
		Westermann, Claus	35, 192, 195
Shemesh, Aharon	182	Whitters, Mark F.	127
Simmons, W. Kyle	215	Willitts, Joel	152
Skeggs, Beverly	85	Winninge, Mikael	17, 63–64, 98–100, 142, 144, 146, 149, 166, 171, 175–76, 191, 203
Smolar, Leivy	217		
Steck, Odil Hannes	39–41, 51		
Steins, Georg	147	Wischmeyer, Oda	159
Stenhouse, William	4	Wise, Michael O.	71, 208
Steudel, Annette	178	Wold, Benjamin G.	95
Stone, Michael	69	Wolfson, Elliot R.	206
Stuckenbruck, Loren T.	74–75, 93	Wolter, Michael	157
Sollamo, Raija	113	Wright, Benjamin G.	91–92, 94–95
Striker, Gisela	31	Wright, N. T.	160–61
Swartz, Michael D.	205, 207	Wright, Robert B.	3, 71, 73, 81–82, 97–98, 105–6, 114, 124, 130, 140–41, 151, 165–66, 203, 226, 244
Talmon, Shemaryahu	78, 178		
Tauberschmidt, Gerhard	27		
Theissen, Gerd	150	Wyatt, Nicolas	217
Throop, C. Jason	206	Yerushalmi, Yosef	231
Tigchelaar, Eibert	94	Zacharias, H. Daniel	125
Toomer, G. J.	5		
Toorn, Karel van der	108, 186–89		
Torijano, Pablo A.	14		
Tov, Emanuel	27, 59, 71, 73		
Trafton, Joseph L.	36, 96, 104, 144, 151, 171, 203–4		
Tromp, Johannes	36, 100, 111–12, 114, 116–18, 121–24, 129, 133–34, 136		
Tsouna, Voula	102		
Tzoref, Shani L. [Berrin]	21–22, 74, 99, 179, 182, 191, 196–97, 250, 252–55		
Udoh, Fabian E.	88–89		
VanderKam, James C.	93–94		
Viteau, Joseph	3–4, 25, 114, 130, 203		
Volkmar, Gustav	113		
Wälchli, Stefan H.	25		
Wallace, David H.	116		

www.ingramcontent.com/pod-product-compliance
Lightning Source LLC
Chambersburg PA
CBHW051208300426
44116CB00006B/476